# BUST HELL WIDE OPEN

# BUST HELL WIDE OPEN

★ ★ ★ *The life of* ★ ★ ★
## NATHAN BEDFORD FORREST

## SAMUEL W. MITCHAM, JR.

REGNERY
HISTORY

Regnery History™ is a trademark of Salem Communications Holding Corporation; Regnery® is a registered trademark of Salem Communications Holding Corporation

ISBN 978-1-68451-030-6

Cataloging-in-Publication Data on file with the Library of Congress

Published in the United States by
Regnery History
An imprint of Regnery Publishing
A Division of Salem Media Group
300 New Jersey Ave NW
Washington, DC 20001
www.RegneryHistory.com

Manufactured in the United States of America

10 9 8 7 6 5 4 3 2 1

Books are available in quantity for promotional or premium use. For information on discounts and terms, please visit our website: www.Regnery.com.

# CONTENTS

Introduction     ix

**CHAPTER 1**
FRONTIERSMAN TO MILLIONAIRE     1

**CHAPTER 2**
FIRST BLOOD     21

**CHAPTER 3**
I'LL BE DAMNED IF I'LL SURRENDER     33

**CHAPTER 4**
SHILOH     45

**CHAPTER 5**
THE MURFREESBORO RAID     53

**CHAPTER 6**
THE WEST TENNESSEE RAID     75

**CHAPTER 7**
FAILURE AT FORT DONELSON     89

**CHAPTER 8**
THOMPSON'S STATION AND BRENTWOOD     95

**CHAPTER 9**
THE PURSUIT OF THE JACKASS BRIGADE     103

**CHAPTER 10**
RIVER OF DEATH     121

**CHAPTER 11**
FORREST CREATES AN ARMY: THE SECOND WEST TENNESSEE RAID    137

**CHAPTER 12**
OKOLONA    149

**CHAPTER 13**
THE THIRD WEST TENNESSEE RAID    163

**CHAPTER 14**
FORT PILLOW    173

**CHAPTER 15**
"THE MOST PERFECT BATTLE": BRICE'S CROSS ROADS    193

**CHAPTER 16**
"THERE WILL NEVER BE PEACE": TUPELO AND THE MEMPHIS RAID    215

**CHAPTER 17**
RIDING AGAINST SHERMAN    235

**CHAPTER 18**
THE NASHVILLE CAMPAIGN    259

**CHAPTER 19**
THE LAST BATTLE    277

**CHAPTER 20**
AFTER THE WAR    291

NOTES    319

BIBLIOGRAPHY    341

ABOUT THE AUTHOR    351

INDEX    353

*Lieutenant General Nathan Bedford Forrest*

# INTRODUCTION

*No great man lives in vain. The history of the world is
but the biography of great men.*

—Thomas Carlyle

I grew up in Mer Rouge, Louisiana, in the 1950s and '60s. It was a
world different from today—in some ways better, and in some ways
worse. Overall, though, I am quite satisfied with my small Southern
town upbringing. Early in life, I developed a passionate interest in the
Civil War. This, however, did not extend to Nathan Bedford Forrest,
who reminded me too much of my grandfather, whom I loved but sometimes wasn't sure I liked. Grover Mitcham had a fierce temper and would
lash out violently at the slightest provocation. He carried a cane of
pressed cypress and did not hesitate to use it. Like Forrest, he employed
two-fisted business methods and rose up from a sharecropper's cabin (or
worse, in Forrest's case) to owner of "the Big House."

As a graduate student, my research carried me into World War II.
After writing a number of books on that era, however, I decided to retool
and return to my first interest—the War Between the States. I now plan
to spend the rest of my life writing about this conflict.

My interests had shifted westward, and my first Civil War book dealt with the 1864 Red River Campaign in Louisiana. My interest in Nathan Bedford Forrest remained minimal until I came across a quote from Robert E. Lee who, when asked to name the best general in the Civil War, picked Forrest, despite the fact that they had never met and never would. That prompted me to read a biography or two about him. I was hooked. Although existing Forrest biographies are good, they are more military history and less biography. Napoleon once said: "In war, men are nothing. The man is everything!" Although I don't buy this completely, there is some truth to it. Alexander the Great said that he did not fear an army of lions led by a sheep, but he did fear an army of sheep led by a lion. And with an army of wolves led by a lion, you get astonishing results. Had Jefferson Davis and his advisers recognized Forrest's genius in time, I might today be writing this book from the Confederate state of Louisiana. So, although military history and biography are to a degree inseparable, this book will emphasize the latter. I want readers, upon finishing this book, to feel like they know Nathan Bedford Forrest, *the man*.

Nearing completion of this book, I feel much the same as I did when I finished my three-volume biography of Field Marshall Erwin Rommel, the famed Desert Fox of World War II: sadness. Like many historians, I always write an Introduction last. I have learned that if you go into a project without preconceptions, you never know what you will find. Like Rommel, Forrest had his flaws, but getting to know him well has been a pleasure—and, in many ways, I'll miss him.

The average reader might be surprised at how much Forrest's frontier upbringing played in his life and campaigns. My biggest surprise in this effort is the abiding admiration I now feel for Forrest's wife, Mary Ann. She was an awesome Christian woman. She would have to have been, to put up with her husband for all those years. Mary rather reminds me of my grandmother, who put up with Grover Mitcham. Both eventually achieved their long-range goal and saw their husbands convert to Christianity, but, in both cases, it was a long, hard ride.

Now, a warning, to my liberal friends. Forrest's world view was that of a Nineteenth Century Southerner, a Confederate patriot, and a man who grew to manhood in the raw, tough, and often violent world of the antebellum American frontier. I firmly believe that it's a mistake to judge the past entirely by the standards and values of today, a practice some historians call "Presentism," in which the past is always wrong because it is not the present. I hold that we can learn a great deal from the past and from the people who populated it, people like Forrest, even though we might not want them as neighbors.

The structure of this book is different from all my others. The first hardback books I ever owned were Douglas Southall Freeman's four-volume Pulitzer Prize-winning *R. E. Lee.* I have tended to follow Dr. Freeman's pattern of footnoting. Now, after reading books by Winston Groom and others, I have decided to go in the opposite direction. The footnotes in this book will be mostly informational in nature, so as to convey additional data, such as military details or biographical material on secondary characters who do not fit neatly into the flow of Forrest's major endeavors. Those interested in the finer details of his operations, his times, or the people with whom he interacted should find them interesting. There is a full bibliography included as well.

The first four maps are patterned after those in Robert S. Henry's 1956 book, *"First With the Most" Forrest.*

I thank Texas A & M for the use of its outstanding library. Major thanks also go to my agent, Dr. Al Zuckerman, who, as usual, performed yeoman service. The major thanks, however, goes to my family, especially my extremely tolerant Christian wife, Donna, who is an inspiration to all who know her. Take heart, dear. You might have had to put up with a lot, but at least you didn't have to put up with Nathan Bedford Forrest!

Dr. Samuel W. Mitcham, Jr.
Monroe, Louisiana
December 2015

# CHAPTER 1

# FRONTIERSMAN TO MILLIONAIRE

*A great man may commence life in a hovel.*
—Publilius Syrus

*It is fortunate to be of high birth, but it is no less so to be of such character that people do not care to know whether you are or are not.*
—Jean de la Bruyere

On June 13, 1943, Brigadier General Nathan Bedford Forrest, the chief of staff of the Eighth Air Force, led a squadron of B-17 bombers against the U-Boat submarine base at Kiel, Germany. Alerted by radar, German fighters met the American planes over the North Sea. Their main target was Forrest's lead aircraft, which they fatally riddled with 20mm shells. Forrest courageously ordered his co-pilot and crew to bail out, while he remained at the controls to ensure they got clear. No American witnessed the ensuing crash, and for a time hope remained that somehow Forrest had survived. Weeks later, his body finally washed ashore near the German seaplane base at Ruegen Island, where the Germans buried him with full military honors on September 28, 1943. He was thirty-eight years old.

A West Point graduate, Forrest the first American general officer killed in action in World War II. He posthumously received the Distinguished Flying Cross, and he was reinterred in Arlington National Cemetery after the war. His death ended a line of legendary military leadership that extended back more than eighty years to his great-grand-father, also named Nathan Bedford Forrest, who blazed a trail of fire and blood across the American Civil War. General Lee's praise of Forrest as the greatest battlefield commander of the war reverberated widely. P. G. T. Beauregard, whose favorite general was himself, remarked that "Forrest's capacity for war only seemed to be limited by the opportunities for its display," and General Joseph E. Johnston, commander of the Confederacy's Western Front, named him the greatest soldier the war produced and said, "Had he the advantage of a thorough military education and training, he would have been the great central figure of the war." Revered historian Bruce Catton called him "one of the authentic military geniuses of the whole war." Jefferson Davis also proclaimed him a "genius," and regretted not turning him loose against Sherman's supply lines sooner. "I saw it all after it was too late," he lamented. Noted historian Shelby Foote once commented that the Civil War produced two geniuses: Abraham Lincoln and Nathan Bedford Forrest. Forrest's campaigns were studied by European field marshals, ranging from the British Viscount Wolseley (who visited America during the war and became head of the British Army under Queen Victoria) to Lord Wavell (supreme British commander in the Middle East and India during World War II) to France's Ferdinand Foch (Allied Commander in World War I) to Germany's Erwin Rommel, the "Desert Fox."

During the war, Ulysses S. Grant, the General-in-Chief of the United States Army, both respected and feared Bedford Forrest. Newspaper correspondent Sylvanus Cadwallader, who spent three years with Grant, wrote that Forrest "was the only Confederate cavalryman of whom Grant stood in much dread." Grant generally dismissed reports about Confederate raiders, but "if Forrest was in command he at once became apprehensive, because the latter was amenable to no known rules of procedure, was a law unto himself for all military acts, and was constantly doing the unexpected at all times and places." Another Union general complained: "We never know where Forrest is, or what he is going to do, but he always knows where we are, and what we propose to do."

After the war, Union General William Tecumseh Sherman called Forrest "the greatest cavalryman America ever produced." During the war, he was a bit more pointed, famously saying that Forrest had to be killed, even if it cost ten thousand men and bankrupted the public treasury.

And Sherman had reason to fear Forrest. Not only did the Confederate raider burn or make off with Sherman's wagon trains, rout his cavalry, spread terror in rear areas, cut his communications, smash his railroads, burn his warehouses, blow up his bridges, steal his horses, sink his boats, destroy his supply depots, raise entire cavalry divisions behind Yankee lines, overrun his forts, spread destruction and disorganization everywhere he went, and crush Union general after general who was sent to suppress him, and then disappear like a ghost so that he could do it all again later, he almost managed to kill Sherman personally. This incident occurred on April 8, 1862. The Confederates had been decisively defeated at Shiloh the day before, and the Union Army was now chasing after them, with Sherman personally assuming command. The beaten Southern infantry retreated rapidly in the face of the Union pursuit. Forrest, however, did not think himself defeated nor did he conform to conventional ideas about how and when to fight.

In his haste to run down the fleeing Rebels, Sherman allowed his cavalry to become separated from his infantry. He had no idea that Forrest was lurking in the woods off his left flank, waiting for an opportunity to strike. When Sherman's vanguard crossed a stream and became separated from his other troops Forrest seized the moment. He and hundreds of Confederate cavalrymen burst out of the woods, firing their revolvers and screaming their Rebel yells. To Sherman's dismay, his shocked vanguard fled in terror, and Sherman himself was caught up in the panic. He recalled: "As we approached the ridge, down, with a yell, came Forrest's cavalry firing right and left with pistols, over the skirmish line, over the supports, and right among me and my staff...My Aide-de-Camp, [Captain] McCoy, was knocked down, horse and rider, into the mud, but I, and the rest of my staff ingloriously fled, pell-mell, through the mud, followed by Forrest and his men." The opposing generals came within a few yards of each other, and Forrest narrowly missed bagging the Union commander. Nineteen years later, Sherman told a reunion of the veterans of the Army of the Tennessee: "I am sure that had he [Forrest] not emptied his pistols as he passed the skirmish line, my career would have ended right there."

Forrest continued to torment Sherman for the next three years. Even the Union enlisted men on the Western Front feared Forrest. They knew that when they outnumbered the Rebels three-to-two or greater, they always won—unless the enemy commander was Forrest. Then the odds didn't matter—until the last week of the war, they almost always lost. His command cut supply lines and communications, destroyed railroads and bridges, and made off with dozens of herds of cattle as well as thousands of horses and mules. His riders captured wagon trains, supply depots, and river transports; cut telegraph lines; took hundreds of artillery pieces, and sank gunboats. They also routed thousands of men sent against them and captured more than thirty-one thousand prisoners. Forrest took so many Federal supplies that, during the last three years of the war, his men were furnished with the best horses, arms, and equipment Uncle Sam could provide. And he did all this, despite the fact that only rarely did he command more than three thousand men at any time. Several high-ranking Union officers had their forces smashed and their careers ruined in their fruitless attempts to destroy a man who was known as "the Wizard of the Saddle." Others were captured, one was killed in personal combat with Forrest, and one Union general only escaped capture by fleeing out the back door of where he was staying in Memphis, dressed only in his nightshirt.

This very American saga began roughly four decades before the start of the Civil War. He and his twin sister Frances (called Fannie) were born near the present-day hamlet of Chapel Hill, Tennessee, on July 13, 1821, on the edge of the Western frontier. He was named for his grandfather and the county of his birth, and was called "Bedford" by his family. His family's story was intertwined with that of the American frontier. Initially residing in Virginia, his ancestors moved to North Carolina in 1740, and to Sumner County, Tennessee, on the Kentucky border, in

1806. The original Nathan Forrest moved to the Duck River country in south-central Tennessee around 1807, where he raised eight children. His oldest son, William, became a blacksmith. Like his future son, William was tall (about 6' 2") and muscular.[1] He married Nathan Bedford's mother, Miriam Beck, in 1820. She was 5' 10" and also muscular. She weighed 180 pounds and had dark hair and bluish-gray eyes, and she was just as tough as her husband. Her first set of twins was born a year later, and eight other children followed—by her first husband.[2]

Forrest inherited Miriam's hair, eyes, physical strength, endurance, and character. She was a gentle, kind-hearted woman until aroused, in which case she was implacable—she was a strong and loving wife and mother, and a devout Christian, which her son was not.[3]

The Forrest home was a small (eighteen by twenty feet), crudely built log cabin beside a rough, rutted dirt road. Its floor was made from logs cut in half, with the split side up. The cracks between the logs which formed the walls and the poorly fitted doors made the place hot in summer and cold in winter. Massive beams supported the roof and the loft, where everyone slept. Its large stone fireplace provided warmth and doubled as a stove.

Napoleon once said that poverty is the best military school and, if so, young Forrest was very well educated. Little is known about his early years but one revealing story has survived. He and some other children were picking blackberries when they suddenly discovered a rattlesnake. All of the other children dropped their baskets and ran away. Bedford grabbed a stick and beat the snake to death. That was his reaction to danger and would be his entire life: face it, fight it, and kill it. It was a frontier mindset and one he kept until the day he died.

At an early age, Bedford was noted for his abundant energy and his lungs. He could out-yell any of the other kids at play—or when he was being beaten by his parents or his teacher. When he was old enough, William and Miriam sent him to a log schoolhouse run by Colonel John Laws. Forrest attended two three-month terms, both conducted in the winter, when the children—the main source of labor on frontier farms—were least needed. Later, during the Civil War, Bedford ran into his old teacher in Corinth, Mississippi, and asked the colonel if he remembered him. Laws replied that he did not. Forrest declared that you should remember me, since "you've whipped me often enough!" Laws later recalled that Bedford had plenty of sense but was interested only in athletics and would not apply himself to books. Forrest was not studious as his rudimentary grammar, spelling, and punctuation prove. During the war, for example, a soldier made a written request for a furlough after verbal appeals failed. Forrest wrote back: "I told you twist [twice] Goddamnit know." Typically, he dictated his dispatches and reports. He once declared that he never saw a pen without thinking of a snake.

Meanwhile, Southern society was changing thanks to the genius of Eli Whitney, who invented an improved cotton gin in 1793. Whitney's invention would process green seed cotton without tearing the fiber. Prior to that, a worker had to carefully hand pick thirty to forty seeds from one pound of cotton, which typically took all day. Now, a single slave could clean fifty pounds per day. The invention made cotton an extremely profitable crop which made Southern planters and New England cotton mill owners extremely rich. The more prosperous planters began to acquire more slaves and to construct mansions of cedar and brick.

In 1830, when Forrest was nine, his father bought a tract of land near Chapel Hill. It included a better constructed log cabin (built in 1825), a double crib log barn, a log corn crib, a smokehouse, a stone-lined well, and several barbecue pits, which General Forrest reportedly used later to hold recruiting parties. The property also had an orchard with apple, peach, and pear trees. Fresh and canned fruit was stored in a limestone cavern, which can still be seen today. Although all seemed well, William Forrest heeded the call of the frontier again in 1835. The government's removal of the Cherokee and Chickasaw Indians had opened good farmland in northern Mississippi, and he moved his family there.

William Forrest died two years later, leaving his fifteen-year-old son as the man of the house. This term meant more on the frontier in 1837 than it does today. Forrest had to support his pregnant mother, six brothers, Fanny Beck (an unmarried aunt), and three sisters. Although his father had built a cabin, there was still land to be cleared and fences to be constructed. So, everybody worked. Hard. Under their older brother's supervision, the Forrest boys plowed, cut wood, and took care of the livestock. Bedford tanned hides and made shoes for the family by the light of the fireplace. His sisters operated the spinning wheel, did the washing, took care of the chickens and ducks, and tended the garden. The family also made their own lye soap and candles. This new responsibility forced Forrest to grow up fast—perhaps too fast—but he adapted well. Being a young patriarch also made him accustomed to being in charge and to having everyone around him look to him for direction, especially in crises. It was an experience that made him a leader and extremely self-confident.

In the late 1830s and 1840s, northern Mississippi remained very much an untamed wilderness. One day, Miriam Forrest and her sister Fannie were riding back to the cabin with a basket of chicks that the family's neighbor had given to them. Unfortunately, the women could not cover the nine miles before sunset. Darkness had just fallen when she reached the creek about a mile from her cabin. There, she heard the blood-chilling roar of a panther, which had smelled the chicks. Fannie urged her sister to drop the chickens but she refused. As their horses entered the water, the panther sprang from the bushes and ripped into Miriam's back and shoulder. Her horse's panicked jerks caused the panther to fall into water, and Miriam was able to make it to her cabin. She never cried out, despite her pain.

Forrest carried her into the cabin and dressed her wounds. He then removed his father's flintlock from above the fireplace and announced that he was going to kill the panther. Miriam urged him to wait until daybreak, but he refused. The panther would be gone by then. Forrest unleashed his hound dogs and headed out into the night. Sometime after midnight he treed the panther. He waited until dawn and, in the pale morning light, killed it with a single shot.

This was the frontier world Forrest grew up in, a merciless world of kill or be killed. Forrest never completely left that world—or perhaps it would be better to say that it never left him. Hard conditions breed hard men—and Forrest became one of the hardest.

Young Bedford also learned to think on his feet. On one occasion the family was traveling home by wagon. It was raining heavily and they got stuck in a creek. Water was rising rapidly and though the boys pushed hard on the wheels, no amount of effort could dislodge the vehicle. Conditions became dangerous. Bedford then walked over to the ox, bent down, and bit off a half inch of its ear. The wagon and its cargo were safely on dry land in no time.[4]

Despite danger and death (typhoid fever would claim one of Forrest's brothers and all of his sisters in 1841), the family prospered. In time, Bedford built his mother a new cabin—one with the dog run and a smokehouse in the back.

Meanwhile, a new neighbor built a house nearby. He owned an ox which liked to cross the fence and eat the Forrest family's corn. In the Old South, the typical small farmer had two main crops: corn and cotton. Cotton was the cash crop, and corn was the main food crop for both humans and animals. Corn was used to make corn meal, cornbread, Johnny cakes, corn grits, and in many families, corn liquor. Corn silage was also used to feed the animals. The loss of the corn crop, therefore, was more serious than the loss of the cotton crop. Cotton could not be eaten. An ox could do a large amount of damage and knock down or eat a lot of corn. Forrest asked the neighbor to restrain the animal. It was not his fault, the neighbor declared, that Forrest's fence was too weak for his ox. If Forrest wanted to protect his corn, he should build a stronger fence. Bedford bluntly replied that he would shoot the ox if it got into his crops again. The neighbor threatened to shoot Forrest if he did that.

A few days later, the ox pushed through the fence again. Forrest shot it dead and sent word of what he had done to the neighbor. The man grabbed his rifle and headed to Forrest's place, bent on revenge. As he was climbing the fence between the properties, Forrest fired at the man, sending his bullet so close to him that he went tumbling back over the fence. He came up almost instantly—and ran for his life. The Forrests never had trouble with him after that.

In early 1841, it appeared that Texas and Mexico were about to come to blows again. A company of volunteers formed up in Holly Springs,

Mississippi, to go to Texas and help the Texans fight for their independence. Forrest, then twenty, joined them. Problems arose when they reached New Orleans. They ran out of money and could not afford a boat to Galveston. Most of the boys turned around and returned home. Forrest proceeded overland to Texas, but when he and his few remaining companions arrived, they found that the crisis had passed and Texas did not need them. With no money to return home, Forrest took a job splitting rails for $.50 per hundred. After several weeks, he had enough money to get back to Tippah County.

When he finally did get back, he carried a disease with him. History does not record what it was, but he was laid up for several months.

One day, the young backwoodsman wondered what it was like to be drunk. He had seen several men make fools of themselves when inebriated in public, and he was afraid he might hurt or kill someone if he got into a brawl, so he went into the woods with a jug of whiskey, where he could do no harm to anyone. When he woke up, he did not remember what had happened, but he was sick. He had typhoid fever, which turned into a severe case of pneumonia. Forrest promised God that, if He allowed him to recover, he would never take another drink. He recovered, and he never drank alcohol again, except during the war, when he was wounded and the physician used it as anesthetic.

Forrest remained at his family's house until the autumn of 1842, when his uncle Jonathan, who lived in Hernando, Mississippi (population four hundred), offered him an interest in his mercantile business. Forrest jumped at the chance. Bedford soon became a successful horse trader, and eventually would expand his operations to include cattle and slaves. His mother, meanwhile, married James Horatio Luxton of Marshall, Texas, in 1843, eventually giving birth to four more children.[5]

Most Americans today associate the frontier with the Wild West of the post-Civil War era. But the South had its frontier era too, and even though many Americans do not associate the South with the frontier, they do know Southerners who were leading frontiersmen, with Davy Crockett, Daniel Boone, and Jim Bowie being three of the most prominent examples.

The cattle culture, in fact, was not born in the West. Its birthplace was the South. Colonial records for South Carolina, for example, speak of round ups and cattle drives, brandings, and rustling. More profitable forms of agriculture (especially cotton) gradually displaced the cattle business, although it lingered on in places not suitable for crops. Southwest Louisiana, for example, was cattle country until the mid-1880s, when Seaman A. Knapp introduced mechanized rice production. The Southern frontier had everything the Western cattle region would later have except the Spanish saddle horn, to include Indian wars, vigilantes, and gunfights.

In 1845, Jonathan Forrest became involved in a quarrel with a planter named William Matlock. Matters reached the point where words became superfluous. On March 10, Matlock, his two brothers, Jefferson and James, and an overseer, a man named Bean, walked through the mud of the main street of Hernando toward the Forrest store,[6] carrying guns. All business ceased in anticipation of the coming fight.

Forrest, now twenty-three, intercepted the men on Main Street and told them that, while the quarrel was none of his business, four against one was not fair, and he would not allow them to murder his uncle. Jefferson Matlock quickly drew his pistol and shot at Bedford, but missed. Forrest also made a quick draw with his double-barreled pistol and fired. One of the Matlocks went down, critically wounded. Another of the attackers wounded Forrest, but not seriously. Forrest fired again and a second Matlock fell into the mud. Now, Bedford stood empty-handed, with no time to reload. Fortunately for him, a friend rushed forward and tossed him a Bowie knife. He grabbed it with his left hand and charged the remaining gunfighters, stabbing the third Matlock, who fell into the muddy street, severely wounded. Bean decided he had enough and took to his heels, with Bedford in hot pursuit. Forrest found him hiding under a bed. He dragged him out and held him by the collar. "You deserve death at my hands," Forrest declared, "but I am too brave a man to murder one so completely in my power; I give you your life." Tragically, one of the shots meant for Bedford hit his uncle, who died a day or so later.

One of the Matlocks died of his wounds and Jefferson Matlock's right arm had to be amputated. The two surviving Matlocks and Bean were arrested and tried for murder. However, after great expense, they were acquitted in spite of the evidence. Apparently most of the expense involved bribing jurors. A firm believer in the law, Bedford turned himself in, but the authorities immediately released him.

Shortly thereafter, young Forrest was involved in another life-or-death situation. He was riding with a friend and prominent local attorney, James K. Morse; they encountered James Dyson, a planter who disliked Morse intensely. Without warning, Dyson pulled out a double-barreled pistol and put a ball in Morse's heart, killing him instantly—and leaving Forrest alone with a murderer—and him the only witness. Coolly, Bedford told Dyson that, if he pulled the trigger and had a misfire, he would kill him. At this, Dyson paused a moment, during which Forrest drew his own pistol and pointed it at him.

Dyson lowered his weapon. It was the first time that bluffing saved Forrest, but it would not be the last.

On Forrest's word, James Dyson was arrested and tried for murder. But through bribery he also escaped justice.

One bright Sunday in April, shortly after the Hernando gunfight, Bedford was riding down the road when he encountered a buggy stuck in a creek. It was carrying nineteen-year-old Mary Ann Montgomery and her widowed mother to church. Nearby, two young men were laughing at the ladies' plight and the driver's fruitless efforts to move the vehicle.

Bedford rode up and asked the women if he could help. When they accepted, he tied his horse to a tree, waded into the creek, lifted up each woman in turn, and carried them to dry ground. Then he and the driver put their shoulders to the wheels and pushed the wagon out of the mud. Forrest then turned to the two spectators.

"Why didn't y'all help these ladies?" he demanded.

The pair didn't say a word.

"I suggest that you remove yerselves from this vicinity at once," Forrest growled, "or I'll give you a thrashin' you won't soon ferget!"

Perhaps they had heard about the Hernando gunfight, or maybe they were just afraid of the tall, muscular frontiersman. In any case, they immediately rode away.

The two ladies thanked Forrest profusely, who introduced himself and asked permission to call on Mary. He appeared at the home of Mary's uncle and guardian, the Reverend Samuel Cowan, the very next day. Incredibly, he found the same two rude spectators waiting in the parlor. He ordered them to leave immediately, and they did.

Mary Ann Montgomery was pretty, petite, gentle, well-educated, quiet, well-mannered and introverted. Mary was a cousin of Sam Houston and was related to General Richard Montgomery, a hero of the American Revolution. Her father, William H. Montgomery, had died when she was three, leaving her mother (then twenty-seven) with four small children. The family nevertheless managed to send Mary to the prestigious Nashville Female Academy, where she received a fine education and learned the social graces.

Forrest's family had nothing approaching the Montgomery's pedigree, and he was extroverted, rough, tough, badly educated, hot tempered, dominating, violent, confrontational, and profane. Yet, he also was unquestionably a fine physical specimen. He stood at 6' 2" and weighed 210 pounds, with broad shoulders, a well-muscled body and good, white, even teeth, which he took care of, unlike quite a few on the frontier. He was well groomed, too, with a dark mustache and chin beard and long, thick, black hair, cut in the Cavalier style. And she already had first-hand proof of his gallantry and his deep respect for women, so she did nothing to discourage his obvious interest in her.

On his second visit, Bedford proposed. Mary hesitated.[7] Forrest told her that if she accepted either one of the two men he had twice sent off, she would be making a serious mistake. They had not taken care of her when she and her mother were stuck in the creek that Sunday, and they would behave the same way as husbands. He, on the other hand, now had a successful business and would be both willing and able to support her, and he knew how to treat a lady.

She accepted his proposal the fourth time they met, contingent upon her uncle's approval. A Presbyterian minister, Cowan was not at all excited about the prospect of having Forrest in the family. He asked Bedford why he wanted to marry Mary. She was a good, pious Christian girl, whereas he cursed, fought, and gambled. She was nothing like him.

I don't want to marry anybody like me, Forrest replied. I want to marry a Christian girl. He promised to be a faithful husband and a good provider. He also offered himself as a protector, a major consideration on the frontier.

It is not known what happened to change Cowan's mind, but he eventually relented. Mary and Forrest were married in Hernando on September 25, 1845. The Reverend Cowan performed the ceremony. "The above came together in hand, accompanied by a good, sweet morsel of cake and a bottle of the best wine," the Hernando newspaper reported.

The happy couple was, as the Bible says, unequally yoked. While Forrest believed in God and respected Christians, he certainly wasn't one himself, and didn't intend to be. He thought Christianity was a fine religion—for women. He would focus instead on the pursuit of wealth, land, material possessions, and the respect of others. For her part, Mary lived her life for the glory of the Lord. Forrest always behaved well around women and treated them with respect, and he expected other men to do likewise. Although an occasional profanity of his slipped out in Mary's presence, he tried to speak civilly when she was around. He did not allow dirty talk in her presence, or in the presence of any woman. He would not tolerate dirty jokes or humor which degraded women. He once fired one of his best friends for engaging in sex outside of marriage, saying he would not tolerate in his army any man who would "do that" to a woman. Trifling with a woman's affections was dastardly in Forrest's book.

His worst vice was gambling, and his affection for it caused some stress within his marriage. Mary Ann considered it a sin and an offense to God. She would often beg him not to go out to gamble, but he went anyway. She would stay at home and pray for her husband until he returned. He usually won—sometimes hundreds of dollars. At least three times, he won the modern equivalent of $50,000 in a single evening, but this meant nothing to his wife. She said she would rather live on half rations than have him gamble. Her concern was the salvation of his eternal soul.

The newlyweds moved into a small log cabin not far from the center of Hernando. He worked hard to earn more money, because of his new responsibility and because his Uncle Jonathan was heavily in debt when he died. He expanded into slave trading, starting with six blacks he inherited from Jonathan. He also traded horses and cattle, ran his uncle's mercantile business (specializing in the sale of farm supplies and equipment), and founded and operated a stage coach line between Hernando and Memphis. He also started a brickyard in Hernando in order to meet the growing demand caused by the region's increasing population and prosperity. Forrest was even elected coroner—a position which involved serving warrants and collecting fines.

Mary gave birth to their two children while they were living in Hernando. William Montgomery ("Willie") Forrest was born on September 28, 1846, and Frances Ann ("Fanny")—named after his lost sister—came on February 5, 1849 (like her namesake, she would die as a child in 1854). By 1850, their household was somewhat crowded with the two children, Ann Cowan (Mary's aunt), Joseph F. Forrest (probably a cousin), and a boarder, James Patton Anderson, a future Confederate general, under their roof. Bedford also provided support for his brother, John Nathan Forrest, who had been partially paralyzed during the Mexican War, when a bullet ripped through his spine.

By 1851, Bedford moved to Memphis, then a sprawling, brawling river city of twenty-three thousand. There he ran a real estate business and slave market, with four of his brothers as partners. Soon he was taking slaves and horses as far north as Kentucky, although his main customers were Louisiana sugar growers and east Texas cotton planters. He opened branch offices in Vicksburg (run by his brother Jesse) and Jackson, Mississippi (run by his brother Aaron). When Bedford was out of town, his brothers Bill and John ran the Memphis office.

As Memphis slave traders went, Forrest was the best of a bad lot. He would not separate families and, if he acquired a slave without his or her spouse, he tried to buy the other, and then sell them as a family. He would also purchase the children. He never beat his slaves. Several authors have cited this fact as proof of his benign nature. Well—yes and no. Mostly no. His refusal to use the whip was not entirely humane. If a potential buyer saw that a slave had been beaten, he assumed that there was a reason for the beating. Logic suggested that this slave must be a trouble-maker. The last thing a Southern master wanted was a troublesome slave. If a slave had been beaten, his economic value dropped, drastically reducing the slave trader's profit margin. This was the last thing Forrest wanted, so he did not whip his slaves. Still, he treated his slaves well by the standards of the day.

When Forrest acquired a slave, the first thing he did was hand him over to his valet, Jerry, who saw to it that the slave washed thoroughly and put on clean clothes. Clean and healthy slaves promoted customer satisfaction, free and effective word-of-mouth advertising, and repeat business. Forrest made sure that they bathed regularly, were well groomed, well housed, and well fed. He encouraged his slaves to learn to read and write (which was illegal in some states), and kept a list of vicious slave dealers, to whom he would not sell. He even allowed certain trusted slaves to go out in Memphis and find their own masters. This was a big plus in the eyes of a slave. Forrest's slaves seemed to have respected and liked him (as much as they *could* like a slave trader), and preferred to be owned by him rather than his more brutal counterparts. But those who knew his reputation for having a volcanic temper or had witnessed it first-hand feared him, too.

In 1852, not long after he started this business, Forrest traveled to Houston and Galveston. He booked passage on the leaky steamboat *Farmer* for the last leg of his journey. That night, the often angry voices of gamblers in the adjoining saloon kept him awake. Annoyed, he burst into the bar and peremptorily ordered the gamblers to be quiet. Perhaps he was also concerned that the argument might end in gunfire, which could send bullets through the thin walls and into his room. They did

Forrest & Maples slave poster.

not wish to fight the angry, red-faced Tennessean, and agreed to hold it down.

Fully awake by now, Forrest decided to take a walk on the deck, which was cooled by the fresh air of the Gulf of Mexico. He was startled to find that the chimney stacks on the boat were red hot and the adjoining cabins were kept from burning only because of the constant line of men who were throwing water on their wood surfaces. He immediately approached the captain and protested. The man—who was drunk—declared that he was racing another steamboat, he was winning, and was only six miles from the landing. He intended to win or blow up the boat in the attempt.

Forrest retreated to the extreme aft of the steamboat and waited for the explosion. It was not long in coming. As the ship neared the Rockfish Bar, the boilers blew up, killing about sixty people, including the captain. Forrest suffered an injured shoulder, but nevertheless helped get survivors to shore. Fortunately, the explosion occurred in shallow water, and the other steamboat rendered assistance.

Forrest made numerous trips from Texas to Kentucky, trading livestock and slaves. Frequently he camped for the night across the road from Mr. Hubbard's home on the Grenada to Greensboro road in Mississippi. Hubbard's son, John Milton Hubbard, was a child in the 1850s, but he remembered Forrest's visits. He recalled that the first creosote he ever saw, Forrest used on him to sooth a toothache. "He was a man to impress even a stripling, as I was then," young Hubbard recalled more than fifty years later. "I should have carried his image in my mind to this day even if there had never been a war." He remembered him as "A man of commanding, but pleasing personality, with grayish-blue eyes who spoke kindly to children."

Hubbard later spent four years with the Seventh Tennessee Cavalry Regiment, two of them with Forrest. Although he saw the rougher side of Forrest's personality, his affection and admiration never dimmed. Forrest always commanded and kept the respect of others. This talent, exercised without conscious effort on his part, stood him in good stead in the years ahead.

In the 1850s, Memphis was still a frontier settlement, populated by robbers, thieves, thugs, desperados, and all sorts of adventurers, as well as law-abiding citizens. A river town and a trading center, it was in many ways "wide open." One of the city's more notorious gamblers was Joseph Able, who had killed a man in a saloon and fled Memphis one step ahead of the law. He left behind his wife and daughter in the care of his ne'er-do-well son John. John has his father's temperament and, one day, accosted a man named Everson on a public boardwalk for insulting his mother. They came to blows, and John struck the man with his pistol. The blow caused the gun to discharge, according to Able, and the bullet killed Everson instantly. John walked to the jail-house and surrendered.

That night, a lynch mob formed to deal with John Able. It was blocked, however, by the mayor and several prominent citizens, including Forrest. He stood on the balcony above the Worsham Plaza and told the mob that this was not a matter for them to settle. The mayor had called a meeting for the next day, and they should wait until then. The speech had its desired effect, and the mob dispersed.

The next day, the promised meeting was held, but the mob was not satisfied. Angry men stormed out of the meeting hall, broke into the jail, carried out Able, and prepared to hang him. The young man, who was not yet of age, argued that he had been provoked, and that he would be acquitted if given a fair trial. His mother also tearfully pled for his life, causing the mob to waiver. Then Forrest appeared, cut the rope, and he and his friends escorted the young prisoner back to the jailhouse.

The crowd followed Forrest and the others to the jail, surrounded it, and demanded Able. They threatened to break down the door and storm the place if he was not handed over. Forrest threw open the door and walked out with a six-shooter in each hand and a knife in his belt. He spoke earnestly and coldly. "I'll kill any man who tries to enter this jail," he growled. At first, no one moved. Then they decided that the prisoner was not worth dying for, and they all went home.

The next day, Forrest's courage was the talk of Memphis. The following year, 1858, he was elected alderman and soon became head of the city's Finance Committee. He set up Memphis's first paid fire department. He also brought a refreshing honesty to a self-serving city council. On one occasion, a councilman wanted to condemn a bridge so that he could award the rebuilding contract to a friend of his—and almost certainly receive a kickback. After inspecting the bridge, Forrest declared that, except for some minor repairs, it seemed to be in good shape and he saw no reason to condemn it. The councilman then made the mistake of telling Forrest his true plan.

"You infernal scoundrel!" Forrest roared. "Do you dare to ask me to be as damned a rascal as yourself? I have a big notion to pitch you into the Mississippi River. Now, I warn you if you ever presume to address such a damnable proposition to me in the future, I will break your rascally neck!"

On another occasion, the city council considered selling its stock in the Memphis & Charleston Railroad. Even though retaining it was against his personal financial interests, Forrest firmly opposed the sale, because he believed the sale price was too low. When the council voted to sell anyway, Forrest purchased $50,000 worth of M & C stock. He later sold it for $70,000.

Forrest was easily reelected in 1859, but having no political ambition, he resigned later that year. He also gave up the slave trading business and moved to Coahoma County, Mississippi, and became a cotton planter. In the Old South, it was considered more respectable to own slaves than to trade in them. It had been a high income but low prestige occupation so, now that he had made his fortune, Forrest decided to remake his reputation.

While in Memphis, Forrest attended a free lecture given by Dr. Orson G. Fowler of New York, a noted phrenologist.[8] At the end of his speech, Fowler asked the audience to choose someone to be examined. The crowd chose Forrest.

Dr. Fowler studied his head and ran his fingers over his skull. "Here is a man who would have been a Caesar, a Hannibal, or Napoleon if he had had the opportunity. He has all the qualities of a great military genius. If he could not go over the Alps he would go through them." He went on to predict that, if he had the opportunity, he would yet make a mark on the world stage. As the audience applauded, Forrest returned to his seat. He had no idea that Fowler's prediction would soon come true.

Forrest continued to enjoy economic success. On one occasion, he bought 1,900 acres of good cotton land for $47,500 ($1,200,000 in 2015 dollars). A few months later, he sold it for three times that. By 1858, he was making $96,000 a year or $2.5 million by today's standards. The following year, he sold about one thousand slaves for an average of $1,100, grossing $1,100,000 ($30 million in 2015 dollars).

Forrest moved his family to his Green Grove plantation (near Sunflower Landing) in Coahoma County, Mississippi in 1859. The Grove covered 1,900 acres, and included a six-room house and twelve servants' cabins, which housed thirty-six slaves.[9] He subsequently purchased an additional 1,445 acres of prime farmland adjacent to his plantation. Green Grove produced one thousand bales of cotton that year, for a profit of about $30,000 ($800,000 today). The following year, he had two hundred field hands working Green Grove, but Forrest owned several other plantations in Tunica County as well. He and Dr. A. K. Taylor of Memphis owned a plantation in Arkansas, twelve miles from the mouth of the St. Francis River. In 1861, Forrest estimated his worth at $1.5 million (about $34 million in 2015 dollars), but he almost certainly understated his wealth. He was happy, healthy, prosperous, and married to a beautiful woman whom he loved and to whom he was totally devoted. But he saw dark clouds on his horizon. The U.S. sectional conflict—which had been brewing for decades—had finally boiled over.

Forrest was a strong Union man until Abraham Lincoln was elected President of the United States with 39.8% of the popular vote. He agreed with Tennessee's overwhelming anti-secession vote on February 9, 1861. On April 12, 1861, however, Confederate guns fired on Fort Sumter. Three days later, President Abraham Lincoln called for seventy-five thousand volunteers to "suppress the 'Rebellion.'" Public opinion in Tennessee immediately swung strongly in favor of secession as did Nathan Bedford Forrest, who now decided to join the Confederate Army.

# CHAPTER 2

# FIRST BLOOD

*The bravest are surely those who have the clearest vision
of what is before them, glory and danger alike, and not-
withstanding, go out to meet it.*

—Thucydides

On June 8, 1861, by a margin of 108,339 to 47,233, Tennessee
voted to join the Confederate States of America. Six days later,
Bedford Forrest, along with his son Willie (age fifteen) and his
youngest brother Jeffrey (age twenty-four), walked into the recruiting
office in Memphis and enlisted in Captain Josiah S. White's Tennessee
Mounted Rifles, which later became part of the famous Seventh Tennessee Cavalry Regiment.[1]

This act was the result of a great deal of soul-searching on Forrest's
part. He was a Union man, but he also believed in States' Rights, and he
was a Constitutional conservative, a free trader and a practical businessman. He realized Lincoln's high taxes (the tariffs) would bankrupt many
Southern plantations, farms and businesses, and would derail the economic boom the South enjoyed for more than a decade. As soon as the
Deep South seceded, the Republicans (now a majority in Congress)
passed the Morrell Tariff, which increased the tax to an astronomical
47 percent. The South, which contained less than 30 percent of the

Isham G. Harris (1818–1897) succeeded Andrew Johnson as governor of
Tennessee in 1857. Reelected in 1859
and 1861, he led the state out of the
Union in 1861. During the war, he
served as a volunteer aide to generals
Sidney Johnston, Joseph E. Johnston,
Braxton Bragg, John Bell Hood, and P.
G. T. Beauregard. Although his state
was completely overrun by Yankees in
1863, Harris was still issuing edicts as
governor as late as November 1864. He
fled to Mexico after the war, but was
elected U.S. senator in 1877 and served
until his death. Prior to the war, he was
a lawyer, state legislator, and a member
of the U.S. House of Representatives.
Commissioning Forrest a lieutenant
colonel was the most fortunate
appointment of his career.

country's population, was already paying 85 percent of the taxes. (There was no Federal income tax in 1861 and the tariff was the main source of Federal revenue. Over three-quarters of the money went for internal improvements in the North.) The new tariff inadvertently played into the hands of the fire-eating secessionists, because it was a contributing factor to the secession of the upper Southern states of Arkansas, Virginia, North Carolina, and Tennessee.

There was no snobbery in Forrest's makeup. Most men in Forrest's position would have used their power and influence to obtain a commission. He, however, was content to be a private. Others, however, did not see things that way. Several prominent citizens—individually and as part of delegations—visited Governor Isham Harris, and urged him to give Forrest a commission, as did General Gideon Pillow, the commander of the Provisional Army of Tennessee, and Major General Leonidas Polk, commander of the Confederate forces in western Tennessee. Governor Harris, a Memphis lawyer, knew Forrest, agreed and made one of the smartest moves of his career. On July 10, he summoned Bedford to Memphis, promoted him to lieutenant colonel and authorized him to recruit a battalion of mounted rangers.

Tennessee, and indeed the entire Confederate government, was short on money, horses, and equipment of every kind, and Bedford Forrest had deep pockets. He did not mind spending his own money to arm and equip his men, correctly reasoning that, if the South lost the war, he would lose his fortune anyway. He spent $20,000 ($450,000 in 2015 dollars) to purchase top-of-the-line pistols (Navy Colts) and other supplies for his troops and went to Kentucky to recruit and buy more equipment from Yankee merchants, who were not so committed to the Union cause that they were averse to making a serious profit.

Kentucky was "neutral" in the summer of 1861, and Forrest was followed by Union agents. He nevertheless recruited two companies of Kentucky cavalry, bought five hundred Navy Colts and smuggled them south in boxes marked "potatoes." He smuggled saddles out in boxes labeled "leather" and other equipment in "coffee" boxes. U. S. Congressman and former Governor John J. Crittenden rightly suspected his actions and publicly called for his arrest. Forrest used his notoriety to his advantage. He sent his men and weapons south from Louisville while he headed north, followed by Northern operatives. Then, after nightfall, he shook his pursuers and turned south to rejoin his men.

Forrest was a superb recruiter. Tall, vigorous, alert, charismatic and physically impressive, he seemed born to command and radiated self-assurance. Young men instinctively had confidence in his ability to lead, and they flocked to his banner.

As Forrest was preparing to return home, a woman warned him that the pro-Union cavalry was waiting for him at Munfordville, blocking his escape route. Forrest then ordered a parade, consisting of all of his men, their families and loved ones, and any other Southern sympathizers who wished to join. He deliberately pranced them by the railroad station as a train passed by. By artificially inflating his numbers, Forrest hoped to avoid a fight. The ploy worked. When he arrived in Munfordville, the road to the south was clear.

By the first of August, Forrest was back in Memphis. He had raised eight companies, totaling 650 men that was organized into the Tennessee Mounted Ranger Battalion. It was transferred to Confederate service in October. Later called "Forrest's Tennessee Cavalry Battalion," it grew into a regiment, which was dubbed "Forrest's Cavalry Corps" and later "Forrest's Tennessee Cavalry Battalion." In January 1862, the War

Department redesignated it as the Third Tennessee Cavalry Regiment, but, to many, it was always simply "Forrest's Old Regiment."

Although he never commanded more than about ten thousand men at any one time, over the course of the war, Forrest commanded more than one hundred different organizations (divisions, brigades, regiments, battalions, batteries, and independent companies). As many as fifty thousand different soldiers came under his command during the next four years.

Forrest's second-in-command was Captain David C. Kelley, a former Methodist missionary to China, and an extremely brave man. He also served as the battalion and later regimental chaplain. His assistant, at Mary's request, was William Forrest, the general's son.

Willie Forrest was competent and courageous but quiet. A strong Christian at an early age, he was much more like his mother than his father. Bedford managed to get General Polk—an Episcopal bishop in civilian life—to transfer a couple of clean-living young men (Mercer Otey, the son of an Episcopal bishop, and Samuel Donelson, the son of Brigadier General Daniel S. Donelson) to his staff. Forrest did not really need these boys. They were there to provide Christian friends of his own age for Willie.

Forrest was assigned to General Albert Sidney Johnston's Military District of the West, which included Kentucky, Tennessee, Arkansas, and Missouri. Johnston had forty thousand troops,[2] many of whom were not even armed, as opposed to ninety thousand Federals. Johnston was, in fact, running a huge bluff. Most of his three-hundred-mile front could only be covered by patrols. He assigned Forrest and his Rangers the task of screening the gap between General Polk's garrison at Columbus and the western flank of the Bowling Green concentration. Here Forrest's men came under fire for the first time.

One day, a woman came to Forrest because her husband, a Confederate sympathizer, had been arrested by three Unionists. Her plea for help touched a soft spot in Forrest, who always had the deepest sympathy for women in distress. He tracked down two of the three Unionists and, with a column of cavalry, went to arrest the third, a man named

Jonathan Bell, at his home. Riding beside Forrest at the head of the column was Dr. S. M. Van Wick, the battalion surgeon.

Van Wick was extremely well dressed with a new uniform and cape. As they approached the house, Bell fired his rifle at Van Wick, assuming apparently that the best-dressed Rebel would be the commanding officer. The bullet killed the doctor instantly, and Bell fled.

To obtain the release of the woman's husband and other hostages, Forrest captured ten pro-Union Baptist preachers, who were returning from a conference in the North. Forrest released two of them and sent them to the Federal headquarters in Marion, along with a message to the Yankee commander. He would hang all eight preachers from the same pole if the Confederate sympathizers were not released immediately. They were.

Forrest was probably bluffing. He never hanged civilians unless they were proven spies, and he respected the clergy. He started each major operation with a prayer, led by the unit chaplain. In camp, attendance of church services was mandatory for Forrest's men, whether they were believers or not.

Sometime afterward, Forrest's men captured a Northern chaplain. They brought the terrified man—who expected the worst—to the fierce Rebel commander. To the preacher's surprise, Forrest invited him to sit with him at the dinner table and asked him to bless the food before they ate. The next day, the general set him free, remarking that he did not make war on non-combatants. He could not resist having a little fun at the preacher's expense, however. "Parson," he smiled, "I would keep you here to preach for me if you were not needed so much more by the sinners on the other side."

As fall turned into winter, Forrest trained and toughened up his men, who quickly learned that he could not be argued with, and that he had a violent temper when aroused. Recruits continued to trickle in throughout the fall and early winter. One of them was Adam R. Johnson of Texas. His reaction to Forrest was typical of many newcomers. "I saw at once that he was a man of great and prompt decision. His muscular, well-proportioned figure, over six feet in height, was indicative of

NORTHERN TENNESSEE and SOUTHERN KENTUCKY

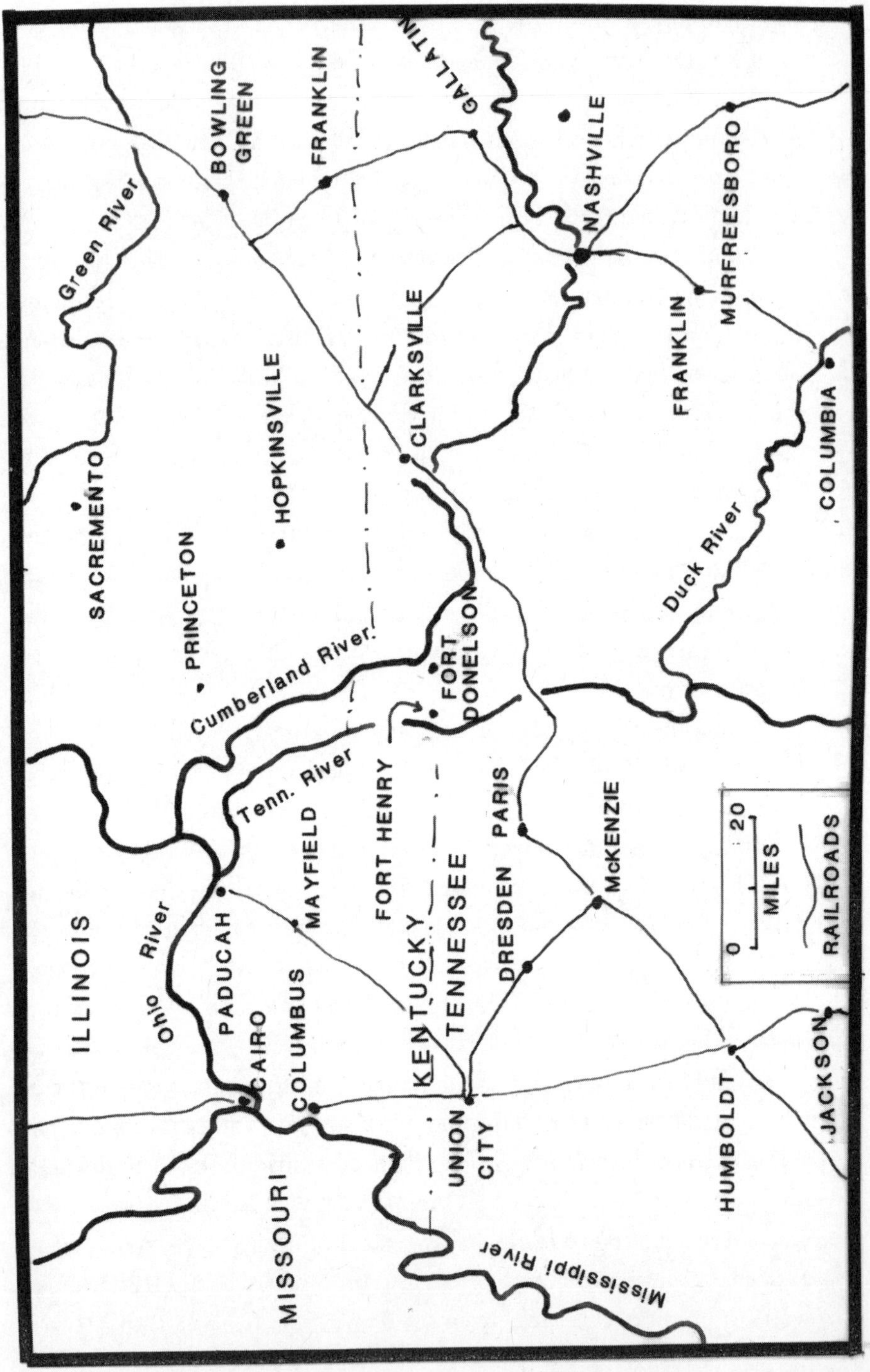

extraordinary physical strength. But it struck me that his most wonderful feature was his piercing blue eyes which flashed and changed so rapidly with every emotion...He was a man to catch the look and hold the attention of the most casual observer, and as we gazed on each other I felt that he was a born leader and one that I would be willing to follow."

All of the men seemed to feel that way. They also noted that he was extremely approachable and he took care of them. "Everything necessary to supply their wants, to make them comfortable, he was quick to do, save to change his plans," Major Kelley recalled.

It was customary to place the battalion's corn in piles in the center of the camp, so after reveille each man could shuck several ears for his horse. One morning, the colonel found that a certain horse had slipped its halter and was eating out of one of the piles. Forrest dressed down the owner of the horse in front of men. The young boy replied that he could not keep his horse in line because it was smarter than any other horse in the regiment and no halter could hold him. Forrest rejected his argument and gave the boy minute instructions on how to halter his horse. The next morning, Forrest found the mount happily munching away at one of the corn piles. Forrest again reprimanded the miserable private and threatened to have him arrested if it happened again. "I done like you said, Colonel, but they ain't no halter that kin hold that critter of mine." That night, Forrest tied up the horse himself, and showed the young man exactly how it should be done. The next morning, the horse had again slipped its halter and was happily eating away. Forrest accepted his defeat gracefully, stating that any horse which was that smart was entitled to more corn than the rest.

Setting up camp in Hopkinsville in southwestern Kentucky (See Map), Forrest led patrols and probes as far north as the Ohio River. At Ford's Ferry on the Ohio, he captured a transport ship and its entire crew. The cargo included coffee, whiskey, bacon, molasses, sugar, and wool blankets—which were particularly important now, with winter coming on. A few days later, he engaged in his first and somewhat unconventional skirmish of the war near Canton, Kentucky, on the Cumberland River. The Union gunboat USS *Conestoga* attempted to capture the

Confederate supply depot there, and Forrest tried to lure the gunboat into an ambush. Neither side succeeded, but Forrest's men received their baptism of fire and had acquitted themselves well. There were no Rebel casualties, and Forrest reported that his men killed four Yankees and a dog.

Forrest saw to it that his men had floored tents before he went into winter quarters at Hopkinsville on December 20. He shared his quarters with Mary and Willie. But he was not in them long. On December 26, Brigadier General Charles Clark, his district commander, ordered him to reconnoiter in the direction of Rochester and Greenville, about thirty miles to the northeast. The weather was horrible—bitter cold with intermittent freezing rain. On December 28, Forrest was on patrol when two of his best scouts, Johnson and Robert M. Martin,[3] reported that there was a Union cavalry regiment at Sacramento, Kentucky, about sixty miles northwest of Bowling Green and seven miles from their present location. Forrest immediately headed for the village at a gallop. When he led his column into town, he was met by Miss Mollie Morehead, a teenaged girl, who begged Forrest for help. She and her sister had been surprised and shocked a few minutes before to find Yankee cavalrymen watering their horses from a nearby pond. Forrest later described the scene this way: "a beautiful young lady, smiling, with untied tresses [of hair] floating in the breeze, on horseback, infusing nerve in my arm and kindling knightly chivalry within my heart." His heart went out to her, as it always did to women in trouble. The Union cavalry was retreating but it hadn't gone far. He headed after it. She fell in alongside the colonel and rode with him several hundred yards, and would have ridden into battle right beside him had not Forrest begged her to return.[4]

Forrest overtook the Yankees about a mile outside Sacramento. They apparently were unsure that the men opposite them were, in fact, Rebels. Forrest grabbed a rifle from one of his boys and personally clarified the matter for them. They moved smartly to the rear.

This was Forrest's first real battle, but he handled it like so many others. The Federals picked a good position on a wooded ridge, at a right angle to the road. Forrest halted just out of range of it and waited impatiently for his men to catch up. They had ridden more than thirty miles that day, at least ten of it at a gallop, and were strung out along the road to Sacramento. When about 150 of his men arrived, Forrest broke his command into three groups. He ordered Major Kelley to move around the Union right with sixty men, while Lieutenant Colonel James W. Starnes, M.D., outflanked the Union left with thirty men. Part of these groups advanced on foot. (Specifically, Forrest ordered Kelley and Starnes to "take 'em in both ends!" because he did not yet know the term "flank.") Forrest and the third group (about sixty men) remained mounted and probed the Northern line in the face of brisk enemy fire. When it appeared that the Yankees were about to retreat, Forrest pulled back and impatiently waited for Kelly and Starnes to strike. When they did, there was uncertainty in the Northern ranks. At the first sign of confusion, Forrest drew his sword, stood up in his stirrups, shouted "Blow the charge, Isham!" to his bugler, and personally led an attack against the Union center. "The Southerners, led by this impetuous chieftain, swooped down upon their foes with such terrific yells and sturdy blows as might have made them believe a whole army was on them, and turning tail, they fled in the wildest terror," Private Johnson recalled. The men in gray were not yet disciplined enough to maintain their formation, but that did not matter in this battle. Most of the Yankees kept running, but some of their officers rallied a good many of them and Colonel Forrest, who was ahead of all the Rebels, was soon fighting for his life. "I believe there was [sic] at least fifty shots fired at him in five minutes," Private James H. Hamner recalled. "One shot took effect in his horse's head, but did not kill him. He [Forrest] killed 9 of the enemy."

"Never in any battle did [a] leader play a fiercer individual part than did Forrest on this day," one of his men recalled. "With his long arm and long sword, once during the fight and chase he was some distance ahead of his men, making a pathway as he cut and slashed on this side and on that."

Forrest's path was blocked by a Union cavalryman, a former blacksmith whose physical strength probably rivaled the Confederate commander's, and they were soon engaged in hand-to-hand combat. Another Yankee came in behind him and was on the point of running the colonel through the back with his saber when a Southern lieutenant shot him off his horse. Meanwhile, he slashed the blacksmith and down he went. Almost immediately, Forrest was attacked by a private and two captains, Albert G. Bacon and A. N. Davis. The private fired at Forrest and missed, although the bullet did go through his collar. Forrest put him down with a single bullet. Captain Bacon also tried to kill him but fell mortally wounded by a quick saber thrust. Beside Forrest, a Rebel captain fell dead with a Union bullet in his brain. A moment later, a Confederate private died when Federal Captain A. N. Davis ran him through with his sword. Forrest shot Davis, knocked him and his horse down, and rode over them. The captain's shoulder was dislocated in the fall so he quickly surrendered. Forrest's horse tripped over two other horses and went down. The colonel landed ten feet further north. Private Johnson thought he was injured and rode to his rescue, jumping dead and wounded men and animals in the process. Just as he arrived, Forrest popped up. "Johnson, catch me a horse!" he cried. Meanwhile, up came the rest of the charging Rebels—moving so rapidly they couldn't stop. Horses tripped over men and other horses and created a great pile-up of Rebs, Yanks, and animals. The remaining Yankees took to their heels, and the Southerners followed for some distance, picking up the rifles the Federals threw away. The captured Yankees were paroled and local citizens took care of the wounded on both sides.

Forrest later reported that the battle was "a promiscuous saber slaughter" and that the Yankees left "their bleeding and wounded strewn along the whole route." They lost about one hundred men, including thirty-five captured. Forrest lost two killed and three wounded. Ironically, one of the wounded was shot by his own men. He was wearing the uniform he wore in the Mexican War, and in the confusion someone mistook him for a Yankee.[5]

"This battle had a splendid effect in our regiment [sic]," Private J. C. Blanton recalled. The men were convinced that Forrest was an outstanding leader. General Clark was also convinced. "For the skill, courage, and energy displayed by Colonel Forrest he is entitled to the highest praise, and I take great pleasure in calling the attention of the general commanding...He was at one time engaged in a hand-to-hand conflict with four of the enemy, three of whom he killed, dismounting and making a prisoner of the fourth." General Johnston was so pleased by Clark's report that he wrote Forrest a letter of commendation.[6]

Like many other men in the Civil War, Major Kelley was awestruck by the sight of Forrest in combat. During battle or times of stress, Forrest underwent a glandular or cardiovascular surge, in which blood flooded into his face, causing it to darken and swell, and his eyes took on a different look. Kelley wrote later of the remarkable physical change: "I could scarcely believe him to be the man I had known for several months. His face flushed till it bore a striking resemblance to a painted Indian warrior's, and his eyes, usually mild in their expression, were blazing with the intense glare of a panther's, springing upon its prey." Even his speech changed. Ordinarily it was slow and somewhat low, but in battle, one of his veterans recalled, "the whole man changed; his wrath was terrible, and few, if any, dared to brave it." Another soldier said, "I'll swear I never heard such a voice. It penetrated you through and through and made you move."

At Sacramento, the standard tactics that Forrest would apply during the war made their debut. Field Marshal Viscount Wolseley noted that his methods were "the common-sense tactics of the hunter and the Western pioneer."

1) He always outflanked the enemy on both flanks and got into his rear, creating disorganization and sowing confusion in enemy ranks.

2) At the first sign of confusion on the enemy's part, he always attacked.

3) He almost always attacked with everything he had and never left anything in reserve, except his horse holders, and sometimes not even them. This further perplexed his West Point-educated adversaries, who were taught to keep a reserve (typically about one-third of their strength) and therefore assumed Forrest did also.

4) He often used his cavalry as mounted infantry, meaning that his men would ride to the battlefield, and then attack as infantry.

5) He almost always led from the front, inspiring his men by his example. His personal courage was remarkable, astonishing friend and foe alike. He had nothing but contempt for those who feared danger.

6) He never met a charge standing still. He instinctively understood the psychological disadvantage of waiting for an attack. If the Yankees attacked first, he always met them halfway. "Never stand and take a charge," he once exclaimed. "Charge them too!"

7) He trusted his own instincts. "Forrest seemed to know by instinct what was necessary to do," Captain James Dinkins recalled.

8) He generally treated his prisoners well. "He fought to kill but he treated his prisoners with all the consideration in his power," Dinkins recalled. "So did his own men."

9) He was always the aggressor.

10) He always did what the enemy least expected.

Finally, fighting seems to have excited him. Most men don't like combat but do it when they have to, out of a sense of duty, obligation, or comradeship. But some people do like war—General George S. Patton, Jr., being a very prominent example. Forrest did not like war nor did he romanticize it. He knew it was a serious business. But he was one of the few who enjoy the actual fighting. "Come on, boys!" he wrote in one recruiting advertisement. "Let's have some fun and kill some Yankees!" He meant that. Fighting was a primitive form of fun for him. He got a thrill out of combat. That was a good thing, because he would be under fire 179 times during the war.

# CHAPTER 3

# I'LL BE DAMNED IF
# I'LL SURRENDER

*Sooner or later, every bluff is called.*
—Luftwaffe Lieutenant General Herbert Rieckhoff

As 1862 began, Forrest was operating in front of the Green River. He reported to General Albert Sidney Johnston that the Yankees were preparing an offensive. On January 10, Forrest burned the bridges on the Pond River, a deep tributary of the Green, and fell back to Hopkinsville.

General Johnston, the commander of the Confederacy's Western Front, was continuing his bluff along a three-hundred-mile "line" from the Cumberland Gap to the Mississippi River with woefully inadequate forces. The most vulnerable point was in western Tennessee, near the Kentucky border, where the Cumberland and Tennessee Rivers come within ten miles of each other and flow parallel through southwest Kentucky until they enter the Ohio near Paducah.[1]

The Confederate defense of the Tennessee River hinged on Fort Henry, while Fort Donelson guarded the Cumberland. Union General Ulysses S. Grant began an offensive against these two forts on February 2, 1862. He commanded the ground forces, while Flag Officer Andrew

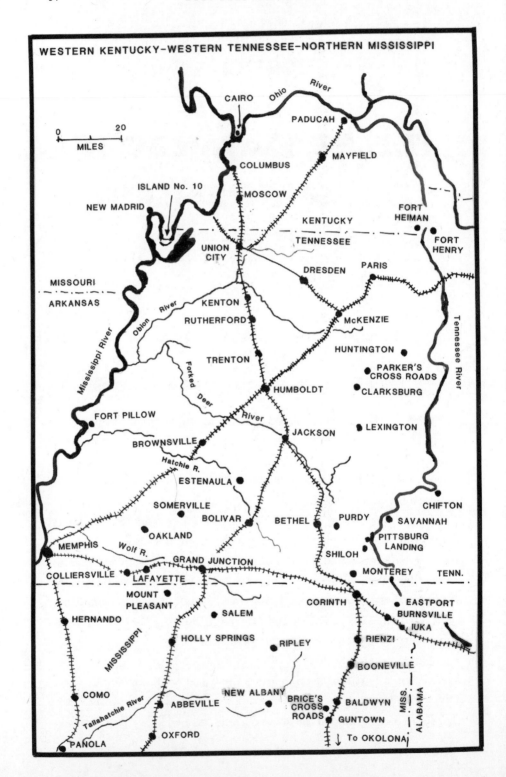

WESTERN KENTUCKY–WESTERN TENNESSEE–NORTHERN MISSISSIPPI

H. Foote directed the gunboats. They captured Fort Henry after a brief struggle on February 6.[2]

Johnston ordered the remaining forces on his western flank to concentrate at Fort Donelson. These included the infantry brigades of Brigadier General Gideon J. Pillow, Simon B. Buckner, and John B. Floyd. Forrest's cavalry covered their retreat from western Kentucky.

Johnston now made the worst mistake of his military career. Despite the fact that he thought Fort Donelson was doomed in the long run, he decided that the best way to defend Nashville was to hold Donelson. Perhaps he was emboldened by the size of the garrison. Counting the troops already there and the survivors of the Fort Henry garrison (both under Brigadier General Bushrod R. Johnson), the brigades of Pillow, Buckner, and Floyd, and Forrest's cavalry, Donelson was defended by nearly fifteen thousand men commanded by Pillow until Floyd, the senior officer, arrived on February 13.

Forrest's men arrived on the east bank of the Cumberland on Sunday, February 10, and Pillow appointed him acting brigadier general and commander of all of the cavalry within the fort (1,300 men). His Third Tennessee Cavalry ferried across the river the next day. Forrest conducted one of his usual quick inspections as they crossed. He was constantly inspecting, especially the horses and their equipment. "In Forrest's command, a sore-back horse was a felony," one veteran recalled. As soon as his steeds' hooves hit dry ground, Forrest reconnoitered toward Fort Henry. He sent word to General Pillow that the Yankees were preparing to advance.

Forrest was right. Grant began the twelve-mile drive from Henry to Donelson on February 12. He covered the first ten miles without opposition. Then he ran into Nathan Bedford Forrest. Taking maximum advantage of the rough terrain, Forrest's dismounted cavalrymen launched several sharp attacks that threw the Union cavalry back on its infantry. Despite being outnumbered ten to one, the boys in gray held up Grant's army for hours, until General Buckner ordered Forrest to retire. Grant then cut the main road to Nashville, and nearly surrounded Fort Donelson. The only road left in Rebel hands ran along the river and was

Brigadier General Gideon Pillow (1806–1878) was a Tennessee lawyer, slave owner, and land speculator before the war. He was a U.S. major general of volunteers during the Mexican War, where he performed well and was wounded twice. Antebellum, he was the law partner of Isham G. Harris, Tennessee's wartime governor. Forrest served under him at Fort Donelson. Although Forrest admired him, Pillow's career was ruined when he fled the doomed fort and left the garrison to its fate. He is buried in Elmwood Cemetery, Memphis.

partially inundated. Grant completed his encirclement of the garrison on February 13. The Rebels dug in, Forrest and Bushrod Johnson digging side-by-side with their men.

Several Federal attacks were turned back that day and Union sharpshooters were particularly active and annoying, prompting Forrest to grab a rifle from one of his men and, at a distance of several hundred yards, knock a Federal sniper out of a tree.

On February 14, the unusually mild weather turned bitterly cold. Floyd and his generals decided to attack and reopen the road to Nashville but, for reasons never made clear, Floyd put the attack off until afternoon.

From a hill, Forrest and most of the rest of the garrison watched a great land-sea battle. At 3 p.m., six Federal gunboats (four of them ironclads) attacked the water-facing batteries of Fort Donelson. "Parson, for God's sake, pray!" Forrest called to Major Kelley, "for nothing but God Almighty can save the fort!"

If God saved the fort, the instrument He used was a serious Yankee blunder. With their heavy naval guns, the Northerners could have stayed out of range of the fort's cannons and smashed the Rebel batteries with no danger to themselves. The Western Flotilla, however, pushed to within three hundred yards of the lighter Confederate guns—well within their range. The Southern gunners proved themselves better than the enemy thought, scoring hit after hit. Foote's flagship, the *St. Louis*, was struck several times in rapid succession. One solid shot blew away the pilot house, killed the pilot, and carried away the wheel. Another hit the flag officer in the foot and critically wounded him. The *St. Louis* drifted downstream, out of control and out of the battle. The USS *Louisville* was hit thirty-six times and the *Carondelet* fifty-four, and both were disabled. The *Pittsburg* was hit twenty times and was taking on water. It withdrew to keep from sinking. In all, the six Yankee gunboats were hit 147 times, and fifty-four men were killed and wounded. The garrison suffered no casualties, and Forrest learned a valuable lesson. While the ironclads had a fearsome reputation, they were far from invincible.

But while Forrest was, as ever, eager to fight, the normally aggressive General Pillow apparently lost his nerve after an aide standing next to him was killed by a Union sharpshooter. Pillow postponed his attack until the next day.

By dawn on February 15, Grant had twenty thousand men besieging the fort, with seven thousand more nearby on transports or within easy marching distance. All during the night of February 14/15, the Confederates silently shifted units to their left flank, with the goal of crushing U.S. General John A. McClernand's division, and opening the road to Nashville.

The Rebel regiments struck at 5 a.m. Forrest's cavalry formed the extreme left flank of the Southern line and advanced over terrain that was difficult for horses. After slow progress, however, he discovered that he had turned the Union right flank and was in McClernand's rear. Forrest rose in his stirrups, drew his sword, and charged. Coupled with the attacks of Pillow and Johnson, this was too much for the Yankees. They fell back to their second line, which held temporarily, thanks largely to a six-gun artillery battery. Forrest attacked and captured it, killing most of the artillery horses and the gunners, but not before both he and his brother Jeffrey lost their horses. Jeffrey was severely injured when his horse went down, but Forrest carried on, joined the Confederate infantry in the attack, and remounted and had two more horses shot beneath him. One of them died when an artillery shell hit the animal just behind Forrest's leg. In all, Forrest had twenty-nine horses shot out from under him, eighteen fatally, during the war.

In the midst of confused attacks and counterattacks, Forrest's aggressive strategy remained the same. At one point, seeing a Yankee advance, Forrest told General Pillow, "We can't stop 'em, but we can ride over 'em." The Yankees got the worst of it. By 9:30 a.m., the Union right was in full retreat. One Illinois brigade left 836 dead and wounded on the field.

Of all the senior Southern commanders, Forrest alone realized that a general advance would push the Federals back into Hickman's Swamp and possibly destroy Grant's army. He rode to General Johnson and begged him to issue the orders for a general attack, but Johnson (who was Pillow's second-in-command) refused. He thought the Yankees were trying to lure them into an ambush. Forrest desperately searched for Pillow, but couldn't find him. Pillow had gone over to the Confederate right flank, to see why Buckner had not attacked the Union left, as they had planned. It was several hours before the disorganized Rebels could advance again. By then, the Yankees had reinforced McClernand with two brigades from their left flank, which should have been pinned down by Buckner. Thus passed the only chance Floyd would ever have had to destroy Grant's army.

By mid-day, Forrest's cavalry had been pulled back into reserve. The temperature was twelve degrees Fahrenheit. The men were so cold and exhausted that scout Robert Martin fell asleep in a bed of snow. Fearing that he would die of exposure, Forrest and Adam Johnson picked him up, carried him in to a tent, lay him down, and covered him with blankets, during which time Martin remained fast asleep.[3]

If the Confederates could no longer inflict a decisive defeat on the bluecoats, they could escape with their army intact down to Nashville if Buckner's brigade could seize the Wynn's Ferry Road. Part of this road was covered by a Union battery, amidst a line Federal infantry, on a steep hill. "They must be silenced!" General Pillow cried. "Forrest must do it!"

Forrest decided to attack in columns of squadrons supported by Colonel Roger Hanson's Second Kentucky Infantry Regiment.

Hanson's men were green but they acted like veterans. They advanced to within fifty yards of the Union position at right shoulder arms, sustaining heavy casualties in the process. But when they did fire, the volley was awesome. As the Union line staggered, Forrest's men charged on foot, with their commander personally leading the attack. He was wounded seven times (none seriously) and his coat was punctured by fifteen bullets, but he overran the battery and put the escape route for the entire Confederate army firmly in Rebel hands. This brought the total of guns Grant had lost to Forrest to ten. He would carry off another 115 over the next three years, bringing the total to 125—about the same number as the Army of the Potomac turned on Pickett's Charge at Gettysburg. Remarkably, however, at about 2:30 p.m., Pillow ordered his troops to withdraw to their original positions. Forrest's men remained behind, collecting weapons and helping the wounded. He then returned to camp for some well-earned rest.

About 11:30 p.m. on February 15, an aide woke Forrest from a heavy sleep, with orders to report to Pillow's headquarters in the Dover Hotel, about a mile south of Fort Donelson. He found Floyd, Pillow, and Buckner sitting at a table. He walked in, saluted, and was told that the enemy had

Brigadier General John B. Floyd (1806–1863), former governor of Virginia (1848–1852), U.S. secretary of war (1857–1860), and an open opponent of secession before the election of Abraham Lincoln. Unfortunately for the South, he was an inept and inexperienced field commander. He was defeated in western Virginia in 1861 (where he was wounded), and decided to surrender the Confederate Army at Fort Donelson, rather than to launch a breakout attempt, which would very likely have succeeded. Later he mishandled the evacuation of Nashville, after which Jefferson Davis sacked him. He died a year later.

reinvested the fort. Taken aback, Forrest categorically refused to believe it. He and some of his scouts had crossed that ground at 9 p.m. and had not seen the enemy. Besides, Forrest asserted, Grant's right flank had been so badly battered it was in no condition to reinvest so quickly. The colonel argued that the garrison was not "penned up, surrounded or whipped." Buckner and Pillow, who had known each other in the

Mexican War—and hated each other ever since—were divided. Pillow sided with Forrest. Buckner had convinced Floyd to be much more pessimistic.

The three generals conferred briefly and ordered Forrest to send out scouts. When the scouts returned, they reported no sign of the enemy, but added that Federal campfires were still ablaze. Forrest argued that these were old campfires, and in fact he had seen Confederate relief parties helping wounded Yankees to the campfires earlier.

Nevertheless, to Forrest's astonishment, the Confederate generals decided that their last escape route was cut. Floyd and Buckner wanted to surrender. Pillow wanted to launch another breakout attempt or at least to hold out one more day. He was hoping for boats that could ferry most of the men to Clarksville.

Buckner believed that Grant had fifty thousand men surrounding the fort and that Foote's crippled fleet was, despite appearances, invincible. Buckner also averred that there was not enough ammunition for the men to defend Fort Donelson, disregarding a telegram stating that a steamboat load of ammo would arrive from Clarksville that very night. (It did. Several other boats carrying ammunition and provisions arrived around daylight.)

General Floyd was a professional politician. He deferred to Buckner (a West Point graduate and hero of the Mexican War). He opted for surrender. Bedford growled, "There is more fight left in these men than you think," before he stormed out of the room.

A few minutes later, Forrest's scouts reported that the river road, though flooded, was definitely open. Forrest returned to headquarters with this news, but the chief Confederate doctor advised that the men would die of pneumonia if they waded through freezing water in this bitter weather. Floyd dismissed any plan to escape, but added that he could not surrender to the Yankees personally. He was under Federal indictment for moving large quantities of arms to Southern arsenals just prior to secession. The charges were untrue but they sounded plausible, and Floyd was not about to go before a Northern jury. He turned command over to Pillow, who, in turn, handed command over to General Buckner.

As the generals debated who would surrender, Forrest announced, "I'll be damned if I'll surrender!" He had promised the parents of his soldiers that he would look after them, and he intended to keep his word. "I did not come here to surrender my command!" he roared. "I would rather my bones bleach on the hillside than go to a Yankee prison!" Forrest returned to his regiment. "Boys," he said, "these people are talking about surrendering, and I'm going out of this place before they do, or bust hell wide open!" He announced, "We're going out even if we die in the attempt!" In the darkness, he formed up most of his battalion—about five hundred men. He was joined by about one thousand men from other commands, including an artillery battery. At one point, the road was completely covered by water. There was no way to determine how deep it was. Forrest called for volunteers to test it. No one came forward. The colonel applied the spurs to his horse and checked it himself. It was not too deep.

Simon Bolivar Buckner (1823–1914), the man who surrendered Fort Donelson. Buckner was a West Point graduate and personal friend of Ulysses S. Grant. Although largely responsible for the disaster, his career was not ruined by it—unlike those of Floyd and Pillow. Exchanged after several months in prison, he later took part in the invasion of Kentucky, the defense of eastern Tennessee, and commanded the Department of Western Louisiana. He was promoted to lieutenant general in September 1863. He later was governor of Kentucky (1887–1891).

Shortly thereafter, a lieutenant and three other scouts reported that the enemy had blocked the road and was in line of battle. Forrest turned command over to Major Kelley (in case he did not come back) and, with his brother Jeffrey, rode out to see for himself. A cold, gray dawn was breaking as they moved closer to where the enemy was reported. The "Yankees" turned out to be a line of fence posts. The two brothers moved cautiously forward to the enemy campfires. They found only wounded men. The fires had been kept burning by small parties from both sides and a few farmers, so that the wounded would not freeze. Forrest later recalled that, after two hours on the road, "Not a gun had been fired at us, not an enemy had been seen or heard." Later, Forrest said: "I am clearly of the opinion that two-thirds of our army could have marched out without loss, and that, had we continued the fight the next day, we could have gained a glorious victory." But it was too late now to prevent Buckner from capitulating or to save Floyd and Pillow from ignominy and dishonor. Floyd escaped by steamboat and took his two Virginia regiments with him. Pillow fled aboard a small boat that ferried him to the west bank. Buckner surrendered 10,271 men. The total Confederate losses at Fort Donelson were about twelve thousand.[4]

What if the twelve thousand men lost at Donelson had been present on the first day of Shiloh, two months later? Grant's army would probably have been destroyed and the South might have won the war. But there was no use discussing might-have-beens. Kentucky and most of Tennessee was now lost to the Confederacy. Forrest turned his horse in the direction of Nashville, the fall of which, after the debacle at Fort Donelson, was only a matter of time.

Later, certain officers said that by leaving Fort Donelson Forrest was guilty of insubordination. Others, out of a strange sense of propriety, felt he should have remained with the garrison and surrendered with the army. Forrest ignored these criticisms. "He cared nothing for petty cabals, jealousies, and messroom talk," Captain James Harvey Mathes wrote later, "but would set out before breakfast and win a victory while others were drawing maps, or waiting to get a newspaper..."

It was eighty miles to Nashville. The weather was terrible, the animals were exhausted, the roads were bad, and there was no shelter at night; the army's tents were at Fort Donelson.

On the road, Forrest received word that Nashville had fallen. "I shall never forget the remark of that daring Col. Forrest just before he got to the bridge of the Cumberland River," Private John C. Lilly recalled. He told his men: "I am going in to that town. I don't care if there is ten thousand Yankees in there and any of you that don't want to follow me fall out of the ranks right here. Forward march!"

No one fell out. The rumor was false. There were no Yankees in Nashville—yet.

Nashville, a huge Confederate supply depot and manufacturing center eighty miles southeast of Fort Donelson, was in a state of panic. Mobs rioted and took over the doomed capital. General Johnston put Floyd in charge of the city and ordered him to bring off as many supplies as possible but, as usual, the former governor failed completely. When the first rumors arrived that General Grant was approaching the place, he fled for Murfreesboro, and command devolved onto Colonel Forrest.[5] No more fortunate event could have occurred, from the Confederate point of view. Arriving in the town on Tuesday, February 18, he encountered complete bedlam. Forrest immediately rode into the surging mob, found its leader, and knocked him out, smashing his head with a revolver. (Bedford always knew the quick way to handle a mob.) Bedford occupied a warehouse where an Irishman accosted him, demanding a share of the supplies. Forrest poleaxed him as well. He ordered his men to draw their swords and expel any unauthorized people from the depots at the point of their blades. When this was done, he put guards over the warehouses, countermanded orders to burn the railroad trains, restored civil government, telegraphed for more rolling stock, and commandeered every vehicle and wagon in the city. "Forrest had great common sense and a clear head for business and was a good quartermaster and commissary as well as a soldier," Adam Johnson recalled. "His genius for turning small things to account was something wonderful, and his commanding air always inspired confidence and made people think that he knew what he was about." With order restored, Forrest organized wagon trains of supplies and sent them south. Floyd had ordered Forrest to leave the city by Friday, February 21, at the latest, but the colonel saw no reason to obey this order. He and his men worked for three days, virtually without rest, and emptied most of the warehouses.

When mobs threatened his men, Forrest brought up fire engines and turned the hoses on the crowd. The cold water did the trick, and the evacuation continued, with supplies sent to Murfreesboro. Among other things, Forrest saved six hundred boxes of clothing, 250,000 pounds of bacon, forty wagons full of ammunition, and rifling machinery from a local factory. He destroyed five hundred barrels of liquor that belonged to the Confederate government and left the city only at the mayor's request. Don Carlos Buell's army had occupied Edgefield, across the Cumberland River from Nashville, twenty-four hours before. The Yankees entered the city on February 25, while Forrest galloped off to join Johnston's army, which was now moving west.

# CHAPTER 4

# SHILOH

*Take time to deliberate, but when the time for action has
arrived, stop thinking and go in.*

—Napoleon

orrest reported to General Johnston on February 24, 1862, and
was greeted most cordially. Johnston recognized, especially after
Fort Donelson and Nashville, Forrest's merit. In March, Forrest's
command was reorganized as the Third Tennessee Cavalry Regiment
and Forrest was elected colonel without opposition.

In the meantime, Ulysses S. Grant concentrated five of his six divisions in the vicinity of Pittsburg Landing on the Tennessee River, with
most of his troops located about two and a half miles south. Sherman's
division bivouacked around a little country church called Shiloh (See
Map on following page).

General Henry Halleck, the senior Union general in the west,
planned to reinforce Grant's Army of the Tennessee with Don Carlos
Buell's Army of the Ohio (five divisions), take personal command, and
advance on the major Confederate railroad junction of Corinth, Mississippi. General Johnston, however, preempted him.

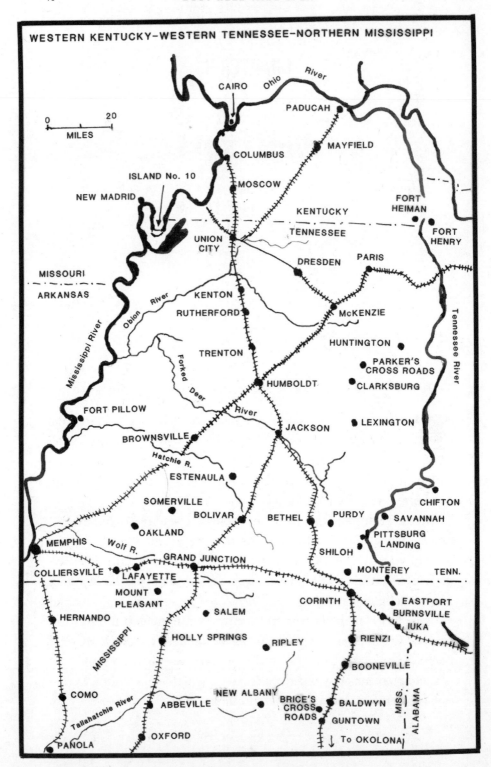

WESTERN KENTUCKY–WESTERN TENNESSEE–NORTHERN MISSISSIPPI

He hit the Yankees with his full force at dawn on April 6, and took them completely by surprise. After severe losses, the Northerners rallied and fought back stubbornly. Both armies were green, and at times, the fight was more a violent clash between two armed mobs than a battle between two well-organized armies. By the end of the day, Grant was in his final defensive position at the edge of the landings but, with dusk falling, the Rebel leaders decided not to attack again.

The terrain at Shiloh was wooded and not suitable for horses, so Johnston placed the Third Tennessee Cavalry in reserve behind his far right flank, near the confluence of Lick Creek and the Tennessee River. In the morning, the Confederates slowly pushed the Yankees back in hard and often fierce fighting. To his chagrin,

Albert Sidney Johnston (1803–1862), the former secretary of war for the Republic of Texas and commander of the Confederate Army of Mississippi at Shiloh. Jefferson Davis considered his death to be the turning point of the war.

an impatient Forrest was left out of the battle. He sent a dispatch to General Johnston, asking for orders. None came. About 11 a.m., he could stand it no longer. He drew up his regiment in line of battle.

"Boys, do you hear that rattle of musketry and the roar of artillery?"

"Yes, yes!"

"Do you know what it means? It means that our friends and brothers are falling by the hundreds at the hands of the enemy and we are here guarding a damn creek! We did not enter the service for such work and the reputation of this regiment does not justify our commanding officer in leaving us here while we are needed elsewhere. Let's go and help them! What do you say?"

"Yes! Yes!"

Without orders, Forrest moved his command forward, into the area that became known as the Hornets' Nest, right behind Major General

Benjamin F. Cheatham's division. Cheatham's men had just been driven back, and Forrest asked Cheatham if he should attack. Cheatham would not grant permission; if Forrest attacked, he would do so on his own initiative and on his own responsibility without Cheatham's support. Undeterred, Forrest ordered his men to move from marching formation to battle formation and led a charge at a gallop. His unit quickly overran a Union battery and took dozens of prisoners. One gun and some of the bluecoat infantry escaped into the blackjack thickets. Not long thereafter, other Rebel forces surrounded General Benjamin H. Prentiss's division on the Sunken Road, and after a fierce battle, compelled it to surrender. Forrest was ordered to guard the prisoners and take them to the rear. He turned two-thirds of the regiment over to Lieutenant Colonel Kelley and delegated this duty to him. He continued to push forward with the remaining squadron.

On April 6, only Brigadier General James R. Chalmers's Mississippi Brigade advanced as far as did the Third Tennessee Cavalry Regiment. From a small hill beside the river, they saw the enemy crowded on the banks and in great confusion. But the losses on both sides were severe. Among the Confederate dead was Albert Sidney Johnston.[1] Command devolved onto General P. G. T. Beauregard, who learned that Grant had lined up fifty-two guns for a last stand at Pittsburg Landing. The Little Creole hesitated. He decided to finish off the Yankees the next day.

As night fell, Forrest made a personal reconnaissance of the Union far left flank, crawling forward close enough to hear the Yankee soldiers talking. To his dismay, he learned that the vanguard of General Buell's army had arrived and that more reinforcements were on the way. The noise from the direction of Pittsburg Landing confirmed what Forrest heard: troops were definitely crossing the river. He went in search of Beauregard, to tell him he must launch a night attack at once if he had any hope of winning this battle, because he would be heavily outnumbered by morning. He never found the Louisianan, but he did find General William J. Hardee, the commander of III Corps. Hardee brushed off Forrest's warning, saying that the plans for tomorrow had been made and could not be changed. They had better be changed, Bedford retorted, or the Army of Mississippi would be "whipped like hell" in the morning.

After a fruitless argument with Hardee, Forrest returned to his camp and received the news every parent dreads. Willie, his only son and only surviving child, was missing. A deeply worried Forrest went out into the horrors of the night looking for him but to no avail. When he finally gave up and returned to camp, Willie was there. Not only was he unhurt, he and another boy had brought in fifteen Yankee prisoners.

When dawn broke on April 7, Forrest's men were still on the far right flank, under the command of Breckinridge's Reserve Corps. It turned back three attacks and Forrest's cavalry played a prominent role in checking the last one. Grant, however, had been reinforced with twenty thousand fresh troops and now heavily outnumbered the Army of Mississippi. Grant kept up the pressure and pushed the Confederates slowly back until 2:30 p.m., when Beauregard admitted defeat and withdrew in the direction of Corinth.

The losses at Shiloh were tremendous on both sides. Grant and Buell lost 13,047 men (26.8 percent of their men) and the Rebels suffered 10,699 casualties (24.3 percent of their army). These casualties exceeded the total American casualties in the American Revolution, the War of 1812, and the Mexican War combined. The Yankees lost fifty generals and regimental commanders, while the Rebels lost forty-five, including General Johnston, the highest ranking officer killed in action during the Civil War.[2] One historian wrote that, after Shiloh, the South never smiled. A Northern soldier commented for both sides when he said that no one who was at Shiloh ever spoiled for a fight again.

Former U.S. Vice President John C. Breckinridge, now a major general, C.S.A.,[3] took charge of the retreat with five thousand infantrymen and Forrest's cavalry acting as his rearguard. They bivouacked four and one half miles south of Pittsburg Landing on the night of April 7/8. That night, Grant and Sherman planned the pursuit of the defeated Rebel army.

Sherman pursued with two infantry brigades and two squadrons of cavalry, backed by a division of Buell's army. Six miles southwest of

Pittsburg Landing, Breckinridge's men covered the road with fallen trees for two hundred yards. Sherman was in a hurry to catch the Rebels and, in his haste to run them down, allowed his cavalry to become separated from his infantry, and his advanced guard of two battalions became separated from the main body as it crossed a stream. Forrest was lurking in the woods off his left flank, waiting for just this kind of opportunity. As soon as Sherman made his mistake, Forrest launched an all-out attack. Three hundred fifty Southern horsemen burst out of the woods, firing their revolvers and screaming their Rebel yells, and Forrest narrowly missed bagging William Tecumseh Sherman personally.

Sherman and his entourage ran through the lines of an Ohio regiment. Forrest's men reined in, but their commander—at the front as usual—barreled right into them and found himself alone and surrounded. There are two versions as to what happened next. One is that several dozen Federals fired at him and all but one missed. At point blank range, one of the Ohioans shot him in the side and the bullet lodged just above his hip and an inch from his spine. His right arm was temporarily useless. His horse was also shot but kept on going. Forrest used his revolver and cleared an escape path back to the woods. His reins were probably between his teeth, as was the usual procedure employed by Rebel cavalrymen in combat situations.

The other version of the story is that Forrest grabbed a Union N.C.O. and used him as a human shield until he got out of range of Yankee muskets. When he was out of danger, he let the sergeant go. This version seems even more unlikely, especially for a man with a temporarily paralyzed arm. But, without a doubt, one of these unlikely accounts is true. I tend to believe the first version.

Either way, Forrest made his escape, but he suffered his first serious wound of the war. He headed for Corinth but, due to the pain of his injury, was forced to stop and get into a buggy. This ride proved to be even more painful than the horse, so he remounted, despite a driving hail storm. He turned command of the regiment over to Kelley and went into a hospital. Dr. J. B. Cowan, a cousin of Mary's, performed surgery on the wounded colonel without anesthetics, but he could not find the bullet. Meanwhile,

Sherman's disorganized vanguard recovered but only advanced a few hundred yards more after the Battle of Fallen Timbers, in order to capture a Rebel hospital. Sherman only allowed cavalry scouts to go beyond this point. He returned to the rear and told Grant that further pursuit was inadvisable. Thus ended the Shiloh campaign.

On April 10, Colonel Forrest was feeling much better and was given a sixty-day furlough. His toughness and his iron constitution enabled him to leave almost immediately for home and his wife. Nineteen days later, however, Colonel Kelley asked him to return to Corinth. There was discontent in the regiment over a lack of food—especially good food. Forrest returned at once and quickly solved the problem. Private John C. Lilly recalled: "one day we were surprised when Col. Forrest arrived in Camp. Although he was looking a little pale, we were glad to see him back to take command of his Old Regiment. Col. Forrest was considered somewhat ruff [sic] with his men, but there never was a better officer to provide for his men. In camp or on a march we always had plenty of grub and horse feed. He would make the Quartermaster hustle."

A week after he returned, while reconnoitering the advancing Yankee lines, his horse jumped a log. The jolt jarred the bullet, which touched a nerve, causing severe pain. Forrest was taken to the hospital, where, this time, surgeons found the bullet and removed it in a complicated and dangerous operation.

Forrest was in the hospital for two weeks, but his wound had not dampened his ardor. He had gotten a thrill out of the Battle of Shiloh. He wrote a friend (apparently from a hospital bed) and declared that he could not wait for the next big battle—the bigger, the better.

# CHAPTER 5

# THE MURFREESBORO RAID

*Losers make promises they often break.*
*Winners make commitments they always keep.*

—Denis Waitley

O n April 11, 1862, General Henry W. Halleck arrived at Pittsburg Landing, assumed command of the forces Grant had led at Shiloh, and, on May 2, began a drive on Corinth, an important railroad junction twenty-five miles to the south.[1] Outnumbered more than two to one, Beauregard conducted a brilliant delaying action. When the Northerners finally entered Corinth on May 30, everyone was gone, including the civilians. The Little Creole, in the meantime, fell back toward Tupelo, forty miles south of Corinth. Meanwhile, Colonel James C. Saunders, a prominent north Alabamian, turned up at Beauregard's headquarters and asked that Forrest be named commander of the Confederate cavalry in Major General Edmund Kirby Smith's Chattanooga district. Saunders, who was over sixty, was too old to do the job himself. Beauregard was reluctant to transfer Forrest but, in the end, relented. On June 11, Colonel Forrest said goodbye to his regiment and headed for the gateway city of Chattanooga. He arrived on June 19, and began forming a brigade of cavalry.[2]

General P. G. T. Beauregard (1818–1893), victor of Fort Sumter and First Bull Run and commander of the Army of Mississippi. He recognized Forrest's value long before most of the Confederate high command, but his poor relationship with Jefferson Davis minimized his value to the Confederacy. Davis relieved him of his command in June 1862 for going on sick leave without bothering to inform Richmond. He later did a good job defending Charleston, South Carolina, and Petersburg, Virginia.

Forrest's new command was a rag-tag outfit and part of it, the First Kentucky Cavalry, virtually dissolved itself. Its men had enlisted for twelve months in 1861, their enlistments were up, their state had been overrun by invaders, and they understandably wanted to go home. Most of them did. The strength of the regiment plummeted to 120 men. All totaled, Forrest had around one thousand horsemen by July 9.

In June 1862, while Beauregard held off Halleck north of Tupelo, Buell drove on Chattanooga with thirty thousand men. If the Yankees seized Chattanooga, with its east to west railroad connections, it might be a body blow from which the Confederacy could not recover. Kirby Smith, with fewer than ten thousand men, delayed the Yankee advance, but he needed help. Forrest knew that an army does not have to be defeated in the field to be forced back. If its supply lines are severed, if it has no food except what is with the line regiments, it will retreat on its own accord to avoid starving, even if there is little resistance in front of it. This is what Forrest had in mind on July 9, when he left Chattanooga for the Union rear. His target was Murfreesboro. It was Buell's main supply depot and the railroad from Nashville to Chattanooga ran right through it.

From his scouts, Forrest knew the route he should take to reach Murfreesboro undetected.

Forrest kept his new command's ranks well closed up and, about 11 p.m., July 12, rode into Woodbury, nineteen miles from Murfreesboro.

The women of the town were, in the words of Andrew Nelson Lytle, "moving about like mad hornets." Captain Oliver Cromwell Rounds, the U.S. Army's provost marshal in Murfreesboro, had that afternoon taken away the men and boys of the town and locked them in the Murfreesboro jailhouse. Six were to be hanged in the morning as retribution for a Union soldier who had been killed nearby. Among those marked for death was the Reverend William Owens, the local Baptist preacher, and a much loved and very pious man. The ladies, and their crying children, were almost hysterical. They pleaded for help.

Any abused woman who needed Forrest's help was sure to get it. He promised them that their husbands and sons would be back with them by sundown the following day. The women—fearful, grateful, and hopeful, all at once—brought out hams and chicken, black-eyed peas and cornbread, cakes and pies. They had cooked this food for their families' Sunday dinners, but now they gave them to the hungry riders, who gobbled them down with profuse thanks. Forrest gave his boys just enough time to eat and rest and water their horses. Then the angry colonel applied the spurs to his steed and rode off into the night, followed by his entire command. He had a promise to keep!

The Murfreesboro garrison consisted of the Ninth Michigan Infantry Regiment (Colonel William Duffield), the Third Minnesota (Colonel Henry C. Lester), a Kentucky artillery battery, and a squadron of Pennsylvania cavalry—1,500 men and four guns in all. But it was a divided command. The Michiganders and Minnesotans could not get along, so the Ninth (plus the Pennsylvania cavalry) was posted a half mile east of the town, while the Third Minnesota and the artillerymen camped on the Stone River, just off the Nashville Turnpike, one and a half miles northwest of the courthouse. Murfreesboro itself was held by one company of Michigan infantry, various provost and supply units, and the staff of Brigadier General Thomas T. Crittenden. He had just arrived and was not slated to take command until later that morning.

Forrest knew about the flawed Union dispositions from his scouts. He ordered them to eliminate all fifteen Federal pickets without firing a shot, which they did. A second party would storm the courthouse and the jailhouse, while a third dealt with the Yankees in the rest of the town. A fourth would attack the Michigan regiment outside Murfreesboro.

At 4:30 a.m. on July 13, the Reverend Owens was on his knees, praying for deliverance from the hands of the Philistines (that is, the Yankees), when he heard the low rumble of thunder. But it didn't stop; in fact, it grew in volume. It was the sound of the horses' hooves. God (or at least Forrest) was answering his prayer. The Yankees fled, but not before one of them set the jail on fire and took the keys with him. Rebel cavalry swiftly rounded up the fleeing Northerners while Forrest and his men broke down the cell doors and freed the prisoners.

One of the freed Southerners was Captain William Richardson of Alabama, one of two spies in the jailhouse who had been captured behind Union lines and whom the Yankees therefore had every right to hang. Forrest asked Richardson if anyone had abused or mistreated them. Only one, Richardson replied: the same man who set the jailhouse on fire and tried to roast them alive. Richardson noticed that Forrest's face turned red and his eyes "flashed like fire," but he said nothing.

While Forrest dealt with the jailhouse, Colonel John Wharton and part of his Texas regiment charged straight through the town, into the Michigan soldiers' camp and right over their tents. The dashing and gallant Wharton personally shot Colonel Duffield in the groin and left thigh, but was himself wounded a few moments later. Duffield soon passed out from loss of blood and his second-in-command, Lieutenant Colonel John G. Parkhurst, bravely rallied the regiment, which fought well, despite having been so rudely awakened. In violation of the plan, half of the Texans had veered off into the town, leaving Wharton with only two hundred men. They were not able to destroy the Michigan regiment, which created a strong position amid baggage wagons and forage bales and behind a cedar fence. The Texans and Michiganders continued to snipe at each other all morning, but there were no more major charges.

Meanwhile, the Second Georgia and the errant Texans cleared the town. They were spurred on by the ladies of Murfreesboro, who ignored enemy fire to greet and cheer on the boys in gray. A Michigan infantry company defended the courthouse and turned back two uncoordinated Confederate attacks. Forrest then took personal command. He ordered the Georgians to attack the rear of the courthouse while he and a mixed bag of Texans and Georgians dealt with the front door. "Long live the women!" the cavaliers cried as they battered down the doors and carried the position after some hand-to-hand fighting. As was the case in the jailhouse, they found dozens of civilian hostages. More than 150 citizens were freed from the two places, including the men from Woodbury.

Despite being over sixty years of age and not being subject to military service, Colonel Saunders joined Forrest as a volunteer aide and took part in the fighting for the courthouse. A Union bullet struck him in the chest, passed through his right lung and out his back. Everyone thought he was mortally wounded, but the tough old bird made a full recovery, rejoined the Confederate Army and lived until 1898.

Meanwhile, detachments of Rebels were looking for Crittenden and Rounds. They found the general hiding in a private apartment behind a saloon. They treated him with the dignity befitting his rank. The captain would be another matter.

Oliver Cromwell Rounds did not duplicate the morally upright behavior of his namesake. When one of the ladies learned who Forrest was looking for, she gleefully told the general and his entourage that Rounds stayed in the house of a woman of doubtful morality. She gave the cavalrymen the exact location of the house, which was only a couple of blocks away. "And don't stop at her bedroom door!" she cried as a group of young graycoats headed off in the direction she indicated.

Forrest's detachment found the captain hiding under the woman's bed. They pulled him out but reportedly did not let him dress. The miserable officer was unceremoniously plopped on a horse and spirited off to captivity clad only in his nightshirt.

Now that the town was secure, Forrest turned his attention to destroying the Ninth Michigan and Third Minnesota. Colonel William J. Lawton's Second Georgia blocked the front of the Minnesota regiment around the beautiful Oaklands Plantation,[3] while Forrest sent six companies of Kentucky and Tennessee troops to attack the wagon trains in their rear. The Yankees repulsed them twice. Forrest was furious. He reformed his companies and gave them a world-class dressing down. So harsh and profane were his remarks that no man forgot what, for many, was the worst cursing out of their lives. But they now understood that Forrest would not tolerate their leaving the field in the face of the enemy. Forrest then personally led the next charge, which carried the position.

During this attack, a black man (probably a teamster) picked up a pistol and shot at Forrest five times. The colonel turned his horse and, from thirty paces, fired a single shot, killing him instantly.

Forrest left Colonel Lawton with seven companies to keep watch on the battered Third Minnesota, while turning most of his command against the Ninth Michigan. Some of Forrest's officers, however, were worried that the large Union garrisons along the railroad (ten regiments of them!) had been alerted and were likely sending relief columns. These officers asked Forrest to be content with a partial victory and to pull out while he still could. "I didn't come here to make a half job of it!" Forrest snapped. "I'm going to have them all!"

When he had his troops in position, Forrest raised a flag of truce and sent a message to Duffield. It read:

> COLONEL: I must demand an unconditional surrender of your force as prisoners of war or I will have every man put to the sword. You are aware of the overpowering force I have at

my command, and this demand is made to prevent the effusion of blood.

I am, Colonel, very respectfully, your obedient servant,
N. B. Forrest
Brigadier-General of Cavalry, C. S. Army

Forrest deliberately overstated his rank to impress the Yankees and
help intimidate them into surrendering. He would not officially be promoted for another eight days.

Lieutenant Colonel Parkhurst passed this note to Duffield, who was
in bed in a nearby residence, but the wounded commander left the decision to him. By now, half of Parkhurst's command had been killed,
wounded, or captured, and there was no evidence that help was on the
way. Besides, he, Duffield, and the rest of the Union army had been hard
on the citizens of middle Tennessee, and they feared Confederate ven-
geance. Parkhurst, himself seriously wounded, surrendered to the Confederates around noon.

Forrest now turned his full attention to Colonel Lester. Another flag
of truce went up. Lester wanted to speak with Duffield, and Forrest
readily acceded. After their conference, he too surrendered. Forrest had
bagged virtually the entire garrison. He had 1,200 Yankee prisoners,
including a general; three hundred mules; 150 horses; arms and equipment of all kinds; and four pieces of artillery. Forrest estimated that he
lost about twenty-five killed and forty to sixty wounded, which was
probably a low estimate. And, as promised, the men of Westbury
returned to their families before nightfall.

In the town square after the battle, a sergeant called the roll of prisoners. Captain Richardson[4] recalled that only one was missing. The
sergeant called the name again.

"Pass on. It's all right," Colonel Forrest ordered.

The missing man was the Union jailer who abused the prisoners and
set the jailhouse on fire. No one ever saw him again.

The Southerners loaded all the supplies they could in the captured
wagons and burned everything else, including the supply depot outside

of town, burning bridges and ripping up railroad tracks. They left Murfreesboro about 6 p.m. and traveled nine miles toward McMinnville. In the last thirty hours, they had ridden about sixty miles and had fought a twelve hour battle.

Bedford Forrest had celebrated his forty-first birthday by capturing almost as many prisoners as he had men.[5] There were, in fact, so many captured wagons that he could not carry them all off. So he segregated the Northern officers from the enlisted men and offered the enlisted men a deal: if enough of them volunteered to drive the wagons to McMinnville, he would parole all of them once they got there and let them go home. One Yankee shouted: "Three cheers for General Forrest!" The Union POWs responded lustily. It was almost a unique occurrence in the Civil War—Yankee soldiers cheering a Southern general.

Bedford's men captured or burned 150,000 rations and knocked the Nashville and Chattanooga Railroad out of commission for two weeks. Buell could not feed his army, which he immediately put on half rations and decided to withdraw. The Federal drive on Chattanooga was over, at least for the time being.

The affair at Murfreesboro was more than a brilliantly successful cavalry raid: it completely changed the strategic balance of power in middle Tennessee and Kentucky. When it occurred, Braxton Bragg (who replaced Beauregard on June 17), was in the process of moving his army east from Tupelo to Chattanooga. He and Kirby Smith had come up with a brilliant strategic plan: outflank Buell and invade Kentucky. Now they would have time to execute it.

After the Murfreesboro victory, Forrest's reputation spread like wildfire, both nationally and internationally. Emperor Napoleon III was so excited when he heard the story that he sent Forrest a fine pair of binoculars, which he carried with him for the rest of the war. Also, the women of the southwest[6] now felt that they had a knight and protector in General Forrest. (He was officially promoted on July 21.) They would actually threaten Union officers who acted improperly with him, saying things like "I'll tell General Forrest on you!" or "Ol' Forrest will get you for that!" Soon many Yankees began to believe it also. He became sort of a bogeyman to Northern soldiers. Much like Erwin Rommel in World War II, he became a psychological threat to the Federal troops. Like Rommel, enemy soldiers developed a begrudging respect for him, which sometimes crossed the line into outright appro- bation. The enemy generals, on the other hand, hated him. "His meth- ods were not calculated to impress his foes with admiration," Judge Young wrote later. "The many reverses they had suffered at his hands, the wholesale fear of his presence, his desperate courage, boundless resources [resourcefulness], rapidity of movement, rapidity of onslaught, recklessness in facing death, and insensibility to fatigue made failure practically unknown in his campaigns, and he became a terror to his foes and a tower of strength to his comrades." Many agreed with Cap- tain John W. Morton, who wrote that Forrest had "a massive brain, an inflexible purpose, unflinching courage, tireless energy, and a will that could brook no opposition…truly a combination of characteristics and attributes rarely found in one man."

Forrest never lifted a finger to advance his own reputation, publicize himself, or court a journalist, however. His reputation nevertheless grew with amazing speed and spread throughout the southwestern Confed- eracy, which desperately needed a hero. The ladies loved him, the enemy feared him, and his own troops did both. None of this affected Forrest one bit. He never sought promotion. Had Governor Harris not called upon him to raise a battalion, he would have been content to remain a private in the ranks. Forrest's fame and reputation extended down to his men, who were extremely proud to be part of Forrest's cavalry, which was now being called "winged infantry" and "lightning infantry."

The harshest detractors of the Confederate cavalry were, without a doubt, the Confederate infantrymen. They poked fun at them, usually with one-liners, like "Whoever saw a dead cavalryman?" or "Dead men don't wear spurs." Another popular joke went:

Infantryman: Have you ever seen a dead Yankee?

Cavalryman (impatiently): Yes!

Infantryman: Did you stop and look at him?

Cavalryman: Yes!

Infantryman: What was the matter? Did your horse fall down or was your spurs broken?

But when the infantry found out that a particular horse soldier rode with Forrest, the tone instantly changed to one of respect. They wanted to know all about the man who was now called "the Wizard of the Saddle" far and wide, what raids had the cavalryman been on, and was he with Forrest at Fort Donelson, Shiloh, Fallen Timbers, Nashville, Murfreesboro. And there were no more jokes.

The Murfreesboro operation was not the end of Forrest's operations in middle Tennessee. He wanted to neutralize Buell until Bragg completed his move to Chattanooga, and Buell wanted to run Forrest down and kill or capture him.

Union forces were marching in all directions. They thought Forrest might have as many as seven thousand men. Buell sent an entire division under Brigadier General William "Bull" Nelson to suppress the Wizard of the Saddle, along with 1,200 cavalrymen. Pursuing Forrest's swift horsemen with infantry was fruitless. He captured Lebanon, Tennessee on July 20 (the garrison escaped the night before) and the jubilant citizens of which threw a huge party at which Forrest was the guest of honor. The next day, Forrest and his men visited the Hermitage, the home of President Andrew Jackson, a man Forrest greatly admired,[7] a few miles outside of Nashville. It was the first anniversary of the Confederate victory at Bull Run and a good number of the prominent citizens of Nashville were celebrating there, so the Rebels got to attend another party. That afternoon, Forrest rode down the Lebanon Pike to within sight of the capitol building, causing anxiety among the Yankees, but doing no damage, other than capturing a few prisoners. Nelson chased him, but Forrest doubled back to the railroad, which the Yankees had been repairing for two weeks, and did another two weeks' worth of damage. The Wizard then disappeared again.

From Washington, D.C., where he had returned, Halleck, now the general-in-chief of the Union Army, telegraphed Nelson to express his displeasure that Forrest had not been apprehended. Nelson signaled back that "to chase Morgan and Forrest, they mounted on race horses, with infantry in this hot weather is a hopeless task." Forrest rode around, through, and occasionally over the Army of the Ohio, capturing pickets and patrols, burning bridges, and tearing up railroad tracks. "Our guards are gathered up by the enemy as easily as he would herd cattle," General Buell moaned. Forrest marched and countermarched between Nashville and Murfreesboro three times and burned up to three bridges a day.

Buell reinforced Nelson with two more infantry brigades, but it was not enough. With John Hunt Morgan, another Rebel raider, striking between Nashville and Louisville, Nelson moved north of the Cumberland to chase after Morgan and George H. Thomas took command of the troops chasing Forrest. Although he turned out to be one of the best Union generals in the Civil War, Thomas had no success against Forrest, who doubled back and destroyed Thomas's wagon train.

Despite (or because of) his success, a rift developed between Forrest and Braxton Bragg. Bragg suggested that Forrest use his cavalry as an observation force and retire east to the Sequatchie Valley if pressed by the Federals. Forrest decided that the best way to check Buell was to operate in his rear.

Bragg was very jealous and insecure, and he sent Forrest a mild letter of reprimand for not honoring Bragg's suggestions. Bragg did not restrict his criticism of General Forrest to his correspondence. He told Brigadier General St. John Liddell: "I have not a single general officer of cavalry fit for command…look at Forrest! The man is ignorant and does not know anything of cooperation. He is nothing more than a good raider."

Meanwhile, Thomas doggedly pursued Forrest with four columns of troops. At one point, it looked like he had him, too. The Wizard was isolated in a mountainous area with few roads. Thomas went so far as to report that Forrest had been captured, along with eight hundred of his men. Forrest, however, eluded capture by leading his men into a dry creek bed at the base of a mountain and hiding there until the Union infantry marched past. After night fell, the men silently led their horses

past the Federal picket line, which was only six hundred yards away.
They then took the road to McMinnville, which was fifteen miles to the
west. About halfway there, they ran into a Union roadblock. Forrest's
men shouted and galloped around it. The startled Yankees fired a few
shots, but no one was hurt on either side. Forrest's total losses in the
entire operation were a few mules and one wagon.

After operating behind Union lines for two months, Forrest linked
up with Bragg and the rest of the Army of Tennessee (formerly the Army
of Mississippi) on September 3. Bragg now had two choices: drive west
into middle Tennessee or northwest into Kentucky. He chose the second
option. Kirby Smith had already crushed and routed Nelson's forces at
Richmond, Kentucky, on August 30, killing or capturing 5,194 out of
the 6,500 Yankees engaged.[8]

Bragg ordered Forrest to delay Buell's retreat by harassing and
attacking his rear. To help accomplish this task, he allowed Bedford to
keep the four cannons he captured at Murfreesboro, and reinforced
him with four companies of Alabama cavalry from his old regiment.
Forrest succeeded brilliantly. He hung very close to Buell's rear guard
and forced him to deploy several times to save his wagon trains, while
Bragg's hard-marching infantry raced ahead of the Union vanguards.
On September 14, Bragg attached Forrest's brigade to General (and
Episcopal Bishop) Leonidas Polk's I Corps of the Army of Tennessee.
That same day, Forrest invested Munfordville, Kentucky—where the
Louisville & Nashville Railroad crossed the Green River—and isolated
the Federal garrison. Polk's infantry joined him shortly thereafter, and
the garrison surrendered on September 17. More than four thousand
prisoners were taken, and Buell's main route of retreat was in Southern
hands.

Braxton Bragg had won the race. His army was between Buell and
the Union supply base at Louisville. He was in a position to destroy the
Army of the Ohio. There was panic in Louisville, and Cincinnati, where
the citizens blocked roads, fortified businesses and stores, and prepared
for a presumed looming battle. At the same time, following his crushing
victory at Second Manassas, Robert E. Lee swept northward into

Maryland. The Confederacy appeared to
be in the ascendant.

But, as was frequently the case, Braxton Bragg lost his nerve. He stepped aside
and allowed Buell to retreat through Munfordville to Louisville.

Forrest was disgusted that this great
opportunity had been wasted, and he said
so in outspoken and profane terms. Forrest's own health may have had something
to do with this. Out on patrol, his
exhausted horse collapsed. Taken by surprise, Forrest was not able to get off in
time. The animal landed on him and then
rolled over him. Although not seriously
injured, he still hurt—and he was not a
good patient. His physical ailments always
affected his temper.

Bragg had promised to make Forrest
chief of cavalry for the army, but he bris-
tled at Forrest's criticism. As a result, on

Major General Don Carlos Buell (1818–
1898) saved the Union Army at Shiloh
and won the Battle of Perryville. He was
less successful against Bedford Forrest.
Not favorably disposed to the Lincoln
administration, he was sacked for political reasons in October 1862 and was
replaced by William S. Rosecrans.

September 25, the same day Buell reached Louisville, Bragg summoned
Forrest to army headquarters at Bardstown and relieved him of his
command. He ordered the Wizard to return to middle Tennessee and
raise a brigade of six new regiments—four infantry and two cavalry.
He was allowed to keep his four Alabama companies, his Escort Company, and his staff. Bragg selected Major General Joseph Wheeler of
Georgia as his chief of cavalry. A twenty-six-year-old West Point graduate, Wheeler was energetic, gallant, courteous, likeable, friendly,
selfless, devoted to duty and the cause, and unquestionably brave. He
also was more deferential to his commander than Forrest could bring
himself to be.

Bragg continued to maneuver against Buell until October 8, when
the Army of the Ohio won a less than overwhelming victory at Perryville

over the Army of Tennessee. Bragg retreated back to middle Tennessee. Lee's attempt to capture Maryland, meanwhile, came to a bloody end at the Battle of Sharpsburg (Antietam) on September 17, and he fell back into Virginia.

In the meantime, Forrest rode 165 miles in five days. As soon as he arrived in Murfreesboro, which was again in Confederate hands, he began recruiting. Instead of four infantry and two cavalry regiments, however, he formed four cavalry regiments and ten unregimented cavalry companies—the equivalent of another regiment without a regimental headquarters.[9] Excited by the opportunity to serve under Forrest, men rushed to his banner. He soon had more than two thousand horsemen in his new command.

Finding volunteers was one thing; equipping them was another. The Confederate government was able to furnish only enough good Enfield rifles and low quality Belgian muskets for Colonel George G. Dibrell's Eighth Tennessee to arm a single company (perhaps sixty men), but he was also given four hundred ancient flintlock muskets, similar to those used in the American Revolution. Some of the men brought shotguns and revolvers from home. Other men went into their first battles with no arms at all.

Braxton Bragg had promised Forrest that he would be in charge of middle Tennessee, but as soon as Forrest organized his forces, Bragg sent General Breckinridge to supersede him. Forrest took it like a good soldier, although he lost what little respect he had left for Bragg. On the other hand, he admired Breckinridge and might have voted for him when he ran for president of the United States in 1860. The Kentucky politician was also a fairly good general who improved over time, and he had three thousand infantrymen with him.[10] When Forrest suggested that they take Nashville, Breckinridge was all for it. They drove to the edge of the city and probed its defenses but found them too strong to attack.

Meanwhile, the Wizard's fame was causing trouble at home. Memphis fell on June 6. A few weeks later, a Union sailor (the master's mate on the gunboat *Carondelet*) and a detachment of men showed up at Bedford's mother's house, a few miles northeast of the city. The NCO insulted Mrs. Luxton (nee Forrest) and spoke rudely and abusively to her. All her sons except John were in the army, so she went to see him the next day.

John was the second oldest Forrest boy after Bedford. He was not in uniform because during his service in the Mexican War, an enemy bullet had shattered his spine, leaving him permanently paralyzed from the waist down, but able to walk with crutches. A few days later, the sailor and his men turned up at the boarding house were John lived. John reprimanded him for upsetting his mother. The Federal was unrepentant and cursed John. John threatened to break his crutches over the mate's head if he did not shut his mouth. The bluecoat wouldn't let up and began lambasting the entire Forrest family, whereupon John arose, raised a crutch and attempted to wallop the sailor, but another Yankee kicked the other crutch out from under him and he fell. Apparently it amused this particular group of Federals to see a crippled man on the floor, struggling to recover his crutches. But John wasn't struggling for his crutches; he was reaching for his Derringer. He pulled it before they could react, and a moment later there were two men on the floor, and the abusive sailor was in critical condition, although he would eventually pull through. The paralyzed Mexican War veteran was taken to a gunboat, where he was chained up in solitary confinement.

When word of John's plight reached General Forrest, he immediately wrote the commandant of Memphis, demanding that the Yankees release his brother, or at least give him humane treatment and a fair trial—or they would wish they had. John was released immediately. He was eventually tried in front of a panel of Union officers who did not think verbally abusing mothers and kicking crutches from under handicapped war heroes was at all amusing, and he was acquitted.[11]

Forrest formed a fine staff when he got his first brigade, and it would remain largely unchanged throughout the war. Captain (later Major)

John P. Strange of Memphis, the sergeant major of the original battalion, was the adjutant. Captain Mathes called him "a gentleman of polished demeanor and dauntless spirit" who had great influence with General Forrest. He later turned down a promotion to colonel to remain with "the Wizard."

The chief of artillery was Samuel Freeman, an overweight attorney and school teacher from the Nashville area. He was also very good at his job and was very popular with the staff and men.

Captain (later Major) Gilbert V. Rambaut, a former Memphis hotel manager, was the son of a refugee from the French Revolution was chief commissary officer.[12] Young Rambaut had been born in Petersburg, Virginia, but moved to Memphis in 1857. Originally opposed to secession, he followed his adopted state out of the Union and enlisted in Forrest's original battalion in 1861 at the age of twenty-five. Forrest dictated his reports to Rambaut until Charles Anderson joined his staff. It was said that Rambaut never missed an opportunity to get into a fight. In late 1862, he turned down a promotion to lieutenant colonel in order to remain with Bedford and, like Strange and Anderson, remained with him until the end of the war.[13]

Bedford's son, Private (later Lieutenant) William (Willie) Forrest was his father's principal aide. He was promoted to captain near the end of the war.

Captain Adam "Stovepipe" Johnson was his first chief of scouts, but Johnson left the regiment soon after Fort Donelson. Eventually rising to the rank of brigadier general, he received his nickname when he forced two thousand Indiana militiamen to evacuate the town of Newburgh, Indiana, by mounting pieces of stovepipe on the running gear of a wagon, making the militiamen think he had a cannon. Johnson had only twelve men with him at the time. His storied career ended tragically in the Battle of Princeton, Kentucky, on August 21, 1864, when he was accidently shot by one of his own men. Totally blind for the rest of his life, he nevertheless directed several successful business operations and founded the town of Marble Falls, Texas. He died in 1922 and is buried in the Texas State Cemetery at Austin, not far from Stephen F. Austin, Albert Sidney Johnston, and John Wharton.

Bill Forrest, the general's brother, replaced Johnson as chief of scouts. His temper was as fierce as Bedford's, perhaps even more so, but he was very good at his job. Captain Thomas Henderson, another excellent scout, replaced Bill when he was promoted to major of the Eighth Tennessee Cavalry Regiment in late 1862. Henderson was a typical Forrest officer. Even when he was wounded and could not walk without the aid of crutches, he continued to ride out on missions, saying that one did not have to be able to walk in order to ride a horse.

Forrest's assistant adjutant general, inspector general and *de facto* chief of staff was Captain (later Major) Charles W. Anderson. A resident of Nashville, he was a merchant in Cincinnati and later an officer with the Nashville & Chattanooga Railroad. He started the war as a member of the Confederate transportation department and first distinguished himself shortly after the fall of Fort Donelson. About 1,200 sick and wounded soldiers had to be evacuated from Nashville to Chattanooga, but there was not a single military hospital in that city. Albert Sidney Johnston delegated to Anderson the task of creating hospitals. With the help of the citizens of Chattanooga, he took over three large buildings and set about converting them into hospitals. Mrs. Benjamin Hardin Helm, Abraham Lincoln's sister-in-law, oversaw dozens of women who sewed sacks stuffed for mattresses, while Anderson saw to the building of bed frames, the acquiring of medical supplies, and the construction of mess halls. Thanks to Anderson, Helm and the lady volunteers, the well-supplied and clean hospitals were fully operational within a week.[14]

Shortly thereafter, Anderson returned to his home, which was within Union lines, to tend to his seriously ill wife. He was captured and sent to a Union jail. He was, however, a prewar friend of Andrew Johnson, the U.S. governor of Tennessee and future president of the United States. Johnson ordered that Anderson be released on parole. But war still had an interest in Anderson. He recalled:

The day Buell passed my home myself and family were on a visit to a neighbor some four miles away. McCook's cavalry formed in front of my house, and soon every building as well as my residence was in flames. They took my portraits out, of which I had two, smashed the frames, tacked the canvas to trees, and jabbed their sabers through the eyes. They drove my negroes out of their houses and fired the buildings ...

Charles Anderson, shortly after he was promoted to major, near the end of the war.

Suddenly, however, the Yankees beat a hasty retreat with Forrest right on their heels. Anderson asked Forrest if he could join his command. When the general discovered Anderson could compose clear and exacting orders, he assigned him to his staff. In addition to other duties, Anderson became Forrest's private secretary.

Other staff officers included Major George Dashiell of Memphis (paymaster); Major Dr. James B. Cowan, who was Forrest's chief surgeon throughout the war; Captain Matthew C. Gallaway (aide); Captain John G. Mann of Jackson, Tennessee (chief engineer officer); Captain Charles S. Hill of Mississippi (chief of ordnance); C. S. Severson and Alexander Warren (quartermasters),[15] and Lieutenant Samuel Donaldson of Nashville (aide).

Being a member of Forrest's staff was not an easy job. He was a hard taskmaster and sometimes a harsh one, and he expected all his staff officers to join in the fighting. There was little turnover. They were proud to ride with Forrest, and most of them stayed with him until the end of the war.

A new member of his staff showed up about this time, one who, initially at least, was entirely unwanted: Lieutenant John Morton. An eighteen-year-old cadet at the Nashville Military Academy when the war broke out, he distinguished himself at Fort Donelson, when he took over a battery after its captain was wounded. Captured when Buckner surrendered, Morton spent a few months in Yankee prisons. He greatly admired Bedford Forrest for taking his command out of Donelson, and he wanted to work for him. Through Bragg, he arranged to become Forrest's chief of artillery. The move did not sit well with Forrest. He resented what he rightly saw as Bragg's interference in his command, and he thought that Morton might be a spy for Bragg. He subjected the startled lieutenant to a barrage of the famous Forrest profanity in which he categorically refused to accept Morton as his chief of artillery. Entirely ignorant of the enmity between Bragg and Forrest, Morton was shocked and

John Morton, seen here after his promotion to captain. Morton, who was only twenty-two when the war ended, was like a son to Forrest.

confused by Forrest's reaction. Yet, he was determined to ride with Forrest. He told the general that he would work for Freeman, if that was what Forrest wanted. He only asked permission to accompany Forrest on his next raid. He was confident, he said, that Forrest would capture some guns for him to command. Forrest reluctantly agreed to consider it if Morton could get General Wheeler to endorse the order. The lieutenant immediately set out and—after riding 104 miles in twenty-three hours without sleep or food—returned with the signed order. This effort impressed Forrest, and he eventually allowed Morton to come along, but he clearly wasn't enthusiastic about him, referring to him as "the tallow faced boy."

Over time, however, Forrest's opinion changed. The "boy" proved faithful, fearless, and extremely competent. Before long, Forrest referred to him as "the little kid with the big backbone." For his part, Morton proved utterly devoted to Forrest and remained so for the rest of his life. After Sam Freeman was murdered, Morton became chief of artillery. Later, but before he was old enough to vote, he was a chief of artillery for a Confederate cavalry division. He celebrated his twenty-first birthday commanding a battalion of Southern horse artillery at the Battle of Chickamauga.[16]

The Confederacy allowed every one of its generals to have an escort. Not every general took advantage of this privilege. Forrest took it one step further; he turned his escort company into a special battle group, which he committed to action at key moments under his personal leadership. It became an elite force within an elite force.

Formed in September 1862, the Escort Company was initially led by Montgomery Little of Bedford County. An orphan, he became a planter in Mississippi and was in business in Memphis when the war began. Like Forrest, he was a Union man until Lincoln called for troops to invade the South.

Little's second-in-command was Nathan "Nat" Boone of Booneville in Lincoln County. A descendant of Daniel Boone, the famous pioneer, he joined the Tennessee Volunteers in 1846, when he was sixteen years old, and fought in the Mexican War. He was described as "fat, fair, forty and fearless." Although a good soldier and leader, he had absolutely no ambition for elevated military rank. He was acting commander of the Escort Company on more than one occasion but was never a candidate for permanent command.[17] He started and ended the war as a lieutenant.[18]

Another interesting member of the Escort Company was Luke E. Wright (1846–1922). Originally a heavy artilleryman, he fought at New Madrid and Vicksburg, where he was captured. After he was exchanged, he refused to rejoin the artillery and enlisted in the Escort Company and served with it until the end of the war. Later, he became a lawyer in Memphis, and served as governor-general of the Philippines and U.S. secretary of war under President Theodore Roosevelt.

It will surprise some readers to know that a number of Forrest's soldiers were black. In his after action report on the Battle of Murfreesboro, U.S. Lieutenant Colonel John G. Parkhurst reported that he was attacked by Wharton's regiment, Morrison's First Georgia, and a large number of Rutherford County civilians. He wrote: "There were also quite a number of negroes attached to the Texas and Georgia troops, who were armed and equipped, and took part in several engagements with my forces during the day." According to an African-American who fought with Forrest at Shiloh and Brice's Cross Roads, seven blacks were in the Escort Company.

There were also quite a few non-white non-combatants in Forrest's cavalry. He took forty-three slaves with him when he went to war. He made a deal with them. If the South won, he would set them free at the end of the war. If the South lost, they would be free anyway. Only one of these men deserted. "Those boys stuck with me," he recalled. "Better Confederates never lived."

Three years into the war, Forrest decided that the South was likely to lose, and he might be killed before he freed these men. So he freed them early. They stayed in the Confederate Army and continued to serve until the very end. At least twenty of them returned to northern Mississippi with Forrest and worked on his plantation after the war.

Private Louis Napoleon Winbush (1846–1934) with his grandson, Nelson, at a United Confederate Veterans' reunion. At various times, Winbush was a Confederate Army chaplain, cook, and combat cavalryman with Company M, Seventh Tennessee Cavalry Regiment. He fought with Forrest at Brice's Cross Roads and several other major battles. Certain of the self-ordained "politically correct" deny that there even were any black Confederates, but the historical record proves they existed—just as it shows the Northern critics of Lincoln and his conduct of the war (usually called "Copperheads") existed as well. Those interested in this topic can search the Internet, where they will find many photographs of black Confederates, or consult some of the books on it that I list in my bibliography. The notion of black men serving the Confederacy will make some quite uncomfortable and others downright angry. Honest history often has that effect.

# CHAPTER 6

# THE WEST TENNESSEE RAID

*The courage of the soldier depends upon the*
*wisdom of the general.*

—Publilius Syrus

*Fortune favors the bold.*

—Latin Proverb

Following the aborted attack on Nashville, Forrest returned to base. There were now essentially three major fronts: Virginia (Lee vs. Ambrose Burnside); middle Tennessee (Bragg vs. William S. Rosecrans, who replaced Buell); and the Mississippi Valley (John C. Pemberton vs. Grant). All three experienced major battles in December 1862, but the most dangerous threat was that posed by Grant and his chief lieutenant, Sherman. Their objective was Vicksburg.

In November 1862, Grant advanced in overwhelming numbers. Pemberton fell back and wired Bragg for help. On November 21, Bragg signaled that he was sending Forrest with a large cavalry force into west Tennessee, to cut Grant's supply lines and force him to withdraw.

Grant's supplies came by boat to Columbus, Kentucky. From there, they were transported by rail to the main supply depots at Bethel and Holly Springs, Mississippi. Grant himself headquartered at Oxford, 280 miles south of Columbus.

Forrest's mission was a dangerous one. He would have to cross a major river at flood stage, three-quarters of a mile wide, patrolled by gunboats, in the dead of winter, without any boats assigned to him. If he succeeded in crossing the river, he would be in the middle of Union-controlled territory with several large federal garrisons. Half of his two thousand men were armed with ancient muskets, some dating back to the War of 1812, and quite a few of these had no flints. Many men weren't armed at all. Others were armed with shotguns, but they were of limited value because of a severe shortage of percussion caps. There were other problems as well, including the region's dirt roads, which became muddy pits in winter, a lack of forage, and a shortage of winter clothing and supplies of all kinds.

Forrest protested against this mission. He was convinced Bragg hated him and was deliberately sacrificing him and his command. But the order stood. He left for western Tennessee on December 11 and, after a march of seventy miles, reached Clifton, a town on the east bank of the Tennessee River, on December 15. Forrest's advanced party, which was composed mainly of carpenters, had arrived on December 13 and built two flatboats, each capable of carrying twenty-five men. Forrest sent out patrols to warn of approaching gunboats and began ferrying men across at once. In a cold, driving rain, the ferrying continued all night, until every man and horse was across.

Even before the crossing Yankee scouts had spotted Forest and kept close tabs on him. Rosecrans sent Grant a warning that Forrest was on his way. On December 15—the very day the crossings began—Brigadier General Jeremiah C. Sullivan, the commander of the Union garrison at Jackson, Tennessee, wired Grant that Forrest was crossing the river at Clifton. Grant ordered his troops in western Tennessee to concentrate at once at Jackson, where three railroad lines joined.

Sullivan had ten thousand men and outnumbered Forrest five to one, but Forrest, a master of deception, made Sullivan wary of attacking. Forrest had men beat drums calling assembly, lights out, and so on, where there were no units. Bugles relayed orders where there was no one to receive them. Union scouts reported seeing hundreds of campfires, without knowing that no one warmed themselves there, except one man, whose job it was to keep perhaps a dozen camp fires going. Units—especially artillery—exposed themselves to Union outposts, but far enough away that the Federals did not realize that the same guns were repeatedly parading in front of them. Quaker guns—logs that were painted black to resemble cannons—were deployed in large numbers. Confederate guards misled Yankee prisoners about Forrest's intentions and strength, and then turned their backs and let the prisoners escape. Union sympathizers were rounded up, given disinformation, and then released. "Dismount and remount" tactics were practiced, so a unit would be counted twice or more, as cavalry *and* as infantry, while prisoners and detained civilians watched at a distance the night before they were released or paroled. Forrest was especially fond of capturing U.S. telegraph offices, intercepting their dispatches, and then sending false transmissions— allegedly from Union commanders—concerning his strength, movements, and presumed intentions (which were usually the opposite of what he actually intended to do).

General Forrest soon discovered that he had a number of born actors in his Escort Company. These men often became "deserters." They would go over to the Yankees and spread whatever stories Forrest wanted them to tell. Frequently these men were interrogated by Union generals, who thus received a totally distorted picture of the tactical situation. Often they thought Forrest was ready to attack with entire brigades that did not exist or were a hundred miles away. While in the Yankee camp, the "deserter" would get a pretty good picture of the size, condition, and morale of the Union forces. When the deserter was released to go home, he reported everything he learned to General Forrest.

In winter, a favorite tactic was to send mounted troops through cornfields, shouting orders to non-existent units. One horse could make enough noise in a dried out cornfield to sound like ten, even if the rider didn't want him to.

These tactics saved Forrest and his men in western Tennessee in December 1862, as well as in other times and places. On December 16, General Sullivan reported that he was facing eight thousand Rebels. Two days later, he revised this figure to ten thousand men and seven batteries—about twenty-eight guns. Even General Grant was fooled. On December 17, he telegraphed Admiral David Porter that Forrest had five thousand to ten thousand men. Forrest actually had two thousand men and four guns.

General Forrest was also pretty good at undercover operations. On December 17, one of Forrest's spies showed up with ten thousand percussion caps for shotguns. We still don't know who he was, where he came from, where he disappeared to, or anything about him.[1]

Sullivan, meanwhile, sent out a column of eight hundred Illinois and Ohio cavalry and Tennessee Unionists on December 16, all under the command of Colonel Robert Ingersoll, a famous agnostic. Forrest's men spent most of December 17 drying their clothes and grooming their horses. The next day, Forrest attacked Ingersoll near the hamlet of Beech Creek, five miles from Lexington. Ingersoll fell back to a strong position in a stretch of woods behind a deep creek. Forrest sent Colonel James W. Starnes north, to outflank the Union left.

Starnes found an undefended bridge over the creek. The flooring had been removed, but Dr. Starnes replaced it by dismantling a nearby snake-rail fence. His regiment soon poured across, together with those of Colonel Jacob Biffle, Colonel George G. Dibrell, and Captain Samuel Freeman's guns. They quickly broke Ingersoll's left and swung over to attack his right. The Tennessee Unionists—called "Homegrown Yankees"—ran away immediately, allowing Forrest to enfilade the dismounted Illinois and Ohio troops in the center. Before he could react, Ingersoll was partially surrounded, and Rebels were firing into his ranks from all directions. "Ingersoll made a good fight," one of Forrest's boys wrote later, "but if he really believed that there was no hell we convinced him that there was something mightily like it." After offering some stiff resistance, the rest of the Yankees gave way, and the rout was complete. Forrest captured the colonel, 150 men, three hundred small arms (mostly excellent Sharpe carbines), a generous supply of ammunition, seventy horses, and a pair of three-inch Rodman rifled cannon, which became the nucleus of John W. Morton's famous battery. Forrest lost three men killed and five wounded.

Ingersoll was an affable guest at General Forrest's mess for the next three days. He even joined the nightly four-card draw poker game with Forrest and his officers, but lost all of his money by the end of the second evening, so Dr. Cowan loaned him $100 in Confederate money. Years after the war, Ingersoll gave a lecture in Nashville, Tennessee, which Cowan attended. Ingersoll recognized him and remembered the incident. He wrote Cowan a check for $100 in U.S. money on the spot—a huge profit for the physician.[2]

U.S. Colonel Robert "Bob" Ingersoll (1833–1899), a lawyer, political leader, attorney general of Illinois, and Union cavalry commander, was the son of an abolitionist Congregationalist preacher. Later known as "The Great Agnostic," he was one of the most eloquent speakers of his day, but he was no match for Bedford Forrest on the battlefield.

After disposing of Ingersoll, Forrest boldly rode to the outskirts of Jackson, Tennessee, throwing General Sullivan into a panic. He called on all nearby garrisons for reinforcements. He also signaled Grant:

> JACKSON, December 18, 1862—7:10 p.m.
>
> My cavalry was whipped at Lexington to-day. Colonel Ingersoll taken prisoner and section of artillery captured. The enemy [Forrest] are reported to be ten thousand to twenty thousand and still crossing the river. They are now within six miles of my outposts. I will try and find their numbers by daylight.

Even though he was outnumbered five to one, Forrest loosely surrounded the place and captured several outposts, bringing his total number of prisoners to five hundred. He also cut every telegraph wire going in or out of Jackson, completely isolating the town. This greatly alarmed Grant, who suspended his offensive against Pemberton and sent more reinforcements to west Tennessee. Although the operation was far from over, the Wizard had already accomplished his mission.

Now that the Yankees at Jackson were cowered, Forrest used the night of December 18/19 to do as much damage as possible. He sent one battalion south along the railroad, where it tore up tracks and captured a rail station, bringing in another seventy-five prisoners. Colonel George G. Dibrell's Eighth Tennessee Cavalry turned north and, at 2 a.m. on December 19, overran Carroll Station, bagging another 101 Yankees. In the meantime, Colonel Jacob B. Biffle's men dashed down the railroad toward Bolivar, where he captured an outpost and another fifty men.

Later that day, Sullivan sent out a detachment of the Forty-Third Illinois Volunteer Infantry Regiment to test the Rebel positions. Forrest hit it on both flanks with the Fourth Alabama, under his personal command, and Freeman's artillery. The Yankees fell back into Jackson, convinced that Forrest had many more men than he did.

That night (December 19/20), Forrest withdrew to Spring Creek, where the rest of his brigade rejoined him. Once again, he divided his command. He sent Dibrell (along with Morton's guns) to destroy the stockade and railroad bridge at Forked Deer Creek, while Dr. Starnes was ordered to seize Humboldt.

Dibrell was unsuccessful. The ground was too wet for him to bring up his artillery, and the stockade was too strong to take without it. Starnes overran Humboldt, however, and took one hundred prisoners, along with five hundred small arms and three hundred thousand rounds of ammunition.

Forrest, meanwhile, turned north with the rest of his command.[3]

His target on December 20 was Trenton, Tennessee. Memphis and Jackson aside, it was the home of the largest Union garrison between Mississippi and Kentucky. Trenton's women, waving their handkerchiefs, pointed Forrest to the Yankees, who had fortified the supply depot with eight hundred bales of cotton but without any cannon. Forrest led the attack, supported by Freeman's guns, and the garrison surrendered quickly. When Northerners tried to burn the depot, Captain J. P. Strange and Bedford Forrest captured the arsonists and made them quench the fire.

With 275 men, Forrest captured four hundred men at Trenton, including two colonels, as well as three hundred contrabands (former slaves), one thousand horses, thirteen wagons and ambulances, seven caissons, one hundred thousand rations, twenty thousand rounds of artillery ammunition, and four hundred thousand rounds of small arms ammunition, among other things. The garrison commander sadly handed his sword over to Forrest, wistfully adding that it was a family relic. Forrest examined it and handed it back to him, saying that he hoped the next time he drew it, it would not be against his own people.

There were so many captured weapons that the entire command could have rearmed itself. Those men who were carrying old flintlocks and shotguns discarded them in favor of the Federals' Enfield rifles.

Forrest learned that the Federals had forced the residents of Trenton to sign Oaths of Allegiance to the United States. He ordered Captain Charles Anderson to collect all of these papers. They were piled on the courthouse lawn and burned. Southern soldiers and civilians celebrated until dawn.

The Rebels had also captured a large quantity of counterfeit Confederate money. It had no value because the engraving and printing were so perfect and the quality of the paper was so high that any Southerner would immediately recognize it as bogus. Forrest and his men kept it as poker money.

The most significant item Bedford kept from the booty at Trenton was a U.S. Dragoon model saber, made of Damascus steel. He used it for the rest of the war.

The Union commanders now estimated that Forrest had twenty thousand men, with Sullivan reporting that Cheatham's division and Colonel Theodore A. Napier's brigade had crossed the Tennessee to reinforce Forrest. In fact, neither Napier's small guerrilla battalion nor Cheatham's division were at hand.

As of Christmas Eve, Forrest had taken 1,300 prisoners. He paroled them after distributing disinformation about reinforcements joining his command. He then headed north, where his brigade captured the Federal outpost at Union City (250 men), two U.S. infantry companies at Rutherford Station, 272 men at Kenton Station, and a few smaller garrisons. The Confederate brigade also destroyed fifteen miles of railroad in a single afternoon.

More than ever, Ulysses S. Grant wanted Forrest killed or captured. He ordered Thomas A. Davies, the garrison commander at Columbus, Kentucky, to attack the advancing Rebels. Davies had more than five thousand men, outnumbering Forrest two to one. He was, however, thoroughly intimidated by the Wizard of the Saddle. He signaled Halleck for help. Halleck ordered Major General Samuel Curtis in Missouri to immediately dispatch everything he had available from St. Louis to Columbus.

Forrest's men destroyed a major railroad bridge at Moscow, Kentucky—only ten miles south of Columbia—without interference. As of Christmas Day, Forrest had destroyed all but one railroad trestle between Jackson, Tennessee, and Moscow, Kentucky; and the Mobile & Ohio Railroad—Grant's main supply route—had been thoroughly wrecked. Grant had to put his army on half rations.

On December 20, Grant's massive supply depot at Holly Springs was destroyed by Confederate cavalry under Major General Earl Van Dorn, Pemberton's chief of cavalry. Now Grant was in double jeopardy. In his memoirs, General Grant wrote: "At the same time [as Van Dorn's Holly Springs raid] Forrest got on the line of railroad between Jackson, Tennessee, and Columbia, Kentucky, doing much damage to it. This cut me off from all communications with the North for more than two weeks, and that interval elapsed before rations of forage could be issued from stores in a regular way."

On December 24, a panicked Davies signaled Halleck that he believed Bragg was driving on Columbus with forty thousand men. Davies wanted to evacuate the town, spike his guns, and dump his powder into the river. He actually ferried his supplies across the Mississippi before General Samuel Hurlbut, the commander of XVI Corps, assured him that evacuating Columbus was not yet necessary.[4]

Forrest feinted at Columbus—so that Starnes's regiment, using five hundred axes they captured at Trenton, could destroy the large railroad bridge at Obion—and tore up another fifteen miles of track.

Except for Starnes's bridge wreckers, Forrest gave his boys Christmas Day off. He visited almost every company, joking, talking with junior officers, and singling out individual soldiers for special praise. The unit's morale, which was already high, rose even higher, even though ten thousand Yankees were trying to close off Forrest's only line of retreat to the south.

On December 26, the last phase of the west Tennessee campaign began—the escape. Captain Anderson later recalled that, of all Forrest's marches, this was the worst. The weather remained cold, rainy, and just plain nasty. The Yankees had thrown a tight net around Forrest, with Brigadier General Grenville M. Dodge coming up from Mississippi, every bridge in the sector destroyed, and Union gunboats patrolling the Tennessee River with greater frequency than ever.

To get back home, Forrest had two major rivers to cross: the Obion and the Tennessee. The Obion (which at this point ran generally east to west) was swollen by winter rains and was at flood stage. Strong Yankee forces blocked the way and held or destroyed the bridges—except for one.

The bridge at McLemoresville was abandoned and was so old and rotten that it was about to fall down. It was so decrepit that the Yankees did not bother destroying it or guarding it. And it was here that Forrest did cross. His men arrived after nightfall on December 28 and, by torchlight, ten men from each regiment cut timber and began to repair and strengthen the dilapidated structure. The general himself swung an axe. Within an hour, the ancient bridge was reinforced to the point that some of the cavalry could cross, but it was still dangerous.

As the Rebels worked, a Union column bivouacked a few miles to the east of McLemoresville and another a few miles to the west. But neither one realized that Forrest and his entire command were between them.

It was cold and a light rain was falling. While horses crossed the bridge easily, wagons, heavy with captured loot, were another matter.

The teamsters hesitated. Forrest jumped aboard the lead wagon and drove it across. No one hesitated after that, but the next two wagons ended up in the river. Fortunately, they were in the shallowest part. Forrest made the men wade into the bone-chilling water, right the overturned vehicles, and get them to shore.

The last wagon crossed at 3 a.m. Then came the artillery. By 6 a.m. on December 29, the entire command was across.

General Sullivan, scouring the northern side of the Obion in pursuit of the Rebels, signaled Grant that he had Forrest "in a tight place," but Sullivan was now on the wrong side of the river.

Forrest wasn't done. He decided to destroy the U.S. supply depot at Bethel, thirty-five miles south of Jackson, putting further pressure on Grant, perhaps even forcing him to abandon northern Mississippi. As part of this mission, Forrest planned on destroying or neutralizing the Federal forces under General Sullivan and General Dodge. The Union generals accommodated him by operating in widely separated columns: Colonel William W. Lowe from Fort Henry, General Dodge from Corinth, Colonel Michael K. Lawler from Jackson, and General Sullivan, who, by the afternoon of December 29, was south of the Obion. General Davies refused to leave Columbus, despite Sullivan asking him to join the chase with four thousand of his men.

Sullivan's division advanced with three brigades, commanded by Colonels Lawler, Cyrus L. Dunham (1,800 men), and John W. Fuller (2,000 men). Lawler was too far west to be a factor, but Dunham was lured into a trap, pursuing "the forty thieves," as Forrest's scouts called themselves. In order to cut off Forrest's retreat, Dunham occupied Parker's Crossroads, seven miles below Clarksburg, on December 30, and called for reinforcement. Sullivan refused, but Colonel Fuller disobeyed orders and marched for the crossroads.

Before daylight on New Year's Eve, Forrest moved against Parker's Crossroads. Anticipating that Sullivan and Fuller might decide to crash the party, Forrest sent four companies under Captain William S. McLemore to cover his rear and warn him if Sullivan and Fuller tried

*THE WEST TENNESSEE RAID*  85

anything. Unfortunately, McLemore misunderstood his instructions and took the wrong road. Forrest thought his rear was covered, but it wasn't.

Forrest's artillery led his dismounted troops in action—a unique tactic for the Civil War. Forrest had eight guns to Dunham's three. He placed Freeman's guns on the flanks and Morton's in the center. Morton, the former "tallow-faced boy," soon dismounted one of the Union guns—much to Forrest's delight. The Rebels drove the Yankees back to a ridge, which they then charged and captured. Dunham led an immediate counterattack but failed to retake the position. Forrest then executed one of his favorite tactics: Colonel Russell and his Fourth Alabama, along with Napier's battalion, outflanked the Union right and poured into its rear, while Starnes did the same to its left, smashing the Thirty-Ninth Iowa Infantry. The Northerners fell back to a cornfield at the edge of the woods, pursued by Colonel Dibrell and Forrest in the center. Napier was killed in the charge[5] but his men captured Dunham's guns, Starnes took his supply wagons, and, about three hundred Yankees were captured. Nearly surrounded, and pinned down by Rebel crossfire, white flags popped up among the Federals. Forrest rode out and began negotiating Dunham's surrender when, to his astonishment, three regiments of Ohio infantry plowed into his rear.

For the first and only time in the war, Forrest was taken by surprise. The first Rebels the Ohio regiments ran into were the horse holders. (When dismounted cavalry attacked in the Civil War, one out of every four men was normally left behind to hold the mounts.) Fuller's brigade netted several prisoners and three hundred horses.

Yet, thanks to leaders' quick action and willingness to take the initiative, Forrest's command was saved. When they heard the firing in their rear, Starnes and Russell launched immediate counterattacks on both of Fuller's flanks. Dibrell turned most of his men around to face Fuller and prepared to charge, as did Captain Montgomery Little with the Escort Company. Forrest rushed to join them but rode right into a squad of Yankee infantry, which demanded he surrender. Forrest calmly replied that he had already surrendered and was on his way to order his "few remaining men" to lay down their arms. He then put spurs to his horse and was gone before the Yankees could react.

As soon as he reached his main body, he stood up in his stirrups and shouted: "Split in two and charge 'em both ways!" They did. Forrest personally led Escort Company out of the trap.

Forrest's brigade escaped, although twenty-five rebels were killed, seventy-five were wounded (among them Lieutenant Morton), and 250 were captured, including Major N. N. Cox and Captain J. P. Strange (who had personally seized eighteen wagons in Dunham's rear). In addition, Forrest's command had lost three hundred horses, five guns (including three that had been captured from Dunham), five wagons, and two ambulances. The Northerners had fifty killed and 150 wounded. Forrest's brigade limped into Lexington, Tennessee, at 6 p.m. After pushing on another ten miles, they camped for the night.

The Battle of Parker's Crossroads likely saved Grant's supply depot at Bethel. Sullivan sent the Sixth (Union) Tennessee Regiment to block Forrest from reaching the Tennessee River, but, as often would be the case, the homegrown Yankees performed poorly and the Rebels quickly scattered them on New Year's Day, 1863. There was only one Rebel casualty: Forrest's forage master. He was talking to the general when a spent ball hit him squarely in the forehead. He fell stunned, but the ball did not penetrate the skull and he suffered no permanent damage, although he did have one heck of a headache.

When they got to the river, Major Jeffrey Forrest and his men quickly raised the flatboats, which they had sunk in shallow water two weeks before. They also constructed several improvised rafts. From noon until 8 p.m., Forrest (fearing gunboats) hurriedly ferried his men across the Tennessee, which was 1,800 feet wide at this point. The guns crossed first, then the wagons, then the horses' saddles. The horses were pushed into the river and forced to swim. There were as many as one thousand horses in the river at one time. The soldiers crossed last. One regiment was left as a rearguard, supported by a section of guns under Lieutenant Edwin Douglas. Preparing for combat, Douglas unlimbered his guns and, acting according to tactics of the day, Sergeant Max Baxter withdrew the caissons and horses obliquely out of range. Forrest, who knew little about artillery, mistook this move for an act of cowardice. He rode up and hit Sergeant Baxter on the back with the flat of his sword. "Turn those horses around and git back where you belong or, by God, I'll kill you!" he roared.

"General, I'm moving in accordance with tactics."

"No, you are not. I know how to fight, and you can't run away with the ammunition chest."

Forrest was wrong. A few days later, Lieutenant Douglas brought a copy of the Confederate Army artillery manual to the general's tent and explained why Baxter maneuvered the way he did. Douglas also offered to conduct a demonstration drill, which Forrest immediately agreed to attend. The general kept the manual and mastered it within a week. He also went to Baxter's tent and apologized. Later, he made it a point to commend the sergeant in front of the entire battery. Baxter was eventually promoted to lieutenant.

During his first west Tennessee campaign, Forrest killed, wounded, or captured more than 2,500 men, including four regimental commanders. He captured a net total of four guns, eleven caissons, fifty wagons and teams, ten thousand stands of arms, a million rounds of ammunition, 1,800 blankets, and other supplies and equipment. He had destroyed fifty railroad bridges and twenty stockades, and left the Union rear in shambles. His success had a strategic effect as well in that Grant decided to abandon the railroads as his main means of moving supplies and rely on the Mississippi River instead. Forrest had started the campaign with raw recruits, poorly armed and poorly equipped. Now it was a brigade of self-confident veterans who had absolute faith in themselves, their general, and their officers, and who were armed and equipped with the best weapons and supplies that the Lincoln administration could provide.

Now that Forrest had his brigade well-armed with rifles and six shooters, he forbade enlisted men for carrying swords. Officers could still carry swords if they wished, as symbols of their rank. Forrest would continue to carry a sword. But, for him, it was not just a symbol of rank, it was a weapon, too. He was going to use it for its designed purpose—killing at close quarters. When he got back to base camp, he put a sharpened edge on the sword he had captured at Trenton. Regulation officers' swords at this time were only sharpened three or four inches from the point. Forrest sharpened his all the way to the hilt. When someone pointed out to him how it was supposed to be sharpened, according to the customs of the day, Forrest growled one of his most famous aphorisms: "War means fightin', and fightin' means killin'." He continued to grind away.

# CHAPTER 7

# FAILURE AT FORT DONELSON

*Never fight a battle when you don't gain
anything by winning it.*
—Field Marshal Erwin Rommel, the "Desert Fox"

*Never fight a battle when you don't gain
anything by winning it.*
—Lieutenant General George S. Patton Jr.

W hile Forrest was rampaging through western Tennessee, Braxton Bragg and his Army of Tennessee fought William S. Rosecrans and the Army of the Cumberland in the Battle of Murfreesboro (called the Battle of Stone's River in the North), which lasted from December 31, 1862 to January 2, 1863. The fighting was very heavy and bloody. Rosecrans's army suffered more than thirteen thousand casualties out of forty-four thousand engaged, while Bragg committed thirty-four thousand men to the fight and suffered 10,300 killed, wounded, and captured. Bragg retreated on January 3, but overall the battle was inconclusive. After Murfreesboro, Bragg occupied a line extending along a ridge eighteen miles southeast of the town. His entire front was eighty miles long. Its flanks were covered by cavalry units at McMinnville on the right and Columbia on the left. Forrest commanded the left flank and Wheeler the right.

Bragg sent Wheeler along with John Wharton's brigade and part of Forrest's command to obstruct river traffic on the Cumberland. A short

Joseph "Fighting Joe" Wheeler (1836–1906), shown here as a West Point cadet, just a few years before he became a Confederate general. He graduated in 1859. Wheeler fought Indians in New Mexico before joining the Confederate Army as a first lieutenant in 1861. Promoted to colonel in September, he led the Nineteenth Alabama Infantry at Shiloh. He was a favorite of Braxton Bragg, who promoted him above Forrest and gave him most of Forrest's second command during the Kentucky campaign. Bedford refused to serve under him after the Fort Donelson debacle of 1863. After the Civil War, he was a planter, lawyer, congressman, and U.S. major general during the Spanish-American War. He is buried in Arlington National Cemetery.

while later Bragg ordered Forrest and his remaining force to join Wheeler immediately.

En route, Forrest's brigade camped at Dickson, Tennessee, and their commander spent the night at the home of James Larkin, a nearly blind ninety-year-old farmer and devout Presbyterian minister. Originally a Unionist, Lincoln's call for seventy-five thousand volunteers to suppress the Southern Confederacy turned him into a Confederate. Several of Larkin's grandsons were in the Confederate Army and at least one of them was a preacher. The next morning, the general again thanked Larkin for his hospitality and mounted his steed, but Larkin asked him to dismount and kneel. Larkin wanted to pray for him. The general did as requested. Larkin put his hand on Forrest's head and asked God's blessing on him, his men, and their cause. The prayer must have been powerful and eloquent, because tears poured down Forrest's cheeks as he rode away.

After two days of hard riding, Forrest caught up with Wheeler fifteen miles from Dover. As soon as time allowed, he inspected his regiments and found that they did not have enough food or ammunition. Forrest asked Wheeler to conduct a general inspection of the entire command. They discovered that Wharton's men had only twenty rounds of ammunition per man and fifty rounds for his two guns. Forrest's men had twenty rounds per man and forty-five for each of his four guns. Haste had put the Confederates in a desperate situation.

Wheeler hoped to ambush Federal transports on the river near Palmyra. The Yankees, however, had been tipped off, and after two days passed and no boats appeared, Wheeler decided to recapture Fort Donelson.

General Forrest protested that an attack was unlikely to succeed, and even if it did, the fort could not be held against U.S. gunboats. If the first attack failed, there would not be enough ammunition for a second. They were also one hundred miles from their base. What if they were cut off? They would not have enough ammunition to fight their way back. Scouts had already reported that a large body of Union cavalry had left Franklin to capture Wheeler and Forrest. Wheeler, however, was not moved. He insisted on the attack. Forrest pushed the issue as far as he could without being insubordinate and told Captain Anderson and Dr. Ben Wood of his medical staff that if he was killed he wanted them to make it known that he opposed this attack from the start.

On February 3, 1863, Forrest began the battle by attacking the Cumberland Iron Works (nine miles from Dover) and capturing two detachments of Union infantry, but three Yankees escaped and warned the garrison at Fort Donelson.

Fort Donelson's commander, Colonel Abner C. Harding, had pickets established in front of the fort.[1] He recalled a steamer, off-loaded a company of infantry and two field guns, and impressed them into his defense. He had Dover fortified, ready for Wheeler's attack, and summarily rejected Wheeler's demand for surrender.

Forrest was better as an independent commander than as a subordinate. The plan called for Wharton and Forrest to attack simultaneously from the west and southeast, respectively. As Forrest moved into position, he saw a body of Yankees moving toward the river. Mistaking the maneuver for a retreat, he attacked at once, without waiting for Wharton. He charged across the hollow, through which he had escaped the year before, and had his horse shot from under him. When they saw their general go down, the Rebels halted and their attack failed.

Forrest mounted another horse and ordered his men to charge as infantry. Again his horse was killed beneath him. His men reached the

Joseph Wheeler, circa 1863.

parapet of the main Union redoubt but could go no farther. Wharton's men were rebuffed at the edge of Dover. Confederate losses were heavy—about six hundred of the two thousand engaged, which included a quarter of Forrest's men and sixty from Wharton's command. Colonel Harding lost 126 out of his approximately one thousand soldiers.[2]

As night fell, Forrest placed Captain Anderson in charge of the rearguard as the Confederates retreated. Wheeler, Forrest, and Wharton withdrew to a crude log cabin four miles from the battlefield where Wheeler dictated his report to headquarters.

That night, when Forrest heard Anderson's voice outside, he went out and helped him off his horse. (Anderson was too frozen to dismount by himself.) Forrest helped him into the cabin, rousted two unwounded officers from the only bed, pulled off Anderson's boots, wrapped him in blankets, and helped him lie down.

Wheeler was still dictating his report. Forrest interrupted and warned Wheeler not to say anything negative about Forrest's men. Wheeler replied that he had not.

"General Wheeler," Forrest snapped. "I advised against this attack, and said all a subordinate officer should have said against it, and nothing you can now say or do will bring back my brave men lying dead or wounded and freezing around that fort tonight. I mean no disrespect to you. You know my feelings of personal friendship for you. You can have my sword if you demand it, but there is one thing I do want you to put in that report to General Bragg. Tell him that I will be in my coffin before I fight again under your command."

"Forrest," General Wheeler replied quietly. "I cannot take your saber, and I regret exceedingly your determination. As commanding officer, I take all the blame and responsibility for this failure."

Wheeler arranged to transfer Forrest out of his command. True to his word—although they remained friends and even socialized together after the war—Forrest never served under Wheeler again.

# CHAPTER 8

# THOMPSON'S STATION AND BRENTWOOD

*Courage is the first of human qualities because it is the quality which guarantees the others.*

—Aristotle

fter the Fort Donelson debacle, Forrest returned to the duty of covering Braxton Bragg's left flank. He refitted his command in the vicinity of Columbia, Tennessee, scouted in the direction of Franklin, and reported that the Yankees were rebuilding the railroads and preparing to advance south of the Duck River.

General Joseph E. Johnston, the Confederate supreme commander in the West, ordered General Van Dorn and most of Pemberton's cavalry transferred from the Vicksburg sector to join Forrest on Bragg's western flank. Van Dorn arrived with three brigades and 4,500 men, and Forrest's brigade came under his command.[1] Wheeler remained in command of the cavalry on Bragg's eastern flank.

Forrest spent the rest of February and early March drilling his troops, making sure the horses were properly shoed, and conducting parades twice a week. Discipline and organization had not seemed very important to Forrest in 1861, but that changed. Now he was determined to have his command well drilled and well organized—and ready the next time he met the enemy.

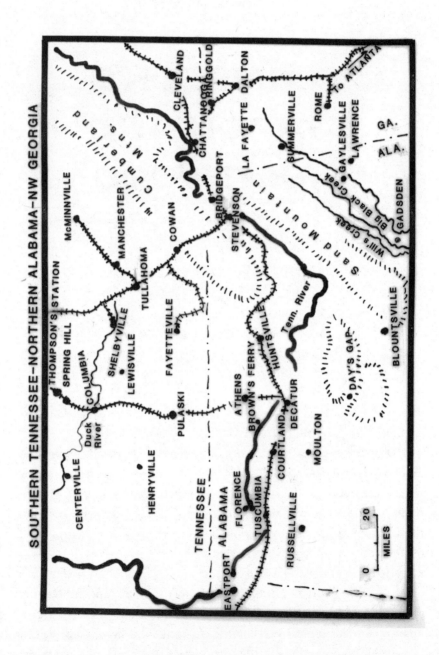

SOUTHERN TENNESSEE–NORTHERN ALABAMA–NW GEORGIA

On March 4, a strong Federal force from Franklin advanced south along the Columbia Turnpike in the direction of Thompson's Station. Commanded by Colonel John Coburn, it included four infantry regiments, an artillery battalion, and some cavalry—2,837 men in all. Simultaneously, a second column under Brigadier General Philip H. Sheridan advanced west from Murfreesboro. It was obvious that they intended to link up at Spring Hill, twelve miles north of Columbia. Van Dorn decided to destroy Coburn before Sheridan could join him.

John Coburn (1825–1908) was a lawyer, judge, and a former member of the Indiana House of Representatives. He joined the Union Army and became colonel and commander of the Thirty-Third Indiana Infantry in 1861. Captured by Forrest, he was later exchanged. His men were the first Union troops to enter Atlanta in September 1864. Brevetted brigadier general in 1865, he served in Congress from 1867 to 1875.

The clash occurred at Thompson Station on March 5. Coburn was only four miles from Spring Hill when he was hit in the left flank by four hidden Rebel guns, directed by Captain Freeman. Forrest then led an attack against the Union cavalry, which panicked and disappeared over the horizon. Other Van Dorn units, however, were roughly handled by the Union infantry. The Third Arkansas Cavalry was hit especially hard and its commander was killed, along with the regimental color guard. The regiment wavered until a local seventeen-year-old girl, Alice Thompson, rushed forward, grabbed the fallen battle flag, and rallied the command.

Forrest's favorite horse, Roderick, was a casualty of the battle. The animal loved Forrest and often followed him around camp like a dog. Roderick was wounded three times at Thompson's Station and the general ordered his son to take him to the rear. Once they got there, Willie unclenched the saddle but did not halter him. From the front came the sound of another volley. Roderick immediately headed back to the battle, seeking his master. He jumped three fences to get there. As he approached Forrest, a stray Yankee bullet killed him.

General Forrest bent over Roderick, tears pouring down his cheeks as the animal died. Forrest had him buried near where he fell, and a monument now marks his final resting place. Today, a statue in Memphis stands above Forrest's grave. It is of the general sitting astride his beloved Roderick.

With Van Dorn checked, Forrest swung the Ninth and Tenth Tennessee far to the right, outflanking Coburn, and coming up behind him. Forrest ordered his men to dismount and personally led a charge. When he was within twenty yards of the Yankee line, the Federals dropped their weapons and surrendered. About two thousand Yankees were captured, 1,800 of them by Forrest. These included Colonel Coburn and Major William R. Shafter who, as a major general, would be the American commander in Cuba during the Spanish-American War. Of the nearly one thousand Confederates engaged that day, 108 were killed, wounded, or missing. Forrest lost a total of sixty-nine men. Captain Montgomery Little, commander of the Escort Company and a grand-nephew of Daniel Boone, and Lieutenant Colonel Edward B. Trezevant, commander of the Tenth Tennessee, were among the dead. Little was at Forrest's side when the fatal bullet struck him.

Upon hearing the heavy firing around Thompson's Station, Philip Sheridan turned tail, and the Federal operation against Van Dorn ended.

After Thompson's Station, Van Dorn reorganized his command into two divisions: one under Red Jackson and the other under Forrest. Bedford commanded Frank C. Armstrong's brigade and his own former brigade, now under Colonel Starnes.

The sparring for this agriculturally rich part of middle Tennessee continued for four more months. The Northerners, who needed food and forage, began another advance on March 9, this time in overwhelming force. They were directed by Major General Gordon Granger, a very capable corps and divisional commander. Van Dorn wisely did not give battle but conducted a delaying action and fell back behind the Duck River. Then Granger, who decided that he was in an exposed position, fell back to the Franklin area.

"Where is Forrest?" Everyone from President Lincoln to the lowliest private wanted to know. To everyone's surpise, Forrest popped up at Brentwood, nine miles north of Franklin, and well behind Union lines, on March 25.

The hamlet of Brentwood, located on the Nashville & Decatur Railroad, was garrisoned by more than five hundred men from the Twenty-Second Wisconsin Infantry Regiment. A mile and a half to the south was a stockade, garrisoned by the three hundred men of the Nineteenth Michigan. The stockade guarded an important railroad bridge over the Harpeth River. Forrest planned to take both positions.

Forrest had Captain Anderson tie his staff's sole white handkerchief to his sword and demand the surrender of Union com-

Earl Van Dorn, who was born near Port Gibson, Mississippi, in 1829, was known as "the Terror of Ugly Husbands." He graduated from West Point in 1842, ranking fifty-second out of fifty-six graduates, and fought in the Indian and Mexicans Wars (where he was twice brevetted for courage), and was part of the Second Cavalry when it was led by Sidney Johnston and Robert E. Lee. He proved to be over his head as an army commander in 1862, but did well commanding cavalry forces. Forrest strongly disapproved of his womanizing.

mander at Brentwood, Colonel Edward Bloodgood. Bloodgood refused—until he saw Lieutenant Morton deploying the Confederates' guns. Having no artillery of his own and no hope of relief (the Confederates had already cut the telegraph wires), the colonel changed his mind and capitulated. Working quickly, the Southerners loaded wagons with captured supplies and headed south with their prisoners. Everything they could not carry they burned. To paralyze the nearby garrisons, Rebel vanguards demonstrated against Nashville and pushed to within three miles of the capitol building. In the meantime, the main body turned toward the stockade.

Forrest again ordered Anderson to carry a surrender demand. To his horror, he could not find the handkerchief he used at Brentwood. Forrest laughed and told him to use his shirt—maybe the Yankees could tell that it once was white. Apparently they could, because another three hundred Federals surrendered.

Back at Franklin, General Granger learned that something was happening in Brentwood, so he ordered Brigadier General Green Clay Smith to investigate with seven hundred cavalrymen. About a mile from the stockade, he attacked the Fourth Mississippi Cavalry of Armstrong's brigade and routed it; then Colonel Starnes hit him in the flank and scattered his command. Forrest brought off eight hundred prisoners and a good number of wagons. As had happened in previous actions, after Brentwood, his unarmed men armed themselves, and those who were poorly armed traded their weapons for some excellent Northern weapons. The most unusual capture was made by the First Tennessee. It made off with a beautiful set of twenty-four silver band instruments, which it used for the rest of the war.

Earl Van Dorn had some very positive traits, including courage, gallantry and boldness. On the other hand, he was high-strung, a womanizer, jealous, and sometimes quite petty. Forrest, who had zero tolerance for adultery, did not like him and once commented that he would like to cut his heart out.

After Brentwood, Forrest, as was his custom, let his men have their pick of the best Union arms and equipment. He believed that this was only right; after all, they were the ones who captured it. Van Dorn's quartermaster, however, saw things differently and complained that not all of the captured equipment had been turned over to his department. Van Dorn backed his staff officer, which led to a confrontation at Van Dorn's headquarters at Spring Hill. Major Minnick Williams of Van Dorn's staff was the only witness.

The disagreement over the spoils of Brentwood got increasingly out of hand. Van Dorn accused Forrest of being behind a series of newspaper articles in a Chattanooga newspaper, which gave the lion's share of the credit for recent victories to Forrest. He asserted that the articles were, in fact, written by members of Forrest's staff.

Forrest's temper boiled over. He heatedly denied the charges and demanded to know where Van Dorn had gotten his information. He added that, if Van Dorn could not produce the author, he would hold him personally responsible. Van Dorn accused him of treachery and falsehood; then, he reached for his sword, which was hanging on the wall of his office. Forrest went for his sword and drew it halfway out of the sheath. Then he stopped and dropped it back into the scabbard.

"General Van Dorn," he said, "you know that I am not afraid of you. But I will not fight you. And I leave it to you to reconcile with yourself the gross wrongs you have done to me. It would never do for two officers of our rank to set such an example to our troops and I remember—if you forget—what we both owe to the cause."

Van Dorn later said that he was never so ashamed in his life. He at once realized that he was wrong and apologized. He and Forrest shook hands and parted amiably. They would never meet again. Earl Van Dorn was shot dead by an angry father on May 7, 1863. [2]

Skirmishing, minor forays and reconnaissance operations continued in middle Tennessee until April 10, when Van Dorn launched a major reconnaissance in force and came within four miles of Franklin. In accordance with the plan, Forrest approached the town from the south, in column formation, with Armstrong in front and Starnes two miles behind. Meanwhile, Rosecrans's cavalry corps, Major General David S. Stanley, commanding, crossed the Harpeth and advanced south of Franklin. As luck would have it, they struck right between Forrest's two brigades. The only Confederate unit here was Freeman's artillery, which unlimbered but did not have a chance to fire. Most of the battery was captured, including Captain Freeman. Seeing that he had made an error by not sending out flank guards, Starnes personally led an immediate counterattack. The Yankees hurriedly abandoned the captured guns and caissons, and some of the prisoners escaped in the confusion. The blue-coats ordered Freeman and some of the others to double-time to the Harpeth, a mile and a half away.

Freeman was a large, overweight man with an injured knee who was not able to keep up with the Federal horses. Dissatisfied with his slow pace, members of the Fourth U.S. Regulars murdered him. Lieutenant Morton succeeded Freeman as chief of artillery. The Regulars also shot a surgeon, Dr. Skelton, but he survived.

Messengers quickly informed Forrest that Stanley was behind him, had captured Freeman's battery and was now in Armstrong's rear.

If Forrest was startled, he didn't let it show. "That's where I've been trying to get him all day, damn him!" he roared. "I'll be in *his* rear in about five minutes!" He ordered Armstrong to about face and charge. So confident did Forrest sound that many of the men present believed until their dying day that Stanley had fallen into Forrest's trap. But Stanley quickly realized that he was between two large Confederate forces. He hastily retreated across the Harpeth before Forrest could close the jaws of the trap on him.

Forrest galloped up to the scene of Freeman's murder only a few minutes after his death. "Brave man," he said in a breaking voice. "None braver."

They buried him the next day, Sunday, April 11. Forrest's men never forgot the scene. The general trembled with grief and wept freely, his body shaking with anguish, and he made no attempt to hide his pain. As a result, something positive came out of the funeral. In the eyes of the boys in gray, Forrest became more human. There was more to him than the harsh taskmaster and relentless warrior. It was as if he was a patri-arch, his division was one huge clan, and he was mourning the loss of one of his children. The men knew that such a person would take care of them and would never take a needless chance with their lives.

# CHAPTER 9

# THE PURSUIT OF THE JACKASS BRIGADE

*Victory belongs to the most persevering.*

—Napoleon

The victories won by the Confederate cavalry caused annoyance and friction between Rosecrans and Lincoln's high command. Rosecrans sent telegrams to Washington every day demanding more horses and cavalry so he could deal with Van Dorn, Wheeler, Forrest, *et al.* He also pressured Granger to whip Van Dorn and Forrest. Granger wrote back, "You do not seem to understand why it is so difficult to surprise and crush Van Dorn. In the first place, he keeps every road and lane and hilltop picketed; the country people are his friends and are always ready to give [him] information."

As a result of all this, when thirty-four-year-old Colonel Abel D. Streight proposed an idea for a raid through his division commander to Rosecrans and his influential chief of staff, Brigadier General (later President) James A. Garfield, they were ready to listen. His idea was daring. He wanted to destroy the Confederate line of communications in northern Georgia, smash Bragg's railroads, and blow up all the ammunition factories in Georgia. With his railroad gone, Bragg would have to

Colonel Abel D. Streight (1828–1892), the commander of the Independent Provisional Brigade (a.k.a. the "Jackass Cavalry").

abandon middle Tennessee and retreat to the mountains of east Tennessee, where he could not feed his army without breaking it into small groups, which would be much easier to defeat. The only other alternative Bragg would have would be to abandon Tennessee altogether and retreat to northern Georgia. Rosecrans would then have the agriculturally rich middle Tennessee and would not have to depend as much on a 220-mile long supply line.

According to Streight's plan, he would join General Dodge at Eastport, Mississippi, with a brigade of mounted infantry. From there, Dodge would advance eastward and threaten Tuscumbia. Streight would move east behind Dodge's and, at the appropriate moment, would break away, turn south and east again and dash for the mountains of northern Georgia. En route, he would cut the Western & Atlantic Railroad near Rome, Georgia (160 miles from Tuscumbia), and destroy as much track as possible. The Northerners thought this would force Bragg to retreat because they believed his army was drawing its supplies via the Western & Atlantic. They were wrong Bragg's food came from the area around Shelbyville west to the Columbia region. The W & A was actually supplying General Lee in Virginia, so it was still very important.

The plan was approved on April 7, and Streight hurriedly outfitted his brigade.[1] For some reason which surpasses human understanding, the Northerners decided to mount most of Streight's brigade on mules. This was a disastrous move. While mules are more sure-footed in mountainous terrain than horses and are excellent beasts of burden, paradoxically they are poor at carrying riders and wear out quickly when forced to do so—especially if required to move faster than a walk. This is the root of why an axiom developed generations before: "A good farmer never rides the working stock." It was also impossible for a cavalry unit equipped with mules to keep its location secret. This is because when one mule brays, other mules follow suit. Fifteen hundred braying mules made a deafening noise which could be heard for miles—and made stealth and surprise impossible. The mules also tended to run away, were legendarily stubborn, and were fond of biting people they didn't like and they didn't like anybody. Before long, Streight's men unofficially changed the name of their unit from the Independent Provisional Brigade to "the Jackass Cavalry."

On April 10, the same day Forrest was fighting at Franklin, General Garfield ordered Streight to embark at once. His brigade boarded eight steamers and arrived at Palmyra the next day. Then they marched to Fort Henry. First, however, they had to catch and saddle the mules. Streight recalled: "I then for the first time discovered that the mules were nothing but poor, wild, and unbroken colts, many of them but two years old, and that a large number of them had the horse's distemper" (a fatal equine disease). Some were "so wild and unmanageable that it took us all that day and part of the next to catch and break them." The fact that the Yankees were infantrymen—not horsemen—worsened to the delay. The mules tossed them high into the air without much difficulty. About fifty mules died aboard the boats or were too near death to travel. Another dozen or so died the first day of the march. Streight replaced them by impressing 150 horses and mules from local citizens. This, of course, took even more time, so it was April 15 before the expedition finally reached Fort Henry and the 19th before it reached Eastport—a week behind schedule.

That same day, Dodge began advancing from Corinth across northern Mississippi with almost ten thousand men. He was opposed by Colonel Philip D. Roddey, who had only one regiment.[2] Dodge pushed Roddey back to the Mississippi-Alabama border the first day. Roddey retreated to Bear Creek, where he took up an excellent defensive position and called for help.

In accordance with the plan, Streight moved behind Dodge. That night, Roddey's men heard the mules braying in Dodge's rear. Some of

George Dibrell (1822–1888), shown here after his promotion to brigadier general in 1864. A highly capable officer, he commanded the Eighth Tennessee Cavalry Regiment and then a brigade under Forrest. After the war, he was a U.S. congressman (1874–84) and president of a railroad.

the Rebels infiltrated into Streight's camp, started firing their pistols, and stampeded the mules. The next day, four hundred of Streight's 1,250 remaining mules were missing. His men spent April 21 and 22 chasing them down, but could find only two hundred of them. Most of the rest were picked up by Roddey's scouts.

On April 23, the day Dodge finally pushed Roddey out of his positions on Bear Creek, Bragg ordered Forrest to ride to Roddey's rescue. By forced marches, Forrest's command arrived on April 27, and they were in the battle line by dawn the following day.

Unknown to Forrest and Roddey, Streight broke off from Dodge, marched past the Rebel left flank, and headed for Sand Mountain, Alabama, on April 26. The column was already in poor shape, in spite of the fact that General Dodge had given Streight's men some of his animals. About 150 of Streight's men were without mounts and another 150 walked beside their mules, which were so sick that they were barely able to carry their saddles.

Although Streight was behind the Confederates and as yet undetected, heavy rain on April 27 and 28 slowed his progress. On the morning of the 28th, Roddey's scouts reported that Streight's column sixteen miles due south of Courtland and driving on Moulton, well behind Rebel lines. Forrest reacted immediately. He ordered Roddey to fall back to Courtland. He sent Dibrell's regiment to attack Dodge's rear, a detachment of cavalry with Morton's guns to fortify Decatur, and the Eleventh Tennessee to take up blocking positions between Dodge and Streight. To himself he assigned the task of pursuing and destroying the Federal raiders. Realizing how demanding the pursuit would be, he selected only his toughest men with the best horses to go with him. To command them, he picked Roddey, Colonel Biffle, Major McLemore and his brother, Bill Forrest.³ He ordered three days of rations cooked and enough corn shelled to feed the horses for two days. He made sure that the guns and caissons were double-teamed with the best horses. The animals were also inspected and shoes tightened.

Forrest set out in a cold drizzle at 1 a.m. on April 29, heading south. He reached Moulton at noon and learned that the Union column had left, heading southeast. This suggested that Colonel Streight's objective was either the Georgia railroads via Sand Mountain or Decatur. The latter seemed more likely. To get to the railroads, Streight would have to cross a barren, sparsely populated region. Even if he reached his objective, escape would be problematic at best. Since Decatur seemed to be the most likely target, Forrest initially headed in that direction himself and sent Roddey toward Sand Mountain.

Meanwhile, Dibrell performed brilliantly. He raised havoc in Dodge's rear, seized the main river crossing and spread the rumor that Van Dorn was on his way with his entire command. Alarmed, Dodge headed back to his base in Corinth. Streight was on his own.

Forrest camped at Danville—not far from Decatur—that night. Bill Forrest and his "forty thieves" silently pushed to the edge of Streight's camp and captured ten videttes.⁴

In the saddle well before dawn on April 30, Forrest rode fast and soon rejoined the main body. Streight had left camp with his main force at dawn, but his rearguard, along with a number of stragglers and escaped slaves, remained behind, cooking breakfast, unaware that the Wizard of the Saddle had covered fifty miles in a day and a half. They were still hanging around the campfires when, out of nowhere, Forrest's artillery opened up on them. Then dozens of Rebels suddenly burst out of the woods and overran the camp. It is doubtful if any of the Yankees would have escaped except for the fact that breakfast was too great a temptation for the hungry Southerners. Meanwhile, Streight retreated to Day's Gap, a ridge three miles from the top of Sand Mountain. He took up a strong position with his right anchored on a steep ravine, his left on a marshy stream, and his men were dismounted and well concealed. Meanwhile, Bill Forrest, chasing the Yankees who had been routed at breakfast, ran into an ambush. Several scouts were killed or wounded, including Bill, whose thighbone was shattered.

As the rest of Bedford's men came up, Forrest ordered them to dismount. He had only one thousand men with him, but he ordered them to attack anyway. Roddey's men were too anxious and advanced well ahead of Forrest's. They received a full volley and lost 40 out of 350 men. Roddey fell back, and Streight counterattacked, capturing two of Forrest's guns. Forrest was furious, and tried to recapture the guns but failed. He regrouped for another attack and beat any straggler he saw with the flat edge of his sword. He ordered the horse-holders to tie the animals to bushes and join the line of battle. This increased his strength by twenty-five percent. A junior officer pointed out that, if the attack failed, the Yankees could counterattack and take their mounts. Forrest declared: "If we are whipped, we'll not need any horses" because they would be dead.

Meanwhile, more of his men caught up, so Forrest attacked at 3 p.m., only to find most of the Yankees had gone. Streight had only left small detachments of skirmishers, which he basically sacrificed. Forrest's men captured forty Northerners. The general ordered his men to "shoot at everything blue and keep up the scare." Among those captured were Colonel James W. Sheets, commander of the fifty-first Indiana, who was mortally wounded.

For all intents and purposes, Colonel Streight was now on the run. He told his men that the most dangerous man in the whole Confederacy was on their trail. He was forced to abandon his hospital, which Forrest promptly took. Forty or so Confederates captured at Sand Mountain were liberated, and sixty-eight Yankees were captured and paroled.

The forty-three miles between Day's Gap and Blountsville were mostly uninhabited, and most of the few people who lived there were Unionists. Streight had plenty of good guides who knew the country well, and there was an abundance of good ambush sites. Forrest continued the pursuit, even though it was dangerous, because the Yankees could be anywhere. He lost one horse killed from under him and two more wounded.

Forrest sent Roddey back to Decatur, because he did not know that Dodge had retreated. This left him with less than half as many men as Streight. On the other hand, Streight had to gather most of his forage from the local countryside—a dangerous business. Local militiamen captured and murdered at least two members of the Seventy-Third Indiana and probably others as well.

An hour before sundown, Streight deployed for battle on Hog Mountain. Forrest launched a rare night attack. The Union fire was mostly high, so there were not many casualties, but the Yankees escaped in the darkness, abandoning the two guns they had captured from Forrest, but they had been spiked.

Under the light of a full moon, the Rebels continued their pursuit. The trail of the Union retreat was littered with pieces of paper: the Yankees were destroying their letters and private papers—another indication that they realized the seriousness of their deteriorating situation.

Private Granville Pillow of the Ninth Tennessee was slowly riding down the road at the point of the pursuit when his horse suddenly stopped. Pillow gently nudged him onward, but the animal balked, threw up its head, drew its ears back and sniffed suspiciously. Pillow knew what this meant. He immediately galloped back and told his lieutenant that there was an ambush ahead. The officer sent him directly to Forrest, who quickly deployed his command and attacked. The fighting was heavy but short. Streight fell back rapidly.

And so it went for four days. Streight would set an ambush, Forrest would foil his plot, and the Yankees would retreat. In doing so, they showed excellent discipline. There was little straggling, despite the fact that they were exhausted and many mules broke down. They trudged along on foot, with the Rebels nipping at their heels.

Meanwhile, Forrest manufactured another advantage for himself. He used a relatively few fresh troops to harass the Union rear, while his own fighters got a few hours rest. Then he would rotate his men. This way, at least some of the Southern troops were partially rested, while all of the Northern soldiers had to keep pushing on. These tactics also mitigated one of Forrest's disadvantages: when he lost a horse, he also lost a man. A Union soldier who lost a horse or mule at least might be able to pick up another from local sources, but the Rebels followed over country which had been picked clean by Streight's raiders.

On May 1, Streight got lucky. He entered Blountsville to find a May Day celebration in progress. The Federals crashed the party and took all the food, and many of the celebrants' horses. Suddenly, Forrest appeared at the head of the Fourth Tennessee, igniting a fierce battle in the streets of the town. Forrest personally attacked the Union front while Biffle got into their rear and routed Streight's horse holders. The steeds scattered in all directions. Colonel Streight had to withdraw again, and his men wearily turned east. More and more were now on foot, but their endurance was remarkable.

A scout approached Forrest and reported that a column of Union cavalry was marching on him via a parallel route. Forrest realized immediately that this couldn't be true. He asked if he had seen the Yankees. No, the scout replied, he got the report from a civilian. Forrest grabbed him, jerked him off his horse, and beat his head against a tree. "Now, God**mn you, if ever you come to me again with a pack of lies, you won't get off so easy!"

Forrest hung on his opponent's coattails so closely that Streight had to abandon what was left of his supply train. He had his men load their corn, ammunition and rations into saddle bags and set his last six wagons on fire, but Forrest's men were pursuing so closely that they put out the flames before they did much damage. This began a running fight to the Big Black River, also called the Big Fork of the Black Warrior River. Streight crossed the stream at 5 p.m. and kept marching east. Probably because of exhaustion, the Yankees got most of their powder wet during the crossing. As night fell, Forrest sent Colonel Biffle and one hundred of his best men to continue harassing Streight's rear. He let the rest of his command sleep until midnight. Then they caught up with Biffle at dawn on May 2. Forrest and his men had now been moving and fighting for nine consecutive days.

Streight wanted to let his men rest near Will's Creek, fifteen miles east of the Black Warrior River. Forrest would not allow this—and struck immediately. The Yankees beat back the attack, but had to keep moving east. On both sides, the pace was punishing. Horses and mules continued to break down, collapse and die. Some of Streight's men procured replacement mounts along the way—usually at gunpoint.

After he crossed Will's Creek and the Federals had resumed their march, Forrest let his men rest. When he called upon them to mount, several simply could not get up. Forrest culled the weakest horses and men and sent them to Decatur. He gave the remainder a pep talk, full of warmth and sympathy. Six hundred men responded and rode off with their commander, chasing the remaining 1,700 Yankees.

The next obstacle was Black Creek, which was formidable. It was small but deep, with steep banks and supposedly was crossable only by boat or bridge. Streight hoped to put it between his men and Forrest. If he succeeded, he could rest his soldiers and animals, and begin his final push on Rome, Georgia. This, he thought, would give him half a day's head start over Forrest. If he could then cross the Oostanaula River at Rome and burn the bridge there, he would gain another day—perhaps two. He could then destroy the Confederate railroads in Georgia.

On the morning of May 2, the war reached a dogtrot house, which was inhabited by the widow Samson and her two daughters.[5] The Yankees used her fence rails to burn the Black Creek Bridge. The women had tried unsuccessfully to pull them off the bridge before they burned and now, at 10 a.m., were returning from the effort. Suddenly, a single Yankee rider appears with a lone Rebel in full pursuit. Seeing the bridge on fire, he suddenly halted, screaming "I surrender! I surrender!" Then the ladies noticed that the Rebel had three stars on his collar with a wreath around them. He took the Yankee prisoner and turned to the women. "I am a Confederate general," he said. "I am trying to capture and kill the Yankee soldiers across the creek yonder."

The women walked outside the gate to touch the bridle of his horse and pet its sweat-covered neck. "Ladies, don't be alarmed," the man said.

"I am General Forrest. I and my men will protect you. Where are the Yankees?"

On the other side of the creek, Mrs. Samson replied, ready to shoot you if you try to cross. She did not mention that the Yankees had searched her house but found nothing of value except a side-saddle, which one Federal had maliciously cut to pieces with his knife.

As the Rebel skirmishers came up, dismounted, moved forward and started exchanging fire with the Yankee snipers, Forrest realized nothing could save the bridge. He asked Emma, the youngest daughter, where he could cross the creek. There was an unsafe bridge two miles downstream, she said, but there was a ford just a few hundred yards away. She had seen the cows use it, but only she and her family knew where it was. If the general would saddle her a horse, she would show him.

Forrest replied that there was no time for that. He extended his hand and she mounted the horse behind them. Her mother objected, but Forrest assured her that he would bring her back safely.

They rode across a field and into a ravine, where they dismounted and crawled through the bushes until they could see the ford, which was about three quarters of a mile from the bridge. She pointed out the entrance and where it came out. In doing so, she placed herself between Forrest and the Yankees. "Get behind me! Get behind me!" the general cried as he placed his own body between Emma and the Federals. "You can be my guide, but not my breastwork."

As they crawled back to safety, the Yankees fired at them. Then Emma stood up and the Northern boys realized she was a woman. All firing ceased immediately. She headed back toward the horse, with Forrest behind her, acting as a human shield. The Northerners opened fire again, trying to kill the big Rebel. Forrest trembled in fear—not for himself, but because he was afraid one of the bullets would hit Emma. He was terrified by the thought of having to carry her lifeless body back to her mother. A couple of wild shots did rip through her dress, but she was not touched.

Forrest was most impressed by Emma Samson's courage. He took her back home, asked her name and for a lock of her hair. He also asked her to see to the burial of Robert Turner, one of his bravest men, who had fallen near Black Creek.

The Southern artillery came up half an hour later and covered the cavalry as it crossed the ford. Streight, who was busy rounding up fresh horses and mules in Gadsden, was shocked to learn that Forrest had penetrated the Black Creek line. His only hope now, he realized immediately, was to capture Rome and burn the bridges there. He remained in Gadsden only long enough to destroy some Confederate Army supplies.

After Black Creek, Emma Samson was hailed as a heroine throughout the South. The Alabama legislature honored her with a resolution of commendation and then gave her more tangible token of their esteem—an entire 640 acre section of land.[6] The original Samson farm is now the site of Alabama City, Alabama.

Forrest's crossing of Black Creek finally shook the confidence of Streight's brave men. Up until now, in spite of all they had been through, their morale had remained high and they had hung together. Now their spirits sagged and, with visions of a Confederate prison dancing before their eyes, they began to straggle. The grayback cavalrymen picked them up one by one. Streight nevertheless decided to make his third all-night march in three days. His scouts reported that a Confederate column was advancing parallel to them to the north. Assuming that they were trying to beat him to Rome, Streight sent Captain Milton Russell and two hundred of his best-mounted men to seize the bridge at Rome. Like all the Federals at this point, however, Russell and his men were low on ammunition.

Forrest reached Gadsden on May 2 and asked for volunteers to rush to Rome, to warn the Home Guard of the approaching Yankees. John H. "Deacon" Wisdom, a rural mailman, played Paul Revere and performed this task. Revere rode eighteen miles. Wisdom had to cover sixty-seven. Riding like a madman, he reached Rome in eight and a half hours, screaming "The Yankees are coming!" Church bells were soon ringing, even though it was midnight. Forrest also sent a rare personally composed dispatch to the citizens. (Usually his adjutant or an aide did the writing.) It read: "Prepare your selves to Repuls [repulse] them—they have two Mountain howitzers. I will be close on them. I have kild [sic] three hundred of their men. They air running for their lives."

The Home Guard, Governor Joseph E. Brown's Georgia Militia and convalescing Confederate soldiers immediately turned out and prepared the town for defense. They were joined by dozens of local men, armed with shotguns and hunting rifles. The men also took up the flooring from the bridge over the Oostansula. When Captain Russell arrived outside of the town shortly after sunrise, he found it too heavily defended to attack.

Meanwhile, Streight's men captured a prisoner and took him to the colonel. The man quite possibly was a plant, sent by the Wizard himself to deceive the Yankee colonel. He told Streight that Forrest had Roddey's brigade and Armstrong's brigade with him, as well as several others whose names he did not know. Streight apparently believed him and now suspected that he was outnumbered three to one or more.

Forrest caught up with Streight at Blount's Plantation, twelve miles from Gadsden. Colonel Gilbert Hathaway, the commander of the Seventy-Third Indiana Infantry, set a clever ambush with five hundred men, but Forrest spotted it in time. He aligned three hundred of his men in column of fours. He ordered them to advance and fire left and right with their revolvers. They overran the ambush and killed several men, including the brave and highly capable Hathaway.

Some of Hathaway's officers thought he should receive a decent burial. Despite the nearness of the enemy, they asked Mr. Blount to see to it that he was buried in a metallic coffin.

"There are no metallic cases in this country," the plantation owner replied.

"Then give him a plain pine coffin."

"We have no coffins," Blount sadly replied.

"Then take some planks and make a box and bury him and mark his grave."

"You have burned all my planks, and I have nothing with which to make even a box."

The officers persisted, even though Confederate bullets were flying about their heads. "Then wrap his body in an oil cloth and bury him, for God's sake, where he may be found."

This the Alabamian promised to do. He buried the colonel in his garden and put a marker above his grave.

Streight was now forced to detour in the direction of Gaylesville, Alabama, about eleven miles away, where there was an intact bridge over the Coosa. (Captain Russell had earlier crossed the main bridge on route to Rome but had not posted guards, so Forrest's scouts were able to loop behind Streight and burn it.) On the way, the colonel ran into a charcoal manufacturing plant, from which wagon trails radiated off in all directions. Not knowing which of the many roads was the one to Gaylesville, he split his command into groups, which wandered every which way. It was daylight before he found a bridge across the Dyke River, a tributary of the Coosa. Once on the other bank, he burned the bridge.

Forrest arrived at the Dyke shortly after—about 5 a.m. on May 3. He ordered his men to ride into the stream to see how deep it was. They crossed holding their paper cartridges above their heads. By 9 a.m. he was across. It had taken him four hours to cross a stream that it had taken Streight eleven hours to cross.

Streight's men were simply not able to go any further. They stopped to rest at Lawrence's Plantation near Gaylesville, twenty miles from Rome. Here, after riding 119 miles without sleep in eighty-three hours, Forrest's cavalry finally caught up with them. Streight's officers had already told him that, if Forrest caught them again, it was all over. Confederate Captain Henry Pointer conveyed Forrest's usual demand for surrender "to avoid the further effusion of blood." A courier arrived from Captain Russell, saying he had been unable to recross the Coosa or take Rome. Streight asked for a personal interview with Forrest, which was quickly granted. The Rebel general demanded "Immediate surrender. Your men to be treated as prisoners of war, officers to retain their side-arms and personal property." Negotiations proceeded. In Streight's presence, Forrest gave dispatch riders orders for several regiments, which were nowhere near Lawrence's. Captain Pointer also played a role in the act. He offered Streight a drink of whiskey, commenting that it might be the last drink the colonel ever got.

Several times, Forrest's artillerymen drove their guns across an opening in Streight's line of sight. Colonel Streight looked over Forrest's shoulder and asked: "How many guns have you got? There's fifteen I've counted already."

"I reckon that's all that has kept up," the chieftain remarked. "But I've got enough to whip you out of your boots."[7] The artillery continued its show until Streight had counted twenty-three guns.

During the truce, Streight held an officers' call. He wanted to fight on, but his officers had had enough. They unanimously voted to surrender.

One of Forrest's aides rode up, announced the arrival of another regiment, and dropped the remark that the field was getting crowded. Forrest ended the negotiations by pretending that his patience had run out and he was ready to attack again. "Sound to mount!" he snapped at his bugler. Streight capitulated immediately. He had only one condition: his men were to be allowed to give three cheers for the Union. Forrest consented to this last act of defiance, and Streight surrendered 1,540 men and a battery of mountain howitzers.

After the surrender, Streight learned that Forrest had been bluffing. He demanded that his guns be returned to him, so he could resume the battle. Forrest laughed and said: "You know what they say, Colonel...all's fair in love and war!"[8] Captain Russell arrived a few minutes later with his two hundred men, who also surrendered.

Of Streight's original mules, only about twenty were still standing. Many of Forrest's horses were also at the end of their strength. The best animals from middle Tennessee and Kentucky, they had been trained almost from birth not to stop until the race was won. They had been pushed beyond their endurance and, now that it was over, many of them died. Of the 550 Confederate horses that entered Rome, three hundred perished over the next two days. Forrest had captured 1,600 horses and mules in the pursuit and surrender of the Jackass Brigade. He ordered them returned to their owners, but only 450 of them could be located.

The citizens of Rome welcomed Forrest's soldiers as conquering heroes. They threw flowers in front of the Rebel horses and greeted their riders with food of all kinds. Someone fired one of the town's two ancient cannons in salute to Forrest. Unfortunately, he had forgotten that it had been loaded for the defense of the town. Fortunately, no one was hurt.

When Forrest asked for food for his prisoners, the Romans treated them to ham, chicken and roast beef. "We were quite willing to feed the Yankees when they had no guns," a local lady recalled. The citizens presented the general with a wreath of flowers and a beautiful horse named Highlander, which was paid for by a popular subscription that was oversubscribed within two hours. Forrest asked that the excess money be used to benefit the sick and wounded. On the night of May 5/6, he received word that another Union column had entered Alabama and was moving between Elyton (now Birmingham) and Talladega. Forrest and his men mounted and headed off to meet it. At Gadsden on May 7, however, his scouts arrived with the news that the rumor about the column was false.

That night, Forrest stayed at the home of R. B. Kyle and spent the entire evening playing with Kyle's two-year-old son. The next morning, he insisted upon carrying the child two or three miles on the saddle of his horse. As they parted, Forrest kissed the youngster and exclaimed to his father: "My God, Kyle, this is worth living for!"

From Gadsden, Forrest made a leisurely march to Decatur, picking up stragglers, the wounded, abandoned Union supplies, and a great many slaves who had followed Streight's column in hopes of reaching freedom. He then proceeded to the north bank of the Tennessee. On May 11, he turned command over to Jacob Biffle and traveled by rail to army headquarters in Shelbyville. On the way, he was stopped by the people of Huntsville, then the most important town in northern Alabama. The citizens cheered him and presented him with "King Philip," a twelve-year-old gelding horse that he kept long after the war. Forrest was now a hero throughout the Old Southwest. Even Braxton Bragg greeted him almost with affection and said he was recommending him for promotion to major general. He even spoke of making him chief of cavalry. Meanwhile, an angry husband and father entered the amorous Van Dorn's headquarters on a pretext and shot him dead. Forrest and Brigadier General William H. "Red" Jackson, another cavalry division commander, urged Bragg to name General Gideon Pillow his successor. Bragg appointed Forrest instead. His corps consisted of his own division and Jackson's. Shortly thereafter, however, Jackson and his men were transferred to Mississippi, leaving Forrest with a division of two small brigades (his own and Armstrong's). James Seddon, Jefferson Davis's Secretary of War, wanted to send Forrest to Vicksburg in order to stave off Grant's offensive against that critical city.[9] Davis, however, assigned the task to General Joseph E. Johnston, and the city fell on July 4.

Meanwhile, General Forrest decided to transfer Lieutenant Andrew Gould out of his command. Gould was in command of the two guns lost at Sand Mountain, and Forrest held the young officer responsible. Lieutenant Morton, who was friendly with both men, knew that they both had violent tempers and tried to keep them apart, but he was not successful.[10]

At 3 p.m. on June 12, Gould showed up at Forrest's headquarters (the Masonic Building in Columbus, Tennessee) and demanded to speak with him. Forrest was meeting with his quartermaster and whittling with a pocketknife when Gould turned up. The general folded up his knife, put it in his pocket and walked out into the hall to talk with Gould. The lieutenant strongly insisted that his transfer be rescinded or at least the wording in the letter of transfer be revised, because it implied Gould was a coward. Forrest refused to do either. One word led to another and the argument became more and more acrimonious. Then Gould made a move for the pistol in his pocket. Forrest grabbed his hand, reached for the knife in his pocket, and opened it with his teeth. He stabbed the lieutenant in the side, just as Gould fired his pistol through his pocket. Gould escaped Forrest's grasp and fled, followed by the wounded general. After hearing the shot, several officers rushed to the scene, intervened, and convinced

Forrest to see a doctor. The physician examined him and declared that he believed the wound would be fatal.

"No damned man shall kill me and live!" Forrest roared. He jumped off the operating table and made his way into the street. Pulling a gun from a saddlebag, he began looking for Gould. One soldier told him that the lieutenant's wound was mortal; another said it was not bad at all. The young artilleryman had gone into a tailor's shop, he said, and pointed the way.

An enraged Forrest burst into the shop, where doctors were working on Gould. Seeing the general, Gould fled into the back alley. Forrest fired at him but missed; his bullet grazed the leg of an innocent bystander ("a big Dutchman" from Armstrong's brigade). He continued his pursuit and finally caught the young man, who had collapsed in some tall grass. Determining that he was near death, Forrest left him there without inflicting any further injuries on him.

The physicians who had been helping Gould now took charge of the general and got him back to his hotel room, where his wife and son were waiting. As soon as he saw Mary, Forrest calmed down. Fortunately for him, the ball had lodged in a muscle and missed anything vital. When he learned that he was going to live, the general ordered the doctors to take care of Gould and do all they could to save him. "It's nothing but a damned little pistol ball!" he said of his own wound. "Let it alone and go get Lieutenant Gould. Take him to the Nelson house and make him as comfortable as you can. Spare nothing to save him! And, by God, when I give an order like that, I mean it!" He joked that, had Gould shown the same kind of bravery at Sand Mountain, this incident would not have occurred. For several days, it seemed that the lieutenant would recover. But pneumonia set in and he died. With Mary and her sister serving as nurses, the general recovered rapidly. Meanwhile, his cavalry returned to outpost duty and resumed patrolling in the vicinity of Spring Hall, on Bragg's left flank.

# CHAPTER 10

# RIVER OF DEATH

*Rough diamonds may sometimes be mistaken for worth-less pebbles.*

—Thomas Browne

fter they arrived in Spring Hill, May 1863 was a month of daily skirmishes for Forrest's men. On June 1, after scouting the Nashville and Murfreesboro areas, Forrest sent a dispatch to General Bragg, informing him that Rosecrans was preparing to move. Later that week, he learned that Granger had left Franklin with some of his units. He rode into Franklin long enough to discover what formations were still around, get some supplies, and release a few political prisoners. As he neared the Union fort just outside the town, he saw what he took to be a white flag. It was really a signal flag, calling upon General Granger for help. As he approached the fort, a Union officer stood up. This man had been captured at Murfreesboro and had been well treated by Forrest and his men. Now he paid the general back. "General Forrest," he shouted, "I know you and don't want to see you hurt! Go back! There is no truce. That is a signal flag!"

Forrest raised his hat in acknowledgement and withdrew quickly, waving at the Yankee as he left.

Granger had moved to Triune, about twelve miles southeast of Franklin. Forrest launched a probing attack on June 20, but discovered a large infantry force there, so he quickly withdrew. While Granger's men's attention was diverted, Major Jeffrey Forrest stole a herd of cattle from them.

On June 23, Rosecrans began a major offensive. Despite the fact that Forrest had warned him, Bragg was caught flat-footed, and the Union general pushed heavy columns through gaps in the Cumberland Mountains, turning Bragg's right flank. On June 26, as his Duck River line collapsed, Bragg ordered Forrest to fall back and link up with Wheeler's cavalry at Shelbyville.

Joe Wheeler covered the retreat of Polk's corps, but the Yankees were right on his tail. He was about to burn the Duck River bridge at Shelbyville when Major Rambaut of Forrest's staff rode up and announced that Forrest was within sight of the town. Wheeler, with four hundred volunteers and two guns, re-crossed the bridge but could not complete his dispositions before the Northerners attacked and captured the artillery.[1] In the confusion, a caisson overturned on the bridge, cutting off Wheeler's retreat. He rode his horse to the riverbank and jumped fifteen feet into the water, followed by about one hundred of his command. The Yankees followed them and fired on them as they swam away. Between forty and fifty Confederate cavalrymen were killed or were wounded and drowned. Forrest, meanwhile, heard the sound of the battle. Realizing his route of retreat was probably cut, he veered away and eventually crossed the river four miles to the west.

General Granger did not know it, but Bragg's main wagon train was only nine miles away. It was raining heavily and the train was making slow progress on the muddy roads. He had a window of opportunity to inflict a terrible blow on the Confederate Army, but halted the pursuit instead. Moving as rapidly as he could through the mud, Forrest inserted his command between Granger and the wagon train, and the opportunity was gone.

On June 28, General Bragg evacuated Tullahoma and fell back to the Elk River. Forrest's cavalry formed the rearguard as Bragg retreated toward Chattanooga. The Northern cavalry had greatly increased in numbers since 1862 and was also more assertive. Colonel John T. Wilder's Mounted Infantry Brigade—which was armed with Spencer Repeating Rifles—was particularly aggressive.[2] On July 3, the rearguard fought a delaying action through the town of Cowan, Tennessee, and was hard pressed by the Yankees. It was under Forrest's personal command and he was dressed like a private. As the men retreated, an old woman gave Forrest a tongue-lashing. "You big ole rascal!" she screamed. "You cowardly cur! If Ole Forrest was here, he would kick your butt and make you fight!" The Escort laughed out loud at the general's expense. Later, sitting around a campfire, someone brought up the incident again. Forrest joined in the jollity and said: "I would've rather faced Yankee artillery than that fiery dame!"

Rosecrans's brilliant Tullahoma Campaign had not resulted in a major battle, but it was nevertheless a significant Northern victory. In nine days, he had pushed the Rebels back one hundred miles and secured agriculturally rich middle Tennessee. Also, the average Confederate soldier lost any faith he may have had in General Bragg. Morale plummeted, and thousands of men deserted. Unfortunately for his future, Rosecrans concluded that the morale of the Army of Tennessee was broken and would never recover. His only worry was Forrest. He was at the end of a very long supply line and was mostly resupplied by rail. He was concerned that Forrest would fall upon his lines of communications and cut them, as he had done to Buell, so he stationed several brigades along his route to prevent this. Forrest, however, attempted nothing of the sort, due to the rough nature of the terrain, the lack of roads, the worn condition of his horses and men, the gains the Union cavalry had made in both quality and quantity, and the fact that he had been given other missions, such as guarding potential river crossings on the Clinch and Tennessee Rivers, to make sure Bragg was not surprised again. In addition, he and his men were just plain tired. They badly needed a rest.

The next few weeks were generally quiet. Due to the mixing of units during the retreat, Wheeler now covered Bragg's left flank while Forrest guarded the right. He headquartered in the beautiful town of Kingston

William S. Rosecrans (1819–1898), the commander of the Army of the Cumberland.

on the Clinch River, seventy miles north of Chattanooga and forty-five miles west of Knoxville. Here Forrest's men had a six-week respite, during which they enjoyed horse races, dominoes, card games, swimming in the Clinch and playing in the clear mountain streams.

At the start of the war, he (like many other volunteers) had an elevated opinion of West Pointers. Working with Bragg and Wheeler had severely undercut this view. Bedford now believed that they thought their four years' education, coupled with years of garrison duty, gave them a divine right to command (President Davis, himself an alumni, seemed to support this view.) But two years into the war, Braxton Bragg had hardly ever won a victory, while Forrest, an amateur, had almost never tasted defeat. Now he began to think strategically.

Forrest spent at least part of his time looking at the big picture. On August 9, 1863, he sent a letter to General Samuel Cooper, the adjutant general of the Confederate Army, through regular military channels—to include Bragg. The Federals had conquered the Mississippi River Valley, Forrest said. All right, let's use that against them. He asked to be given his Escort Company, Major Charles McDonald's battalion (150 men) and Colonel Thomas G. Woodward's Second Kentucky (250 men). He also asked for long-range Enfield rifles for the men, an artillery battery of Dahlgren or three-inch Parrott guns and plenty of ammunition. With this command, and with the authority to raise additional forces and take charge of several companies and battalions operating behind Union lines, he believed he could create an army of five thousand to ten thousand men. With it, he claimed that he would cripple Union shipping on the Mississippi and Tennessee Rivers, if he did not shut it down entirely. Even if these, the main Federal supply lines, could not been closed, dozens of Northern brigades and regiments would be required to guard the valley and thus could not be used against Bragg or Robert E. Lee.

Had Forrest's plan been adopted, it might have prolonged the war by a year. And, that year might have enabled the embattled South to gain its independence. U.S. Grant himself wrote, "Anything that could have prolonged the war a year beyond the time it did finally close would probably have exhausted the North to such an extent that they [the Northern people] might have abandoned the contest and agreed to the separation."

Ten days later—fearing that Bragg would not forward the proposal—Forrest went over his head and sent it directly to President Davis.

He was too late. Bragg, who had known Davis since the Mexican War, advised Jefferson Davis to reject Forrest's plan, and Davis accepted his recommendation.

Adam R. "Stovepipe" Johnson (1834–1922), Forrest's chief of scouts in 1861. He rose from private to brigadier general in three years. Totally blinded and captured in 1864, he never allowed his handicap to stop him. After he was exchanged, he attempted to return to active duty. Following the war he was a successful businessman, founded a town, and helped harness the waters of the Colorado River.

Famed historian Ludwell Johnson called it the worst mistake of Davis's presidency.

On August 16, Rosecrans advanced again with three infantry corps: Thomas's XIV, Alexander McDowell McCook's XX and Thomas L. Crittenden's XXI, as well as Stanley's Cavalry Corps. Once again he outmaneuvered Bragg, but this time Rosecrans's contempt for Bragg was so great that he was convinced the Rebels would not offer battle. He separated his infantry corps and even some divisions from the rest of the army and from each other, so that they were not in a position to help one another if attacked. They were subject to destruction in detail if the

Rebels concentrated against them. Had Rosecrans been opposing Robert E. Lee and Stonewall Jackson, most of the Army of the Cumberland would almost certainly have been destroyed. Fortunately for the North, he was opposing Braxton Bragg and a set of mediocre corps commanders, so no such thing happened.[3]

Meanwhile, the animosity between Forrest and Braxton Bragg increased. During the Kentucky campaign, Braxton Bragg conceived a hatred for the state in general, which led to friction between him and the Kentucky cavalry leaders, including Brigadier Generals John Hunt Morgan and Basil Duke. When Stovepipe Johnson, Forrest's former chief of scouts, and his partisan rangers joined the Army of Tennessee in September, Bragg ordered them dismounted and converted to infantry. Fortunately for the Kentuckians, they were in Forrest's sector, and he flatly refused to obey the order. "He well knew the fighting qualities of Kentucky's sons," General Johnson recalled, "and they in turn admired and loved him, and would have done anything he asked, no matter what the odds against them." Bragg swallowed this insubordination, but he chalked up another black mark against Forrest.

Meanwhile, outmaneuvered again, Bragg ordered Forrest and Buckner to pull closer to his right flank, forcing Buckner to evacuate Knoxville. It was occupied by Ambrose Burnside and his twenty-four thousand men on September 4. Forrest suggested that this was an opportunity. The Army of Tennessee could concentrate against Burnside with vastly superior forces and destroy him before Rosecrans could react. Bragg ignored his recommendation and began evacuating Chattanooga. Rosecrans's men entered the gateway city on September 9. The next day, they pushed into the rugged Cumberland Mountains.

Despite the rough terrain, Rosecrans persisted in his unwise policy of dividing his army. Forrest, in the forefront as usual, correctly reported that Crittenden's corps was alone and isolated; even worse, he had two divisions across the small Chickamauga Creek and a third several miles away at Lee and Gordon's Mill. Bragg was only six miles away and his army was concentrated. So sure was Forrest that Bragg would fall on Crittenden and destroy him that he made detailed plans for seizing the

Red House Bridge in the Northern rear, to cut off the Union retreat. But Bragg took off the other direction and another opportunity was lost.

Forrest continued to fight the advancing Yankees and, taking maximum advantage of the terrain, slowly fell back. He was joined by his old brigade (three thousand men), which he deployed as infantry. More and more as the war went on, Forrest's men used their horses to get them to the battlefield where, once there, they fought as infantry. Checked in the mountains, Crittenden threw in Wilder's Lightning Brigade with their Spencer Repeating Rifles. Forrest stopped them, but he was wounded in the process. With little anesthetic available, the surgeon, Dr. J. B. Cowan, prescribed liquor. So, for the first time in many years, Forrest actually took a drink.

Rosecrans finally woke up to the fact that his wildly dispersed army was in danger on September 13. He hurriedly ordered his forces to concentrate, but that would take four days. Bragg and his corps commanders thus had four more days to destroy all or part of Rosecrans's army, but they were unable to take advantage of them. Forrest, however, created his own advantages, as usual. On September 18, with a force of fifty men, he attacked a Pennsylvania cavalry regiment. The charge was so sudden and so violent that it caused considerable confusion in Union ranks, but the Yankees soon rallied and pursued the Wizard. Forrest, however, had posted the rest of his command a short distance away and led the bluecoats straight into an ambush. He turned on the Federals and personally split the skull of a captain with a saber stroke. He pursued the survivors for four miles and downed several other enemy horsemen, stopping only when he reached Chickamauga Creek.

By the morning of September 18, most of the Army of the Cumberland was concentrated near the Chickamauga. Now that he had lost all of his advantages, Bragg at last decided to launch an all-out offensive, so he moved toward the creek. Counting reinforcements he had just received from Mississippi and was getting from Virginia, he had sixty thousand men as opposed to Rosecrans's fifty-eight thousand. It was the largest battle in the Civil War in which the Confederates had a numerical advantage, even though it was a slight one.

"Chickamauga" allegedly is an Indian word for "River of Death." This creek separated the two armies and would form the eastern boundary of the battlefield, which covered about four square miles. It was heavily wooded. Sometimes movements fifty feet away could be heard but not seen. Narrow dirt roads led to various fords and bridges. There were a few clearings around very modest farms.

For the next two days, Forrest may as well have been an infantry general. The battle began on September 19. The morning was characterized by heavy fog. Forrest was up before dawn, feeling his way around the Union left. He discovered that the federal left flank (General Thomas's XIV Corps) overlapped Bragg's right, putting Rosecrans in a position to roll up Bragg's entire front. Forrest immediately sent a dispatch to Bragg, requesting strong and immediate infantry reinforcements. He also sent Captain Anderson to see General Polk, six or seven miles to the rear, with a request that he (Forrest) be given Armstrong's division. For the moment, however, all Forrest had available was one brigade of Brigadier General John Pegram's small division.

In order to buy time for Bragg, Forrest attacked Thomas's flank, which was held by Major General John M. Brannan's division. So fierce was his attack, and so closely was it supported by Morton's and Jacob Huggins's batteries, which were firing grape and canister, that Brannan reported he was under attack from two full divisions.

At one point in the battle, one of Forrest's men lost his nerve and headed for the rear as fast as he could run. Forrest ordered him to halt but the panicked soldier did not heed him. The general drew one of his six-shooters, cocked it and aimed. Just as he was about to fire, Captain Anderson cried: "Oh, General, think!"

Forrest paused long enough to consider and allowed the private to escape.

Pegram held the line despite suffering twenty-five percent casualties. He was reinforced just in time by Forrest's own brigade (now commanded by Colonel George G. Dibrell), which Forrest deployed as infantry. Still it was not enough to defeat the overwhelming tide of bluecoats. Ordering Pegram to hold at all costs, Forrest dashed to the rear, where he found a brigade of Major General W. H. T. Walker's Reserve Corps. Without bothering to ask Walker's permission, he took charge of it and threw it into battle.

The fighting on September 19 was brutal. "I had been in sixty battles and skirmishes up to this time," Confederate Captain Thomas F. Berry recalled, "but nothing like this had I ever seen." General Thomas finally managed to push the Rebels back but, alerted by Forrest, Walker joined the fight and, on his own initiative, threw in the rest of his small corps. Thomas now had five divisions in action, minus a brigade, which ran out of ammunition and prudently left the field. Walker, who, as senior commander, took charge of the fighting, had two infantry divisions and Forrest's cavalry, but the fighting was so fierce that Thomas thought he was outnumbered.[4]

Now it was Thomas's turn to call for help. More Yankees joined the fighting. So did the five brigades of Cheatham's division. The battle lasted until after nightfall but, thanks largely to Forrest, Thomas's attempt to turn the Confederate right had been thwarted.

At one point, Captain Berry of Morgan's old command led a charge near Chickamauga Creek with 570 men. He lost 362 men killed and wounded in an hour. He suffered a wound in his side, and his horse was killed and fell on him, crushing his left leg below the knee. That night, medical orderlies from the ambulance corps found him and left him for dead, telling him that he would not last an hour.

Fortunately for Berry, some wandering infantrymen pulled his horse off of him and dressed his wound, but he still could not walk or crawl. He rolled over and over until he reached the Chickamauga. The water was blood red, but he filled his canteen and shared it with a wounded South Carolina soldier. He lay in a stupor for hours before he heard the sound of hoof-beats. It was General Forrest, taking care of his boys. He dismounted, knelt beside Berry, and felt his heartbeat. He sharply ordered the ambulance personnel to place him on a litter and drive him to a hospital. Berry's admiration for Forrest knew no limits after that. "He rose supreme to every situation; everywhere he astonished friends and foes alike," the captain later declared.

Berry's adventures were far from over. In the hospital, the surgeons decided to amputate his leg. As they tried to operate, Berry thrust a doubled-barreled derringer into the doctor's face, cocked it, and dared him to try. The surgeon then refused to remove the bullet from Berry's side. So, Berry operated on himself and extracted it, with the help of a beautiful nurse, with whom he promptly fell in love. She refused to return his affections, however. She had lost her husband at the First Bull Run and was not about to get romantically involved until after the war.

Berry did not walk on crutches until November 15, He returned to duty on January 1, 1864, and immediately headed for Forrest's cavalry.[5]

Meanwhile, on September 20, Bragg planned to begin the battle anew at dawn but could not get his disorganized army moving forward until 9:30 a.m. The Confederates on the right flank were checked, except for Forrest, who got into Thomas's rear and captured his hospitals.

Lieutenant General D. H. Hill saw Forrest's men advancing and asked what infantry brigade it was. He was so impressed when he was told that it was Forrest's cavalry that he rode over to Bedford and said, "General Forrest, I wish to congratulate you and these brave men moving across that field like veteran infantry upon their magnificent behavior. In Virginia I made myself extremely unpopular with the cavalry because I said that, so far, I had not seen a dead man with spurs on. No one can speak disparagingly of such troops as yours."

Meanwhile, the Confederacy got very, very lucky.

Unknown to anyone on the Northern side, Bragg had appealed to Richmond for help on August 22. Robert E. Lee sent him James Longstreet's I Corps, which consisted of John Bell Hood's and Lafayette McLaws's divisions.[6] After a nine-hundred-mile train ride, it began to arrive on the night of September 18. They were preparing to advance, just as Rosecrans made a fatal mistake. He ordered General Thomas J. Wood to move his division to cover a gap, which in fact did not exist. In doing so, he created a gap where none existed before. Just at that moment, Longstreet attacked with three divisions at the very spot Wood had just vacated. Wood's division was practically destroyed, Jefferson C. Davis's brigade was smashed, and Sheridan's division streamed rapidly to the rear. Several Union brigades were routed, and Longstreet captured forty guns. McCook's XX and Crittenden's XXI Corps were caught up in the panic and were swept away—as was Rosecrans.

Longstreet wanted to pursue, but Bragg wanted to destroy the Union left, where General Thomas occupied the crest of a position called Horseshoe Ridge. General Granger tried to reinforce Thomas with four thousand of his five thousand men. This move Forrest tried to prevent. Despite the fact that he was outnumbered more than two to one, Forrest got behind Thomas and blocked the road with fourteen guns. He held Granger up for two hours, but General Hill refused to send him any reinforcements and Polk would not act. Granger broke through to Thomas, just in time to turn back a strong Rebel attack. The battle was ferocious but the desperate Northerners held their positions, although just barely. Thomas finally retreated as the sun was setting. Although the moon was bright, there was little attempt at pursuit. Wheeler did make a belated effort to follow Rosecrans down the Dry Valley Road and took one thousand prisoners.

Forrest was in the saddle at 4 a.m. on September 21. Unlike Bragg, he had pursuit on his mind. He gave Pegram, Dibrell and Armstrong each a separate line of march. Forrest rode with Armstrong, who had four hundred men. They met and attacked a Union cavalry force near Rossville. A bullet severed an artery in Forrest's horse's neck, covering the general with blood. Bedford leaned over, stuck his finger in the wound, and continued the charge. When the attack was over and the Yankees were routed, Forrest removed his finger and dismounted. A few minutes later, the horse—Highlander, the wonderful animal the citizens of Rome had presented him—dropped dead. It was the second horse Forrest had lost in three days.

Forrest continued to push on toward Missionary Ridge. At 7 a.m. he climbed a tree and witnessed the disordered flight of the Yankees. He sent a message to General Polk in which he strongly recommended an immediate pursuit. Polk agreed and sent a message to Braxton Bragg. Bragg hesitated. After several dispatches went unanswered, Forrest went to Bragg personally and found him in his tent, sound asleep. He woke him up and forcefully urged an immediate pursuit. If he attacked now, Forrest said, both Chattanooga and the Union army could be captured. Bragg, however, could not be moved. His excuse: a shortage of supplies. There were plenty of supplies in Chattanooga, Forrest retorted. Bragg did not answer. Furious, Forrest stormed out of his tent, screaming: "What does he fight battles for?" and rode off at a gallop.

When Forrest returned to his corps, he caught up with Martin's Kentuckians, who had pushed to the very edge of Chattanooga. He took off his hat to honor them and cried, "Any man who says that Morgan's men are not good soldiers and fine fighters tells a damn lie!" This was a direct verbal shot at Bragg and all the boys knew it. They loudly cheered their commander. "This characteristic speech of Forrest gave the boys more genuine delight than if he had made them the most eloquent and eulogistic address," Stovepipe Johnson recalled.

Meanwhile, Rosecrans used every available minute to organize a defense. The terrain already gave him major advantages. In desperation, Forrest pushed forward with the Fourth Tennessee Cavalry, now under McLemore.[7] He penetrated to within three miles of Chattanooga. When Forrest recalled him, he was "burdened" with prisoners.

The next day, September 22, Lafayette McLaws's division was on picket duty on Missionary Ridge. Forrest tried to persuade him to attack, but McLaws wouldn't do so without orders, so Bedford took matters into his own hands. He assembled his entire cavalry corps on Missionary Ridge and descended into the Chattanooga Valley. He pushed forward two miles and drove the U.S. infantry and cavalry pickets to within half a mile of the town, but he could not take it without infantry.

And so passed the last opportunity the South would ever have to destroy the Army of the Cumberland.

Braxton Bragg's record of command was characterized by indecisiveness and anxiety. He was unable to stay the course once a plan was decided upon. General Leonidas Polk described him as "a poor, feeble-minded irresolute man of violent passions...uncertain of the soundness of his conclusions and therefore timid in the execution." A member of Polk's staff called him "obstinate...ruthless without enterprise, crafty yet without stratagem, suspicious, envious, jealous, vain, a bantam in success and a dunghill in disaster." A dozen generals, including William J. Hardee, Pat Cleburne, Leonidas Polk, James Longstreet and Ben Cheatham, had called for President Davis to replace him.

Bragg did have one undeniable talent—finding scapegoats. He was not afraid to relieve an officer of his command in order to protect his own position—even if it harmed the Confederacy. He ran Hardee off, relieved and arrested Thomas C. Hindman[8] and Leonidas Polk, and fired D. H. Hill—another scapegoat. Pat Cleburne was too good a commander to fire and everybody knew it, so all Bragg could do was see to it that he was never promoted to corps commander, as he probably should have been. He also sacked Nathan Bedford Forrest.

On September 28, Forrest received an order to turn his division over to Wheeler and take a ten-day furlough to LaGrange, Georgia. Forrest took his leave begrudgingly, but he had not seen his wife for weeks, and he always enjoyed his time with her. While there, on October 3, he received another order from Bragg:

> Headquarters, Army of the Tennessee
>> Missionary Ridge, September 28, 1863
>> Brigadier General Forrest, Near Athens
>> GENERAL: The general commanding desires that you
> will without delay turn over the troops of your command
> previously ordered to Major-General Wheeler.
>> I am, general, very respectfully,
>> George Wm. Brent, Assistant Adjutant General

Forrest took this order as a personal affront. It was well known throughout the army that Forrest refused to serve under Wheeler.

Polk, Hindman and Hill took being relieved from command with grace. They filed official protests, asked for courts of inquiry, had their requests ignored, and quietly withdrew from the stage. Forrest was not cut from the same cloth. He at once dictated to Captain Anderson a scalding letter to the army commander. He charged Bragg with duplicity

Braxton Bragg (1817–1876), the incompetent commander of the Army of Tennessee and later military advisor to his good friend, Jefferson Davis.

and lying, and promised to visit him soon, to say to him in person what he had written.

Accompanied by Dr. James B. Cowan, his chief surgeon and Mary's cousin, he paid a personal visit to the general, who was in his tent when Forrest found him. He stormed passed the guard and burst inside. Bragg extended his hand, but Forrest slapped it away. "I am not here to pass civilities or compliments with you, but on other business." He pointed his index finger into Bragg's face.

"You commenced your cowardly and contemptible persecution of me soon after the battle of Shiloh, and yet kept it up ever since... You robbed me of my command in Kentucky, and gave it to one of your favorites—men whom I armed and equipped from the enemies of our country. In a spirit of revenge and spite, because I would not fawn upon you as others did, you drove me into west Tennessee in the winter of 1862 with the second brigade I had organized, with improper arms and without sufficient ammunition, although I made repeated applications for the same. You did it to ruin me and my career. When in spite of all this I returned well-equipped from captures, you began again your work spite and persecution, and have kept it up; and now the second brigade, organized and equipped without thanks to you or the government, a brigade which has won a reputation for successful fighting second to none in the Army. Taking advantage of your position as commanding general in order to further humiliate me, you have taken these brave men from me. I have stood your meanness as long as I intend to. You have played the part of the damned scoundrel, and are a coward, and if you were any part a man I would slap your jaws and force you to resent it. You may as well not issued any orders to me, for I will not obey them, and I will hold you personally responsible for any further indignities you endeavor to inflict upon me. You have threatened to arrest me for not obeying orders promptly. I dare you to do it, and I say to you that if you ever again tried to interfere with me or cross my path it will be at the peril of your life!"

Bragg was shocked, and Cowan was terrified. Forrest turned on his heel and stormed out, followed by the mortified physician.

"Well, you're in for it now!" Cowan declared as they rode away.

"He'll never say a word about it; he'll be the last man to mention it; and mark my word, he'll take no action in the matter," Forrest snapped. "I will ask to be relieved and transferred to a different field, and he will not oppose it."

General Forrest was right.

# CHAPTER 11

# FORREST CREATES AN ARMY: THE SECOND WEST TENNESSEE RAID

*The word "impossible" is not in my dictionary.*

—Napoleon

President Jefferson Davis arrived in Georgia on October 9 and spent five days interviewing Bragg's senior generals. Despite the consensus among some pretty solid officers (and some who weren't) that Bragg should go, Davis could not bring himself to relieve his old friend. During his trip, however, Davis did take some steps which worked out very well for the Confederacy. He asked Bragg about Forrest's August proposal. Bragg replied that he had been loath to release such a distinguished soldier at that time, but now he felt he could do so "without injury to the public interest." As Forrest predicted, he did not mention their confrontation in Bragg's tent.

Forrest and the president met in Montgomery on October 27. They had a long and gratifying talk. Davis gave him permission to raise an independent command in northern Mississippi, western Tennessee and western Kentucky. He promised to supply the Wizard with horses and weapons for the men. Two days later, Forrest received a letter from Davis approving his request for a transfer to Mississippi and naming him

Jefferson Davis (1808–1889), President of the Confederate States of America.

commander of the Cavalry Department of West Tennessee and North Mississippi.

Forrest returned with Davis as far as Atlanta where he assembled the units he would take to Mississippi. The Confederate high command did not allow him many and refused to allow Forrest's old brigade, which he had taken into western Tennessee in 1862, to go with him.

They gave him his staff (eight men); the Escort Company (sixty-five men); McDonald's Battalion (139 men); and Morton's battery (sixty-seven men)—279 men and four guns in all.[1] Colonel Jeffrey E. Forrest's Fourth Alabama was scheduled to go with him until word arrived that Forrest's favorite brother had been killed in action near Tuscumbia, Alabama. Because they were Alabama troops, Forrest was content to let them remain in Alabama.[2]

This time, Forrest had a direct superior he could work with or at least tolerate. Forrest's specific department commander was Major General Stephen Dill Lee, who was absolutely delighted to have him. "No longer than yesterday I wrote General Bragg stating that if you were unpleasantly situated," Lee wrote to Forrest, "west Tennessee offered a good field...whether you are under my command or not, we shall not disagree, and you shall have all the assistance and support I can render you. I would feel proud either in commanding or cooperating with so gallant an officer as yourself."

Unlike Stephen Lee, however, the commander of the Department of the West and the Army of Mississippi, Joseph E. Johnston thought of Forrest as little more than a successful raider. Before Davis announced that Forrest had the command, Johnston has asked the president to send him Wade Hampton to direct the cavalry in the northern district of Mississippi, so he could use Stephen Lee in the south. Sherman and General

Samuel A. Hurlbut, the senior Union commander in the sector, also were unimpressed. Sherman wrote to Hurlbut: "Forrest may cavort about that country [western Tennessee] as much as he pleases. Every conscript they now catch will cost a good man to watch." Hurlbut did, at least, note that, with Forrest in command, he expected the Rebel attacks to have "more dash" in them.

To reinforce Forrest—who faced the U.S. XVI Corps of twenty thousand men under General Hurlbut—Joe Johnston ordered Robert V. Richardson's brigade, reported to be two thousand men strong, of west Tennesseeans to join him. When he arrived at Okolona at the end of November, however, Richardson brought only 240 men, a quarter of whom were unarmed. Forrest waited several days for the weapons Jeff Davis had promised him, but they never arrived. He nevertheless decided to push into western Tennessee, even though a shortage of horses forced him to leave fifty men and two guns behind. He had already sent Colonel Tyree Bell, a prominent West Tennessean, ahead of him, to spy on the Yankees and to tell people that Forrest was on his way.

The weather was terrible. It had literally rained for forty days, and the rivers and creeks of north Mississippi were out of their banks. The "brigade" reached the Tallahatchie River at New Albany on November 27, but had to repair the bridge. This job was finished on November 30, when six days' rations were issued. Lee's men accompanied him for two days, but they parted company on December 2, and Forrest was behind Union lines and on his own—and with only 450 men.

Forrest, however, would soon tap into the local manpower pool. There were Southern horsemen who were ready to do battle against the invaders—under certain circumstances. "At this time west Tennessee was full of little companies of from ten to thirty men willing to fight but unwilling to go far from home or into the infantry," Forrest recalled.

Largely due to Forrest's reputation, dozens of men rallied to his standard. "I determined to cast my fortunes with the daring and dashing Forrest..."one veteran recalled. "He was constantly receiving recruits...wherever he went many old, seasoned, wounded soldiers joined him from choice." On December 8, he wrote Lee and the War

Department from his headquarters in Jackson, Tennessee: "I am highly gratified with my success so far...troops and men are flocking to me in all quarters."

Hurlbut remained unconcerned. He signaled Brigadier General John D. Stevenson, commanding the Union front line troops and headquartered at Corinth, that he would deal with Forrest once the roads dried. Hurlbut also asked Grant to reinforce Major General A. J. Smith at Columbia, Kentucky. He intended to advance against Forrest from the north, south and west—once the rains stopped and the roads dried.

Forrest did not wait for the roads to dry. He dispersed his officers all over the region to raise more men, and they began bringing in bands of recruits, each numbering twenty-five to two hundred men. Within three weeks, they brought in enough recruits to form the Sixteenth, Eighteenth, Twenty-First, and Twentieth Tennessee Cavalry Regiments.[3] "The Wizard" had lived up to his name and had literally created a brigade out of nothing.

On December 6, Forrest wrote to General Johnston, stating that he expected to have eight thousand men by the end of the year. After that, he would begin conscripting for the infantry. Recruits were coming in at a rate of fifty to one hundred per day. He also had a herd of four thousand beef cattle, as well as thousands of pounds of bacon, leather and clothing. He asked Johnston to loan him Generals Pillow and Armstrong when he returned to Mississippi, to help organize the recruits, and he pointed out that he was short on weapons and asked for more arms and artillery. On December 18, Forrest wrote Johnston again and asked for $100,000 for his paymaster and $150,000 for his quartermaster. He mentioned that he had already spent $20,000 out of his own pocket. Finally, he asked for two of Stephen Lee's cavalry brigades to aid in taking out his cattle herd.

Events, however, had shaken up the Confederate command structure. Grant had routed the Army of Tennessee at Chattanooga, forcing Bragg to resign on November 30. Johnston assumed command of the Army of Tennessee on December 16, leaving a command vacancy in

Mississippi. This was filled by Lieutenant General Leonidas Polk, who took charge of the Army of Mississippi on December 22.

Meanwhile, the Yankees finally began to act. On December 18, they advanced against Forrest from all directions. Fifteen thousand Northerners converged on the town of Jackson, which was garrisoned by 3,500 Rebels, of which one thousand had no arms. "I think we shall cure Forrest of his ambition to command West Tennessee," Hurlbut, the overall commander, claimed. Brigadier General James M. Tuttle, commanding the strong Union garrison at La Grange, agreed. "It looks to me like we will get them sure this time," he cheerfully wrote to Hurlbut.

Forrest's scouts, however, had warned him of the enemy movements. Characteristically, he decided not to escape to the south or southeast, as the Yankees expected; instead, he would head southwest, cross two major rivers (the Hatchie and the Wolf), and get away under the very noses of the XVI Corps and the Memphis garrison.

On the night of December 22/23, the citizens of Jackson threw them a huge going-away party on the courthouse square, complete with bonfires, torches and candles. Bands were out in full force; fiddlers played the Virginia reel, and there was dancing until dawn. Then the bugle blew and boys in gray mounted up. Nathan Bedford Forrest was the last man to leave the town.

Lieutenant Colonel Dew W. Wisdom, meanwhile, surprised one of Hubbard's columns at Mifflin, fifteen miles southeast of Jackson. The fighting was moderate to heavy all day.[4] Finally, the outnumbered Rebels fell back toward the Hatchie River. The Yankees did not pursue, but retreated to Purdy instead, leaving a corridor open for Forrest, his wagons, cattle, and a herd of three hundred pigs.

Forrest's command crossed the Hatchie near Estenaula on the night of December 24/25. At one point, a ferryboat capsized and a wagon and team fell into the river. Forrest jumped into the stream, cut the mules out of their harnesses, and saved them. A draftee on the bank loudly proclaimed to his friends that there was no way he was going to get into that icy water. As soon as he finished rescuing the mules, General Forrest scurried up the bank and, without saying a word, grabbed the slacker by the throat and pants, lifted him high, and threw him into the river. One of the Escort troops recalled that the dissenter made a pretty good worker after that.

The crossing of the Hatchie was nevertheless a nightmare. Private A. C. McLeary recalled:

> The river was almost bank full, the water running swiftly and the boat was pulled across by a rope stretched bank to bank. The poor, weak horses were put on the boat and the best ones were pushed into the water. Their owners would hold to them from the boat until they passed the middle of the river and then turned them loose, as they could then swim to the landing place without being carried downstream. Our battalion was the last to cross. It was Christmas morning, 1863. I knew my horse would have to take to the water, so I took my saddle and blankets off and put them in a little dugout. The other boys did the same. I paddled across with two loads, threw them out on the bank, and had gone back after another load. Everything was done in a rush. We could hear the guns of the fight that was going on by those who had crossed before us. General Forrest came to where I stopped the little canoe and asked me if I could carry him across in that thing. I told him I could if it did not turn over, and he then stepped in and squatted down with his back to me. He was a large, heavy man, and when I turned the little craft around it was in a quiver, but we made it all right until we reached the middle of the river. When the ferryboat passed us and all the horses were turned loose, the big waves from the boat I thought would knock us over, and every horse looked like he wanted to get to our dugout. The General said: 'Bear downstream; bear downstream.' I told him to take up the paddle and knock them in the head. He did as I told him, and we got to land all right. I had to bear upstream with all the power I had to keep from being carried downstream by the swift current. We all

got across the river. It was then a fight every day and night until we got back into Mississippi. Instead of any of us being captured in getting out of West Tennessee, we captured several of the Yankees and took them out with us.

By the evening of Christmas Day, all of Forrest's men and supplies—with the exception of a wagon loaded with bacon—were across the Hatchie and heading for the next obstacle, the Wolf. Between the two rivers near Summerville, they defeated six hundred cavalrymen under Colonel Henry Prince. Although the Southern force of 650 men outnumbered Prince's force, about one third of the Rebels remained unarmed. To gain the advantage, Forrest resorted to deception. Lieutenant Boone, temporarily commanding the Escort, cried out: "Brigade!" His sergeants picked up the cry and shouted out orders to their "regiments." To add to the deception, the attack was not made in any standard formation; instead, Bedford spread his men out in a long line, with ten paces between each cavalryman, and again with no reserve. When he attacked, his line was a quarter of a mile long, causing the Yankee commander to abandon the field in the face of what he thought was an overwhelming force. Prince left behind seven dead, thirty wounded, and eighty captured. He lost six wagons loaded with supplies, an ambulance, and one hundred horses and mules. On the other side, Lieutenant Boone was wounded and his brother, Sergeant Boone, was killed.

As the Union columns converged, Forrest moved through Summerville and spent the night six miles to the west. If he were to break out and escape, it would have to be done on December 27, the next day.

Well before dawn, Grierson had patrols out everywhere between Memphis and Corinth. When at last they discovered Forrest's location, Grierson telegraphed it to the other Union columns. It did him no good: the wires had already been cut. The Yankee general scrambled his dispatch riders. But they were also too late. Forrest crossed the Wolf just northeast of Memphis, pushed his flank guards to within four miles of the city, and headed south.

Tyree Harris Bell (1815–1902). An excellent training officer, Forrest placed Bell in charge of a brigade in January 1864. He did a fine job, which led to his promotion to brigadier general on February 28, 1865. His personality was said to be very much like that of Bedford Forrest.

A journalist from the *Cincinnati Commercial*, stationed with the U.S. XVI Corps in Memphis, expressed astonishment at Forrest's performance, writing:

Forrest, with less than four thousand men, has moved right through the Sixteenth Army Corps, has passed within nine miles of Memphis, carried off a hundred wagons, two hundred beef cattle, three thousand conscripts, and innumerable stores; torn up railroad tracks, destroyed telegraph wires, burned and sacked towns; run over pickets with a single derringer pistol...and all in the face of ten thousand men.

The weather turned cold and a hard rain fell. But Forrest was between his base and the Yankees, so he was able to follow his supply train and withdraw through Holly Springs via a series of short, slow marches. He reached Como, Mississippi, by the end of the year. In a little more than a month, Forrest had ridden around the U.S. XVI Corps, raised an army of 3,500 men, and defeated a substantial Federal force.

Meanwhile, he was promoted to major general on December 4, 1863, and the Confederate Senate confirmed the promotion on January 25, 1864.

In January 1864, Forrest headquartered at Oxford, Mississippi, between the Union forces at Memphis and Vicksburg. Here he organized his command into four brigades under R. V. Richardson (1,500 men); Black Bob McCulloch (1,600 men); Tyree Bell (2,000 men); and Jeffrey Forrest (1,000 men). McCulloch and Jeffrey were placed into a division under Chalmers. Supply shortages, however, dogged him although General Polk was sending all the arms and supplies he could.

Undaunted by the logistical challenges, Forrest whipped his command into shape, teaching them war as he waged it and drilling it at least once a day. Colonel Bell, who was much like Forrest in temperament, was particularly good at these activities, and Forrest relied heavily on him.

The hard training might have had another positive effect: taking the men's minds off of the rigors of camp life. There were few latrines, no soap, and horse manure was everywhere. It was also cold and the men stayed so close to the campfires that wood smoke permeated their skin, hair, and clothes. Lice were abundant, and diseases such as measles, dysentery, typhoid, and "camp fever" were rampant. The food was monotonous, consisting mostly of hardtack and/or cornmeal, with occasional poor-quality bacon or beef. Sometimes even this meager fare did not arrive and the men had to eat raw corn. Some troopers cut steaks from dead horses and mules, and a few even cooked rats.

Before long, the cold, the food, and the boredom took their toll, and the new recruits (especially the conscripts) began to desert. Forrest sent his veterans in pursuit, and they brought many of them back, but the desertions continued and dissatisfaction grew.

The issue came to a head one day in early February, when nineteen men from Bell's west Tennessee brigade deserted together, but were brought back to camp by some of Forrest's veterans. Forrest ordered that they be shot. The residents of Oxford were horrified by the thought of a mass execution, and prominent citizens, including numerous ladies and clergymen, appealed to the general to revoke the sentence—all in vain. The men in the ranks were so upset that some officers suggested there might be a mutiny. Forrest remained unmoved. He was determined to make an example of these men. On the day set for the execution, Bell's command marched to a large field and formed up in a line on three sides of a hollow square. The deserters were ordered to sit on their coffins and were blindfolded. Behind each coffin was a freshly dug grave. The firing squad moved into position. The commands were given. "Present—arms! Make ready! Take aim…"

At that moment, a staff officer galloped up and stopped the executions. Addressing the guilty men, he said, "General Forrest has requested me to say to you that it is unpleasant to him to shed blood in this manner, and that, through the petitions of the clergy, the prominent citizens of Oxford and your officers, if you will now promise to make good and faithful soldiers, he will pardon you!"

"We will! We will!" cried the men. The entire brigade broke out in cheers. The men were spared, but a hard lesson had been learned. "There were no more desertions," Captain Dinkins recalled, "and the men learned that General Forrest was not cruel, not unnecessarily severe, but they also learned that he would not be trifled with."

Meanwhile, Forrest obtained another fine regiment: the Second Tennessee which was part of Brigadier General Samuel W. Ferguson's brigade of S. D. Lee's command. A wild bunch, they did not like Ferguson, who was a strict disciplinarian. Also, they wanted to serve in Tennessee and believed that, if they rode with Forrest, they had an excellent chance of doing so. Finally, they wanted to serve under the bold and charismatic Wizard of the Saddle. So, when the brigade was ordered to prepare to move to Jackson, Mississippi, the regiment petitioned to be assigned to General Forrest's corps.

Petitions of this kind are usually ignored by higher military headquarters, but General Polk approved this one. When word arrived of the transfer, he Second Tennessee cheered. It would remain with the general for the rest of the war and turned out to be a top-notch combat unit.

Another aspect of Forrest's life changed now that he was back in Mississippi—Mary was with him. She had not seen her husband or her son very often during the preceding three years. In 1864, she stayed with the army as long as the military situation permitted, ministering to the boys and giving comfort to "my soldiers," as she called them. They soon looked upon her as a mother figure, just as they looked upon Forrest as something of a father figure—a tough and sometimes harsh one to be sure—but a father figure nevertheless. They paid her a tremendous compliment by bestowing upon her the sobriquet "the Ole Miss." In the Old South that term meant the lady who kept the family together while the men were away at war, running the farms and plantations and taking care of the family and the slaves. They also served as the nurses, the comforters, and substitute mothers for lonely boys far from home. Although there are those who believe otherwise, the nickname of the University of Mississippi—Ole Miss—appears to have been coined to honor those remarkably

Bedford Forrest, circa 1864.

capable, selfless, tireless and heroic women, not the state—and Mary Forrest was one of those women.

# CHAPTER 12

# OKOLONA

*How formidable is he who has no fear of death!*

—Publilius Syrus

On February 3, 1864, General Sherman left Vicksburg with four infantry divisions—thirty thousand men—advancing toward Meridian, Mississippi. At the same time, General William Sooy Smith was supposed to leave Memphis with seven thousand cavalrymen and twenty guns. His mission was to crush Forrest, ravage northern Mississippi, and drive the 250 miles to Meridian in order to meet up with Sherman. Then together, so the plan lay out, they would push on to Selma, Alabama—perhaps as far as Mobile—devastating all that was in their path. A third column, consisting of gunboats and infantry on transports, pushed up the Yazoo River, to create a diversion. Operating out of New Orleans, Major General Nathaniel P. Banks created a second diversion by feinting toward Pascagoula, Mississippi (in other words, by appearing to threaten Mobile).

Sooy Smith's men were handpicked from the best cavalrymen in the Union Army. They were armed with Sharp's carbines, one of the best cavalry weapons available in 1864, as well as Colt Repeating Rifles and

Sooy Smith (1830–1916), another Union cavalry commander whose forces were crushed by Forrest.

"Navy Sixes." They were also stripped for action. Their horses were well rested, in excellent condition, and well shod. Each man had an extra set of horseshoes in his saddlebags, complete with nails. Baggage was limited to ammunition, five days' rations and blacksmithing equipment—all on pack mules. There were no wheeled vehicles except ambulances, cannons, and caissons. Artillery was double-teamed. It was an impressive formation, so much so that Sherman described Smith's troops as "the best and most experienced troops in the service."

Sooy Smith was a thirty-three-year-old Ohioan who graduated sixth in the West Point Class of 1853, ranking above Philip Sheridan, John M. Schofield, and John Bell Hood. He was a great engineer[1] and had done well commanding infantry in western Virginia, at Shiloh, at Perryville and at Vicksburg, where he led a division. This was his first major cavalry command but he was eager to "pitch into Forrest."

Smith's second-in-command was Brigadier General Benjamin Grierson, a former music and voice teacher, songwriter, and bandleader. Apparently, he was more than just an artist because Sherman called him "the best cavalry officer I have yet had." Grierson's reputation had been greatly enhanced by a raid through Mississippi and Louisiana during the Vicksburg campaign, in which he travelled eight hundred miles through the heart of the southwestern Confederacy in seventeen days.

Due to the threat to Meridian, Forrest was forced to send more than two thousand men to reinforce General Lee in eastern Mississippi. To make matters worse, he initially had to scatter his command all across northern Mississippi, to protect against several possible routes of advance. It was rumored (falsely as it turned out) that another Union column from Vicksburg would advance against Forrest's rear, and the Wizard sent a brigade to Grenada, to guard against this contingency. He also had to send another regiment to the Yazoo. This left him with 2,500 men to defend northern Mississippi. Most of these were new recruits, and six hundred were unarmed.

Smith's cavalry corps was supposed to leave for Meridian on February 3. The Yankees, however, overestimated Forrest's strength, as usual. Grant had promised to reinforce Smith with Colonel George E. Waring's cavalry brigade from Columbus, Kentucky.[2] It was late, partially due to swollen streams and muddy roads, but Smith waited on it anyway. When Waring's men did arrive, their horses had to be reshod and rested for two days. As a result, Smith did not leave Memphis until February 11. He was supposed to be in Meridian on February 14, but it was 250 miles away. Worse still, there was no way he could tell Sherman what had happened, why he was late, or when he might arrive. Sherman was and would remain "in the dark."

Hurlbut feinted against Forrest's front near Abbeville with an infantry brigade while Smith swung east and marched through Holly Springs, New Albany, Pontotoc, and on to Okolona. At first, he faced only scattered opposition from Brigadier General Samuel J. Gholson's Mississippi State Troops, which he classified as "rabble." Forrest did not take Hurlbut's bait and began to concentrate his men in order to defend the vital Mississippi prairie region called "Little Egypt."

Northern Mississippi is what in the South is known as "red-clay country." In the 1860s, there were few plantations in the area, and most of the people were plain country farmers. Forests and swamps surrounded its hills, and the dirt roads were very difficult to travel on in wet weather. Okolona marked a dividing line between Mississippi's hill country and its prairies (Okolona is Indian for "Queen of the Prairie.") South of Okolona is the region called Little Egypt, an agricultural area that produced huge amounts of corn, and hundreds of corn bins lined the Mobile & Ohio Railroad. Each belonged to a farmer, who was responsible for filling it at a certain time. The several supply depots in the region were full of unshucked corn, meal, bacon and beans. This was the place Smith was sent to destroy and Forrest had his heart set on defending. Forrest knew that he was outnumbered three to one. When he attacked, his timing must be perfect, or the entire region would be lost, Smith would join Sherman, and the consequences for the South would be immeasurable—and all bad. Part of Little Egypt, therefore, would need to be sacrificed.

Smith reached Okolona on February 18 and began a systematic program of destruction. He tore up the railroad, and set fire to supplies, cotton gins, barns, and houses. He then turned south toward West Point, Mississippi. When he did so, his column was burdened by about three thousand escaped slaves, who had fled their masters and had taken wagons, mules, and their entire families and formed a large caravan, which slowed Smith considerably. It was February 20 before he took Aberdeen and West Point.

As they moved through the area, Smith's soldiers seemed to be possessed by pyromania. Colonel Waring recalled, "the sky was red with the flame of burning corn and cotton," all the way down to West Point. The blacks, "driven wild with the infection, set the torch to mansion houses, stables, cotton gins and quarters…leaving only fire and absolute destruction behind them." The devastation was so bad that it embarrassed Smith, who wrote to Grierson, "I am deeply pained to say [the operation] has been disgraced by incendiarism of the most shocking kind. I have ordered the first man caught in the act to be shot and have offered a $500 reward for his detection." The burning continued, however. When the army left Egypt, Mississippi, only two houses were still standing.

The flames also outraged the Rebels. Private R. R. Hancock of the Second Tennessee wrote in his diary on February 20, "That night the whole country northward was illuminated by burning homesteads, cotton-gins, corn-houses and stockyards, inspiring the Confederates with a passionate resolution to do all in the power of men to punish such an unmanly heathenish method of warfare."

The Yankees had now covered more than half the distance from Memphis to Meridian and, even slowed by the thousands of escaped slaves, would reach Sherman in three or four days. General Smith, however, was becoming nervous, and a painful attack of arthritis did not help calm him. The source of his nerves: Nathan Bedford Forrest, who was clearly concentrating against him. Smith's vanguard had clashed with Jeffrey Forrest's men just south of West Point, and Black Bob McCulloch's brigade had been identified nearby. Up to his old tricks, Forrest spread disinformation and rumors. One of them particularly frightened Smith—Stephen D. Lee from Polk's army was about to join Forrest with his cavalry. He would be outnumbered, isolated in the middle of Mississippi, and could easily be cut off. On February 21, he halted his drive at Ellis Bridge on the Sakatanchee Creek, three miles south of West Point.

This was the moment Forrest had been waiting for. He ordered his command to concentrate there. Bedford and Jeffrey Forrest were already present, skirmishing with the Federal cavalry. In the confusion, with Union bullets flying all around, Forrest saw a Confederate soldier, dismounted, unarmed and hatless. He had thrown away his rifle and was fleeing to the rear in panic. Forrest galloped over to him, dismounted rapidly, grabbed him by the collar, threw him to the ground and dragged him to the side of the road. He picked up a limb and, as General Chalmers recalled, "proceeded to give him one of the worst thrashing I have ever seen a human being get." Forrest was an immensely powerful man and he beat the private until his temper was spent or his arm got tired. "Now, God**mn you," he roared, "go back to the front and fight; you might as well be killed there as here, for if you ran away again, you will not get off so easy." A sketch of the incident later appeared in Northern newspapers under the headline: "Forrest breaking in a conscript."

The first unit to join Jeffrey's brigade and the Escort Company was Colonel William Falkner's Twelfth Kentucky.

This particular group of Kentucky horsemen had a poor reputation as being good only for guerilla warfare, and the men of the Escort Company were wary of how they'd behave in a stand-up fight. "Jesus Christ," one man exclaimed. "Those are the Kentucky Go-rillers. They won't fight." Black Bob McCulloch challenged the Escort.[3] "Ride into the fight with them one time and see what they will do," he pleaded. This sounded fair to the Tennesseans, who joined the Kentuckians as they surprised the elite Yankee cavalrymen, routed them, and pursued them several miles. Forrest was in the middle of the fight and personally shot and killed a Yankee soldier. In the confusion of the fighting, one Southern trooper fired on General Forrest. The bullet went through his clothes but did not touch him.

"I think they are badly scared..." Forrest commented to Chalmers. "If they fall backward toward Pontotoc I will follow them as long as I think I can do any good." Colonel Waring recalled: "No sooner had we turned tail than Forrest saw that his time had come, and he pressed us sorely all day and until nightfall." That night, Forrest heard that the Federals were crossing the creek at Siloam. He took McCulloch's brigade and galloped four miles up the creek, where he found the enemy's crossing thanks to the smoke and flames coming from the buildings they had set on fire. He overran an isolated detachment, killing a few and capturing 23.

On February 21, Forrest's vanguard was commanded by Captain H. A. Tyler of the Twelfth Kentucky.[4] He captured a few prisoners and signaled back that the Yankees were definitely retreating. Six miles beyond West Point, General Smith made a stand at the end of two open fields, lining both sides of the road. After he scouted the position, Forrest came up with his Escort Company. The captain told his commander that it was death to charge up that lane. Follow me, the general said, and personally led the charge. The Yankees fell back. Forrest gave Tyler the Escort, which was temporarily under the command of Lieutenant Thomas Tate, and ordered him to dog the Yankees while he hurried up Chalmers's men.

Tyler pursued them to the Evans Plantation, where an entire Union regiment made a stand. Tyler's men took a volley and the captain was about to order a retreat, when he heard, "Close in with your revolvers, Tyler, I am here." Then, Forrest, saber drawn, led the charge, riding a full thirty yards ahead of McCulloch's brigade. The Northerners fell back across a narrow causeway and bridge that could not be outflanked. Black Bob dismounted his men and ordered an attack, while Forrest rushed ahead.

The fighting was heavy and Bedford killed another Yankee in personal combat.

During the night of February 21/22, the Federals retreated into what was left of Okolona, while Forrest's men enjoyed the food and campfires they left behind. Colonel Waring continued to fall back to Ivey's Farm, five miles north of the town, where he formed a strong blocking position, while General Grierson made a stand at Okolona with two brigades. Forrest, meanwhile, was joined by Colonel Barteau and 1,200 men from Bell's brigade.

Clark R. Barteau became one of Forrest's most important subordinates in 1864. Although born near Cleveland, Ohio, in 1835, he had visited Tennessee in 1858, to see slavery firsthand, liked what he saw and

Colonel Clark R. Barteau (1835–1900), a native of Ohio who embraced the South and secession.

stayed there. He was principal of the Hartsville Male Academy and a newspaper editor when the war broke out. An extreme secessionist, he joined the Southern army and excelled as a cavalryman. An aggressive warrior, he became colonel of the Second Tennessee Cavalry in 1863 and was acting commander of Bell's brigade at Okolona.

Hundreds of Forrest's 2,500 men were still unarmed but he put them into the line of battle anyway. "I have no arms for you yet," he declared, "but fall in here behind, and you shall have plenty of good Yankee arms presently."

Like many other great commanders, such as George S. Patton and Erwin Rommel, Forrest had an indefinable charisma that worked wonders on his men. As one regimental historian noted, "his immediate presence seemed to inspire every one with his terrible energy, more like that of a piece of powerful steam machinery than a human being." Much like the Desert Fox, his charisma grew over time. In 1864, it was at its zenith.

The Wizard was in the saddle before 3 a.m. on the morning of February 22. Barteau's brigade faced Grierson on the open prairie just outside of Okolona when Forrest rode up and joined them. Sergeant Hancock recalled, "Every countenance irradiated with confidence, courage and enthusiasm, which found immediate expression in loud cheers and prolonged shouts of mingled joy and defiance, in recognition of which Forrest lifted his hat and politely bowed to us as he passed our front..."

"Where is the enemy's position?" he asked Barteau.

"You see it, general, and they are preparing to charge."

"Then we will charge them!" He wheeled Barteau's three regiments into column formation and charged into the town via two different streets. The Yankees' breech-loading rifles were more effective than Forrest's long rifles, however, and the charge staggered. Forrest dismounted two of Barteau's regiments (Robert Russell's Twentieth Tennessee and Andrew N. Wilson's Twenty-First Tennessee) and ordered them to advance on foot. "We dashed into the town by two different streets," Colonel Barteau recalled, "and struck the enemy in his very face just as he was preparing to execute the same movement on us. He seemed astonished and confounded, and his partially executed movements were turned into confusion and disorder." Grierson had sent his Third Tennessee (Union) Cavalry to his right flank. Seeing it was badly positioned, Forrest turned on it immediately. He personally took charge of the Second Tennessee, which remained mounted, shouted "Come on, boys!" and led a charge. "I saw Grierson make a bad move, and I rode right over him," Forrest recalled.

The defeat of the Tennessee Unionists caused the Fourth Regulars and Seventh Indiana Cavalry to fall back in confusion. As they did so, Colonels Russell and Wilson seized the moment and urged their regiments forward again. The Yankees were routed. They fled for miles and were in such complete disorder when they passed Waring's blocking position that they endangered the morale of his men. Meanwhile, Barteau's troops had become so intermingled that they had to stop to reorganize. (The colonel himself was temporarily down. A spent ball struck him on his pistol belt and knocked him off his horse. He soon rejoined the battle, however.) Forrest continued the pursuit with Black Bob's and Jeff Forrest's brigades.

During the Okolona pursuit, Forrest had combined the tactics of surprise flank attacks and full-speed charges. He was, as usual, in the forefront of the battle, along with his brother, Jeffrey, who was a brigade commander at age twenty-four.[5] Jeffrey was more of a son to Bedford than a sibling. Jeffrey's father died four months before he was born and sixteen-year-old Nathan Bedford practically raised him. Of all his siblings, Jeffrey was clearly the favorite. Later, he supported Jeffrey and saw to it that he received an excellent education.

At Ivey's Farm on February 22, Jeffrey commanded the Confederate right while McCulloch directed the left. They overran Waring's first line but the second line fired a tremendous volley, dropping several men and horses. One of the bullets struck Jeffrey in the throat, severing his carotid artery. "Jeffrey! Jeffrey!" his horrified brother screamed as he rushed to his side. Forrest held him in his arms as his brother died. He cradled Jeffrey's head in his lap, kissed his brow and sobbed, rocked, and repeatedly called his name. There was a lull in the battle. The tough Rebel fighters stood there awkwardly, not knowing what to say. Colonel Russell, who was present, recalled:

> The moment was too sacred for angry passion to have sway, and catching its inspiration I ordered the men to cease firing, that all might join in sympathy with our suffering General. After nature had triumphed for a while...he rose up, and casting aside those reflections, which had unmanned him for a few moments, by a strong mental effort Forrest was himself again.

Well, not really. With tears streaming down his face, Forrest laid Jeffrey's head gently on the ground, took one last look, and asked Major Strange of his staff to see to the body.[6] Then his expression turned from grief to ferocity. He sprang onto his horse and shouted at Sergeant Jacob

Colonel Jeffrey Forrest, who was killed in action on February 22, 1864.

Gaus, his bugler, "Blow the charge!" And then galloped directly at the enemy.

His men immediately rushed after him but he was in a killing frenzy and had downed three Yankees before they could reach him. (He would kill five men that day and wound a few others.) Dr. Cowan rode up to him and begged him to go to the rear, where it was safe. You may return if you are so worried, Forrest snapped, but he would not. Both Cowan and Major Strange thought Jeffrey's death had driven him temporarily insane. At that moment, as if to underscore the physician's words, a Union bullet killed Forrest's horse. Undaunted, Forrest commandeered a horse from Private J. B. Long of the Escort Com-

pany. This horse was also killed a few minutes later. Forrest's saddle alone was hit by five bullets that day. Meanwhile, an orderly brought up Forrest's last horse, the iron gray, twelve-year-old gelding King Philip.

King Philip was an unusual horse. Not only was he completely fearless, he also became another combatant when the bugle blew. Normally sluggish, he came alive during battle. He would set his ears back, throw up his tail and charge, with the intent of personally doing as much damage as possible to anyone wearing blue. Horses are said to be color blind, but this one seemed to know the difference between blue and gray or butternut. During the war, several Yankees were stepped on, stomped, kicked, or had large hunks of their flesh bitten out by King Philip.

At one point in the pursuit, Forrest and his Escort outran all support and, with sixty men, engaged five hundred Yankees in hand-to-hand combat. Fortunately, McCulloch's brigade was coming down the road at full speed, trying to catch up. When they saw the situation, however, they hesitated. Black Bob, who had been shot in the hand earlier that day, raised his bandaged hand dramatically above his head and, with the blood dripping down, cried: "My God, men, will you see them kill your General? I'll go to the rescue if not a man follows me!" He stuck his spurs into his horse's flanks and rushed forward, followed by his entire brigade. But even now, General Forrest was consistent. As he led his men forward, he noticed a terrified mother and her children, seeking shelter in the middle of the fighting. Somewhat earlier, he had noticed a depression in the ground, which would give them protection. He stopped and ordered Dr. Cowan to place them there, where they would be safe.

Near the end of the day, Forrest had fought and pursued the Yankees for nine miles. Many of his men had dropped out of the pursuit due to exhaustion or lack of ammunition. Some of the Rebels were totally out of ammunition when the Northerners launched a counterattack. One of Forrest's men, Lieutenant Tom Tate, soon found himself in serious trouble. His horse was down, his carbine was empty, and a Union officer was looking right at him, cocking a revolver. Tate thought he was dead when, suddenly, the Federal's head disappeared. Forrest had all but completely decapitated him with his sword. Tate grabbed the Yankee's pistol, hopped on to the now-empty saddle, and rejoined the fighting.

At this point, only three hundred Rebels had kept up. In desperation, the Yankees attacked and got within sixty yards of Forrest's position before Southern gunfire broke up their charge. A second Union line charged. It got to within forty yards. The third line charged. Some of them broke through, but not enough to make a difference, and they were captured when their comrades retreated. One of General Grierson's aides showed such extreme courage that he earned the admiration of blue and gray alike. After he was killed, General Forrest ordered that particular attention be paid to his body.

Even in his grief and rage, Forrest could still show compassion. When his spearhead overran a Union hospital, Forrest had heard a man screaming. He investigated and found a Northerner with a saw halfway through his leg. His surgeon had been in the act of amputating the limb when the Rebels closed in, and the doctor fled. Forrest tended to the wounded Yankee, dashed a cloth of chloroform to his nostrils, and summoned Dr. Cowan, his personal surgeon, to complete the amputation.

Black Bob McCulloch (1820–1905). General Chalmers said he "has no equal as a brigade commander of cavalry."

Ten miles from Pontotoc, the Yankees made their final stand. Forrest broke their resistance and turned the pursuit over to General Gholson's Mississippi State Troops. They captured another fifty stragglers. There were no further counterattacks, and the once proud Union cavalry limped back to Memphis.

Of Okolona, Colonel Waring wrote, "The retreat to Memphis was a very disheartening and almost panic-stricken flight, in the greatest disorder and confusion…The Escort and part of the Twelfth Kentucky drove our seven thousand men without difficulty. This expedition filled every Union man with burning shame while it gave Forrest the most glorious achievement of his career."

William Sooy Smith was sacked almost immediately. He never held another command. He was replaced by Grierson.

On the other hand, it may have been a good thing for the North that Sooy Smith turned back on February 20. Two days earlier, in Meridian, Sherman gave up on him. Without cavalry, he feared that Forrest might fall on him and cut him off from his base at Vicksburg, so he retreated to Canton, just north of Jackson, Mississippi. It was a prudent move, under the circumstances.

Forrest was very proud of the performance of his troops, especially the green ones. "Every man became a hero," he told them when he addressed the troops after the battle. He wrote to General Polk on February 26:

> It affords me pleasure to mention the fortitude and gallantry displayed by the troops engaged, especially the new troops from West Tennessee, who, considering their want of drill and

discipline and experience, behaved handsomely, and the moral effect of their victory over the best cavalry in the Federal service will tell in their future operations, inspiring them with courage and confidence in their ability to whip them again. Considering the disparity in numbers, discipline, and drill, I consider it one of the most complete victories that has occurred during the war.

He was right—the West Tennesseans, and indeed everyone in his command—walked with a new confidence and a new swagger. For the rest of the war, they would be a force to be reckoned with.

One general definitely impressed by Forrest's performance at Okolona was Ulysses S. Grant. He called Forrest an "able" leader and wrote that the outcome of battles is often "due to the way troops are officered, and for the particular kind of warfare which Forrest carried on neither army could present a more effective officer than he was."

# CHAPTER 13

# THE THIRD WEST TENNESSEE RAID

*Start by doing what is necessary; then do what is possible; and suddenly you are doing the impossible.*

—St. Francis of Assisi

After Okolona, Forrest moved his command to Columbus, Mississippi, a beautiful town, featuring impressive homes and stately oak trees. The people were hospitable, the young ladies were charming and beautiful, and the food was plentiful and delicious. The soldiers also enjoyed an active social life. Sometimes, there were up to three parties a night that lasted until dawn and were followed by picnics the following day. Invitations were often sent in the form of military "orders" from "Cupid's Brigade," commanding a soldier to report to Miss So-and-So's "headquarters," where he would receive further instructions. Such orders were always obeyed. While Forrest was content to let nature take its course, General Chalmers was an active matchmaker. Thanks in part to his efforts, several young men fell in love with local belles.

Among the many Confederate leaders who were delighted by Forrest's victory at Okolona was his immediate superior, Lieutenant General Leonidas Polk, the commander of the Department of Mississippi and

Lieutenant General Leonidas Polk (1806–1864), the Episcopal Bishop of Louisiana in civilian life.

Eastern Louisiana. In addition to his official congratulations, Polk—the Episcopal Bishop of Louisiana in civilian life—gave Forrest a more tangible reward: a Kentucky brigade. Polk grandly named its three regiments "cavalry," but only one third of the seven hundred men were mounted.[1] But that was alright with Forrest, because he knew where to get horses: the Yankees in western Tennessee and Kentucky had plenty of horses.

The Kentucky commander, Brigadier General Abraham "Abe" Buford was a large, overweight, jolly man. While hardly the image of the *beau sabreur*, like Forrest, he had led an adventuresome life. A West Point graduate, he joined the cavalry, served on the frontier, chased Indians, and fought in the Mexican War, where he was given a brevet promotion for heroism at Buena Vista. After taking part in the Santa Fe Trail Expedition, he served as an instructor at the U. S. Army's Cavalry School at Carlisle Barracks, Pennsylvania, before resigning from the army in 1854 and returning home to raise thoroughbred horses. Forrest also loved horses and had been a horse trader in civilian life, so the two men hit it off immediately. On March 7, Forrest reorganized his corps into two divisions, each of which had two weak brigades. He promoted Buford to the command of the Second Division. Except when he was disabled by wounds, he would remain with Forrest in that capacity until the end of the war.

Forrest's relationship with his other division commander was less amiable. Brigadier General James R. Chalmers was a well-educated attorney whose father had been a United States Senator from Mississippi. Physically small (his men called him "Little Un"), he was a fierce combat officer. Already viewed as a rising political star, he was thirty years old when the Civil War began. Immediately elected colonel of the Ninth Mississippi Infantry Regiment, he was promoted to brigadier general in early 1862, and was senior to Colonel Forrest prior to Shiloh. Chalmers was given command of the District of Northern Mississippi in 1863, but was superseded by Forrest in mid-November. And that was the rub. Chalmers believed that Forrest should be working for him, not *vice versa, and* he would not cooperate with Forrest on even the most trivial matters. Forrest not unreasonably assumed that, if Chalmers would not cooperate on small things, he would not cooperate on the battlefield either. On March 9, Forrest had enough and relieved Chalmers and one of his brigade commanders of

Brigadier General Abe Buford (1820–1884), a fine commander and thoroughbred horse expert whom Forrest liked very much.

their commands. He wrote to General Polk that he was "satisfied that I have not and shall not receive the co-operation of Brigadier-General Chalmers, and that matters of the smallest moment will continue, as they have heretofore done, to be a source of annoyance to myself and detrimental to the service…I deem it both necessary and beneficial that we should separate." With uncharacteristic diplomacy, he added: "I hope you may be able to place him where he will be better satisfied than with me."

Polk thought Forrest had overreacted but did not want to challenge him directly. He turned the matter over to General Samuel Cooper, the adjutant general of the Confederate Army, with his recommendation that Chalmers be restored to command.

Cooper was the senior military officer in the whole Confederacy until February 1865, when Robert E. Lee became general-in-chief. He was also Jefferson Davis's executive officer for military affairs. Although a disappointment in this position, Davis retained him because he liked

Brigadier General James R. Chalmers came from a powerful Mississippi political family. After he and Forrest overcame their difficulties, Chalmers became Forrest's best divisional commander.

him personally, and he could be counted on to obey the president's orders. Cooper ruled that Forrest had exceeded his authority and gave Chalmers back his command. What role the Mississippi politician Jefferson Davis played in restoring the Mississippi politician Chalmers to his command is a matter of speculation. Chalmers, meanwhile, apparently had a "counseling session" with Lieutenant General Polk, and was informed that as incredible as it may seem to a well-educated, highly successful and well-connected lawyer like him, President Davis preferred the semi-literate frontiersmen to be his commander in northern Mississippi, which is why he appointed Forrest to the post in the first place. So, Chalmers now had two only choices: work for Forrest as a cooperative and loyal subordinate or permanently lose his job. He chose the first option.

For his part, Forrest was satisfied. He had gotten what he wanted and, as several days had elapsed since he fired Chalmers, he had cooled down. He was willing to give him a second chance. Forrest had always recognized Chalmers's abilities as a commander. Chalmers soon developed a personal affection for the Wizard of the Saddle and never ceased to praise him, even years after Forrest's death. He went so far as to write a laudatory song about him.[2]

General Forrest realized that his victory at Okolona had changed the strategic situation in northern Mississippi and western Tennessee, and he was determined to take advantage of that fact. He decided to launch what became known as the Third West Tennessee Raid, in order to bring in recruits, obtain supplies, and mount his new Kentucky regiments. Forrest also was determined to rid the area of three Union cavalry regiments, the Sixth Tennessee Cavalry, the Seventh Tennessee Cavalry and the Thirteenth Tennessee Cavalry, the men of which had developed the most unsavory reputations as rapists and looters.

Forrest left Tupelo, Mississippi, for western Tennessee and Kentucky on March 15. He carried Buford's division (2,200 men) with him, as well as the Seventh Tennessee Cavalry Regiment, McDonald's Battalion (i.e., the remnants of his own first command, the Third Tennessee Cavalry Regiment) and his Escort Company—2,800 men altogether. He initially left Chalmers's division in Mississippi to round up deserters and implement the Confederate draft.

Forrest easily got past the Union front line and again liberated the town of Jackson, a railroad hub and second largest town in west Tennessee, on March 20. Here, many of the citizens told the general and his men tales of Union atrocities, including rape. The offenders were mainly from the Sixth Tennessee Cavalry, which was led by Colonel Fielding Hurst. Hurst himself was an extortionist, who demanded money from Southern towns or he would put them to the torch. In fact, the citizens of Jackson had paid him more than $5,000 in gold or greenbacks (more than $100,000 in 2016 currency) to spare their town.[3] Forrest sent a message through the lines under a flag of truce to Hurst's commanding officer, Brigadier General Ralph P. Buckland, and demanded restitution. Buckland passed the demand up his chain of command and, remarkably, the Federal government repaid the money. Hurst, however, reappeared later and extorted money again.

Oddly, one of Forrest's biggest fans in Tennessee at this time was Mrs. Melocky Hurst, the colonel's wife. On his way to Jackson, Forrest captured Hurst's hometown of Purdy, Tennessee. Knowing that many of his men would cheerfully loot and burn Hurst's home, Forrest dispatched Captain Charles Anderson to the Hurst place with five men from his personal escort under orders to safeguard the house until Forrest's command had passed through. When Mrs. Hurst answered the door,

Colonel Fielding Hurst, commander of the Sixth (Union) Tennessee Regiment and noted extortionist.

she expected the worst and was stunned by the news. "Please, sir," she said, with tears of gratitude running down her cheeks, "say to General Forrest, for me, that this is more than I had any right to expect from him, and that I thank him from my heart for this unexpected kindness. I shall gratefully remember it and shall always believe him to be as generous as he is brave!"

Anderson rejoined Forrest in the town square, where they were soon surrounded by civilians. One was the father of Lieutenant Colonel Drew M. Wisdom of Forrest's command.[4] The elder Wisdom gestured toward the burned-out remnants and lonely chimneys of the former homes of Confederates and Confederate sympathizers. Wisdom stated that many of the people here were pro-Union and were greatly worried by Forrest's presence, because they feared he might retaliate by burning their homes.

"I do not blame any man for being exasperated and, especially those whose homes have been laid to ashes, for desiring to revenge such cowardly wrongs," Forrest replied, "but I have placed a guard around the home of Hurst, and others need feel no uneasiness. Orders have been issued to my command that no Union citizen...be insulted, much less harmed...Of one thing, however, the Union friends of Colonel Hurst and his cowardly regiment may rely upon; if we ever are so fortunate as to find them in our front, I will wipe them off the face of the earth!"

After he arrived in Jackson, Forrest learned that Hurst's colleagues were holding several Southern civilians at Fort Pillow (about seventy miles west of Jackson), including sixty-seven-year-old Rev. George W. D. Harris of Dyer County, a highly respected leader of the Southern Methodist Church and brother of the Confederate governor. Forrest wrote General Buckland and cited seven murders committed by members of the Sixth Tennessee Cavalry in the past two months. One of them was Lieutenant William Dobbs of Forrest's command. Dobbs had been captured while on leave at his father's home in Henderson County, Tennessee, and had been hanged—but not before his face was skinned, his nose and genitals were cut off, and he was tortured. For this and other atrocities, Forrest demanded that Hurst be turned over to the Confederate Army for trial. Not surprisingly, Buckland refused.

Forrest also demanded that Reverend Harris be given a prompt trial or be released. He promised to put five U.S. soldiers, now in his hands, in close captivity (i.e., in chains) until Harris was freed. He further swore to execute them if Harris died of ill treatment. Union authorities released Dr. Harris immediately.

Now Forrest assembled the Seventh Tennessee and sent it to capture Union City. "You damn boys have been bragging you could whip half a dozen Yankees," he said. "You are the Seventh Tennessee Rebs. The Union Seventh Tennessee are [sic.] at Union City. I am going to send you there to clean them out. If you don't, never come back here!"

By now, Forrest's method of leadership had created a cohort of "little Forrests" who emulated their commander and used his tactics on the battlefield. Colonel William L. Duckworth, the commander of the Seventh Tennessee, is just one example. Called "one of Forrest's most attentive students," he invested Union City in the predawn darkness of March 24 and soon determined that the place was too strong to capture without artillery, but not so strong that it could not be taken by bluff. After initiating heavy skirmishing in the morning, around 10 a.m., Duckworth ordered his men to shout as if reinforcements had arrived. The black troops and teamsters were particularly loud and enthusiastic. Duckworth then sent a dispatch under a white flag to the Union commander, Colonel Isaac A. Hawkins, commander of the Seventh (Union) Tennessee Cavalry Regiment and a man whom Forrest had captured in 1862, and demanded he surrender the garrison. Duckworth signed Forrest's name to the dispatch.

Hawkins, agreed to consider surrender but he wanted to see Forrest. Duckworth boldly rode up to Hawkins and said that General Forrest was not in the habit of meeting with those inferior to him in rank, and he had delegated that authority to Duckworth. Meanwhile, some of the men mounted a black-painted log on the fore wheels of a wagon, with a box fixed on the other wheels, making it look like a cannon. In Federal view, they maneuvered it into a suitable position to shell the U.S. position. Hawkins asked for time to consider; Duckworth gave him five minutes. Even though several of his junior officers wanted to fight, the Federal colonel surrendered 475 men and three hundred horses at 11 a.m. to Duckworth's five hundred men. Unknown to Hawkins, a relief column of two thousand men and a battery of artillery was only six miles away, stymied by a burned bridge.[5]

When Forrest's men searched their new prisoners, they discovered that Hawkins's troops had just received more than a year's back pay. The Rebels collected $60,000.

The black Confederates took particular delight in taunting the Union prisoners. "Here's your artillery!" they laughed, showing the bluecoats the black log. "Toot! Toot!"

Forrest and Buford, meanwhile, arrived at Paducah, Kentucky, with Thompson's and Bell's brigades on March 25. The garrison commander, Colonel Stephen G. Hicks, was made of sterner stuff than Hawkins.[6] He rushed to Fort Anderson, on the western edge of the town, and refused Forrest's usual threats and demand for surrender. Forrest took the town but had no intention of attacking the fort, which he judged to be too strong. (The garrison consisted of 675 troops, of which 274 were black.) But Colonel Sam Thompson, a native of Paducah, grew too excited. Without orders, he attacked the fort with four hundred men, galloping past his old law office in the process. It was Forrest's first encounter with black soldiers, and they performed very well. The Kentuckians were quickly checked, and Colonel Thompson was hit by an artillery shell which exploded just as it struck him, blowing him to bits. He perished almost within sight of his home. He was replaced by Colonel Edward Crossland, a fine commander who idolized Forrest.[7]

Forrest held Paducah for ten hours, during which he burned a transport, a dry-dock, and at least sixty bales of cotton, and captured sixty-four

Yankees who did not reach the fort in time. He also collected supplies from Union warehouses, burned the rest, and withdrew. Both Fort Anderson and some Union gunboats were shelling the town and he did not want to be responsible for needless civilian deaths. Near Mayfield he disbanded most of Buford's units with orders to go home, visit their families, get or improve their mounts, and rejoin the command at Trenton on April 3. Every man did.

The news that Forrest was on the loose caused fear and consternation throughout Tennessee and Kentucky, and even points further north. The commander of the Union garrison at Cairo, Brigadier General Mason Brayman, an old friend of Lincoln's from Springfield, suspended all commerce in his district; destroyed all ferries across the Ohio; closed all bars, taverns and houses of prostitution; and ordered his pickets to shoot all suspicious people on sight. He declared that Forrest had seven thousand men and was planning to unite with Copperheads in southern Illinois and Indiana, who would then join the Rebellion. Brayman further claimed that Stephen D. Lee was joining Forrest with another six thousand men. Sherman declared all of this "ridiculous nonsense" and ordered him to attack Forrest. But Brayman ignored the order and kept his men north of the Ohio.[8]

Meanwhile, on March 29, Colonel James J. Neely did what Forrest dreamed of: he met Hurst's hated Sixth Tennessee Regiment at Bolivar (seventy-two miles east of Memphis and twenty-eight south-southwest of Jackson) and completely routed it. Hurst fled to Memphis and only escaped because his horse was faster than those of the Rebels who were chasing him. Neely captured Hurst's hat, all of his wagons, ambulances, papers, fifty thousand rounds of badly needed ammunition, all of his mistresses (both black and white), and thirty of his men. Another thirty Tennessee Unionists lay dead on the field. The victory caused a great deal of satisfaction and delight throughout western Tennessee. But the most impressive victory belonged to Lieutenant Colonel James M. Crews, who was commanding what was formerly Forrest's original regiment, now called the McDonald Battalion. With sixty men, Crews met two Union regiments under General Grierson on the Summerville Road, twenty-five miles from Memphis. Crews launched a Forrest-like surprise attack, which he delivered with such fury that the Yankees thought it must be the advanced guard of a much larger force. Grierson—who had 2,200 men—withdrew to Memphis, burning the bridges behind him. "Forrest was a little too strong for me," he reported to General Hurlbut.

Neely and Crews continued to demonstrate and feint against Memphis for some time, convincing Hurlbut that a major attack on the city was imminent. Hurlbut even prepared to burn his supplies, warehouses and public buildings, in case he lost the city.

James McCree of Jackson was a Union man. At the end of March, he notified the U.S. commander on the Tennessee River that Forrest was in the town with six hundred to seven hundred prisoners and a force that was not much larger. It was obvious that he was about to send them south. They could be intercepted, McCree declared, when Forrest sent them out. Forrest found out what he had done (how is not known), had McCree arrested as a spy, and intended to shoot him.

The citizens of Jackson looked upon McCree as a clever but inoffensive man and were surprised by his arrest. Several of the town's best citizens crossed the river and went to the intended execution site, where they pleaded and begged Forrest not to kill him.

Nathan Bedford Forrest was tough, but he was also susceptible to the influence of ladies and highly respected local gentlemen, if they approached him correctly. "I know you to be guilty," he said to McCree, but "through the interception of these good men you are free, but never let me hear any more of your crookedness."

Suspecting that the Federals in the area were temporarily cowed, Forrest sent the prisoners south anyway. He was right. No attempt was made to interfere with the column and rescue the POWs.

# CHAPTER 14

# FORT PILLOW

*It is senseless to fight when you cannot win.*

—Apache Axiom

To date, during his third west Tennessee raid, Forrest had lost fifteen men killed and forty-two wounded, as opposed to a Union loss of seventy-nine killed, 102 wounded and 612 captured. Meanwhile, he dispatched recruiting officers to various locations in western Tennessee and Kentucky. In part because of the romance and adventure of riding with Forrest, and in part to avenge the depredations committed by Hurst and others Unionists, dozens of young men flocked to the Starry Cross. Strengthened by new recruits, fresh horses and the best equipment and supplies Uncle Sam could buy, Forrest decided to return to Mississippi.

En route, he halted at Eaton, Tennessee, where a number of ladies met with him and tearfully begged him to take Fort Pillow before he left the state. The troops here were primarily ex-slaves who had previously belonged to the residents of this area and were now terrorizing the families of their former masters. Several robberies had taken place and a number of women in the area had been raped by blacks and/or Tennessee Unionists. Some of the blacks had made a special point of insulting the wives and sisters, widows and orphans of Confederate soldiers, and some they also physically abused. The former slaves had also inflicted many indignities on Dr. Harris, the Methodist preacher.

"General Forrest was a man of great sympathy, and when he heard the pathetic stories told by the ladies, he changed his plans and decided to capture Fort Pillow," Theodore F. Brewer, one of Forrest's soldiers who fought at Fort Pillow, recalled. Always the self-appointed protector of Southern womanhood, the ladies' accounts threw him into a cold rage. "You may go home and rest assured that I will take the fort if it costs me my life," he said to the women.

Nor was Eaton the only place Forrest heard tales of outrages. When he left Paducah, the Wizard was distressed by "well-authenticated instances, repeatedly brought to his notice of rapine [rape] and atrocious outrages upon non-combatants of the country by the garrison at Ft. Pillow." The Union soldiers, General Jordan wrote, were also accused of "venting upon the wives and daughters of Southern soldiers the most opprobrious and obscene epithets, with more than one extreme outrage upon the persons of these victims of their hatred and lust." It is clear that Bedford Forrest had one major motivation for attacking Fort Pillow: chivalry. Forrest always saw himself as a protector of Southern women and he was not about to put up with *that*.

On April 9 and 10, Forrest met his division commanders, Buford and Chalmers, at Jackson. In a Northern newspaper, Forrest and Buford read an item that stated that the mules and horses Forrest captured at Paducah belonged to civilians, and that the government animals had been hidden in an old foundry nearby. The astute Yankees, the article declared, had outsmarted Forrest and his slow-witted Southerners. The allegedly slow-witted Forrest ordered General Buford to go back to Paducah and capture the horses. He ordered his officers to make simultaneous demonstrations against Columbus, Kentucky and Memphis, to keep the astute Yankees off balance and confused as to his intentions while he and Chalmers headed to Fort Pillow to, as Forrest said, "clean out the nest of outlaws."

Buford arrived in Paducah on April 14 and drove Colonel Hicks and his men back into Fort Anderson. He then sent Colonel William Falkner and his Twelfth Kentucky Cavalry to the foundry, where he and his men captured 140 high quality horses and their equipment from their more astute opponents.

Fort Pillow was located on a sharp turn of the Mississippi River, thirty-eight miles as the crow flies north of Memphis.[1] The site was picked by Colonel (later Major General) Patrick Cleburne and was named for Confederate Brigadier General Gideon Pillow. It was meant to defend the upper Mississippi River (including Memphis) and became the headquarters of the Confederate Navy's River Defense Fleet. It was supposed to include thirteen miles of outer works and five miles of inner works. The fortifications, however, were only partially completed. It was anticipated that it would be defended by fifteen thousand to twenty thousand men, but the actual garrison strength never exceeded four thousand. It did, however, mount forty guns, including a very heavy 128-pounder Columbiad, when the U.S. Navy bombarded it in May 1862. Even though the fort held, General Beauregard (who anticipated the fall of Corinth) ordered it evacuated, which it was on June 5.

The question might well be asked: Why was Fort Pillow garrisoned at all? With the Union in firm control of the Mississippi River and in possession of Memphis, Fort Pillow was militarily irrelevant. In fact General Sherman ordered it abandoned in January 1864 and used the garrison to support his Meridian Expedition. The next month, however, Major General Stephen A. Hurlbut quietly ordered it be reoccupied, without Sherman's knowledge.

Hurlbut was born in Charleston, South Carolina, in 1821, but fled to Illinois in 1845, to escape his creditors. Here he established a law practice and became good friends with Abraham Lincoln. He entered politics, was elected to the Illinois House of Representatives in 1859, and fervently campaigned for Mr. Lincoln in 1860. Although he had no military experience beyond serving as a militia lieutenant against the Seminoles in the early 1840s, Lincoln appointed him a brigadier general in the Union Army in May 1861. To his credit, Hurlbut had "saved the

Major General Stephen A. Hurlbut (1815–1882), the incredibly corrupt commander of the U.S. XVI Corps at Memphis. He ordered Fort Pillow quietly reoccupied after General Sherman had it abandoned in early 1864. Later assigned to Louisiana, his corrupt activities there led to his arrest by General Canby, but his crimes were covered up by the administration of his friend, Abraham Lincoln, and he was honorably discharged. He later served two terms in Congress and was ambassador to Columbia. This photograph was taken around 1878.

day" for the Union during the Battle of Shiloh on April 6, 1862, by blocking the Confederate path to Pittsburg Landing. This action eventually led to his promotion to major general and the command of the XVI Corps when it was formed in December 1862.

War brings out the best in some people and the worst in others. It brought out both in General Hurlbut. Brave enough in battle, he was also charged with drunkenness and corruption on more than one occasion, much to the embarrassment of his friend, Abraham Lincoln. In 1863 and 1864, he arrested the sons of wealthy Southern families with little or no cause and held them in a hellhole called Fort Pickering until their families paid him ransom. He was also an anti-Semite and confiscated the property of Jews in Memphis and restricted their civil liberties. Many of his subordinates followed his bad example, and the entire Union occupation of the region was characterized by blatant corruption.

Hurlbut also had allowed fourteen licensed cotton traders to set up shop in Fort Pillow with apparent motive of war profiteering. During the war, the price of cotton soared from $.06 a pound to as much as $1.09 a pound—and occasionally more. Tennessee's rich bottomlands produced thousands of 450-pound bales of cotton. An unscrupulous Union commander—with the right accomplices, such as transport captains—could get rich in the illicit cotton trade, and several did. Fort Pillow's isolation from Memphis, where there were too many prying official eyes, also made it a perfect outpost for a criminal enterprise.

This motivation might also have played a role in the make-up of the garrison. The black soldiers of the garrison were from the Sixth U.S. Colored Troops Heavy Artillery Battalion and D Company, Second U.S. Colored Troops Light Artillery Battalion. It is doubtful that anyone foresaw a combat role of them. The typical Union heavy artillery battalion had eighteen to thirty heavy guns. Fort Pillow had a total of only six light guns.[2] Little energy was expended training the black soldiers and few resources were devoted to equipping them. In fact, in the coming battle, many were armed only with clubs. Such men might have been seen as no more than laborers whose services cotton dealers could call on—for a price, of course. Or maybe they were just to act as a rudimentary security force.

The other unit at Fort Pillow, Thirteenth Tennessee Cavalry, consisted mainly of outlaws, renegades, Confederate deserters, and assorted rapists and pillagers. Morale was low. Twenty of its men deserted *en masse* on April 10 alone. Seeing as Hurlbut ignored their crimes, it is a safe bet that they would ignore his—or perhaps they participated in them.

All told, Fort Pillow was garrisoned by 557 Union soldiers, 253 of whom were black. This number increased somewhat in April as some of the local white boys fled the Confederate draft, which Forrest was implementing. So, there might have been as many as 605 men in the fort when the battle began.

During the Civil War, black Union units' fatal casualty rates were much higher than their white counterparts. Whereas, on average, fourteen percent of a white unit would die in an action or from disease, from twenty-three percent to thirty-seven percent of a black unit would perish, depending upon the source you consult. There are several reasons for this, but the main one is bad leadership. A case in point was Fort Pillow. The garrison commander was Major Lionel Booth. His second-in-command was Major William F. Bradford, a hated Tennessee renegade who had an unsavory reputation even before he joined the Federals. A twenty-four-year-old lawyer from Bedford County, he grew up less than a mile from Forrest's birthplace, so the general knew the family but not the man.[3] His military skills were wretchedly deficient. U.S. Officer Examining Boards had twice rejected his application for promotion to colonel because of his appalling dearth of military knowledge—and their standards often were not particularly high. He had also promised to promote one of his more experienced lieutenants to captain, but promoted his brother, Theodore F. Bradford, instead. This duplicity led to a fight, during which Bradford shot and killed the lieutenant. Booth replaced Bradford as the fort's commander by order of General Hurlbut, who was concerned about Bradford's youth and inexperience.

Booth's real name was apparently George H. Lanning. He assumed an alias to avoid contact with his family in Iowa. He had enlisted in the Second U.S. Infantry Regiment then stationed at Jefferson Barracks, Missouri just before the war began. He fought at Wilson's Creek. He became the sergeant and quartermaster of Company F, First Missouri Light Artillery and performed well at the Battle of Prairie Grove and the Siege of Vicksburg. He apparently joined the U.S. Colored Troops as a way to achieve promotion, for he skipped all the company grade ranks and was promoted directly to major when he joined the Colored Troops.

That Booth had been promoted far above his abilities is evident from his design for the defenses of Fort Pillow. Since he could only defend a portion of the fort with his small garrison, he selected a thirty-acre sector on the extreme northern end of the second line of the old Confederate works, on a bluff which was surrounded by deep ravines. Within that sector, he constructed a redan six feet high and eight feet thick—his final defensive position, which was one acre in size. It was shaped like a quarter moon, 125 yards in length, with its west end open and facing the Mississippi River. Around the redan, he built a ditch, which was six feet deep and twelve feet wide. There were several rifle pits along the edge of the ravine.

This might seem impressive, but the ditch and the most prominent ravine were so deep that the Union artillery could not be depressed enough to fire into them. Just outside the ditch, on his right flank, Booth permitted the construction of several buildings, including four rows of cabins which served as barracks for the white troops.[4] They were on low ground, and again the Union artillery could not be depressed enough to hit them. They made excellent positions for Forrest's men. One Union survivor later remarked that they had constructed better positions for the Confederates than for themselves.

The position selected by Booth had a number of other major flaws. The most serious was that it was lower than the hills that surrounded it. This meant the Rebel sharpshooters could fire into the interior of the fort and that the only safe place was the inside walls of the redan. Due to this fact and the contour of the land, Rebel forces would get to within thirty yards of the redan without being detected. Nor was there an effective route of retreat to the Mississippi. The only escape route was a two-foot wide path down the bluff. The only other way was a sheer drop of eighty feet from the top of the bluff to the river. Although this was virtual suicide, several desperate men tried it. There is no record of anyone surviving the fall. One Confederate captain who inspected their bodies recalled: "They were too flat to bury."

After an all-night ride of almost sixty miles, Chalmers and his men arrived early on the morning of April 12. Black Bob McCulloch's men sneaked up on the drowsy pickets and took them prisoner or silenced them with their knives. One of them, however, escaped and raised the alarm. The Missouri Rebels immediately attacked, capturing the first two lines of earthworks from the Thirteenth Tennessee Cavalry, who had little stomach for fighting. The Unionists failed to burn the cabins (except for part of one row), and the garrison fell back to its final defensive position, leaving behind the two guns not in the redan. Major Booth was shot dead by a sharpshooter about 9 a.m., and his adjutant was also killed. The inexperienced and less stable Major Bradford now was back in command.

Surrounded on three sides (north, east and south), with his back to the Mississippi River (due west), with no hope of rescue or reinforcements, Bradford should have realized that surrender was his only viable option. Instead, he decided to fight—and to bolster his men's courage by giving them alcohol. He ordered barrels of whiskey, beer and ale, complete with dippers, placed at various spots in the fort, and he gave the men unlimited access to them. When scouts reported to Forrest that they were drinking, he apparently sensed an advantage. "I will give them time to get drunk," he grinned.

General Forrest and his escort company had arrived about 10 a.m. He doubled his line of sharpshooters and with his guide, A. J. Shaw,[5] and Captain Charles Anderson, set out on a reconnaissance. Typically, it was very thorough and took about an hour. It also necessitated coming under Union fire. Suddenly, his horse reared up and crashed to the ground, dead. Forrest did not let on, but he was injured (or at least severely bruised) in the fall. He mounted a second horse, but it was also killed within minutes, bouncing the general off the ground again. His third horse was also shot but survived.

While opposite the Union right (southern) flank, Forrest asked Colonel McCulloch what he thought of capturing the barracks and houses near the fort. "Black Bob,"[6] an excellent commander, replied if he did, he could silence the Union artillery from there. "Go ahead and take them!" Forrest ordered. His men did so quickly and soon were picking off federal soldiers. "From these barracks the enemy kept up a murderous fire on our men despite all our efforts to dislodge him," Lieutenant Mack J. Leaming, a Union survivor, reported later.

During his scouting mission, Forrest realized that a ravine ran in front of the earthworks. If his men took that ravine, they would be able to position themselves for the final assault without interference, because the Yankees could engage them only if they stood above the parapet, in which case the sharpshooters would almost certainly kill them. Advancing in a series of short rushes, and well covered by the sharpshooters, Bell's and McCulloch's men moved into the ravine. Meanwhile, Forrest personally conducted Colonel Clark Barteau's Second Tennessee Cavalry Regiment to the northeast side of the fort, near the mouth of Coal Creek, which emptied into the Mississippi. With ammunition low, there was nothing to do except wait for the ammunition wagons to catch up. The condition of the roads, however, delayed the wagons' arrival until 3 p.m. With his men resupplied, everything was now ready for the final assault. But Forrest did not think this would be necessary. Neither did his chief of staff, Captain Anderson, who later reported: "It was perfectly apparent to any man endowed with the smallest amount of common sense that to all intents and purposes the fort was ours."

Forrest sent Captain Walter A. Goodman, Chalmers's adjutant, forward under a flag of truce. Not knowing Major Booth was dead, the general addressed his note to him. It read: "As your gallant defense of the fort has entitled you to the treatment of brave men, I now demand an unconditional surrender

A fanciful engraving of the Fort Pillow Massacre, as it appeared in Northern newspapers. It seems clear, however, that several blacks and Confederate deserters were shot as they tried to surrender or shortly thereafter.

of your force, assuring you at the same time that they will be treated as prisoners of war. I have received a fresh supply of ammunition, and can easily take your position. Should my demand be refused, I cannot be responsible for the fate of your command."

This surrender demand was in itself a significant concession by Forrest, because he agreed to treat the blacks as POWs. According to Confederate law, these men were property, not people; therefore, they should be returned to slavery. Forrest, however, now agreed to accept them as prisoners of war. This distinction seems to have been lost on the young major, however.

General Chalmers told Goodman: "If he [Major Booth] refuses, say to him, the men are in no humor to be brought face to face with the Negro soldiers who insulted their families." This menacing statement also had no effect on Major Bradford. After a short time, he replied: "Your demand does not produce the desired effect." He signed Booth's name.

Forrest sent a second note, stating that he must have a "yes" or a "no." He added that "if I am compelled to butt my men against their works, it will be bad for them."

The Federal officers carrying the flag of truce responded by demanding proof that Forrest was really present. Forrest duly rode forward, exposing him to the ridicule of the garrison, which had now been drinking about three hours. Trooper Winik later recalled: "the cocky Federals openly taunted Forrest, daring him to try to take the garrison. It was the mistake of their lives." They also taunted the Confederate privates, dared them to attack, threatened no quarter if they did, made faces at them, and made "insulting gestures" with their hands. "If you want the fort, come and take it!" they cried. "Come on, you dirty Rebels! Damn, what are you here for!?" This, of course, made the Rebel furious.

During the truce, several steamboats carrying Northern troops tried to land in the Confederate rear, despite the fact that the white flag flying over the fort was clearly visible from land and water. Forrest ordered Captain Anderson to take two hundred men to prevent landings behind the southern flank, while Colonel Barteux did the same to the north. When the men on the boats saw that the Confederates were ready to meet them, they withdrew without attempting a landing.

Later, this led to the thinnest war crimes charge ever leveled against General Forrest. According to the Radical Republicans, he should have allowed the amphibious assault forces to land in his rear unimpeded, because of the truce. In other words, it was legal for the Yankees to attack men under a flag of truce, but it was not legal for those same men to defend themselves. (The Northerners on the boats could clearly see the white flag over the fort.) This stretches credibility and common sense to the point of being laughable. They also charged that Forrest took advantage of the truce to improve his positions for the assault on Fort Pillow. This was also untrue. He actually diverted four hundred men away from the main assault forces. There were other war crime charges, however, which cannot be dismissed with a chuckle.

The white flag returned again. Once again each side sent a delegation into No Man's Land to discuss surrender. Forrest grew impatient and personally joined the negotiations. He demanded to know "in plain and unmistakable English. Will he fight or surrender?" Bradford asked for an hour to consider the situation. Clearly he was playing for time. "Tell him I will give him twenty minutes, and that is all I will give him," General Forrest said to the Union delegates. "If he does not surrender, I will not be responsible for the conduct of my men. Tell him that plainly."

The Union officers returned to their lines and sent back a single representative, who saluted, handed Forrest a folded piece of paper, and rode away. The general opened it and read: "I will not surrender." Bradford and his officers thought Forrest was bluffing—and had called his bluff. Forrest, however, was not bluffing.

Forrest at once became very stern and angry. Nothing made him madder than the senseless waste of life, which this unnecessary battle was going to be. He turned to one aide and said: "Go to Colonel Bell, commanding on our right, and tell him when he hears my orderly bugler sound the charge, to go over these works if he gets killed and every man in his command, and tell him I don't want to hear of Tennessee being left behind." He turned to another orderly and said: "You go to Colonel McCulloch, commanding our left, and tell him when he hears my orderly bugler sound the charge, to go over the works if he is killed and every man in his command, and tell him I don't want to hear of Missouri being left behind."

While the dispatch runners did their jobs, General Forrest walked up and down the line, shouting encouragement to his men and yelling, "At 'em! At 'em!"

"He was the incarnation of all the destructive powers on earth," Captain Dinkins recalled. "He was to a battle what a cyclone is to an April shower. His voice could be heard by the Yankees. No doubt they trembled, as later events proved."

"Shoot everything blue betwixt the wind and water, until their flag comes down!" Forrest shouted to his men. But, at variance with his customary behavior, he did not go with them into the fort.

After waiting a few minutes, he told his bugler, Jacob Gaus, to go to the center of the Confederate line and then ordered, "Blow the charge, Gaus, blow the charge!"

Firing as rapidly as they could, the sharpshooters poured a hail of lead into the fort, keeping Union heads down as Bell's and McCulloch's men surged out of the ravine, scurried across the higher ground and into the ditch at the foot of the redan. The first men in the ditch used their bodies as human ladders as the next waves climbed to the top of the parapet and poured over it like a flood. It happened so quickly that the Yankees had little time to react as a thousand men "as if rising from the very earth" were suddenly on top of the parapet and then down into the fort, firing into them with their pistols and carbines. The fighting was fierce—often hand-to-hand—and there was terrible slaughter for a few moments. Then the surviving Federals broke and ran out the back of the fort toward the river. The gunboats, upon whom Major Bradford counted, could not fire, because the combatants were too closely intermixed.

Much to the chagrin of some of the Southern enlisted men, as they moved through the fort, Rebel officers kicked over the barrels of whiskey, beer and ale to prevent their men from getting intoxicated. Some of the men were too fast for them, however, and had already filled their canteens. This is why there were later reports of drunken Confederates at Fort Pillow—because there were.

When Major Booth was killed, he was succeeded as commander of the 6th USCHA Regiment by Captain Charles J. Epeneter, a former Iowa brewer and vinegar maker, with whom he had been a sergeant in the 1st Missouri Light Artillery. Epeneter, however, had been busted to private for insubordination before joining the USCT. He was trying to aim a gun at the Confederate when a sniper's bullet hit him in the head. He was dead before he hit the ground.

Bradford panicked and headed down the bluff. Private John Kennedy of the Second Colored Light Artillery, recalled Bradford shouting: "Boys, save your lives!" as he ran away. Now essentially leaderless, some Yankees surrendered, others kept fighting, while still others took the only route of retreat available to them—down the bluff to the river. This was a gauntlet of death, because Anderson's men fired on the fleeing bluecoats from one side and Barteau's from the other. When they reached the beach, they still faced the crossfire. Several men jumped into the river, taking their chances with the current. Many were shot as they tried to swim away. "The river was dyed red with the blood of the enemy for two hundred yards," Forrest reported later. "[N]egro soldiers cannot cope with Southerners," he concluded contemptuously.

Booth, Bradford and Captain James Marshall of the gunboat *New Era* had agreed that, if everything came apart, the garrison would retreat to the beach, while the gunboat covered them by firing canister into the Southern ranks. But they had not expected Forrest to post two hundred men (Barteau and Anderson) on either flank, and these men were pouring fire through the open gun ports and into the exposed interior of the ship. Marshall ordered his men to run in the guns and close the gunports, and steamed away.[7]

Inside the fort, confusion reigned. When the Rebels first surged into the fort, some of the blacks had dropped their guns and raised their hands. When the Rebels swept past them, a few of them had retrieved their weapons and fired at the graycoats' backs. Some of Forrest's men then decided that, in order to keep from being shot in the back, the best policy was simply to kill everybody. Many of the Rebels were seized by what the Romans called *insanitas belli*—the fury of battle. The Germans call it *Blutrausch*—a fury of the blood. Confederate Sergeant Achilles V. Clark wrote his sisters on April 19: "Our men were so exasperated by the Yankee's threats of no quarter that they gave but little. The slaughter was awful—words cannot describe the scene. The poor deluded negros [sic] would run up to our men, fall upon their knees and with uplifted hands scream for mercy but they were ordered to their feet and then shot down…"

Confederate deserters fared no better. They were ordered to their knees and summarily shot. Apparently the Rebels felt that real men died on their feet, whereas these turncoats deserved no such honor. Of the sixty-four known deserters in the fort, only seventeen survived.

Some of the African-Americans who were smarter than the others played dead. Just before they were to be buried, they would plead for their lives. "Marster, for God's sake, spare me!" one of them cried. "I didn't want to leave home; dey 'scripted me! Spare me, marster, and take me home. Dey 'scripted me!"

Since it was easy for the Rebs to believe the Yankees had conscripted this man, and he was in the fort involuntarily, they spared him, along with several others. Quite a few, however, were not spared.

One man played dead a little too long. Realizing the "corpse" was still breathing, some of the Southern boys decided to have some fun. They tossed him into a grave and began covering him with dirt. The result was "the Second Resurrection" as the coughing African-American came straight up out of the grave. The pranksters thought this was hilarious— but they let the "Black Lazarus" live. Not all of them were so lucky.

Contrary to his usual practice, Bedford Forrest did not personally lead the assault on Fort Pillow, but stayed behind for twenty minutes. It could have been because of his injuries. Or was his own blood up, too? Did he think that the garrison had asked for it—and deserved to get it good and hard? Forrest biographer Jack Hurst, however, believes that "His temper may have undergone one of his characteristic waxing and wanings. Angered by the taunts of black soldiers and especially by the Union refusal to surrender, necessitating the paying of more precious Confederate lives for this victory he had to have, he may have ragingly ordered a massacre and even intended to carry it out—until he rode inside the fort and viewed the horrifying result. Then, begged for his protection, he was probably both vain enough to be flattered and sensitive enough to respond." Forrest left no explanation, so we can only speculate.

As soon as he reached the fort, Forrest cut down the flag. He remained on top of the bluff and turned two of the newly captured guns on the gunboats. The garrison's survivors were overwhelmed on the bank of the Mississippi River. They never did formally surrender.

There are conflicting reports about Forrest's orders regarding the treatment of the black soldiers. One black soldier testified that some of the Rebels were shouting "kill the niggers!" while others were shouting no, that General Forrest had ordered them to be taken alive. Sergeant Clark of the Twentieth Tennessee, however, reported that "General Forrest ordered them shot down like dogs."[8]

General Chalmers admitted that several blacks were killed by his overzealous men but that he and General Forrest stopped the massacre as soon as they entered the fort. It seems clear from the subsequent testimony that Forrest tried to stop the unnecessary slaughter once he entered the fort. At one point, sword drawn, he rode between a group of African-Americans who were trying to surrender and some of his men, who were about to shoot them. He also popped several of his men on the back with the flat of his sword, to stop them from shooting. Whether he was complicit in the earlier killings is a matter of speculation. Most of the killing that took place toward the end of the battle occurred at the foot of the bluff, while Forrest and Chalmers were on the top of the bluff, and Forrest was busy trying to sink gunboats. Forrest nevertheless would spend the rest of his life under the accusation that he had ordered "the Fort Pillow Massacre."

At one point toward the end of the battle, Union surgeon, Dr. Charles Fitch, approached the Rebel leader.

"Are you General Forrest?"

"Yes, sir. What do you want?"

Fitch identified himself and asked for protection as a prisoner of war.

"You are a surgeon of a damned nigger regiment?" Forrest snapped angrily.

No, Fitch replied. He was the surgeon of the Thirteenth Regiment.

"You are a damned Tennessee Yankee, then."

Fitch replied that he was born in Massachusetts and currently lived in Iowa.

"What in the hell are you down here for?" Forrest roared. "I have a great mind to have you killed for being down here. If the Northwest had stayed home, the war would have been over long ago!"

After a few uncomfortable moments (for Fitch), Forrest swallowed his anger and ordered one of his boys to take charge of Fitch and ensure his safety.

Later, Fitch became one of Forrest's most credible defenders, saying that the general was so preoccupied with sighting the gun on top of the bluff that he could not have been aware of the slaughter taking place under the bluff.

Forrest lost fourteen men killed and eighty-six wounded, including Colonel Wiley Reed, commander of the Fifth Mississippi Cavalry and the former pastor of the First Presbyterian Church of Nashville who died of his wounds in Jackson on May 1.

Union losses were much higher. John Cimprich and Robert C. Mainfort, Jr., studied the statistics in great detail and concluded that, of the 585 to 605 men at the fort, between 277 and 297 were killed or mortally wounded. Two hundred twenty six men were taken prisoner—168 whites and fifty-eight blacks. Sixty-four percent of the black troops were killed, as opposed to thirty-one to thirty-four percent of the white troops. Of the Union garrison, between forty-seven to forty-nine percent of the total were killed—very high losses indeed. Chalmers's division suffered less than one percent fatal casualties—losses Forrest considered too high, because the battle should never have been fought in the first place.

Ironically, once the killing was over, the African-Americans who survived were treated better than the white prisoners. They were mostly sent to labor battalions in Mobile, where life was no picnic but at least they got food. They also had hope, because the end of slavery was in sight. The white prisoners were sent to Andersonville, where many of them perished.

As soon as Union resistance ended, General Forrest ordered a cease fire, which held. The men were now back under control. Within an hour, unwounded Union prisoners were carrying wounded men to hospitals, burying the dead, etc., all under the direction of their old officers.

Major Bradford continued to exhibit bad judgment until the end. He was caught below the bluff and, even though Forrest viewed the entire Fort Pillow debacle as his fault, he was treated properly. He was allowed to bury his brother, who had been killed in the battle. He was placed in Colonel McCulloch's tent for the night on his word that he would not try to escape. He tried anyway but was later caught in civilian clothes— a crime punishable by death. Forrest and the Confederate leaders, however, did not intend to kill him. He was placed under strong guard (a lieutenant and four men) and was sent to the rear. The guards, however, had their own agenda. They shot Bradford dead, and left his body for the buzzards—and reported to Colonel Duckworth that he was "shot while attempting to escape."

Forrest left the field to seek medical attention. He turned the command over to Chalmers with orders to bury the dead, give the enemy wounded to a passing boat, and police up the plunder: six guns and hundreds of horses. Chalmers carried off seven officers and 219 enlisted men. He turned sixty wounded prisoners (fourteen of them black) over to the U.S. Navy. On Forrest's orders, he sent the captured cannons to Mobile.

Forrest went ahead to Brownsville. All the women in the area gathered at the steps of the courthouse to thank him for eliminating the fort. They collected and melted down their thimbles and had the metal fashioned into a pair of silver spurs which they later sent to him.

A reporter for the *New York Times* wrote an article, dated April 18 from Knoxville, breaking the "news" of the "Fort Pillow Massacre." The propaganda piece was copied all over the North, where the press used it to whip up hatred against the South, and to keep Forrest from becoming a "superman" to the Union soldiers. Besides a lurid account of the battle, the article also provided details on how Forrest and his brothers operated a "slave pen," which was a "perfect horror to all Negroes far and near!" It falsely stated that the Forrest boys beat their slaves with "long, heavy bull whips" until their "blood trickled to the ground." It ended with, "Such are the appropriate antecedents in the character of the monster who murdered in cold blood the gallant defenders of Fort Pillow." The image of Forrest so created remained the way many Yankees perceived him from then on. Northerners who met Forrest personally were almost always surprised that he was nothing like what they expected and soon changed their minds about him, but he became—and remained—the Forrest of the Fort Pillow Massacre to many who never knew him.

But there was no massacre. In military terminology, a massacre is when all or nearly all of the defenders are deliberately killed—such as at the Alamo, Thermopylae or Little Big Horn. Forrest clearly could have killed all of the Yankees had he wished, but he took dozens of prisoners, so Fort Pillow does not fit that definition. There is no doubt, however, that atrocities were committed. Several men who asked for quarter were not granted it, and others were put to death after they surrendered. There were also incidents of wounded African-Americans being bayoneted or beaten to death.

William Tecumseh Sherman (1820–1891), who ordered a separate, impartial military investigation of Forrest's role in the Fort Pillow atrocity. The fact he took no retaliatory action suggests he found that the Congressional report was slanted for political reasons and had little truth in it, insofar as Forrest was concerned.

That might seem a difference without a distinction, seeing as the men were under Forrest's command. But the fact remains that Forrest did not order these acts to be performed and that he stopped many similar acts from occurring as soon as he got into the fort.

The Radical Republicans conducted an investigation into the battle, led by Senator Benjamin F. Wade and Representative Daniel W. Cooch of the Joint Select Committee on the Conduct of the War. Much of the testimony was false and at least two "eyewitnesses" were in Memphis at the time of the battle. The final report's conclusions were exaggerated or distorted, and cannot stand close historical scrutiny. For example, it declared that the Confederates murdered black women and children, even though they had been evacuated by the Union Navy before the battle began. No matter. The report was meant to be a political instrument from the beginning. Forty thousand copies of the report were printed for dissemination to the Northern public, in apparent hopes of swaying their votes for Lincoln and the continuation of the war.

In view of the uproar, and not trusting the Congressional probe, General Sherman ordered his own investigation, to determine if retaliation was in order. After he received the report, he did nothing. William T. Sherman was not the kind of man to shrink from retaliation if he considered it justified. He obviously concluded the Congressional investigation had little merit.

Sherman ordered A. J. Smith from Louisiana to catch Forrest. Hurlbut urged him to hurry. By the time he got the order, however, Smith was too busy trying to escape from General Richard Taylor's Army of Western Louisiana to go to Tennessee in time to be of any help.

Grant wired Sherman, "Forrest must be driven out... Your preparations for the coming campaign [against Atlanta] must go on, but if it is necessary to detach a portion of the troops intended for it, detach them and make your campaign with that much fewer men."

This is exactly what Forrest wanted. While in Jackson, Forrest had written a letter to Joseph E. Johnston, stating that the decisive campaigns would be Grant against Robert E. Lee for Richmond, and Sherman versus Johnston for Atlanta. Nothing else mattered very much. If Forrest could weaken Sherman, he felt that he helped the Confederacy—and he was right. He could have done even more if Jefferson Davis had allowed him to operate against Sherman's supply line, but this the president refused to do.

Grant also wired to Sherman, "Relieve Maj. Gen. S. A. Hurlbut. I can send General Washburn..." Sherman also sent Brigadier General Samuel Sturgis to assume command of the cavalry over Grierson.

Meanwhile, all at once, Hurlbut and his principal commanders in Memphis decided Forrest's operations in west Tennessee were based on one big bluff. On April 13, Hurlbut wrote Major Booth, the commander of Fort Pillow, that he believed Forrest's check at Paducah would cure him from ever again attempting to take the river forts. He was unaware that Forrest's men were about to take Paducah again the next day, that he had already taken Fort Pillow, that the man he was writing to was already dead, or that he (Hurlbut) was about to be relieved of his command.

Finally emboldened, Hurlbut decided to cut off Forrest's escape route to northern Mississippi. He sent Brigadier General James C. Veatch, the commander of the District of Memphis, east to take Purdy and support Grierson, who would play the major role in bagging Forrest. Veatch took Purdy but, after a few days and no word from Grierson, he got cold feet and returned to Memphis without orders—much to Sherman's dismay. Grierson also withdrew to Memphis shortly thereafter, opening the way for Forrest to send out more than eight hundred prisoners and most of his captured supplies.

Cadwallader C. Washburn arrived in Memphis on April 22. He was a former Republican congressman and political ally of Lincoln's but was much more capable than the typical Union political general.[9] As soon as he got to Memphis, he acted energetically and organized a mixed force of 3,500 cavalry and two thousand infantry to prevent Forrest from returning to northern Mississippi. Sturgis, who arrived on April 23, was placed in command of the cavalry.

He was too late. Forrest made good his escape. The Kentucky Brigade, which had seven hundred men when it joined Forrest, now had more than 1,700, and no one had to ride double on the return trip. Chalmers's Division was also stronger, despite its casualties. It was temporarily detached from Forrest's Cavalry and was sent south, to Stephen Lee.

Riding with the rear guard, Forrest followed his brigades toward Mississippi on May 2. Despite being outnumbered two thousand to three hundred, he held off attacks from Sturgis and then followed the heavy wagon train into Tupelo, where he arrived on May 4, ending yet another successful campaign. Two days later, he received a vote of thanks from the Confederate Congress.

# CHAPTER 15

# "THE MOST PERFECT BATTLE": BRICE'S CROSS ROADS

*Power is not revealed by striking hard or often, but by striking true.*

—Honore de Balzac

General Sherman was seriously worried that Forrest would cut his rail line, which ran from Louisville through Nashville to Chattanooga, making his offensive against the South's second most important city impossible. "There was great danger, always in my mind, that Forrest would collect a heavy cavalry command in Mississippi, cross the Tennessee River, and break up our railroad below Nashville," Sherman wrote after the war. He even had nightmares about it.

Sherman's nightmares almost became a reality. On April 15, 1864—only three weeks before the start of Sherman's great drive to Atlanta—Forrest wrote to Jefferson Davis, proposing that his cavalry and Stephen D. Lee's be combined and strike into middle Tennessee and Kentucky and sever Sherman's main supply line. Fortunately for Sherman and the Union, Davis referred Forrest's letter to his senior military advisor, Braxton Bragg, who fussed about minor points and missed the main strategic objective altogether. Forrest's bold proposal died a-bornin'.

Samuel Davis Sturgis (1822–1889), another Union general whose Civil War career was ruined by Nathan Bedford Forrest. After Brice's Cross Roads he was not reemployed until after the war and spent most of the rest of his career on the Western frontier, most notably as commander of the Seventh Cavalry.

On the other side of the line, Cadwallader Washburn prepared for an advance into northern Mississippi. Sherman selected Brigadier General Samuel D. Sturgis to command the expedition. Among the professional soldiers in the Union Army, Sturgis was known for his energy, force, and courage. Born in Pennsylvania in 1822, he graduated from the famous West Point Class of 1846, along with George B. McClellan, Stonewall Jackson, A. P. Hill, George Stoneman, George Pickett and more than a dozen other Civil War generals. A lieutenant of dragoons, he was captured by the Mexicans at Buena Vista but escaped. Later he fought in several Indian campaigns and in the disastrous Union defeat at Wilson's Creek, Missouri, before he was promoted to brigadier general in 1861. Sent to Virginia in 1862, Sturgis fought at the Second Manassas, South Mountain, Antietam and Fredericksburg.

He served in East Tennessee in 1863 and was chief of cavalry for the Department of the Ohio before being sent to Memphis. Sherman handpicked him to command and promised him a promotion to major general if he defeated Forrest. Now the senior Union general in the west, Sherman was intent on killing or capturing the Wizard of the Saddle. "Tennessee will never be safe as long as that Devil Forrest remains," he wrote. Sturgis promised to bring him Forrest's hair (i.e., he was going to scalp Forrest, like the Indians in the Wild West did to their enemies).

Sturgis made the mistake of taking Forrest lightly. He thought Forrest had left west Tennessee in April because he was afraid of facing Sturgis. "I regret very much that I could not have the pleasure of bringing you his hair," Sturgis wrote to Sherman, "but he is too great a plunderer

to fight anything like an equal force..."
After Forrest retired to northern Mississippi, Sturgis returned to Memphis and
took up residence in the luxurious Gayoso
House, where he proceeded to go on a two-
week bender, in which he amused himself
by smashing crockery, breaking furniture,
throwing glasses across the room and into
walls, and making obnoxious and unwel-
come advances to young women, who were
the girlfriends or wives of junior officers.
Meanwhile, Sturgis was too busy boozing
to take care of mundane details, such as
ensuring that his command had adequate
forage for the upcoming expedition.

U.S. Brigadier General Benjamin H.
Grierson (1826–1911) (center, with
chin in hand), and his staff. A music
teacher in civilian life, Grierson was
rated as the North's best cavalry commander by General Sherman. During
the Civil War, he was always successful, except when he faced General Forrest, in which case he always lost. After
the war, he commanded Buffalo Soldiers in operations against Indians,
again with great success.

Nathan Bedford Forrest scattered his
regiments all across northern Mississippi
in order to cover Sturgis's potential routes
of advance. By doing so, he also avoided
overgrazing any single area, and, therefore,
his horses and mules feasted on the rich
spring grass and became sleek and fat.

Colonel William L. McMillen, Sturgis's infantry brigade commander, liked to
drink to the point that he even inspected his troops while he was clearly
under the influence. At least once, he fell down in front of the troops and
could not get up. Colonel DeWitt Thomas, the commander of the Ninety-
Third Indiana Infantry Regiment, was appalled. He ordered McMillen
carried to a private home and put in bed. Thomas assumed command
until McMillen slept it off. Naturally the story spread like wildfire, and
the soldiers' faith in him plummeted.

Forrest was not at all self-indulgent. His first concern was for the
material and spiritual welfare of his men. Although not a Christian
himself, he made church attendance on Sundays mandatory. The troops

were therefore aware that Forrest took an interest in every aspect of their lives. (Non-believers kept their mouths shut.) The general seemed to be everywhere, conducting innumerable inspections of men, horses, guns and equipment. He often slept on the ground beside his boys and saw to their every legitimate need and want. Their confidence and morale, which was already high, soared even higher. "Oh, he was rough," one veteran recalled, "but I'd follow him through Hell!" Most of them felt that way. One cannot understand the ensuing campaign without understanding that.

Sherman suggested that it would take six thousand men to suppress Forrest. Washburn thought it would take more, so he raised the total to more than thirteen thousand, if one includes teamsters, support troops and assorted camp followers. They included a 3,300-man cavalry division under Grierson with two brigades under Colonels George E. Waring and Edward Winslow, both of whom had reputations as hard fighters.

Forrest commanded two cavalry divisions under Chalmers and Buford in which were twenty cavalry regiments, four independent battalions, five independent companies, and a four-battery artillery battalion under Morton. By May 4, it totaled 9,220 men, but the increasingly dire Confederate logistical situation meant that 3,804 of them had no weapons.

Quite a few of Forrest's men were "deserters." Some had been in Bragg's army but were unwilling to serve under him or Johnston or were bored with infantry service. Yet, these men were not cowards or shirkers as they were perfectly willing to ride with the charismatic Forrest. Johnston and Stephen Lee ordered these men to return to the Army of Tennessee, and the former sent several officers to enforce the order. They took 652 men. More than one hundred others deserted again, rather than return to Georgia.

Meanwhile, rumors that Forrest was on the move or soon would be made the Yankee commanders jumpy. On or about May 16, General

Washburn received word that Forrest was in Tupelo with 10,500 men. On May 20, he warned Major General Edward R. S. Canby that Forrest had ten thousand to twelve thousand men in the Corinth-Tupelo area. That same day, he signaled General Halleck that Forrest might be preparing to capture Memphis and should be attacked; otherwise, he would do "incalculable damage." Colonel Waring informed Washburn that Forrest was in Tupelo and had thirty thousand men. On May 25, he signaled that Forrest was opening the railroad north of Corinth, rather than advancing west, as they had previously believed. The next day, Halleck suggested that the Wizard was planning to take Columbus and Paducah, Kentucky, while the day after that it was reported that he had captured Huntsville, Alabama. In other words, the Yankees had no idea where Forrest was, how many men he had, or what he intended to do.

To the east, Sherman began his drive on Atlanta on May 5. He skillfully outflanked General Johnston's army, who countered with equal skill, conducting a brilliant fighting retreat, falling back from Dalton to Resaca to the Oostenaula, to Cassville to the Etowah to the hill country and then to Kennesaw Mountain. Johnston knew, however, that he could not win by retreating, and, in six letters sent from mid-June to late July to President Davis and General Bragg, he urged that Forrest be turned loose on Sherman's exposed supply line. He said, among other things, that Forrest's cavalry would serve the country far better defeating Sherman's invasion than repelling Northern cavalry raids. Johnston's two senior corps commanders, Leonidas Polk (a West Point classmate of Davis's) William J. Hardee, endorsed the idea. Forrest's new department commander, Stephen Dill Lee,[1] also favored the raid, but was rejected. Even Davis's close personal friend, C.S. Senator Gustavus Adolphus Henry of Tennessee,[2] appealed to the president and to Secretary of War James A. Seddon, but his advice was also rejected. Governor Joseph E. Brown of Georgia also urged Davis to call on Forrest, but they were political enemies and the president responded harshly, basically telling the governor that he didn't know what he was talking about and should mind his own business. Ex-governor and former U.S. Secretary of the Treasury Howell Cobb, now a major general commanding the District of Georgia, also pled for the raid. Davis and Cobb were on friendly terms politically so his rejection was more diplomatic than the one Brown received, but it was a rejection nevertheless. Senator Benjamin H. Hill of Georgia appealed to Seddon, calling on him to use Forrest against Sherman's line of communication, but he didn't get anywhere either. As a result of Richmond's shortsightedness, a single-line railroad, 473 miles long, continued to supply an army of more than one hundred thousand men and thirty-five thousand horses and mules.[3]

Thirteen years later, as he rode in Bedford Forrest's funeral procession, Jefferson Davis admitted he was wrong to listen to Bragg and his cronies about the idea. "I was misled by them," he lamented. "I saw all after it was too late."

The Confederate High Command also became concerned about a potential Union cavalry excursion into northern Alabama. To defend against what turned out to be an imaginary threat, on May 23, it ordered the transfer of Chalmers division and Gholson's Mississippi brigade to northern Alabama, cutting Forrest's strength to four thousand men, who were spread all across northern Mississippi from Corinth to Panola.

In 1864, there were two decisive focal points of the war: Atlanta and Richmond. If the Confederacy could hold them until the presidential election of 1864, many believed, a war-weary Northern people might turn against Lincoln, and vote for the nominee of the Democratic Party, the platform of which included a "peace plank." This was not just wishful thinking. In the summer and early autumn of 1864, public discontent with the war in the North was growing, caused in part by the heavy casualties suffered by the Army of Potomac as Grant relentlessly pounded Robert E. Lee's army in Virginia. Before Atlanta fell, even Lincoln thought he would lose the election. If Richmond or Atlanta fell, however, public opinion would likely swing back in Lincoln's favor because it would boost confidence that a Union victory was inevitable. Although his army was being ground down by the fighting against Grant, Lee still stood between Grant and Richmond in the summer and fall of 1864. Everything then depended on holding Atlanta. Jefferson Davis should have moved Heaven and Earth to save the city—even if it meant temporarily abandoning northern

Mississippi and northern Alabama. By failing to do so, he not only violated one of the axioms of Frederick the Great—"He who defends everything defends nothing"—he also doomed the Confederacy.

On June 1, Forrest was at Russellville in northern Alabama, when a courier arrived from Stephen Lee. Large Union forces had left Memphis and were invading northern Mississippi. He was to return immediately.

Unlike the Federal cavalry in northern Alabama, this was no rumor. Sturgis had indeed left Memphis earlier that day with

Nathan Bedford Forrest, circa 1864.

13,200 men, including more than 10,500 combat effectives; twenty-two guns; and a train of 250 wagons. He carried 150,000 rations of bread, coffee, salt and sugar, and 75,000 rations of meat. His own wagon carried, among other things, a ten gallon keg of whiskey. His supply of forage, however, was inadequate, especially for the mules.

Due to rainy weather, flooded streams, heat, and the terrible state of the roads, it took Sturgis nine days to cover ninety miles. Forrest, meanwhile, could not concentrate his scattered forces, largely because he still didn't know what Sturgis's objective was.[4] On June 6, he met with Stephen Lee, who wanted him to draw Sturgis to Okolona, where, Lee suggested, they could join forces, then attack Sturgis and destroy him. He did not, however, forbid Forrest to engage Sturgis before that time.

On June 7, Grierson reached Ripley. His wagons had bogged down in the mud, forcing his exhausted and undernourished mules and horses to struggle under loads that were too much for them. To make matters worse, there seemed no end to the heavy rain. That night, he met with his top commanders and suggested that they turn back to Memphis. General Grierson was all for it, but Colonel McMillen, the infantry commander,

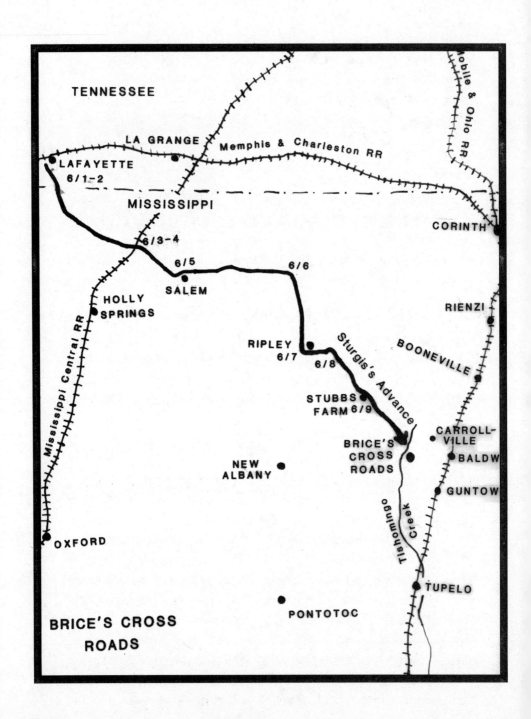

TENNESSEE

LA GRANGE        Memphis & Charleston RR

Mobile & Ohio RR

LAFAYETTE
6/1—2

MISSISSIPPI

CORINTH

6/3—4

6/5        6/6

SALEM

HOLLY
SPRINGS

RIENZI

BOONEVILLE

RIPLEY
6/7

Sturgis's Advance

6/8

STUBBS
FARM 6/9

CARROLL-
VILLE

BRICE'S
CROSS
ROADS

BALDW

Mississippi Central RR

NEW
ALBANY

GUNTOW

Tishomingo Creek

OXFORD

TUPELO

BRICE'S CROSS
ROADS

PONTOTOC

wanted to go on. In the end, Sturgis decided to push forward along a route of advance shown on the map on page 200.

The black troops in Sturgis's command were spoiling for a fight. Just before the campaign began, they swore on their knees to avenge Fort Pillow and not to take any prisoners from Forrest's cavalry. Many wore "Remember Fort Pillow" and "No Quarter to Forrest's Men" patches on their uniforms. Some of them even carried black flags, the traditional symbol of a unit's determination to give no quarter.

They also took their anger out on the locals along the route of advance. On the afternoon of June 7, they entered Ripley where, according to Orlando Davis's diary, "They committed many outrages."[5] They beat a man with a wagon whip and struck the sister of a Confederate General Thomas C. Hindman. They also robbed and plundered houses and businesses, fired randomly through buildings' walls, killed livestock, and stole food, especially corn and meat. They even broke into the cabins of blacks and robbed them of their clothing at gunpoint.

That same day, the Yankee cavalry made first contact with Southern horsemen led by Forrest's newest brigade commander, Colonel Edmund W. Rucker, a civil engineer and railroad man, who was one of the general's favorites. Private Hubbard noted that Rucker had "sort of a bulldog look. We soon discovered that tenacity was one of his characteristics." Like Forrest, Rucker frequently engaged in hand-to-hand combat with the enemy and gained fame within the corps for literally running over Yankees with his horse without a second's hesitation.

On the night of June 9/10, Sturgis camped for the evening at Stubbs' Farm (also called Stubbs' Plantation), eight miles from Brice's Cross Roads (now Bethany, Mississippi). The hamlet consisted of William Brice's store northeast of the intersection and his two-story home, just across the road, a few outbuildings and forty or fifty acres of cleared land, all surrounded by a thick forest of scrub, black-jack thickets, prickly vines and briers. About a half a mile west of the crossroads lay Tishomingo Creek, a north-south running stream with high banks, which would also play a prominent part in the coming fight.

That night, Forrest told his officers that he intended to give battle before the Yankees neared Okolona (in other words, he was not going to wait on Lee to arrive). As soon as the meeting ended, couriers raced to Colonels Bell, Lyon, and others with orders to march at dawn for Brice's Cross Roads.

The forced march was the order of the day. Colonel William L. Johnson's brigade was ordered to join Forrest from northern Alabama. It marched so rapidly that half of its men were not been able to keep up.

It had rained in torrents on June 8 and 9, but the skies cleared that night. The day dawned hot and muggy. The air was so heavy that men and horses started to sweat even before they cinched their saddles. As Forrest rode toward Brice's with Colonel Rucker, he explained his plan to his subordinate. The Union cavalry, he said, would reach the cross roads three hours ahead of the infantry. "We can whip their cavalry in that time. As soon as the fight opens they will send back to have their infantry hurried up. It's going to be hot as hell, and coming on a run for five or six miles over such roads, their infantry will be so blowed we will ride right over them."

For his part, Sam Sturgis did not expect a battle. He knew that Lee was coming up with his cavalry, 3,500 strong, but they were thirty-five miles to the south, and he assumed that there wouldn't be a major encounter until they arrived.

The Yankees were up before dawn. Grierson moved out at 5:30 a.m. with 3,300 men, heading southeast, down the narrow, muddy dirt road. The bluecoat infantry did not start its march until 7 a.m., and not before Sturgis and McMillen shared a drink of whiskey before breakfast. Grierson, meanwhile, ran into the Confederate vanguard, two companies of Kentucky cavalry under the inevitable Captain H. A. Tyler on Tishomingo Creek around 9 a.m. Crossing it was difficult because there was only one bridge and it was narrow and old. Normally the creek would not have presented much of an obstacle, but the recent rains had caused flooding. It was now difficult to cross, and the banks were soft. Superior numbers eventually told, however, and the Kentuckians fell back past the cross roads, which the Federal cavalry took at 9:45 a.m.

Not a mile beyond Brice's, the Union vanguard collided with the bulk of Colonel Hiram Lyon's Kentucky brigade. The battle now began in earnest. The forest was so thick that it was tough for the cavalry to operate. The only open spaces were the roads, and the dense forests concealed Forrest's relatively small numbers. Grierson—not realizing that he had the Rebels badly outnumbered at this moment—dismounted his troops, threw them into action on both sides of the Baldwyn Road, and sent back for help. Forrest sent dispatch riders to his commanders, ordering them to hurry to the battlefield—which the exception of Colonel Clark R. Barteau's Second Tenneseee Cavalry, which he ordered to work its way beyond the Union left flank and into its rear. It would take several hours to complete this maneuver.

Seeing that the enemy was massing, Lyon fell back behind a rail fence. When Forrest arrived, he commanded that every other rail be removed. He wanted to give Grierson the impression that he was about to charge.

Colonel Rucker heard the sound of the battle and came up at a gallop. He found his general sitting on his horse in the middle of the road.

"What is it, general?" he asked.

"Yankees, and lots of them."

"Is it a battle?"

"Yes, it is a battle. Never took a dare from them yet, and won't do it today," Forrest responded. He ordered Rucker to dismount and take positions on Lyon's left. Forrest was now only outnumbered 3,300 to 1,600. But the odds were shifting. Colonel Johnson arrived with about half of his brigade a few minutes later.

At 11 a.m., Forrest was ready to carry out the first part of his plan—defeat the Federal cavalry. To accomplish this, he knew he needed to deal the first blow. He rode along the line, telling his men that, when they heard the bugle again, he expected a full-out charge from them.

He got it. Johnson was on the right, Rucker on the left and Lyon in the center. "The roar of artillery and the fusillade of small arms were deafening," one Rebel soldier from the Seventh Tennessee recalled. "Sheets of flame were along both sides while dense clouds of smoke arose above the heavily wooded field. No language is adequate to paint the verities of the moment." Despite suffering heavy casualties, the Seventh Tennessee broke through, using rifles as clubs and firing pistols at almost point-blank range.

Grierson tried to plug the hole with his reserves, but Rucker held firm, despite the fact that his horse was hit five times and the colonel himself was shot in the abdomen. Forrest, of course, was right in the middle of it. "Mounted on his big sorrel horse, saber in hand, sleeves rolled up, his coat on the pommel of his saddle, looking the very God of War, the General rode down our line," a Southern fighter recalled.

The counterattack was checked in heavy fighting. The Northerners slowly fell back to a second line of defense, still being pressed by the Rebel cavalrymen, who were fighting as infantry. The Federals were still in the line but they had little fight left in them. Forrest kept up the pressure. He sent one of his officers to tell Tyree Bell to "move up fast and fetch all he's got!"

Grierson and Sturgis did exactly as Forrest had hoped. Grierson sent his commander urgent messages, begging him to bring up the infantry quickly. Sturgis ordered them forward at the double. Running for two to six miles down a narrow, muddy Mississippi dirt road in the middle of a hot, sultry June day, wearing wool coats and trousers, and carrying a heavy rifle and pack would take the starch out of well-rested troops. These men, however, had already been marching for ten days through Mississippi rain and sun, and had been on the move for hours in the punishing heat (the thermometer would hit 107°F that day) and humidity that morning. Making matters worse, the thick woods cut off any hint of a breeze and they also had to cross Hatchie Bottom, which was a quarter of a mile of swamp, extremely deep mud and quicksand. Dr. Dyer, the chief surgeon of the infantry division, recalled "the scores and hundreds of men, many of them known to me as good and true soldiers, falling out by the way, utterly powerless to move forward, it was a sad, a fearful reflection, that this condition of so many, would ensure a certain defeat, and terrible disaster."

At 1:15 p.m., Waring's brigade, which made up half of Grierson's division, found itself nearly out of ammunition and so left the field without orders. Sturgis, who had just arrived on the battlefield, committed his reserve (a New Jersey cavalry regiment) and his own escort against the Rebels. Fifteen minutes later, the first Union infantry arrived. Men panted for breath, even when standing still. Some were so exhausted when they arrived that they could not lift their hands to load their rifles.

Yet, Forrest's position was unstable and exposed, and his men were no less susceptible to the heat than Sturgis's. He had two thousand men on the field, but three hundred of them were horse holders. Casualties had been heavy. The Seventh Tennessee had lost one third of its men, Lyon's brigade had lost almost as many, and Chalmers's Mississippi Battalion had lost more than that.[6] A determined attack would likely have won the battle for the Northerners. But they were in no condition to attack. Besides, Grierson thought he was up against six thousand to seven thousand men.

Shortly after 1:30 p.m., reinforcements arrived in the welcome form of Captain Morton and his artillery. His horses had galloped the last six miles, they were covered in mud, and their flanks were bleeding from where the boys in gray had applied the spurs. Then, as Morton deployed his "Bull Pups," as his guns were called, General Buford galloped up with two regiments of Bell's brigade. Forrest placed Buford in charge of the Confederate right (Johnson and Lyon), while he took the left (Bell and Rucker). In a typical Forrest tactic, he sent Captain Tyler and two companies of Kentuckians on a maneuver beyond the Union deep right flank. Forrest was planning to strike the Yankees everywhere at once. Tyler would attack their right rear, Barteau their left rear, and he and Buford their front. But as he waited for all of his units to get into place, a lull gripped the entire battlefield. One soldier later remarked that the waiting and the unnatural stillness was awful. But it didn't last long.

Although Forrest was still outnumbered 7,000 to 2,700, he resumed the battle shortly after 2 p.m., when Bell attacked the Union right.[7] He was checked and the Lincolnites counterattacked against his right and Rucker's left. The Yankees were stopped, but only after Forrest committed his Escort—his only reserves. At just the right moment, Lieutenant Colonel Dew Wisdom galloped up 280 men from the Eighteenth Tennessee and helped stem the tide.

When Colonel Rucker saw the Union bayonets coming through the brush, he yelled: "Kneel on the ground, men, draw your six-shooters, and don't run!" The trees and brush hid the Federal's bodies but not their legs. Few Yankees were killed, but dozens were wounded, and the advance was broken.

For a time, Forrest personally joined the Seventh Tennessee. "I noticed some writers on Forrest say he seldom cursed," one soldier recalled. "Well, the fellow who writes that way was not where the Seventh Tennessee was that day . . . Our movement was too slow to suit Forrest, he would curse, then praise and then threaten to shoot us himself."

Meanwhile, in advance of an Illinois infantry brigade, Colonel McMillen rode up with his staff, and what he saw at the crossroads shocked him. "Everything was going to the devil as fast as it possibly could," he recalled. The cavalry was retreating in disorder, along with wagons and part of the artillery, as Southern cannons were shelling the area. McMillen noted that it was "a scene of confusion and demoralization [which was] anything but cheering to the troops just arriving." The startled McMillen ordered his vanguard to double time from Tishomingo Creek to the crossroads. Again, the weather took its toll—as Forrest had predicted—and about half of the bluecoats still in the ranks fell out before they reached Brice's. These who did arrive were totally spent. Many couldn't even bite a cartridge. Colonel Waring observed that the infantry came up "a regiment at a time, or only so fast as the Forrest mill could grind them up in detail."

At 4 p.m., Forrest received a message from Buford. The Northern cavalry near Brice's house had moved to the rear, and he heard shooting off their left flank, near Tishomingo Creek. It could only be Colonel Barteau and his Second Tennessee Cavalry. This was the decisive moment of the battle. Barteau had only 250 men and could have been stopped; but Forrest ordered his entire command to charge. He rode up to Morton and ordered the twenty-one-year-old captain to advance with his artillery, without infantry support.

Morton's "Bull Pups" led the attack down the road, with the men pushing the cannons. They fired round after round of double-shotted canister into the blue infantry, and advanced to within sixty yards of

Union lines. Meanwhile, Johnson hit the Yankee right flank. With the Union center wavering and Barteux so far in their rear that one Confederate shell landed among his men, confusion gripped the Yankee left. Lyon, Rucker, and Bell pushed back the rest of the Federal line, slowly at first, then rapidly, chasing them back to the crossroads. The Union mass became more and more constricted, and fewer and fewer men were able to fire. But Morton's gunners continued to pound them at point-blank range. Meanwhile, Tyler's men (who had been reinforced by Forrest's Escort) got behind the Union right. General Forrest, pistol in hand, rode up and down the line, yelling to his boys that one more push would sweep the Yankees from the field. He ordered his bugler, Sergeant Gaus, to blow the charge. He personally joined Bell's Tennesseans and waded into the thickest part of the fighting. "[L]ess than five minutes after Forrest joined me, their line broke..." Bell remembered. At last, panic seized the Yankee soldiers, and they began to run.

Meanwhile, in the early afternoon, Colonel Bouton's Colored Brigade[8] crossed the Tishomingo Creek, along with more than two hundred wagons. In the Union army, USCT were often assigned the task of guarding the wagon trains, and Sturgis's expedition was no exception. Sturgis wanted these men to take part in the defeat of Forrest, but nothing worked out the way he planned. As a result of his orders, the wagons were in a muddy cornfield on the wrong side of the creek and most of them were pointed the wrong direction when the Union line collapsed. Bouton ordered them to turn around, but this was very difficult, since each wagon was drawn by four or six mules. Then Confederate artillery shells began landing among the wagons, hitting at least two. The outcome was bedlam. Some of the wagons escaped to the other side of the creek but many were lost as teamsters abandoned their vehicles and joined the rout. Some actually unhitched their teams and rode off on their mules, leaving their vehicles to block the escape route for Sturgis's rapidly dissolving force. Seeing their white comrades pour by in defeat, the blacks joined the cascade to the rear.

A wagon overturned and blocked the only bridge across the creek. The Yankees crawled over the wagon and headed northwest on foot.

Some swam across the creek or tried to (several men drowned in the attempt), leaving behind ambulances, chuck wagons, caissons, cannons, supply wagons and equipment of every kind. The creek, too, was clogged by the debris of the disintegrating army. At this point, another commander might have been satisfied, but not Forrest. One of his principal military axioms was "Git 'em skeered and keep the skeer on!" He was everywhere, now encouraging, now cajoling, now cursing fiercely, and calling on his men to pursue. When Morton reached the blocked bridge with his artillery, his men cleared it by pushing everything into the creek—overturned wagons, ambulances, horse and mule carcasses, equipment, and dead Yankees. The pursuit continued with hardly a pause.

To the north, the Federals opposing Barteau were cut off. They fired a volley into the Second Tennessee and rushed to escape. Some surrendered; others waded into the creek. The Tennesseans were right on top of them and shot several in the back before they could reach the west bank. The rest scrambled across the cornfield on the other side of the Tishomingo and headed for the woods beyond. Many did not get too far. The Escort Company, which had crossed the creek a quarter of a mile below the bridge, charged the mob and made large captures of men and equipment.

About three miles west of the Tishomingo, near Reverend Agnew's house, Colonel McMillen formed a new line of battle with a black regiment and the remnants of two white brigades, about 1,200 to 1,500 men. Then the graycoats arrived. "Here are the d——-d niggers!" someone yelled. It was after 4 p.m. and some of the Rebels had been fighting since 9 a.m., but, as one recalled, "new life, energy and action coursed through our bodies…" The African-Americans fought well initially. They turned back the first attack and even pushed the Confederates back, but when they "saw the maddening rush of the infuriated Rebs," Lieutenant Witherspoon recalled, "they did as mortal men will do under the circumstances—[they] threw down their guns, without firing a shot, and bounded off with the fleetness of a deer." So, too, did McMillen's white troops.

Mrs. Agnew's daughter recalled that, as the black troops had passed the house going into the battle, they shook their fists at the ladies on the porch and said they "were going to show Mr. Forrest they were his rulers." Coming back, with tears in their eyes, they asked Mrs. Agnew what they should do. Would General Forrest kill them? As they ran for their lives, they ripped off their "Remember Fort Pillow" patches, which littered the side of the road.

The white Yankees, meanwhile, were running from the black Yankees *and* the Rebels. They didn't want Forrest's men to catch them with the blacks. They were afraid if they were caught in the company of the African-Americans and the Rebels shot the blacks, as they were prone to do, they might also shoot any witnesses as well (i.e., the white Yankees). Otherwise, they felt that they were probably safe, even if they were taken prisoner. It was well known that Forrest and his men treated regular Northern troops correctly once they were captured. (USCT and Tennessee Tories, of course, were not counted as regular Northern troops.) "The Yanks were afraid to be caught with the n\*ggers, and the n\*ggers were afraid to be caught without the Yanks," one Ripley citizen crudely observed.

The African-Americans were right to be worried. "Most of the negroes were shot, our men being so incensed that they shoot them wherever they see them," Dr. Agnew wrote in his diary on June 13. General Washburn, however, was of a different opinion. He wrote to Secretary of War Stanton and reported that, of the 1,300 colored troops engaged, about eight hundred escaped. "They fought desperately," he said, "and I hear were well treated by their captors."[9] Those who were captured were returned to slavery

Pursuits in the Nineteenth Century were usually halted at nightfall. But Bedford Forrest rarely did what was usual. He continued to push on through the darkness, with the Seventh Tennessee in the lead. Shortly after nightfall, they overtook the remnants of the wagon train. The wagons were full of provisions. The Rebels enjoyed an *ad hoc* buffet and then filled their haversacks with treasures from the Yankees: ham, real bacon, coffee, sugar, cheese, edible beef, etc. The Southern horses also had a banquet: shelled oats, hay and corn. Forrest was impatient, but he let his boys have their feast. Then it was back on the road and after the Yankees. "Come on, men!" he shouted. "In a rout like this, two men are equal to one hundred. They will not stop to fight!"

About midnight, they caught up with another wagon train, which the Yankees were burning. "Don't you see the damn Yankees are burning my wagons?" Forrest howled at his men. "Get off your horses and throw the burning beds off!"

One lieutenant did not dismount. Forrest asked him why he didn't help. The lieutenant responded that he was an officer. "I'll officer you!" he roared as he drew his sword. "[N]o acrobat ever was quicker at that moment than our brave lieutenant in getting to the ground," one of the soldiers recalled. He also noted that the young man was an excellent hand at unsettling wagon beds.

At one point in the pursuit, Forrest came upon a group of Rebels who had halted at a creek and were afraid to cross. To their horror, Forrest lit a candle and held it over his head. The light revealed an abandoned wagon and a cannon in the creek, but no Yankees. "Come on, men," Forrest called as he crossed the creek. "In a rout like this, ten men are equal to a thousand."

The Brice's Cross Roads pursuit was similar to the pursuit of Streight except it was on a larger scale. Forrest would give some of his advanced units a couple of hours rest and then they would gallop up to join the vanguard. Union Colonel Bouton still was intent on saving some of the wagons. He asked for an intact white regiment to at least help lift the wagons off the boggy ground of Hatchie Bottom and form some kind of rear guard, but General Sturgis didn't have one to give him. He could only offer the hope that Forrest might stop. "If Mr. Forrest will leave me alone, I'll leave him alone!" Sturgis cried as he left. But that was't about to happen. Sometime after midnight, as the Yankees crossed a wide creek in the Hatchie bottomland, most of their remaining wagons, some of their ambulances, and all of their artillery bogged down and had to be abandoned. When the Seventh Tennessee arrived, many of the Yankees were perched on logs, reminding Lieutenant Witherspoon of chickens on a roost. The regiment took another 275 prisoners.

The lieutenant pushed on through the darkness until he actually joined the Union rear guard. The rearmost Yankee engaged him in conversation, declaring, "Old Forrest gave us hell today!" The dispirited Northerner also estimated the Rebel general had fifty thousand men, just before Witherspoon took him prisoner.

After the demoralized Federal column passed by, the Southern civilians (mostly women) rushed out, lining the fences and road, cheering on their victorious horsemen and offering them food, water, buttermilk, and, in some cases, real coffee. Captain Morton recalled that even the children of the "poor whites" rushed out with paper sacks of food—all they could afford to give.

Sturgis himself called the rout "one hell of a stampede." The smashed Union column staggered into Ripley, twenty-two miles from the battlefield. Most of them had had no rest and nothing to eat for twenty-four hours. When they were heading for Brice's Cross Roads, Colonel Waring recalled, he had found the women of the town "spiteful." Now that they were beaten, however, the ladies turned out in force to feed them and care for the wounded. Mrs. Falkner, wife of a Confederate colonel and great-grandmother of the famous writer, invited Colonel Thomas to breakfast. Along with her food, she fed him the disinformation that Forrest had twenty-eight thousand men.

If the Federals thought they were safe in Ripley, at 8 a.m., the Sixteenth Tennessee at the head of which rode Forrest and his brother Jesse, disabused them of that notion.[10] Sturgis had tried to reorganize the downhearted mob into companies and regiments. The appearance of Forrest in hot pursuit again disheartened the Yankee army, and it fled from the town in complete disorder, leaving guns, blankets and other equipment behind. Sturgis's own headquarters wagon was captured.

The Rebels continued to pursue throughout the day, but gradually the adrenalin generated by the thrill of such a complete victory began to wear off. During the night of June 11/12, Forrest fell asleep in the saddle. His men were afraid to wake him. Captain Jackson, the commander of the Escort, ordered Private Mack Watson to awaken him. "No, sir!" was the response. "You wake him up!"

Jackson told Watson to see Tyree Bell, who was nearby, and get him to wake the general up. He also refused and told the private to do it. "No, sir! You do it!" came the reply.

Forrest's horse eventually did the job for them, walking into a tree and arousing the sleeping commander.

Later, near the town of Salem, not far from where he had once lived (Salem no longer exists), General Forrest fell off his horse. Practically unconscious, he slept for an hour and then jumped back in the saddle. So rigorous was the pursuit that fifteen horses dropped dead of exhaustion from Morton's artillery alone.

The chase finally came to an end on the morning of June 12, when what was left of Sturgis's men straggled into Collierville. Washburn, meanwhile, had sent an intact brigade there to protect them. It had taken Sturgis ten days to reach Brice's Cross Roads; it took him only sixty-four hours to get back to Memphis. On the return trip, however, he was not held up by wagons, artillery, ambulances and such.

During the preceding three days, General Sturgis had lost a third of his men and all of its trains and artillery. He reported losing a total of 2,240 casualties. The reports of the individual regiments, however, show that he probably left more than 1,200 dead and wounded on the field. He also reported that Forrest had fifteen thousand to twenty thousand men—a figure General Sherman did not believe for a moment. He fired Sturgis shortly thereafter.[11]

Forrest's casualties came to about five hundred.[12] He had captured 1,600 unwounded prisoners (sixty of them officers), 250 wagons and ambulances, five thousand stands of small arms, five hundred thousand rounds of ammunition, tons of baggage and supplies, over a thousand mules and horses, and twenty-two guns. Forrest took what he needed and sent the rest to Johnston in Atlanta. It was a tremendous triumph for a commander who had been outnumbered more than three to one.

Speaking to Captain Morton, Forrest summed up the entire campaign. "In any fight, it's the first blow that counts; and if you keep it up hot enough, you can whip 'em as fast as they can come up."

Field Marshal Erwin Rommel, the "Desert Fox," later reportedly called Brice's Cross Roads "the most perfect battle in world history." The victory at Brice's Cross Roads did not completely upset the strategic balance in the Southwest but it clearly altered it in favor of the South. Sherman had already ordered Brigadier General John E. Smith's division at Huntsville, Alabama, and Colonel J. H. Howe's brigade at Decatur to join him in the drive on Atlanta. Both orders were now cancelled. Brigadier General A. J. "Whiskey" Smith's three divisions in Louisiana had been ordered to prepare for an offensive against Mobile. This operation was also cancelled. On June 14, Sherman ordered him to head for Memphis. Sherman also ordered Major General James B. McPherson, the commander of the Army of the Tennessee, to organize a large force under Smith and Brigadier General Joseph A. Mower to pursue Forrest on foot and devastate western Tennessee and northern Mississippi in the process. Part of the Southern troops earmarked for the defensive of Mobile were thus freed up to join Johnston in Georgia. These included Major General W. W. Loring's entire infantry division. Although Forrest was not allowed to ride to Johnston's aid directly, he at least had managed to improve the odds somewhat, and he had saved the best food producing region the South had left.

Back in Memphis, when Samuel Sturgis learned that other generals were being dispatched to defeat Forrest, he snapped: "It can't be done, sir; it can't be done!"

Asked what he meant, Sturgis replied: "They c-a-n-'-t whip old Forrest!"

All of Washington was made nervous by Forrest's victory. Colonel Waring called the entire region a "Forrest Mill" which grinded up Yankees at a fearful pace, and no one seemed to be able to stop it.

After the battle, Forrest returned to Guntown, set up his headquarters, and began clearing the battlefield. He was now a hero throughout the South and especially in northern Mississippi. At one point, he needed some mules to clear the railroad and, not wishing to go all the way back to his base camp for them, he sent a few of his boys out to scrounge for some. One of the men soon spotted a few on the property of a local civilian and asked the owner if he could borrow them for a few hours.

"Absolutely, yes sir!" the grateful farmer replied. "Ole Forrest can have anything of mine he likes. Except my wife."

# CHAPTER 16

# "THERE WILL NEVER BE PEACE": TUPELO AND THE MEMPHIS RAID

*Great deeds are usually wrought at great risks.*
—Herodotus

On June 15, 1864, William T. Sherman signaled Secretary of War Stanton, "I will order them [Brigadier Generals A. J. Smith and Joseph A. Mower] to make up a force and go out and follow Forrest to the death, if it costs ten thousand lives and breaks the Treasury. There will never be peace in Tennessee till Forrest is dead."

Forrest, meanwhile, took a break and had some fun. He joked with his troopers and played checkers, pitched quoits,[1] watched horse races and played marbles. He was particularly fond of playing poker or "brag and bluff," a frontier card game. As always, nearby towns and cities threw impressive banquets and barbeques for the boys, produced egg nog (heavy on the nog), and held square dances. Sometimes bonfires were set on the town square and fiddles were broken out, and they danced until dawn with the local belles. Forrest never tried to change the "Wild West" character of his men. He liked them and, with a familiarity which did not breed contempt, let it show. The confidence was mutual. They had deep respect for him and knew that he would never risk their lives unnecessarily.

A. J. "Whiskey" Smith (1815–1897), after his promotion to major general in July 1864. Although he was a cruel man, Smith was a good commander who did not take Forrest lightly. His two attempts to destroy Forrest's cavalry were not successful, but his forces were not smashed by the Wizard of the Saddle, and he soundly defeated General Stephen D. Lee at Tupelo.

It would soon become necessary. On June 26, A. J. "Whiskey" Smith moved out of Memphis with more than sixteen thousand men, including 14,700 combat troops and twenty-four guns to face the combined cavalry forces of Forrest and Stephen Lee—eight thousand men.[2]

Two Confederate regiments had been sent from Oxford to Alabama and now had to come back. Charles G. Joy of the Fourteenth Tennessee recalled, "The country was the picture of despair. All of the men were in the army, and many of the farms were grown up with weeds, the houses and fences were dilapidated, and many were deserted because the owner had been killed and the family had moved away."

Rations were short and poor, so food was very important to them. A typical regimental breakfast at this time consisted of corn and watermelon. One morning, they got unsalted goat without bread. The only rations normally issued were flour or corn meal and beef or blue bacon and salt. "Coffee" was made from parched corn or acorns and occasionally barley or okra. They often got raw bacon, which may sound terrible to a Twenty-First Century American, but many Nineteenth Century people preferred it that way.

Private Charles Joy and his hungry squad found a dead pig in front of a blacksmith shop. It had not been dead long, so they dug a pit and barbequed it, borrowing vinegar and red pepper from a nearby home. The horses, meanwhile, ate the ends of limbs from bushes, as well as weeds and leaves. In fact, some of the men actually looked forward to fighting with Mr. Lincoln's army; after all, it would give them a chance to capture better rations.

This column—indeed most of Forrest's cavalry corps—looked very much like a Union Army formation. Most of the mules and horses were branded "U.S.," and their boots and blankets were marked "U.S." Many of their uniforms were formerly blue but had been dyed black. Their wagons were former U.S. Army wagons, and their ambulances were former U.S. Army ambulances. Their cannons, caissons and other accouterments had been manufactured in the North. The sabers their officers carried were U.S. Army sabers.

The fourth expedition sent to destroy Forrest since February was led by Andrew Jackson "Whiskey" Smith. Smith was a pretty good general when he was sober and, by 1864, facing Forrest had a way of sobering up Union generals. He stayed away from the bottle and proceeded with extreme prudence that slowed his advance. Certainly he sacrificed speed for vigilance. He reached LaGrange, Tennessee on the 28th and remained there a week, building up his supplies. He began his drive on July 5.

Smith had studied Sturgis's campaign and was determined not to make the same mistakes. He kept a very tight column, well protected by cavalry on both flanks. Straggling was strictly forbidden because he knew Forrest would gobble up stragglers. He ordered that every canteen be kept full at the beginning of every march so that men would not fall out to get water. The column stopped frequently to rest the horses so that there would be no excuse for straggling. Roll calls were held three times a day to make sure no one had dropped out.

Smith reached Ripley at 7 a.m. on July 8. "The scenes of this visitation were the most terrible of my experience," Rev. Agnew wrote later. Furious because of their previous defeats, the Yankees took it out on the town. They burned thirty-five stores, houses and churches, as well as the court house. The cavalry burned the buildings on the south side of the public square in the morning, and the black troops burned the rest that afternoon. The Cumberland Presbyterian Church, the Methodist Episcopal Church and the Female Academy were all torched, as well as

Colonel William Clark Falkner's home.[3] Reverend Agnew's home was only saved because he had befriended Colonel McMillen during the Brice's Cross Roads campaign, and the Ohioan placed a guard there, to check the arsonists.

Smith then slowly moved on Pontotoc, which he reached on July 12. By now, Forrest was on his flanks, probing and looking for a weakness, but Smith moved so slow and cautiously that he didn't find any. Lee (now a lieutenant general) joined Forrest on the night of July 11, and the two Confederates made plans to defend Okolona, south of Pontotoc. Smith, however, suddenly turned east and headed for Tupelo, eighteen miles away. For once the Rebel generals were caught flat footed, and there were no units available to defend the town. Forrest did break through the Union rear guard once but was turned away after he killed twenty-seven mules. Smith was forced to destroy eight of his wagons as a result, but no serious damage was done, other than the loss of supplies, which was serious enough for Smith. Forrest continued to nip at his heels all day on July 13, which was a tough day for the Northern foot soldiers. The weather was very hot, there were inches of choking dust on the road, and there was not a cloud in the sky. They were delighted when, about 9 p.m., they halted at Harrisburg, an abandoned town four miles west of Tupelo, but there was soon more work to do. General Smith picked a formidable position on a high ridge two miles north of the town. The Union infantry spent much of the night improving the position and literally tore down most of Harrisburg in the process. Meanwhile, Grierson's cavalry continued on and seized Tupelo. They burned part of the town, tore up four miles of railroad track and doubled back to rejoin the main body.

Forrest was also tired when he finally camped that evening. He had several boils and they were causing him a lot of pain. After resting for a time under a tree, he called for Lieutenant Samuel Donelson,[4] and the two men went off on a reconnaissance. Half an hour later, Bedford realized that he had left his six-shooters behind. Donelson offered him one of his, but the general declined, saying he didn't think they would need them. He was wrong. The night was very dark but, after making a thorough inspection of the enemy's position, they blundered into an outpost and were challenged. Forrest, of course, knew how to bluff. He boldly rode over to the Northern picket and demanded to know how he dared to challenge his commanding officer. As the Yankee stood there in confusion, Forrest applied his spurs and the two officers dashed off into the night. The picket fired at him but missed. Forrest later joked that it might have been good if the bullet had hit him. It might have burst one of his boils.

By dawn, the U.S. line was about a mile and a half in length, mostly in the form of a semi-circle. Their two dozen guns were well placed and a cavalry brigade guarded each flank.

After his reconnaissance, Forrest realized that Smith's position was too strong, and he had learned that Smith had only enough rations for two days and would soon have to retreat anyway. But General Stephen Lee felt he must attack and could not wait. The defender of Mobile, Major General Dabney H. Maury, was expecting an attack soon, and Lee wanted to return to Alabama and reinforce him before that happened.

General Lee wanted Forrest to direct this battle but, not believing in it, the Wizard of the Saddle refused. He took charge of the Confederate right (Roddey's Alabamians), while Lee directed the left. Buford led in the center with Rucker's brigade of Chalmers's division in reserve, at least initially.

It was supposed to be coordinated and simultaneous, but the entire Confederate effort was uncoordinated and disjointed. To make matters worse, instead of concentrating his artillery fire on one point, Stephen Lee ignored Captain Morton's advice and scattered his guns along a two-mile battle front, so they had no real impact anywhere.

General Lee lost control of the battle from the beginning. The Kentuckians let their enthusiasm overcome their discretion and charged before anyone else was ready, pitting a single brigade against two full Northern divisions and the USCT brigade, backed by two dozen guns— eight hundred men against eleven thousand. They were cut to ribbons and then bolted. Forrest, who had not yet reached Roddey's command, grabbed a battle flag and rallied the Kentuckians but, seeing that this battle was becoming a disaster, refused to order Roddey's brigade into the slaughter. Other attacks were launched, but they were also piecemeal, although perhaps not quite as bad as the first one. Smith recalled that the entire Rebel attack was "gallantly made, but without order, organization or skill." Rucker was wounded twice within fifty yards of the Union lines and had to be carried from the field. Colonels Barteau, Russell, Wilson, Newsom, and Neely were wounded, and Colonel Isham Harrison of the Sixth Mississippi and Lieutenant Colonel L. J. Sherill of the Seventh Kentucky Cavalry were killed. "Black Bob" McCulloch was shot through the shoulder and lung, while another rifle ball shattered his hand. He would spend much of the rest of the war traveling in an ambulance. Colonel Crossland stopped another bullet and was in critical condition, while Colonel Falkner was wounded twice and had to leave the field. Major Strange was wounded, as was Major Gilbert Rambaut, Forrest's chief commissary officer. An artillery shell exploded over Lieutenant Willie Forrest's head and the concussion hurled him from his horse. He also had to be carried to the rear, but he was lucky to the alive. Officer losses in the Second Tennessee were so heavy that command devolved on a lieutenant, George E. Seay, and he was just plain lucky. A Yankee bullet ripped through his canteen, smashed his watch and bounced off. Every commissioned officer in the Eighteenth Mississippi Cavalry Regiment was killed or wounded. Overall, the Confederates lost about 1,298 men killed, wounded and captured. The Federals lost seventy-seven killed, 550 wounded and thirty-eight captured or missing—665 total.

Stephen Lee broke off the ill-advised battle after two hours. Mabry's brigade and the Kentucky brigade both lost about one third of their men, Bell lost a quarter of his brigade, Buford lost a little more than a third of his division, and Chalmers (who covered Buford's withdrawal) lost more than three hundred killed and wounded. Crossland lost 306 killed, wounded or missing out of eight hundred men on the field (including horseholders). Roddey's losses were negligible. The terrible heat also caused casualties. Eighty men suffered heat stroke from Buford's division alone.

Because of his like for and previous good relations with Lee, Forrest suppressed his temper but only by great effort. One of his men recalled that Forrest was "so mad he stunk like a pole-cat." General Lee called a meeting of his generals that evening. Forrest did not want to talk to him and sent word back that he was ill. Lee ordered him to attend anyway. Forrest came, stomped in, sat down, folded his arms Indian style and didn't speak until Lee was forced to turn to him.

"General, we are in a bad fix," he said. "Anything you'd like to contribute?"

"Yes, we are in a hell of a fix," Forrest snapped. General Chalmers and Colonel Kelley recognized that Forrest was in a foul mood and quickly turned the conversation. After several minutes, Lee asked Forrest if he had any ideas.

Stephen Dill Lee (1833–1908), commander of Confederate forces at Tupelo. He ignored Forrest's advice not to attack, with disastrous results.

"Yes, sir, I've always got ideas, and I'll tell you one thing, General Lee. If I knew as much about West Point tactics as you, the Yankees would whip hell out of me every day!" Then he choked up. "I've got five hundred empty saddles and nothing to show for them."

Not long after the meeting, Lee turned active command over to Forrest, with orders to do the best he could.

Forrest gave Abraham Buford instructions on where to move his division.

"I have no division, General Forrest," the Kentuckian replied.

"Where *is* your division?" Forrest wanted to know.

"They are killed and wounded," he responded, with tears running down his cheeks.

Meanwhile, William Calhoun's home was taken over as a Union hospital. The Yankees learned that he was the brother of the hated John C. Calhoun, and a squad of General Grierson's men came up to shoot him, despite his civilian status and advanced age. He was only saved by the pleas of his wife. Eventually three hundred Union wounded were placed in her home; eighteen of them died.

That night, the Federals burned what was left of Harrisburg.

On the morning of July 15, Smith began his retreat. He did so, he said, because his bread had spoiled. A rumor circulated that Forrest had been killed, so the Wizard mounted his horse and rode about the battlefield, to the relief and cheers of his men. "This is not my fight, boys!" he told them. "When it's my fight, you'll know it!"

Early that afternoon, the pursuit began. At Old Town Creek, about four miles from Tupelo, Bedford Forrest was shot in the right foot near the big toe. It was an extremely painful wound and the worst he received during the war. He was forced to ride in a buggy for several days. When he finally could mount a horse, he had to ride with one foot out of the stirrups for several weeks. Colonel Red Bob McCulloch was also wounded, him in the shoulder.

After Harrisburg (also called the Battle of Tupelo), Forrest's cavalry moved south and camped in the rich soil below Okolona. He scattered his regiments all over the prairie, where the fields were full of green corn, some of which was mature enough for roasting and all of which were suitable for horses. There were also plenty of good watermelons, fat hogs, cornbread, vegetables and "greasy bacon." The health of the horses improved and morale, which had dipped after Harrisburg, recovered quickly.

It was good that morale was rising. Sherman—who was not satisfied with Smith's performance—ordered him to launch another expedition to destroy Forrest. Meanwhile, there was great excitement in Union headquarters. On July 28, Washburn wired Sherman that he had received a report that Forrest had died of lockjaw. "Is Forrest surely dead?" a hopeful Sherman answered. "If so, tell General Mower I am pledged to him for his promotion, and if Ole Abe don't make good my promise then General Mower may have my place."

Lincoln did make good on the promise, although Forrest was not dead. He was, however, in pretty bad shape. One man described him as "sick-looking, thin as a rail, cheekbones that stuck out like they were trying to come through the skin, skin so yellow it looked greenish, eyes blazing."

General Forrest turned command over to Chalmers and recuperated. Elsewhere, Sherman was advancing in Georgia. Still Davis failed to call on Forrest. On July 17, he replaced Johnston with John Bell Hood. Stephen Dill Lee left for Atlanta to take over Hood's former corps, and Dabney H. Maury was temporarily elevated to the command of the Department of Mississippi, Alabama and Eastern Louisiana.[5] He and Forrest met at the Maury's headquarters in Meridian. Maury understood Forrest. He wrote to him, "I reflect that of all the commanders of the Confederacy you are accustomed to accomplishing the very greatest results with small means when left to your own untrammeled judgment." In other words, there would be no interference from higher headquarters in his upcoming operations in northern Mississippi.

People in Mississippi remembered August 1864 as "the wet August" because it rained so much and so often. The rations were plentiful, but there was no dry firewood with which to cook them. The men spent much of the time in their shebangs (make-shift two-man tents), trying to stay dry. A lot of their ammunition, however, was ruined by the dampness.

Forrest had 5,357 men that month. A. J. Smith advanced with four thousand cavalry and fourteen thousand infantrymen. It was obvious to all that the odds were stacked heavily against the Confederates. Sensing trepidation, Forrest sent a general order to his men:

> Whenever you meet the enemy, show fight, no matter how few there are of you or how many of them, show fight. If you run away, they will pursue and probably catch you. If you show fight, they will think there are more of you, and will not push you half so hard…Whenever you see a Yankee, show fight. If there ain't but one of you and a hundred of them, show fight. They'll think a heap more of you for it.

Whiskey Smith concentrated his main body in the vicinity of La Grange, repaired the railroad to Holly Springs, and reached the

Tallahatchie on August 8. Counting three brand new regiments that just arrived from Minnesota, he outnumbered Forrest four to one. Again, he advanced slowly—very slowly—and the rain didn't help. There was constant skirmishing and it took Smith a week to cover the thirty miles from Holly Springs to Oxford. On August 10, he finally pushed Chalmers out of the town. Bedford arrived that night with Bell's and Neely's brigades and attempted to lure Smith into a trap. Forrest wanted Smith to follow Chalmers south, while he looped behind him to the north and east. Smith's scouts warned him, however, so he evacuated Oxford and fell back to Hurricane Creek, six miles north of the pretty little university town, which he had held for only a few hours. Here the Yankees regrouped for several days and advanced again.

Smith would have been even more concerned had he known what Forrest was planning. He knew he could not defeat Smith in the field unless the Northerner committed a terrible tactical blunder, which seemed unlikely; but he could cut his supply lines and leave him with two choices: a precipitous retreat or surrender. Forrest's target was exceedingly bold—he was going to raid Memphis.

On August 18, Forrest inspected the men who had responded to his call for volunteers. Although no one knew where he was going, every man wanted to go with him. After he culled the weak, the sick and those with jaded horses, he set out in a pouring rain, with 1,500 men and four guns. He carried no wagons or supplies. He left behind orders for General Chalmers: "Contest every inch of ground. Do not give it back, unless forced to do so."

The Rebels rode all night. The streams were full and difficult to cross and the invaders had burned most of the bridges. Forrest nevertheless reached Panola that morning. Here Forrest conducted another culling. He sent Morton back with two of his guns and one hundred men. Details had already been sent ahead to ask the women along the route to cook lots of cornbread. As the column passed, the ladies rushed out and fed the cavalrymen. That night, they reached Senatobia, twenty-three miles from Panola and well in Smith's rear.

Forrest had to build bridges over Hickahala Creek (near Senatobia) and over the Coldwater River. At the Hickahala, he ordered his men to make a bridge out of telegraph poles. They objected, saying they had no way of getting the poles to the crossing point. "Yes, you do," Forrest responded, "your horses' tails!" The men braided their mounts' tails and tied them to the poles. Remarkably enough, it worked. Forrest, meanwhile, ordered ten men from each regiment to go to every gin house and cabin nearby and strip the flooring. The planks were brought to the Hickahala. Other details gathered grapevines and muscadine vines, which were used as ropes.

The stream was sixty feet wide on August 20 and was normally crossed by a ferry, which was twenty feet wide. Forrest used the ferry as the central pontoon and anchored it midstream. He made two rafts from the cedar telegraph poles and tied them together with muscadine cables, and on top of these the flooring was spread. The bridge was finished in an hour. It was well under water by the time the last horse crossed, but it had served its purpose.

The Coldwater, seven miles further on, was twice as wide as the Hickahala. It took three hours to build the bridge here, but the last man crossed by nightfall. Another ten-mile ride took them to Hernando, where Forrest halted and let the column catch up. Here, several of his scouts reported in. They gave him an accurate assessment of the Union defenses, the location of their horses, and the exact whereabouts of the headquarters of Generals Washburn, Hurlbut and Buckland.

By this time, the men had figured out what Forrest was up to. Many of them were from Memphis and they were excited. The closer they got to the city, the more excited and louder they became. Forrest had to continually order them to be quiet. "They were making a regular corn shucking out of it," he recalled. "Wet and muddy, but full of life and ready for anything, I never had greater confidence in them. They were great soldiers."

"I never saw a command look more like it was out for a holiday," Private Hubbard commented. They rode all night on August 20/21, but the excitement overcame the fatigue and they arrived on the outskirts of Memphis at 3 a.m. on August 21.

Forrest's plan for the day was for Captain Bill Forrest, with forty men, to charge down the streets to the Gayoso Hotel and capture General Hurlbut. Jesse Forrest, leading part of the Sixteenth Tennessee, was to follow his brother, Bill, down DeSoto Street to Union and capture General Washburn. Colonel Neely's brigade was to take the southern outskirts of the town and smash the Union infantry and Washburn's local militia, which was derisively called "hundred day men." He personally planned to lead an attack on the Irving Block Prison, which housed many Southerners. Colonel Bell, with three regiments, would remain on the outskirts of the city as a reserve. General Forrest told his men to be quiet until they reached the center of town and commanded that any plunderers be shot immediately.

Captain Bill Forrest was an impressive physical specimen, like his brother. His temper was worse than Bedford's, and it was said that General Forrest feared no man, except perhaps Bill. A private described him as "…brave to recklessness. He did not fear one man, nor did he fear a hundred men, and yet he was sympathetic as a woman."

Captain Dinkins of Chalmers's staff recalled, "He never provoked a quarrel, but, when disturbed, would shoot a man on the slightest provocation, and he would give the last cent he had to a person in distress. The writer has known him to do both."

Bill's first job was to overpower the pickets. About 4 a.m., he moved forward with ten handpicked men. He reached the first picket line on the Hernando Road, about two miles from Memphis (near the junction of Trigg Avenue and Mississippi Avenue).

"Halt! Who goes there?" a vidette cried.

"A detachment of the Twelfth Missouri Cavalry with Rebel prisoners," Forrest responded. It was common knowledge that this regiment was with A. J. Smith.

"Dismount and advance on!"

The guard was sitting on his horse in the middle of the road. Instead of dismounting, Bill rode up to him and hit him in the head with his

heavy revolver. He fell unconscious to the dirt.

They reached the first outpost. One of the Yankees fired
on Bill's men as they ran for
their lives. Unable to restrain
themselves, the captain's men
let out a Rebel yell and took
off in pursuit. With the cat out
of the bag, Forrest, who was
following close behind Bill,
ordered Sergeant Gaus to blow
the charge.

A newspaper sketch of Forrest's troops chasing and firing at General Washburn. The sketch is mostly imaginary. The swift corps commander escaped without being fired upon.

And so a peaceful Sunday morning in Memphis was shattered by the crack of gunfire. Bill Forrest and his men came upon a Union artillery camp. They quickly overran it, killed or wounded every Federal who showed himself, and captured six guns. Bill and his men galloped up Beal Street, crossed Main, and Captain Forrest rode—yes, rode—into the lobby of the Gayoso Hotel, followed by several of his men, all of whom stayed mounted. This, Captain Dinkins said later, caused a "panic equal to that at Pompeii when the city was destroyed by Vesuvius." Union staff officers hid in closets and under beds. Forrest's muddy men kicked in the doors and dragged them out. Only two officers fought back. Both were promptly shot and killed. One Confederate soldier stopped long enough to make a cheeky entry in the hotel's guest register "General Forrest and party."

Lieutenant Colonel Alexander H. Chalmers—the general's brother—kicked open Hurlbut's bedroom door, only to be met by a beautiful young woman who begged for mercy. Much of Hurlbut's staff was captured, but the general escaped. He had been to a party and was sleeping in someone else's bedroom that night.

Alec Chalmers, a gallant and handsome young man, went down the halls with several of his boys. They knocked on doors with their pistol butts and sabers, where they were met by sleepy officers or their wives

General C. C. Washburn (1818–1882), the Union commander of western Tennessee and northern Mississippi. He was one of the most competent of the Civil War political generals, but he also was unable to bring Forrest to heel. After the war, he was governor of Wisconsin and the founder of General Mills.

or mistresses. Another beautiful young woman opened the door, saw the mud-covered Confederate, and threw her arms around his neck. "For God's sake, sir, don't kill me!" she cried.

"Not for worlds, madam!" he said, returning the embrace.

Alec Chalmers was having a good day.

Nearby, General Buckland was awakened by a sentry. He dressed quickly and ran to the barracks to turn out his men. General Washburn, headquartered in the elegant Williams Mansion on Union Street, was also awakened by the yelling and shooting. He ran out the back door without bothering to dress. (He would have been captured if he had.) The fleet-footed corps commander and future governor of Wisconsin ran a half a mile to a fort in his nightshirt. Jesse Forrest made off with his best uniform.

Ralph P. Buckland, the commander of the District of Memphis, was the only blue-coat general who reacted promptly and well on August 21.[6] He rallied part of his men and resisted. Colonel Neely saw more than one thousand Union infantry and some cavalry forming just south of Elmwood Cemetery and immediately attacked with six hundred men. The Yankees delivered a heavy volley which halted the first attack. General Forrest, meanwhile, had decided that the prison was too strong to be captured, so he had doubled back, dispersed the Third Illinois Cavalry and captured most of its horses. Seeing that Neely was checked, he rode up with his Escort and Colonel Bell's men, screamed "Forward!" and charged. He routed the cavalry and chased it across the gardens of several local houses. He was riding King Philip that day, and the silver-colored horse again proved that he was a great jumper.

The U.S. infantry and dismounted cavalry retreated to
the building of the State Female
College. Forrest decided that
their position was too strong to
attack. Meanwhile, dozens of
excited women—overcome by
their enthusiasm—rushed into
the streets, dressed in night-
gowns and robes, to greet their

Forrest's cavalry in the streets of Memphis.

muddy heroes. In places, men briefly greeted their families, and Bill Forrest
rode off to visit some friends! Meanwhile, on Georgia Street, Colonel
Logwood, who followed Captain Forrest's detachment, found a line of
U.S. infantry blocking his way. He rode over them with the Twelfth Tennessee. He pushed on to where Wellington Street runs into Mississippi
Avenue, where he found a Union artillery battery hurriedly loading their
pieces. Logwood charged and overran it before the men could finish getting
ready. He reached the Gayoso, posted a squad in each direction, and joined
the search for Federal officers.

The Union garrison and various commands at Memphis totaled
more than ten thousand men. Forrest's raid was the military equivalent
of kicking over an ant hill. By 9 a.m., Union resistance was becoming
organized, and Forrest ordered a withdrawal to the southern suburbs of
the city. He left with six hundred prisoners and hundreds of horses and
mules.

In the meantime, Bill Forrest had finished his social call and decided
to rejoin his command. He found that Colonel Logwood had withdrawn
at 10 a.m., so he turned south down Main Street. Here he ran into a Union
detachment. Bill attacked at once "with such absolute recklessness" that
it broke and ran, Captain Dinkins recalled. Forrest himself, at the head of
his men, shot and killed a Union soldier. The Rebel scouts now galloped
down Union Street, hollering like wild Indians and firing at every Yankee
they saw. When they reached DeSoto Street, they spotted Colonel Logwood's column heading south, so they joined it. Logwood and Captain

Forrest rejoined the main body half an hour later. The Southerners then turned south and headed back toward Mississippi.

Meanwhile, Colonel Matthew Starr's Sixth Illinois Cavalry set out in pursuit. It halted when the Northerners found Forrest's rear guard across their path in line of battle. Because the Rebels outnumbered him two to one, Starr declined to attack. Instead, he drew his sword and dashed out alone, challenging the Rebel commander to a personal duel. Forrest responded immediately, and the two leaders were soon locked in mortal combat in a scene out of the Middle Ages. The fight ended when Forrest ran his saber clear through Starr's chest and out his back, killing him instantly. "He was no more in the hands of General Forrest than a butterfly would be in the claws of an eagle," one Rebel recalled. The leaderless Federals then suddenly remembered that they had an urgent appointment back in Memphis and left for it immediately. Thus ended the pursuit.

That afternoon, Captain Charles W. Anderson returned to Memphis under a flag of truce. Four hundred of Forrest's prisoners had been captured in their underwear. Forrest wanted to exchange prisoners; barring that, he wanted their clothes and shoes. Some of the prisoners were convalescents. Forrest wanted food for them. He waited for an answer at Nonconnah Creek, about six miles from Memphis.

Because it was against Grant's orders, Washburn refused to exchange prisoners. He did send the uniforms and shoes, as well as two wagons full of food. Remarkably, he also asked for his uniform back. Equally remarkably, Forrest returned it to him via Captain Anderson. In return, Washburn later went to Forrest's tailor and had a fine new uniform made for the Confederate general. He also sent him a large bolt of gray cloth and a sizable amount of lace for Forrest's staff, as well as a beautiful sword. Forrest gave the sword to Major Strange.

While two Union officers delivered the wagons of food to the prisoners, Forrest told his men to make themselves comfortable. He made sure he was overheard. He wanted to make the officers (and therefore General Washburn) think that he might attack Memphis again. As soon as the officers left, he mounted his men and headed back toward Panola. He was certain the Northerners in Memphis had telegraphed General Smith concerning the raid (as indeed they had), and he did not want Grierson's cavalry to cut him off. Forrest had deliberately not cut the telegraph wires because he wanted Whiskey Smith to know he was in Memphis and thus encourage him to retreat.

Back in Memphis, General Hurlbut noted that he had been removed from command because he could not keep Forrest out of western Tennessee, but his successor, Washburn, could not keep Forrest so much as out of his bedroom.

The Wizard, meanwhile, was concerned—about Private H. C. Odom, the color-bearer of Company C, Second Tennessee, who had been seriously wounded in the arm. Forrest was mounted and ready to pull out when he realized the young man was about to be left behind. He took the private by the hand, made sure that he was placed in an ambulance and told him "I will see that you are taken care of."

"How far are you going tonight, General?" Odom asked.

"To Hernando."

"I think I can stand it to go that far. I don't want to be left here!"

Forrest assigned four members of the Escort Company to take care of Odom. They took him to a doctor's home, where he remained for three and a half months. Odom never forgot General Forrest's kindness and concern for his welfare. He never completely got over his wound. He was still suffering from it in 1887.

Meanwhile, back at Oxford, Chalmers handled his troops with such great skill and stubbornness that A. J. Smith had no clue that Forrest and his men had left. On August 21, when he first received word that Forrest was in Memphis, General Smith simply did not believe it. The next morning, he finally captured Oxford. Then confirmation arrived that Forrest had indeed been in Memphis. "We are gone up!" he cried. He hurriedly ordered the town burned and prepared to retreat to Holly Springs. He was afraid that Forrest might strike into western Tennessee and cut him off.

Many of the Yankees knew what it was like to have Forrest on their trail and they didn't like it one bit, so their retreat was rapid. One Northerner, a Captain Cannon, sought all of the information he could get about the Confederate general from Mr. Cook, a local resident. Cook described him and asked Cannon if he and a hundred of his men would like to meet Forrest with the same number.

"No," the captain snapped. "I do not care to fight Forrest alone, with my whole company. I hope I may never see him."

One Oxford lady asked a Federal officer why General Grierson did not attack General Forrest with his greatly superior force. The Yankee replied, "Madam, our entire force of seven thousand cavalry would not fight one of Forrest's brigades unless our infantry was there to support them. Not one of our brigades would fight one of his regiments, no regiment would fight one of his companies, and no company would ever charge a pair of Forrest's old boots if they were laying in the road."

The Federal retreat was characterized not only by its speed but also by wanton pillaging, malicious cruelty, and rape. Mrs. Thompson owned a beautiful mansion which contained $100,000 worth of furnishings. General Hatch had already personally pillaged it, stealing silver plates, china, silverware and other items of value, and carried it off in an ambulance. General Smith personally sent one of his staff officers and a detachment of men to destroy it. She was given fifteen minutes to remove her few remaining valuables before it was burned. As she was leaving, a squad of Union soldiers robbed her at gunpoint. She was left with nothing. Other defenseless citizens were whipped or sexually molested. One Federal recorded, "The public square was surrounded by a canopy of flames; the splendid courthouse was among the buildings destroyed, with other edifices of a public character [including churches]. In fact, where once stood a handsome little country town, now only remained the blackened skeletons of the houses, and the smoldering ruins that marked the track of war." Like Sherman and Sheridan, Whiskey Smith was cruel. Many of the women and children of Oxford were left absolutely destitute. They had no food until Chalmers's staff could bring up some poor Confederate rations.

The Yankees began their hasty retreat to Holly Springs about an hour before nightfall. Chalmers was soon informed and moved rapidly to try to cut him off. But Smith's men moved too rapidly and Chalmers was not able get behind them. A few days later, Smith burned the bridges over the Tallahatchie, ending the pursuit.

On August 23, the rumor spread in Memphis that Forrest was back. The news was telegraphed to Sherman, who sent orders for Smith to return to Memphis. He wanted his forces available in case Forrest struck into middle Tennessee. He was still worried that the Wizard of the Saddle might sever his supply lines. He did not know that Smith was already retreating. Union gunboats, meanwhile, shelled the area south of Memphis. They thought Forrest might be regrouping here for another attack. They missed him by about fifty miles. He was already back in Mississippi.

Although Forrest's raid did not accomplish all of its objectives, it was nevertheless an unqualified success. The fifth Union attempt to capture northern Mississippi was a clear failure. The most important agricultural region left to the Confederacy remained in Rebel hands. And in Richmond—now that it was too late—the government at last decided that the proposal to turn him loose against Sherman's supply lines might not be such a bad idea after all.

# CHAPTER 17

# RIDING AGAINST SHERMAN

*The sight of the Confederate battle flag always*
*reminded me of the immense bravery of the soldiers*
*who served under it.*
—U.S. General Josiah Chamberlain (1828-1914)

After A. J. Smith escaped, Forrest took his corps to Grenada, where it spent a week. On August 30, Forrest reorganized his command into two divisions of two brigades each. Chalmers's division had Black Bob McCulloch's men from Missouri, Texas and Mississippi, and a new brigade under Colonel Rucker, made up of Tennessee troops. Buford had Brigadier General Hylan B. Lyon's Kentucky brigade[1] and Colonel Tyree Bell's Tennessee brigade.[2]

Rucker's first brigade had been dissolved after he was seriously wounded at Harrisburg. This new brigade consisted of four old and distinguished regiments, which were led by Colonels Duckworth, Neely, John U. Green and Francis M. Stewart, all of whom were senior to Rucker. They took Rucker's appointment as an affront and refused to serve under him or obey his orders. The result was a near mutiny. A sharp letter from General Chalmers did nothing to alleviate the situation so the general, who was a fine orator, made an earnest appeal to the troops and the officers about the need to disregard personal ambition and the necessity of obeying orders. Chalmers persuaded the brigade to obey Rucker, Forrest and himself. Then Forrest relieved all four colonels of their commands, arrested them, and sent them to Mobile for courts-martial. None of them ever held another command or served under Forrest again except Duckworth, who was restored to the command of the Seventh Tennessee in April 1865—just in time to surrender it.[3]

Rucker's brigade also included McDonald's Battalion under Lieutenant Colonel David C. Kelley. Ironically, Rucker's attempt to return to duty was premature. He had to step down for reasons of health and command devolved on the lieutenant colonel.[4] Any of the four colonels would have become brigade commander had they accepted Rucker.

Meanwhile, the Yankees seized Fort Morgan, Alabama, which controlled the sea access to the port of Mobile on August 23. On August 30, General Maury telegraphed Forrest: "You have again saved Mississippi. Come and help Mobile…We are very weak." Bedford quickly dispatched McCulloch's brigade and ordered Chalmers to move the rest of his division to Alabama. Forrest himself arrived in Mobile in early September. Here he met Mary and was entertained by General Maury and his wife. Mrs. Maury invited several lady friends who wanted to meet the great hero. "His natural deference to the fairer sex gave them all much pleasure," Maury wrote later. "He was always very courteous to women, and their presence was very bright and entertaining. He had for women that manly courtesy and respect that marks the truly brave man. Under all circumstances he was their defender and protector from every sort of wrong. His wife was a gentle lady, to whom he was careful in his deference."

Forrest was in Mobile only briefly. He rejoined to his command and was returning to Alabama, followed by Rucker's brigade, when Lieutenant General Richard Taylor, who had succeeded Maury as departmental commander, ordered that his train be stopped in Meridian, Mississippi.

Richard Taylor was the son of President Zachary Taylor and Jefferson Davis's brother-in-law. Educated at Harvard and Yale, he was a highly successful planter before the war. He superbly commanded the Louisiana Brigade during Stonewall Jackson's Valley Campaign, competently defended Louisiana in 1863, and showed genuine military genius during the Red River Campaign of 1864 when, with 8,800 men, he smashed a Union army of thirty-two thousand. Taylor also knew how to think strategically. He and Forrest first met at his headquarters in Meridian on September 5, and they were very impressed with each other. Taylor said Forrest "was a tall, stalwart man, with grayish hair, a mild countenance, and slow and homely speech." Taylor told Forrest that he considered Mobile safe for the moment and that he thought the priority should be helping John Bell Hood's army. The only way to do this was for Forrest to attack Sherman's communications.

Lieutenant General Richard Taylor (1826–1879) was the son of President Zachary Taylor, the brother-in-law of Jefferson Davis, and a military genius. As commander of the Army of Western Louisiana, Taylor routed a Union Army of thirty-two thousand men and pursued it two hundred miles. He had 8,800 men at the time. Prior to that, he had distinguished himself in the Shenandoah Valley, working for Stonewall Jackson. It was Taylor who turned Forrest loose against Sherman's supply lines.

To my surprise, Forrest suggested many difficulties...and asked many questions...I began to think he had no stomach for the work; but at last, having isolated the chances of success from causes of failure, with the care of a chemist experimenting in a laboratory...Forrest's whole manner changed. In a dozen sharp sentences, he told his wants, said he would leave a staff officer to bring up his supplies...informed me he would march with the dawn, and hoped to give an account of himself in Tennessee.

Taylor immediately telegraphed Jefferson Davis and informed him that he was sending Forrest against Sherman's supply lines. He also telegraphed Braxton Bragg:

> Regarding the campaign in Georgia of paramount impor-
> tance, I have ordered...the operation of General Forrest's
> entire cavalry force on the line of Sherman's communications.
> This will be productive of more benefit than the detachment
> of a portion of it for the defense of Mobile. The former is of
> general, the latter of local, interest.

But it was already too late: Sherman captured Atlanta on September 2.

Taylor's locomotive brought Forrest back twenty miles to the north, where he joined his Rucker's troops. The train picked up the men and headed for Tupelo. Forrest sat in a corner all by himself, lost in contemplation.

A lady who knew him happened to be on the train and, seeing him alone, decided to join him. A staff officer told her not to. He was thinking and not quite himself, and did not want to be bothered. She persisted. When she approached, he growled at her. She fled, to the amusement of the staff, "her face red, and her pin feathers bristling. "I've never been spoken to before like that by any man!" she declared. "General Forrest is a boor!"

Shortly after, the general rejoined his staff. He greeted the lady as if he just saw her for the first time. They were soon busy talking. At one point, the lady asked why the hair on his head was gray and his beard was black.

"I don't know, ma'am, unless it's because I work my head more'n I do my jaws."

Back in Georgia, John Bell Hood was extremely anxious to cut Sherman's line of communications. He sent John Hunt Morgan on a raid into east Tennessee, but that gallant commander was killed on September 4. General Wheeler went on an equally disastrous raid from September 1 to 8. He briefly cut the Nashville & Chattanooga, but the Yankees reacted quickly and Wheeler returned with a decimated command. Now everyone was clamoring for Forrest. On September 11, Hood telegraphed Taylor to "hasten Forrest and get him to operating upon Sherman's communications. It is all-important."

To accompany him on his raid, Forrest selected Buford's division and Rucker's brigade, which was still under the command of Colonel Kelley: 3,543 men, of which 450 did not have horses. He left Chalmers to defend northern Mississippi while he was gone, but he could not spare very much—one brigade, a cavalry regiment and an assortment of state troops. Forrest requested the return of McCulloch's brigade, but he was denied as the high command sent it to western Florida, to guard against a possible offensive by the Union forces from Pensacola against Mobile.

For all his improvisation in battle, Forrest planned everything he could to the most minute detail and left nothing to chance that he didn't have to. When he was planning, he was as intense as a chess master. He either sat immobile, his chin in his chest, or paced up and down, his hands clasped together behind his back. He was doing this at the Tupelo depot when a lieutenant colonel confronted him. Forrest had offended him somehow, and the man wanted an apology or satisfaction. Forrest looked at him, turned around, and walked to the other end of the depot. The colonel followed him and confronted him again. Suddenly Forrest's left fist flew up into the colonel's chin, lifting him completely off the ground and knocking him unconscious. Forrest resumed his pacing, never sparing the officer a second glance.

After ten days of intensive planning, the raid began on September 16. As the command left Verona, Mississippi, each man carried five days' cooked rations, forty rounds of ammunition, a blanket, and one change of clothing. Forrest had been promised help from Roddey and Wheeler. When he met the latter on September 20, he found his command in a rough state. He wrote to Taylor:

> General: I have the honor to state that I met Major-General
> Wheeler today at Tuscumbia…He claims to have about two
> thousand men with him; his adjutant-general says, however,

that he will not be able to raise and carry back with him exceeding one thousand men, and in all probability not over five hundred. One of his brigades left him and he does not know whether they are captured or have returned, or are still in Middle Tennessee... [H]is whole command is demoralized to such an extent that he expresses himself disheartened, and that, having lost influence with the troops, and being unable to secure the aid and co-operation of his officers, he believes it to the interest of the service that he should be relieved from command. General Roddey is sick, but has ordered three regiments—I suppose about nine hundred men—to report to me.[5] You will see, therefore, that I can expect but little assistance, but will nevertheless go ahead; am all ready and will move in the morning and have my command across the river tomorrow night. General Wheeler has turned over to me what he has of my old brigade, numbering sixty men. When I left it with him last November it then numbered over two thousand, three hundred for duty. I hope to be instrumental in gathering them up. I am satisfied that many will flock to me and I shall greatly need the arms telegraphed for to-night.

Apparently, Taylor was concerned that Wheeler might try to pull rank and assume command of the raid. He signaled Forrest that he should rely on his own judgment, "reporting directly to me and acting independently of any officer, regardless of rank, with whom you may come in contact."

As we have seen, Sherman's main supply line was the Nashville & Chattanooga Railroad. By now, his engineers had a secondary supply line, the Tennessee & Alabama Railroad, in operation south of Nashville. To the surprise and consternation of the Yankees, Forrest appeared in their rear at Athens, Alabama, about sundown on September 23, and cut the railroad between Decatur, Alabama and Nashville. He chased the Union garrison into a fort three-fourths of a mile from town, captured two trains, cut the telegraph wires, tore up the railroad tracks and captured one hundred horses.

When dawn broke, Forrest had the fort surrounded but its commander, Colonel Wallace Campbell, commander of the 110th USCT Regiment, refused to surrender. Forrest deployed his men to attack but could not bring himself to do so without meeting with Campbell. The Union colonel refused to capitulate unless Forrest could convince him that he had a much superior force. Forrest, of course, was a master of this game, and soon convinced Campbell that he had eight thousand to twelve thousand men and twenty-eight guns. (He actually had 3,500 men and eight guns.) "The jig is up, haul down the flag," Campbell told his men when he returned. He surrendered at 1 p.m. One reason he gave up was that 469 of his 594 men were African-American, and he did not want to be in any way responsible for another Fort Pillow.[6]

The real fighting that day occurred when seven hundred Michigan and Ohio troops under the command of Lieutenant Colonel Jonas Elliott tried to relieve the garrison. They were checked and then encircled by Rucker's brigade (still under Kelley) and the twenty-four-year-old Lieutenant Colonel Raleigh R. White's Fourteenth Tennessee Cavalry. Elliott was mortally wounded within a mile of the fort, and the relief force was forced to retreat, leaving behind 106 dead and wounded. In this short, sharp engagement, Lieutenant Colonel Jesse Forrest was so badly wounded that he would not return to duty until just before the end of the war.

With the fort conquered and relief column destroyed, Forrest turned against Blockhouses Number Five and Six. Number Five surrendered without a fight. Number Six was located four miles north of Athens and guarded an important railroad trestle. Its commander, Captain Poe, would not surrender and, in fact, fired on Private West when he approached the blockhouse under a white flag. West later joked that his handkerchief was so dirty that perhaps the Yankees thought it was a black flag. Forrest, however, didn't think it was funny at all. He was furious. "Does that damn fool want to be blown up? Well, I'll blow him up then!" He had Morton's artillery fire shells from his three-inch rifled cannons right through it. A white flag quickly appeared but Forrest pretended not to see it until the Yankees broke out a larger white flag. "Hell, we thought it was Roddey," a Union sergeant snapped at one of Forrest's staff officers. "If we had known it was Forrest, we would have quit before the guns opened up." These were the first of eleven block-houses captured and destroyed during this expedition. These surrenders brought Forrest's total haul for the day to 1,900 men, two twelve-pounder howitzers, thirty-eight wagons, two ambulances, three hundred horses, two trains complete with locomotives, and tons of supplies.

Forrest sent the POWs back south of the Tennessee River and turned north toward Pulaski, the next major town on the railroad. The next blockhouse defended the Sulphur Creek Trestle, eleven miles north of Athens. It was seventy-two feet high and spanned a deep ravine four hundred yards wide. It was defended by a square redoubt three hundred feet in length, which was manned by four hundred whites and 620 USCT under Colonel William Lathrop. Its defenses included rifle pits, and two well-placed twelve-pounder howitzers. Two other blockhouses were within supporting distance.

Kelley's brigade, supported by Roddey's men, charged the rifle pits, and the Yankees fell back into the fort. Forrest conducted a personal reconnaissance and it seemed impregnable but, after several hours of maneuvering, Morton got four of his three-inch rifled guns within eight hundred yards of the fort. Forrest sent Major Strange forward with his usual surrender demand, but the Yankees refused in a particularly arro-gant manner. Morton's horse artillery opened up and its aim, as usual, was excellent. Colonel Lathrop was among the first ones killed and his second-in-command, Colonel J. B. Minnis, a Tennessee Unionist, was badly wounded and knocked senseless. One Confederate shell blew up the first Union gun almost immediately and the second one was soon dismounted. In a two-hour bombardment, Morton's guns fired eight hundred rounds into the blockhouse. When Forrest sent another sur-render demand, it was accepted immediately. "You have killed and wounded nearly all my men," the commander told Forrest. "Your shells, sir, bore through my blockhouse like an auger!" Morton said later that the inside of the blockhouse reminded him of a slaughter pen. More than two hundred Federals were killed or seriously wounded, 973 others were captured, twenty wagons and teams were captured and 350 cavalry horses were taken, along with a healthy amount of other supplies.

The next day, September 26, Forrest captured a U.S. Government corral at the Brown Farm near Pulaski, which was occupied by two thousand black civilians. It was filthy. All the former slaves were in dirty rags and many were absolutely destitute. Forrest ordered them to remove their clothes and beds from their "miserable hovels" and then burned "this den of wretchedness." Almost two hundred hovels went up in flames.

Compared to Forrest, all other Civil War generals were amateurs when it came to destroying railroads. Up until this point, Sherman had been almost contemptuous of the way the Confederate cavalry (mainly Wheeler) destroyed railroad tracks. They ruined them the same way Federal cavalry destroyed them. They would uproot rails, set bonfires and throw the rails on top, or heat the rails and tie them around trees. While certainly dramatic, this method demanded a lot of time to destroy even a mile of track, and Sherman's well-practiced engineers would have the railroad repaired in one or two days. (In my opinion, these experts were the unsung heroes of Sherman's advance on Atlanta.) Forrest and his men, however, took a less dramatic but nonetheless more effective approach. They would quickly build small fires all along the length of the railroad. Although not spectacular, these fires were enough to cause the metal tracks to expand, crack, and buckle. Trains could not run on them, miles of rails would have to be replaced, and that process demanded the time-consuming process of uprooting the now-warped and worthless rails. It took weeks instead of days to repair a railroad that Forrest destroyed. To add insult to injury, the wood Forrest's men used was cord wood which the Yankees themselves had cut and stored in order to use it to fuel their locomotives.

There was heavy skirmishing around Pulaski during which Colonel William A. Johnson was seriously wounded on September 27. At the same time, Forrest rode along the railroad almost as far as Pulaski, burning bridges, destroying culverts and ruining rails. Major General Lovell H. Rousseau, commanding the District of Tennessee, signaled, "This is much more than a raid; I regard it as a formidable invasion, the object of which is to destroy our lines, and he will surely do it unless met by a large cavalry force, and killed, captured or routed. The cavalry, supported by infantry, can fight and defeat him, but he must be caught. He will not give battle unless he chooses to do so."

When he reached the outskirts of Pulaski, Forrest pushed the garrison back into its earthworks, but decided the place was too strong to attack. About 10 p.m., he withdrew in the direction of Fayetteville and the Nashville & Chattanooga Railroad—Sherman's main supply route. Unfortunately for the South, the strategic situation had changed, and it was too late. Sherman had defeated Hood's army, which had withdrawn into Alabama and the interior of Georgia. In the more than three weeks during which there was no significant fighting, Sherman had been able to build up a small stockpile of supplies. An army in combat consumes supplies much more rapidly than does an army in camp. It also freed tens of thousands of Yankees for the defense of the main supply route. Had Forrest been turned loose two months earlier, these men would have been tied up fighting Hood and would not have been available for use against the raiders. Additionally, Sherman now had less need for imported supplies. In June, the Georgia countryside had offered little in the way of food. Now, the corn and other crops were ripe, and the Northerners had plenty of food just for the taking.

It rained in sheets in Tennessee during the last week in September, as Forrest's columns struggled eastward over poor middle Tennessee roads. One evening, one of Morton's caissons got stuck and Captain Andrew McGregor of the Fourth Tennessee dismounted and tried to help the gun crew free it. They emptied the ammunition chest to lighten the load and McGregor held the torch while the men tried to push the caisson out of the ruts, but again they failed. At that moment, General

Forrest rode up. He was tired, wet, cold, and angry at the slow progress of the march.

"Who has charge here?" he snapped.

"I have, sir," McGregor responded.

"Then why in hell don't you do something?" Then he unleashed a torrent of the infamous Forrest profanity.

McGregor waited until the general paused.

"I'll not be cursed out by anyone, even a superior officer!" he declared. Without further ado, he opened the lid of the ammunition chest, threw the burning torch inside, and glared at his commander.

Forrest's mouth undoubtedly fell open and his eyes got wide. From his angle of vision, he could not see that the box was empty. He expected an explosion at any second. For the only time on record, Nathan Bedford Forrest hastily turned his horse around and ran away as fast as he could.

When the general reached his staff, he declared that a dangerous lunatic who had just escaped from the asylum was trying to blow himself up, along with the general and the artillery train. He ordered Captain Anderson to go arrest Captain McGregor.

A laughing Anderson returned a few minutes later and told Forrest and the staff what had really happened. Forrest pretended that he, too, thought it was funny, and joined in the general mirth. The officers noticed later, however, that there were only two people around whom the general was very careful not to curse—Mary and Captain Andrew McGregor.[7]

By September 29, Forrest's men had been in action for fifteen consecutive days. They had lost forty-seven killed and 293 wounded. During that time, they had captured more than three thousand prisoners (one thousand of them black), eight hundred horses, eight guns and dozens of wagons, ambulances, weapons, and assorted other equipment. That same day, Forrest pulled to within fifteen miles of Tullahoma, when he received word from his scouts that sizable Union columns were converging on him

General George H. Thomas (1816– 1870), "the Rock of Chickamauga," tried to destroy Forrest's cavalry in 1862, 1864, and 1865. Despite the fact that he had overwhelming forces and may have been the best general in the Union Army, he failed on all three occasions.

from all directions. That same day, Grant ordered Sherman to drive Forrest out of middle Tennessee *before* beginning his "March to the Sea." Sherman replied that he was forming an army under General Thomas to attack Forrest and had dispatched one division to Chattanooga and another to Rome, Georgia, for use against the Wizard of the Saddle. He also asked for reinforcements.

The columns converging on Forrest did, in fact, constitute an entire army— more than thirty thousand men led by George Thomas. There were eight separate columns after him, commanded by Generals Rousseau, John Schofield, James B. Steedman, John T. Croxton, Joseph D. Webster, Granger, Washburn and A. J. Smith. They were later joined by another division under Brigadier General James D. Morgan. General Grant also called off an operation against the Confederate salt works in southwestern Virginia in order to provide more troops to deal with Forrest. The Wizard's command had been reduced to three thousand by casualties, POW guard details and detachments. He was now nearly surrounded and outnumbered ten to one. Even so, Forrest sent Lieutenant Nathan Boone with fifty men to cut the Nashville and Chattanooga Railroad. They did this, but the damage was a pin-prink. Forrest, however, did not believe that he could send his entire command that far east and escape Thomas *et al*.

The Federals thought they finally had the Wizard of the Saddle. Thomas told Sherman "I don't think we will have a better chance than this" to destroy him. Sherman was not completely reassured. He wired Grant on September 29 that Forrest's cavalry "will travel one hundred miles in less time than ours will ten...I can whip the enemy's infantry, but his cavalry is to be feared." He also telegraphed Brigadier General Washington L. Elliott, the chief of cavalry of the Army of the Cumberland: "Our cavalry must do more…We should at least make ten miles to his one hundred."

To meet this new threat, Forrest divided his command in two. He sent Buford to the south toward Huntsville with 1,500 men and orders to destroy the Memphis & Charleston Railroad from there to Decatur. Morton and all of the artillery went with the Kentuckian. With the rest of his command, Forrest moved west north-west in the direction of Columbia. He took Spring Hill by surprise on October 1 and captured the telegraph office, where he learned exact information as to the size, location and intentions of various Union columns. He was particularly concerned that Steedman might cut off his route to the Tennessee River.

Forrest sent the Yankees several confusing telegrams, sent them on a wild goose chase, destroyed the line, and continued west. From October 1 to 5, he destroyed four blockhouses, a large sawmill, and a huge amount of wood meant to fuel locomotives. He also captured thirty oxen, forty mules, six wagons and a stagecoach.

One Federal officer who commanded two blockhouses refused to capitulate because the Southerners had no artillery. Forrest convinced him to give up by demonstrating that he had Greek Fire, an inextinguishable incendiary mixture of fairly common items for which I will not give the receipt for, by tossing it on a stump which exploded into flames. The Northern officer surrendered, leaving Forrest in control of a truss bridge 150 feet long which he burned.

After feinting toward Columbia, Forrest turned south, burning railroad bridges and picking up a good number of recruits along the way. (It would be the latter part of November before Sherman could use the Nashville & Decatur Railroad again.) Forrest reached the Tennessee River at Florence on October 5 and found that Buford had arrived two days earlier. He had already crossed the river with his wagons, the artillery and part of the cavalry. The river was high and rising because of recent heavy rains in the mountains, and Buford had only three small boats and ten light skiffs, so the going was slow. Crossing operations continued throughout the night.

As Forrest feared, Steedman reached Florence the next day and attacked a regiment of Roddey's brigade with twelve thousand men. Barteau promptly joined the battle with his brigade and fought a brilliant delaying action through Florence to Martin's Bluff, a strong position covering the main ferry. He held the enemy off until October 8. Steedman was in the process of outflanking Barteau, and Forrest still had a thousand men on the wrong side of the river. The Rebel general immediately dropped down to where an island lay within seventy yards of the bank. He crossed over, swimming the horses and one hundred head of cattle, which he hid in a cane break on the southern side of the island.

The Yankees arrived three hours later, but they left without reconnoitering the island. The ferrying resumed that night, and Forrest escaped with his entire command except for a regiment of Barteau's brigade. These men broke into groups of companies, single companies or even smaller units, evaded the Yankees, and crossed the river at various points. All but six men rejoined Forrest over the next several days.

One veteran recalled that during the crossing General Forrest showed "considerable disregard for the Third Commandant." On one trip, he noticed a lieutenant who was not assisting with the poles or oars. When Forrest asked him why he was not helping, he replied that he was an officer and he did not feel compelled to perform that sort of duty. This remark was ill-advised to say the least, as Forrest himself was pushing a pole at the time. The general slapped him so hard in the face that he flew off the boat and into the river. Someone held out a pole and rescued him. "Now, damn you, grab hold of an oar and get to work!" Forrest ordered. "The next time I have to knock you out of the boat, I'll let you drown!"

As the last troops boarded the last boat on the morning of October 9, while Forrest checked the cane break for stragglers. He found four. "I thought I would catch some of you damned fools loafing back here," Forrest snapped. He told them they had better come with him, unless they wanted to spend the entire winter on the island.

The crossing of the Tennessee River effectively ended the raid, and Forrest immediately headed for Corinth. He had marched five hundred miles in twenty-three days, most of it behind Union lines. He had inflicted 3,500 casualties on the enemy (including more than 2,300 prisoners), captured eight guns, eight hundred horses, nine hundred head of cattle, 993 contrabands, one hundred wagons, three thousand stands of arms, an unknown number of mules, and a great amount of supplies. He had destroyed six large truss railroad bridges, about one hundred miles of track, two locomotives, fifty freight cars, several thousand feet of trestling, a saw mill, thousands of cords of wood and eleven blockhouses. At the same time, he added one thousand new recruits to his command and picked up seven hundred of Wheeler's stragglers.

But, Forrest was tired. "I have been constantly in the field since 1861," he wrote General Taylor on October 8, "My strength is failing and it is absolutely necessary that I should have some rest." He asked for a furlough of twenty or thirty days. Taylor, however, regretfully rejected his request. The South needed Forrest to in the field. Naturally, the Wizard of the Saddle answered the call.

At Henderson, Mississippi, Forrest linked up with Chalmers's division, which had only 750 men. With hardly a pause, he turned north into western Tennessee. He crossed the border on October 16 and headed for Jackson, arriving there on October 21.

Sherman had set up another primary supply line. Northern transports shipped supplies down the Ohio, Missouri and Mississippi Rivers to the Tennessee River. The cargo was off-loaded at the huge supply depot at Johnsonville.[8] A recently finished military railroad, the Nashville & Northwestern, extended seventy-eight miles from there to Nashville, where it linked up with the Nashville & Chattanooga, and carried supplies to Sherman's three armies in Tennessee and Georgia. Johnsonville was defended by ten gunboats, a fort, heavy artillery and strong ground forces. General Forrest aimed to destroy it nevertheless.

Forrest found that the western Tennessee countryside was devastated, and the attitude of the people had changed since the fall of Atlanta. They now hid their hogs and cattle from both Confederates and Yankees, and a great many men—and certainly not without cause—had given up all hope of winning the war and had deserted. Forrest rounded up many of these men and sent them south, advising Taylor to put them in the infantry at a post a long way from Tennessee. If they were on horseback and near home, they would desert again.

Forrest's presence again spooked Union commanders. Washburn estimated that Forrest had ten thousand men and expected him to plant artillery batteries at Randolph and Fort Pillow, to blockade the Mississippi. Brigadier General Morgan Smith, commandant of Memphis, thought he intended to attack the city with twenty thousand men. He had homes loop-holed for sharpshooters and constructed an inner line of cotton bales as a final defensive position. Having learned their lessons from the earlier campaigns, the Yankees abandoned all of the minor posts in western Tennessee and Kentucky and hurriedly sent their garrisons to the major fortified places, such as Columbus, Kentucky or Paducah. Forrest spent several days rounding up recruits and deserters. When it became obvious that no one from the north, south or west was going to interfere with his mission, the Wizard sent Buford northeast to Fort Heiman on the left bank of the Tennessee River, about forty miles upriver from Johnsonville, near the Kentucky-Tennessee line and 150 miles northeast of Memphis.[9] (Fort Henry was just across the river, on the right bank.) He carried with him Morton's artillery battalion and two twenty-pounder rifled Parrott guns which he had borrowed from Maury at Mobile. When they arrived on October 28, Buford posted one artillery concentration under the command of General Lyon[10] at Fort Heiman and a second one under Morton five miles upstream at Paris Landing.

Bedford's men were guided to their positions by John W. Hinson, a personal friend of Bedford Forrest's and possibly the most successful sniper in the Civil War.

"Old Man Jack" was born in 1807 and became a prosperous plantation owner in the Land Between the Rivers region.[11] Although he opposed secession, had freed his slaves and had even hosted General Grant in his home, he tried to remain neutral in the Civil War. Then, in the fall of 1862, a Union patrol captured two of his sons near Dover. They plead that they were just out hunting, but the Yankees wouldn't listen. They tied the boys to a tree and shot them out of hand. A lieutenant then hacked off their heads with his sword and a malicious sergeant stuck them on the gateposts of Hinson's home.

Men like Hinson lived by the law of the feud. He sent his family west and began studying the topography of the region in great detail. He also had a local gunsmith build him a fifty-caliber sniper's rifle which weighed eighteen pounds. It was fired from an iron tripod and could hit a target more than half a mile away. Firing from ambush, he killed the lieutenant and the sergeant.

Hinson was content to leave it at that, but the Federals learned that one of his other boys had joined the Confederate guerrillas and another marched with the Fourteenth Tennessee Infantry, so they burned Hinson's home. Hinson then took up sniping full time, except when Forrest was in the area. Then he worked fulltime as a scout for him.

Old Man Jack's favorite targets were sailors and soldiers on Federal gunboats. He would not fire on civilian transports, but he killed anyone in a blue uniform. He put a notch on his gun's barrel every time he killed a Yankee, but stopped counting after thirty-six. Estimates of the number of men he killed, however, vary from eighty to more than one hundred. "They murdered my boys," Hinson told Charles Anderson, "and may yet kill me, but the marks on the barrel of this gun will show that I am a long ways ahead in the game now and not yet done." Like thousands of people in western Tennessee and northern Mississippi, Hinson loved Bedford Forrest. After the war, he gave his famous rifle to him.

Four Union steamers from Johnsonville passed Fort Heiman on October 28, but Buford would not allow his men to fire. He wanted loaded cargo ships, not empties. His patience was rewarded the next day, when the steamer *Mazeppe* appeared, towing a barge. Buford let it pass his artillery and into the trap. Morton disabled it with three shots and, out of control, it drifted to the east bank, where its crew fled into the woods. It contained seven hundred tons of supplies, mainly shoes, blankets and warm winter clothing, but also plenty of meat and hardtack. One Rebel paddled across the river on a plank, tied a line to the abandoned vessel, and Buford's men pulled it to the west bank, much to the delight of the boys in gray.

October 30 was also a good day. The steamer *Anna* managed to run the Confederate batteries, but was so badly damaged that she sank before she could reach Paducah. The gunboat *Undine* heard the firing and steamed to its rescue. It was armed with eight twenty-four-pounder brass cannons, four on each side. In general, Confederates were fearful of gunboats; Forrest and his men, however, were not. In an hour-long battle, they beat the *Undine* so badly that its Union captain was forced to ground it on the east bank between Fort Heiman and Paris Landing, out of range of Forrest's guns.

The next ship to appear was the transport *Venus*, heading downriver. It ignored the *Undine's* signals to halt and was battered by Buford's guns. It fell back to a position near the *Undine*. The steamer *J. W. Cheeseman* also ignored the *Undine's* signal flags and was so damaged by the Southern gunners that it landed on the west bank and surrendered.

Colonel Rucker, meanwhile, arrived on the field and, with two guns, found a way through the thick forest and brush. He brought his artillery to bear on the *Venus* and *Undine*. He also brought up sharpshooters, who poured fire through the open gun ports. By 4 p.m. the gunboat was so badly damaged that its captain ordered his crew to abandon ship. The badly damaged *Venus* simply surrendered. Colonel Kelley crossed the river with two companies and soon returned to Paris Landing with the boats.

The *J. W. Cheeseman* contained general cargo, real coffee, candy (especially gumdrops), nuts, and furniture. The Rebels gave the furniture to the locals. Everything else went into their saddlebags or stomachs. "It was remarkable how quickly the boat was stripped of everything worth moving," a staff officer wrote later. The ship was too badly damaged to be of further use, so after they unloaded the cargo, the graycoats burned it.

By now, Forrest was on the field with the rest of his command. He was very pleased with his men's successes. With the captured Yankee vessels, he decided to create his own fleet, which the men dubbed the "horse marines." He offered command of the flotilla to Morton, but the captain

Gunboats of the Union Mississippi River Squadron, 1863. The USS *Key West* is on the left. On November 4, 1864, it was one of the main targets of Forrest's horse artillery. It didn't last forty minutes.

refused to have anything to do with it, so he put Lieutenant Colonel William A. Dawson of the Fifteenth Tennessee in charge. Captain Frank M. Gracey of the Third Kentucky, a former steamboat captain, commanded the gunboat. Dawson's flagship was the *Venus*, upon which Forrest mounted his two Parrott guns. Before the "fleet" sailed, Dawson demanded a private word with Forrest. He said that he would command his ships, but only on the condition that Forrest would not curse him if he lost them. Forrest laughed and told Dawson he would not hold it against him if he came back wet.

The crews practiced the nautical arts on October 31, and, the next day, they steamed for Johnsonville. Forrest planned to keep the ground and naval forces within supporting distance of each other. It rained on November 1, however, and the bad roads became worse. That night, the rain fell even more heavily. On November 2, the horses were slowed by the mud, so the boats got ahead of the cavalry. At 3:30 p.m., six miles below Johnsonville, the flotilla ran into three Yankee gunboats manned by experienced sailors. The outclassed *Venus* was damaged and "Commodore" Dawson was forced to ground it and take to the woods. The Yankees promptly retook it and Forrest lost his two twenty-two-pound Parrotts. Gracey and the *Undine* escaped, but only because Forrest's artillery arrived, deployed quickly and forced the gunboats to retire.

Part of the Union supply depot at Johnsonville.

Two miles below Johnsonville lay Reynoldsburg Island. The eastern channel was impassable and the western channel was narrow, swift and torturous. There were nine Union gunboats in the flotilla defending Johnsonville. Six of them (with a total of seventy-nine guns) steamed north of the island on November 3. Captain Gracey was forced to blow up his ship, but Forrest placed a battery opposite the Reynoldsburg Island chute, effectively bottling up two-thirds of the Union flotilla north of Johnsonville.

From the water side, the supply depot was now defended by only three gunboats, the *Key West*, *Tawah* and *Elfin* (Number Fifty-Four), a total of twenty-eight guns. The *Key West* tried to dislodge the Rebel battery at the south end of the island, but the Southern gunners hit it nineteen times in a twenty minute battle, and it was forced to withdraw.

Meanwhile, on November 3, guided by Old Man Hinson, the bulk of Forrest's artillery stealthily arrived opposite Johnsonville. With the skill of true veterans, the gunners silently placed their artillery just out of sight of the Yankees, who had no clue they were there. Directed by Lyon and Morton, the Rebel guns were perfectly positioned. The fourteen heavy guns of the Union fort at the top of the commanding hill could not be depressed enough to hit them. The gunboats could not easily hit them either.

At 1:59 p.m., in Johnsonville, work crews (mostly former slaves) were unloading barges and transports and were loading two freight trains. Union infantry and artillerymen were idling about, and many of the sailors were lounging on deck.

At 2 p.m., ten Confederate guns opened up. They fired so simultaneously that it sounded like a single loud report. All three gunboats were hit, and the sailors rushed below deck or dove into the water and swam for shore, while everyone else scrambled for safety. Both freight trains were also heavily damaged.

The Union sailors tried to get their vessels underway but without much success. One of the first shells from Captain J. C. Thrall's Arkansas battery hit the boiler inside one of the gunboats. It exploded and steam and smoke enveloped the boat. The graycoats could hear the screams of the scalded Yankees, several of whom dove through the port holes and into the river. Moments later, one of Thrall's rounds hit a magazine, and the gunboat was ripped by a huge explosion. Doomed and sinking, its crew abandoned ship as it drifted toward the barges and transports.

The other two gunboats fared little better. Only one managed to fire its guns and then only briefly. Out of control and burning, they drifted into the barges and transports, catching them on fire as well. Forty minutes later, all three were at the bottom of the Tennessee. The Southern gunners shifted their fire to the cargo ships and barges which were still at anchor. They were soon on fire and, by 4 p.m., all of them were sunk.

The supply depot itself was built up on the slope of the river bank, which rose gently over three hundred yards to an elevation of fifty feet. The huge warehouses and piled-up stores covered dozens of acres and extended for a mile downriver. As fire from the burning boats spread to the outer sheds and warehouses, the gunners shifted their fire to the warehouses. Vast stores of bacon, corn, hay, coffee, uniforms and supplies of every description were soon on fire. One of the warehouses also contained hundreds of barrels of liquor. Several shells hit it, throwing liquor barrels high into the air. Soon a river of liquor was pouring into the Tennessee. It caught on fire and continued to burn after nightfall, looking like burning lava. The smell of burning whiskey, coffee, bacon, sugar and other foodstuffs traveled for miles.

Forrest joined in on the bombardment. He named Colonel Bell and General Buford his assistants, and a major became his spotter. Morton recalled him "handling, loading and firing the piece with the enthusiasm of boy cannoneers on a Fourth of July." Captain Thrall's battery, which was nicknamed the "Arkansas Rats," performed so well that Forrest renamed them "the Arkansas Braves." One battery's sergeant remarked that that was all well and good, but he would prefer something to eat, since "We've been livin' on wind for two days." Forrest ordered an aide to go back to his headquarters wagon, where he would find four boxes of hardtack and three hams and give them to the Arkansans.

The next morning, Forrest surveyed the damage, which was tremendous. Colonel Barteau recalled that "Nothing was left unconsumed; neither gunboat, transport nor barge has escaped, and naught now remained of the large piles of stores that at noon the day before had covered several acres of the surrounding slope." Forrest turned to Morton and said, "John, if they'd give you enough guns and me enough men, we could whip Old Sherman off the face of the earth!"

As the last remaining Rebels[12] prepared to leave on the morning of November 5, a spontaneous demonstration began on the other bank. Most of the men involved were members of a black infantry regiment, but there were a large number of contrabands and white soldiers and sailors. They lined the bank of the Tennessee to swear and curse at the Rebels. Their fierce oaths easily carried over the water. Forrest ordered Lieutenant Briggs to halt and unlimber his guns. The demonstrators did not realize what was happening until Confederate shells exploded in their midst. Simultaneously, Rucker's sharpshooters opened fire. Within two minutes, the bank was clear, except for the dead and wounded.

During the entire raid, Forrest had captured or destroyed four gunboats, fourteen transports, twenty barges, twenty-six pieces of field artillery and millions of dollars' worth of supplies. Particularly gratifying was the capture of nine thousand pairs of shoes.

"Forrest terror" now ran rampant through Union ranks. Colonel Thompson, the commandant of what was left of Johnsonville, estimated that Forrest had thirteen thousand men on the left bank of the river, along with thirty-six guns—twenty of which were twenty-pounder Parrotts. Even the normally unflappable Sherman was alarmed. He signaled Grant that Forrest had twenty-six thousand men and he ordered the entire XXIII Corps to Johnsonville to pursue him. He ordered the commandant of Columbus, Kentucky, that he should burn the town, rather than allow Forrest to capture a pound of provisions. Forrest was reported as far afield as Mississippi, Jackson, Tennessee, Chicago, Michigan City, and Canada. Reports stated that he had between fourteen thousand and twenty-six thousand men under his command. On November 7, it was reported that he was planning to seize Chicago, release the Confederate POWs held there, arm them, sack the city, kill every Yankee he captured, and raise the Copperheads (Confederate sympathizers in the North) in revolt. Major General Joseph Hooker, the commander of the Department of Cincinnati, doubted these reports, but nevertheless sent troops from Indianapolis and St. Louis to Chicago.

The truth was more prosaic, but nonetheless portentous. General Beauregard, now in charge of the Confederate Department of the West, had ordered Forrest to Corinth, Mississippi. He was going to join John Bell Hood's invasion of Tennessee.

# CHAPTER 18

# THE NASHVILLE CAMPAIGN

*Strength of numbers is the delight of the timid. The valiant in spirit glory in fighting alone.*

—Mahatma Gandhi

On November 14, Nathan Bedford Forrest arrived at Florence, Alabama and assumed command of the cavalry of the Army of Tennessee. His command now included Chalmers's and Buford's divisions, plus a third new division under Brigadier General William H. "Red" Jackson,[1] and totaled five thousand men.

Although morale within the Army was high, it had been boosted by Forrest's arrival. The Confederates' material condition was problematic. Equipment and horses were also worn out. Horseshoes and nails were so scarce that Forrest ordered that wheels from farm wagons be forged into shoes and nails. He also found a chronic shortage of ammunition, but he could do little to fix that.

By now, General Sherman was about to begin his famous (or infamous) March to the Sea. His army would push southeast three hundred miles from Atlanta to Savannah, Georgia. From there, he would swing north and trap Robert E. Lee between his army and Ulysses S. Grant's, and end the war.

John Bell Hood (1831–1879). A fine brigade and divisional commander and a very brave man, "the Gallant Hood of Texas" was a mediocre corps commander and a poor army commander.

John Bell Hood did not anticipate the March to the Sea. Instead, he decided that the best defense would be a good offense. He planned, therefore, to drive north from Florence, Alabama, capture Nashville, cut Sherman's supply line, and perhaps push on as far as the Ohio.

Counting Forrest's corps, Hood had about twenty-seven thousand infantry and five thousand cavalry. To defend Tennessee, Sherman detached the Army of the Cumberland under the command of George H. Thomas. It included David S. Stanley's IV Corps (13,000 men), John M. Schofield's XXIII Corps (10,000 men), and Edward Hatch's and John Croxton's cavalry divisions (4,500 men). Thomas also had twenty-six thousand men in sizable garrisons in northern Alabama, and at Nashville, Murfreesboro, and Tullahoma, among other places.

After Forrest's arrival, Hood could not hope for further reinforcements; meanwhile, the Union high command was straining every resource to reinforce Thomas. A. J. Smith soon was *en route* from Missouri with three divisions of the XVI Corps (more than 10,000 men), as was James H. Wilson's cavalry division (4,500 men). Hood nevertheless waited to move until he had stockpiled twenty days' supplies before he moved.

Sherman began his march from Atlanta on November 16. Five days later, Hood began his own campaign. His first target was Pulaski, Tennessee, forty-five miles away. It was defended by the IV and XXIII Corps under Schofield. Forrest commanded the advanced guard which began skirmishing almost immediately with the Union cavalry screen.

CENTRAL TENNESSEE

On November 22, Forrest's men took Lawrenceburg, putting the Confederates in a position to outflank Pulaski. Schofield began withdrawing toward northward Columbia, thirty miles away. (See Map.)

The next day, a Union cavalry brigade blocked Forrest's path. He drew his men up in line of battle and ordered Colonel Rucker to keep contact with the enemy. Meanwhile, he sent Colonel Kelley around one flank, while he led the Escort around the other. Surprised and thinking they might soon be surrounded, the enemy fled to the rear in "a perfect stampede."

Before daylight on Thursday, November 24, Schofield began marching north from Pulaski toward Columbia, hoping to get there before Forrest. Fortunately for the North, a Union infantry division did get there first, giving Schofield command of the Duck River crossings. Forrest's men did not attack—Schofield was too strong—but then held the Confederate front until November 26, when Hood's main body, finally came up. That day, Rucker's brigade probed the Union lines, supported by Captain Edwin S. Walton's battery.[2] Generals Chalmers, Forrest and S. D. Lee, and several members of their staffs observed the operation.

Watching through his spy glass, Chalmers was impressed with Walton's aim and suggested that they ride over to his location for a closer look, which they did.

A few minutes after the generals arrived, Yankee artillery, angered by Walton's goading fire, opened up on Walton with thirty to forty guns. "The earth trembled," one of Chalmers's staff officers recalled. About one hundred shells landed in the area in about a minute. One of Walton's caissons exploded, adding to the bedlam. Everybody quickly dismounted and "hit the dirt," except General Lee. He sat calmly on his horse, not the least bit excited or disturbed. General Chalmers said later that he felt ashamed—until he saw General Forrest on the ground, yelling for one of his officers to "Get away from here!" Then he felt better.

During the evening of November 27/28, Hood met with Forrest and the other senior Confederate officers at a house, three miles south of Pulaski on the Pulaski Pike. Here he outlined a bold and imaginative plan to encircle and destroy Schofield's two corps.

That night, Hood prepared to turn Schofield's position at Columbia. Anticipating this, Schofield evacuated the town and burned the bridges behind him. The next day, Forrest carried out the first phase of Hood's plan. He managed to get Jackson's and Chalmers's divisions across the Duck. (Due to Yankee opposition, Buford did not get across until November 29.) In the meantime, Union Major General James H. Wilson, one of the war's "Boy Generals" (he was twenty-seven years old at the time and the commander of Thomas's Cavalry Corps), arrived and took command of his four divisions (about twelve thousand men).

James H. Wilson was the most successful "Boy General" of the war. Born in Illinois in 1837, he graduated from West Point in 1860, ranking sixth in his class, and had risen rapidly, serving in the Port Royal, South Carolina Expedition of 1861–1862, and then became aide-de-camp to General George McClellan. Soon after, he was assigned to Grant's staff as a lieutenant colonel and took part in the Vicksburg campaign. Promoted to brigadier general in October 1863, he fought at Chattanooga and became chief engineer of Sherman's forces which relieved Knoxville in early 1864. Recognized as an extremely talented young officer, he commanded a cavalry division in Sheridan's corps in the Shenandoah Valley. Then, at age twenty-seven, he was brevetted major general and given command of Thomas's cavalry.

When he took up his command, Wilson wrote, "If only Forrest will wait for us, we shall soon be able to cope with him." But General Forrest never waited for anybody. He seized the initiative and attacked Wilson's cavalry, driving them back five miles. Not only did Rebel horsemen cross the river, but their engineers had placed pontoon bridges over the river and battle-hardened infantry crossed them in force. Wilson advised Schofield to fall back to Franklin as rapidly as possible.

Forrest's goal was to cut the vital crossroads at Spring Hill, cut off Schofield's retreat, and bag his six infantry divisions. Bedford pushed Wilson off the battlefield to the northeast and sent Sul Ross's Texas brigade in pursuit to keep him busy. His plan was foiled when Stanley's corps arrived at the double. Worn down by a week of constant action, and down to four rounds of ammunition per man, Forrest's men were

The Plain of Franklin, which Rebel officers dubbed the Valley of Death, 1864.

in no position to engage a Union corps in a slugging contest.

The next eighteen hours were some of the most controversial in the history of the war. Schofield somehow managed to pass his entire army and his eight hundred wagons north toward Franklin right under Hood's nose, due to conflicting orders, misunderstandings, and timidity. Because Forrest cannot be blamed for Schofield's escape, to go into detail on this controversy—one of the more enduring of the Civil War—is beyond the scope of this book. Suffice it to say that while I believe that Hood, Cheatham and/or John C. Brown were responsible we will never know absolutely for sure who was to blame.

Forrest, for his part, blamed Hood. The army commander called a breakfast meeting at the Nathaniel F. Cheairs House (now the Rippaville Plantation) and blamed his subordinates for allowing Schofield to escape. Forrest was offended and stormed out of the house. Hood followed close behind. On the porch, Forrest turned on the general who had lost a leg at Chickamauga and the use of an arm at Gettysburg, and growled: "Sir, if you were a whole man I'd whip you to within an inch of yer life!"

At Franklin, which is twenty-seven miles south of Nashville, Schofield took an exceedingly strong position south of the town. To close with the Federals, the Rebels would have to cross the Plain of Franklin, an unprotected plateau, in the face of an undefeated and well-entrenched enemy, backed by six hundred pieces of artillery. Schofield was confident that Hood would not attack, but Hood did—and did so without artillery support. The Plain of Franklin was later called "the Valley of Death" by the survivors.

All of Hood's generals objected to the attack, but Hood would not listen. Forrest met with Hood at his command post on Winstead Hill and almost begged him not to strike. He asked Hood to give him one infantry division. He would cross the Harpeth River, he said, and flank the Yankees out of their position within two hours. Hood coldly told him to prepare his cavalry to attack. To make matters worse, General Hood divided the cavalry by placing Chalmers (the strongest mounted division) on the left and Jackson and Buford on the right with whom Forrest rode.

Before the Rebel infantry moved forward, Forrest, Jackson, Buford and three thousand men crossed the river. They attacked Wilson, who had five thousand men present, supported by Wood's infantry division, who had almost as many. For once, the Yankees fought Forrest to a draw. Wilson later admitted that, if Forrest had advanced with his entire command, he might have won the battle.

The Battle of Franklin was a five-hour slaughter, leading Hood's officers to dub the Plain of Franklin the Valley of Death. The Rebels lost, 6,252 men in all, including 1,750 killed. The Northerners lost 2,326. Twelve Confederate Generals were among the casualties, including six who were killed, including Patrick R. Cleburne, and fifty-six regimental commanders were killed or wounded. It was arguably the worst battlefield defeat the South suffered during the entire war. Sam Watkins later wrote that it was "the blackest page in the history of the war...the finishing stroke to the independence of the Southern Confederacy...Would to God that I had never witnessed such a scene!"

Schofield withdrew across the Harpeth that night and headed for Nashville. He linked up with the rest of the Army of the Cumberland the next day, December 1. General Thomas formed a rough semicircle south of Nashville, with both flanks on the Cumberland River. Hood followed mainly because he had to in order to keep his army together. The troops, broken in spirit, were beginning to desert. If he had retreated, they would likely have deserted *en masse*, especially the men from Tennessee. He stopped in front of Nashville and awaited Thomas's next move.

Forrest, of course, never waited for the Yankees to do anything. On December 3, he sent Colonel Kelley with three hundred men and two guns to attack Union shipping on the Cumberland. That same day, Forrest himself suddenly appeared at Blockhouse Number 2 on the edge of

Nashville and captured it. A trainload of African-American soldiers rushing to the rescue ran into an ambush themselves. A shot from one of Morton's guns blew away the locomotive. The blacks took to the woods beside the tracks before Forrest could bring up Buford's division and overrun them, however.

The next day, December 4, Forrest captured two more blockhouses and two stockades, and took 150 more prisoners.

On December 5, Hood sent Forrest to Murfreesboro with Jackson's and Buford's divisions, as well as Major General William B. Bate's small infantry division. He retained Chalmers's command in front of Nashville. This was another bad decision on Hood's part.

As soon as Forrest approached Murfreesboro, the Union garrison commander, Major General Lovell Rousseau, scrambled into Fort Rosecrans on the edge of the town. It was two hundred acres in size and very well constructed, and Rousseau had more than seven thousand men. Forrest conducted a reconnaissance and correctly concluded that it could not be taken by assault; it could only be taken by siege or trickery. He decided to try the latter.

The next day, December 6, Hood sent Forrest two more small infantry brigades, commanded by Brigadier Generals Joseph B. Palmer and Claudius W. Sears.[3] Forrest, who now had 6,500 men, devised a plan to capture the fort by guile. He would advance with the infantry in the center and the cavalry on each flank. According to the plan, the infantry would fall back, luring the Yankees into a trap. When they came out of the fort to pursue the Rebel infantry, it would turn on them. Simultaneously, the cavalry would attack them on both flanks and encircle them. The plan failed, however, because Bate's division, which had been badly shot up at Franklin was in such poor spirits that its feint turned into a full-blown rout. General Bate bravely tried to rally his troops but without success.[4] Only Brigadier General Thomas B. Smith's brigade was not routed.

Forrest plunged in to attempt to stem the retreat. "Rally men, rally! For God's sake, rally!" Forrest cried. Forrest called on one of the regimental color bearers to stop, but he would not. Forrest shot him in the back as he ran away. He then seized the flag, but the infantry would not rally to the colors. Forrest screamed, cursed and even cried. Nothing worked. The retreating men passed around him like a river around a large island. Gaus, who was right behind Forrest, blew his bugle until it was shot from his mouth twice but to no avail. Nothing could stop the rout.

Not all Confederates behaved so disgracefully. Sent to support Buford's division, Morton's battery held until 2 p.m., when Forrest ordered it to withdraw to the north immediately. By that time, almost all of Morton's horses had been killed, and it appeared he would have to leave at least one of his "bull pups" on the field. The young captain would not hear of it. "I will take off my gun or die in the attempt!" he cried. Part of the Second Tennessee helped him push his gun off the field while Lieutenant Colonel G. H. Morton, the regiment's acting commander,[5] launched a mounted counterattack and checked the Union pursuit.[6]

John Morton's coat was penetrated by eleven different bullets and his hat was shot off his head three times. The captain, however, was unscathed.

Some of the other units behaved well, too. At one point in the battle, he had ordered Richard Alley, the short, smooth-faced, bare-footed color bearer of the Fifty-Fourth Virginia Infantry, to hand him his flag. Young Alley would have none of it. Surprised at the rebuff, Forrest explained that he wanted to use the banner to rally the troops. "General," Alley responded, "I can take care of my own flag; just show me where to plant it!" Forrest pointed to a hill that the Yankees had just captured and ordered him to retake it. The boy rallied his regiment, took the hill, and won the respect and admiration of Bedford Forrest. Afterwards, every time he saw Alley, Forrest saluted him and Alley would dip his flag. Forrest would smile and proclaim: "There goes that little feller that totes his own flag!"[7]

Meanwhile, Forrest ordered a charge by Red Jackson's cavalry division, while Buford struck the Union rear and pushed as far as the court house. As a result, the Union advance was checked and the garrison fell back into the fort. The entire battle was indecisive, but it was clear that Fort Rosecrans would not be taken.

For the next week, Rousseau remained in Fort Rosecrans, and Forrest's outposts kept a watch on him, while the rest of his men foraged, captured and burned a train (bagging two hundred prisoners and sixty thousand rations in the process) and destroyed the railroad between Murfreesboro and La Vergne.

On December 9, ice, sleet and snow swept middle Tennessee for five days. Grant and Halleck pushed Thomas to attack Hood, but he wisely refused to do so until he was ready. He particularly concentrated upon building up his cavalry corps to the point it could compete with Forrest's. Grant grew so exasperated that, on December 13, he ordered General John A. Logan to proceed to Nashville to relieve Thomas if he did not attack. Logan was not to take over if Thomas had moved.

Before Logan arrived, however, Thomas launched a massive offense on December 15, throwing his fifty-five thousand men against Hood's force of less than thirty thousand. During the first day of the battle, the Rebels were pushed back but their thin line did not break. At 4 p.m. the next day, however, the Army of Tennessee was routed and Hood lost another 6,000 men, including 4,500 captured.

Colonel Edmund Rucker was among those cut off by the speed of the Northern advance. He ran into a detachment of Michigan soldiers and soon was in hand-to-hand combat with U.S. Colonel George Spalding. He swung his sword with all of his might but missed, and the sword flew out of his hand in the process, so he grabbed the Northern officer and took his sword from him. At that moment, several of the Union soldiers came to the rescue of their colonel and fired at the Rebel. One of the bullets shattered Rucker's left arm. He was quickly captured and carried to the rear, where he was questioned by Generals Wilson and Hatch. He told them that General Forrest had just arrived with his entire command "and will give you hell tonight!" At that moment, one of Rucker's regiments launched a local flank attack and threw the Union front into confusion. Wilson immediately ordered all of his men back to camp for an all-around defense. Rucker's ruse—Forrest was nowhere near the place—may have saved the crippled army from immediate and total destruction.

Spalding, Hatch and Wilson respected Colonel Rucker and took good care of him. He spent the night in Hatch's bed, and General Wilson stayed up all night, tending to the wounded Southerner. The arm, however, could not be saved. When the two men parted company, Wilson gave him a flask of good whiskey. Spalding, meanwhile, picked up Rucker's sword. Twenty-five years later, Rucker was an incredibly successful businessman in Birmingham, Alabama, and Spalding had to make a business trip to the city. He brought the sword with him and returned it to its owner.[8]

On the evening of December 15, Forrest received an order from Hood to prepare for an emergency. Forrest ordered his men to concentrate at Wilkerson's Cross Roads. They had some way to go. Buford was operating against Union gunboats near the Hermitage and Jackson had just captured a wagon train in the Yankee rear, along with 150 prisoners and two hundred thousand rations, most of which would have to be destroyed.

The next evening, Forrest received word that the Army of Tennessee had been routed. Hood ordered him to retreat to Pulaski by way of Shelbyville. He went by way of Lillard's Mills on the Duck River instead. Forrest's disobedience of orders probably saved the army, because it enabled him to join it as a rearguard at the critical moment instead of later. The Wizard also sent Buford to cover his wagon train (including the wounded and four hundred Yankee prisoners), one hundred head of cattle and four hundred hogs.

On December 17, Wilson led the pursuit with nine thousand of his cavalrymen and several thousand infantrymen. Chalmers's cavalry division and part of Stephen Lee's corps were hard-pressed but prevented him from breaking through and falling on Hood's wagon trains and demoralized infantry. The fighting was desperate. In the fighting, which lasted well into the night, General Chalmers personally killed one Yankee and wounded another in hand-to-hand combat, and General Lee

Edward Cary Walthall (1831–1898), one of the South's youngest generals. He led the infantry portion of Forrest's rearguard during the retreat from Nashville.

was wounded in the foot leaving Carter L. Stevenson in command. Chalmers's men spent the night in defensive positions along Rutherford's Creek. Hood encamped for the night at Spring Hill. The next day, the army withdrew toward Franklin, while Forrest rejoined the main army on the 19th and took charge of the rear guard.

Rutherford Creek was almost at flood stage and it was December 19 before Wilson could push across it. The next day, Thomas constructed a floating bridge across the stream, and the pursuit resumed. Forrest retreated behind the Duck River at Columbia, destroying every bridge across the river for miles. He met with Hood at the Vaughn Mansion on the evening of December 20 and told him that the army would be destroyed if Hood did not give him three thousand infantrymen. He asked Hood to send him Major General Edward C. Walthall and his battered but stalwart division. Hood agreed immediately, and he also allowed Walthall to select any troops in the army to go with him. The Mississippian (and at age thirty-three, the youngest major general in Hood's army) picked his own division and the remnants of five brigades. His total strength was 1,900 men, about six hundred of whom had no shoes.[9] This gave Forrest a total of 4,900 combatants to face Wilson, who had nine thousand cavalry and thirty thousand infantry. He had to hold the Yankees at bay until Hood reached the Tennessee River at Bainbridge, almost one hundred miles away.

When word spread that Forrest was in command of the rear guard, many of the tired and exhausted Rebels rushed to join it. Desertions, which had totaled hundreds per day, stopped almost entirely. Forrest's determination spread throughout the rear guard and indeed much of the army, even though he and his men knew the situation was worse than desperate. Throughout the retreat, General Forrest seemed to be everywhere, radiating cheerfulness, and determination. Captain W. A. Goodman, Chalmers's adjutant, recalled, "…at no time in his whole career was the fortitude of General Forrest in adversity, and his power of infusing his own cheerfulness into those under his command, more strikingly exhibited than at this crisis…But he alone, whatever he may have felt (and he was not blind to the dangers of our position), spoke in his usual cheerful and defiant tones, and talked of meeting the enemy with as much assurance of success as he did when driving them a month before. Such a spirit is sympathetic, and not a man was brought in contact with him who did not feel strengthened and invigorated…"

On Wednesday, December 21, Hood's tattered army marched south from Columbia toward Pulaski. General Hatch arrived on the north bank of the river and started shelling Columbia. Forrest sent out a white flag. Shouting across the river, he told Hatch that there were no soldiers in the town, except for the wounded from both sides. He also asked Hatch to exchange two thousand prisoners. Hatch sent the request back to Thomas, who rejected it. The process caused a two-hour delay in the pursuit, which may have been what Forrest really wanted in the first place.

Hatch crossed the river that night and Thomas brought up his pontoon bridges. They were quickly put together by an infantry brigade which was led by Forrest's old antagonist, Abel Streight of Mule Brigade fame. The Union infantry began crossing on December 22, while Forrest took up a strong defensive position six miles south of the town. Wilson regained contact with Forrest's rearguard on December 23, and pushed it back nine miles in heavy fighting.

With inadequate forage and no time to rest, Forrest's artillery teams gave out and he was forced to use oxen, even though he did not have enough of them. He moved most of his wagons and half of his artillery out of danger, unhitched the oxen, and went back for the other half. He thus kept his guns and wagons just out of reach of the enemy.

Although cheerful around his men, Forrest had no patience with Hood's staff. When the general's Quartermaster Department asked Forrest for mules, he refused to send them. The next evening, Major A. L. Landis of the Department came to ask why they had not arrived. Forrest replied, "You go back to your quarters and don't come here again, or send anybody here about mules! The order will not be obeyed." He went on to threaten to come to army headquarters, tie the quartermaster's legs together in a double bow knot around his neck, and strangle him to death with his own shins. He also told the staff officer that Hood should send inspectors to every wagon in the army and throw away all surplus baggage, tents, adjutant's desks, etc. He reminded Landis that he and his men had captured every mule, wagon and ambulance in his command, along with everything else.

"No man in the world ever had greater responsibilities resting upon him than did General Forrest on the retreat from Columbia," Captain Dinkins wrote later, "but he met them with great skill and cheerfulness. With a force of less than five thousand men, he was called to hold in check an army of fifty thousand. The writer does not believe that any other man on earth could have done this. Forrest represented in war what Cicero did in literature. He had a love for right and a sincere respect for any demand for fairness. He was strong in character, profound in strategy, and forceful in battle. We will never see his like again."

The retreat was almost unendurable for the infantry. Snow and freezing rain fell frequently. The roads were slick, and the mud was deep in places. The ice was broken by the wagons, leaving jagged pieces to cut the feet of the barefoot men. Once an ox fell dead from exhaustion. Before its blood could congeal, the men stripped its body of its hide and wrapped it around their feet. But at least the pursuit had slowed, because Wilson outran his supplies and, due to some poor staff work, Thomas's pontoon bridges were sent to the wrong place.

Forrest passed through Pulaski on December 24. He had to destroy some ammunition and wagons and General Buford was seriously wounded in one of the skirmishes.[10] Several miles to the south, Forrest found a fine defensive position at Anthony's Hill—only forty-two miles from Bainbridge—and ordered Jackson to hold Pulaski while he improved it.

Hood was forced to abandon most of his ordnance train fourteen miles south of Anthony's Hill because he needed the horses and mules to transport bridging to Bainbridge. Forrest wanted to save this train if possible.

On Christmas Day, 1864, Wilson's men approached Forrest's position through a defile formed by two steep, wooded ridges. Morton's artillery was placed in hidden positions on the summit, from which it could sweep the ground below. The infantry held the hill, with two four-hundred-strong cavalry brigades (Sul Ross's Texans and Armstrong's Mississippians) in support. Jackson's cavalry division held the flanks, with Chalmers positioned a mile and a half to the right. In contrast to his usual practice, Forrest held three small infantry brigades in reserve.

Wilson's men knew Forrest too well to rush blindly into an attack. One U.S. cavalry brigade advanced cautiously, pushing a twelve-pounder Napoleon by hand up the hill. They were only fifty yards from the crest when Forrest ordered Morton to fire. The Southern infantry whooped and charged down the hill, capturing the gun, 150 Yankees and three hundred horses.

Wilson now brought up his infantry and began a turning movement, only to run into Jackson and Chalmers. The battle lasted three hours. Armstrong's men ran low in ammunition, and their general three times asked permission to retreat, but Forrest would not allow it.[11] Finally, with his men out of ammunition, Armstrong appeared in person and shouted at General Walthall (who was mounted beside Forrest): "Won't you please make that damn man there on that horse see that my men are forced to retire?"

After a few moments of silence, Forrest sympathetically explained to Armstrong that he was only buying time for Hood to cross Sugar Creek, and Armstrong and his boys were playing a noble part in that effort. Shortly thereafter, about 4 p.m., Forrest ordered the retreat, which

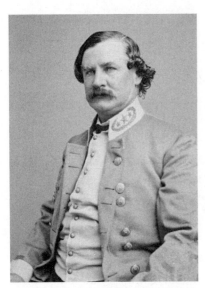

Major General Benjamin Franklin Cheatham (1820–1886). Forrest disapproved of his morals and pulled a gun on him and threatened to kill him during the retreat from Nashville. Cheatham was postmaster of that city at the time of his death.

was well conducted. He destroyed several ammunition wagons Hood had been forced to abandon.

About 1 a.m. on December 26, Forrest's men reached Sugar Creek, fourteen miles south of Anthony's Hill. The men washed off the mud, built large fires, dried clothes and got some rest. Hood, meanwhile, had reached Bainbridge and sent the mules back to retrieve the abandoned wagon train and artillery.

"The weather had become worse and worse," General Wilson recalled. "It was freezing cold during the nights, and followed by days of rain, snow and thaws. The country, which was poor at best, had been absolutely stripped of forage and provisions by the march of contending armies. The men of both forces suffered dreadfully, but the poor cavalry horses fared still worse than the riders. Scarcely a withered cornstalk could be found for them, and thousands, exhausted by overwork, famished with hunger, or crippled so that death was a mercy, with hoofs dropping off from the frost and mud, fell by the wayside never to rise again."

About dawn, Wilson caught up with the Confederate rearguard. This was his last chance to destroy Hood's army, and he knew it. Fortunately for the Rebels, a dense fog covered the landscape, and Wilson's vanguard advanced slowly and tentatively. In the snow, sleet and freezing rain, elements of Walthall's division and Forrest's cavalry launched a sharp local counterattack that stalled Wilson's pursuit.

As Forrest reached the Tennessee, he heard shooting and cannon fire to his right—Union gunboats were shelling Hood's pontoon bridge. Racing ahead, Forrest came upon a quartermaster.

"Any idea who shootin' down thar?" he asked.

"No, I don't. But I reckon it's prolly Ole Forrest. He's the only one fool enough to try an' capture a Yankee gunboat."

"Well, I'm dead certain it ain't Ole Forrest. That's the name the boys call me."

The QM squirmed and hee-hawed. Forrest just smiled and rode off.

Forrest's cavalry and General Cheatham's corps were the only Confederate commands left on the north side of the Tennessee on December 27. Cheatham approached Forrest and demanded that he give way, so Cheatham's infantry could cross the river ahead of the cavalry.

Bedford Forrest did not like Ben Cheatham, who was a drinker and womanizer. Even during the Nashville campaign, he had a tryst with Jessie Peters, the wife of Dr. Peters, the man who had murdered General Van Dorn for "violating the sanctity of my home" by seducing his wife.[12] Early in the campaign, Mrs. Peters had asked for a private meeting with Bedford. He granted the interview, but only within sight of Captain Tyler and other members of his command. He avoided being alone with her. Her spacious mansion was along the route of march and it would have been very convenient for Forrest to headquarter there for the night, with a woman of easy repute within arm's reach, so to speak. But Bedford was not about to be unfaithful to Mary. He selected less commodious headquarters a half a mile away.

Cheatham's demand that his men receive preference aroused Forrest's temper. He went for his gun and aimed it at Cheatham's head. Let the best man cross first, Forrest exclaimed. Fortunately for Cheatham, Stephen Lee (who Forrest respected) was nearby. He galloped forward and broke up the altercation. But Forrest and his men crossed first on December 27, and the campaign ended when Ben Cheatham's command marched over on December 28. Wilson arrived just as the Confederate engineers swung their floating bridge to the southern side. Afterwards, the remnants of the once-proud Army of Tennessee headed toward Tupelo. Before he left, John Bell Hood acknowledged Forrest as the savior of the army.

So did everyone else. Private R. R. Hancock of the Second Tennessee, for example, came upon a Confederate infantryman during the retreat. The man was barefooted but he still had his rifle and a large piece of meat stuck on his bayonet. Hancock rode beside him a while and the soldier asked him to which unit he belonged. Forrest's Cavalry, Hancock replied.

"How I do love Forrest's Cavalry!" the infantryman exclaimed. "I love the very ground that they walk on. Had it not been for Forrest's Cavalry, Hood would not have got out of Tennessee with a single man." As Hancock rode off, the grateful soldier even offered to divide his food with him.

Of Forrest's performance in the thirty-five day campaign, Colonel D. C. Kelley (his second-in-command in 1861) wrote, "The part which he took in the Hood retreat from Nashville...giving the minutes practical details, showed him capable of handling an army of any size. All this while, he was activity engaged in covering retreat, inflicting upon the enemy blow after blow, until his capture of men and artillery induced them to cease pursuit."

Even Forrest's enemies praised his conduct. On January 20, 1865, General George Thomas was at Eastport, Mississippi, where he wrote his official report of the campaign. Of Forrest, he said:

> Forrest and his cavalry...formed a powerful rear guard, made up of detachments from all his organized force, numbering about four thousand infantry, under General Walthall, and all his available cavalry, under Forrest. With the exception of his rear guard, his [Hood's] army had become a disheartened and disorganized rabble of half-armed and barefooted men, who sought every opportunity to fall out by the wayside and desert their cause to put an end to their suffering. The rear guard, however, was undaunted and firm, and did its work bravely to the last.

# CHAPTER 19

# THE LAST BATTLE

*To submit to necessity involves no disgrace.*

—Publilius Syrus

After separating from the Army of Tennessee, General Forrest took his command to Corinth, to defend what was left of that part of the country. During his absence, Grierson had raided the area, smashed the Mobile & Ohio from Corinth south, overran Forrest's camp for dismounted soldiers at Verona, and pushed on to Vicksburg, which he reached on January 5, 1865. He marched four hundred fifty miles, took six hundred prisoners, destroyed eighty miles of track, burned a shoe factory, and inflicted heavy damage on the region's food reserve and infrastructure. During the first week of January, U.S. Colonel William J. Parker led a raid into northern Alabama, defeating Roddey's cavalry, and destroying Hood's pontoon bridge train (eighty-three boats), one hundred fifty wagons and four hundred mules. At the same time, law and order was breaking down as deserters from both sides, newly freed and runaway slaves, jayhawkers, outlaw gangs, and assorted thugs roamed the area. General P. G. T. Beauregard recommended to

General Samuel Cooper, the adjutant general of the Confederacy, that all of the cavalry from the Chattahoochee in western Georgia to the Mississippi River be placed under one commander: Forrest.[1] General Taylor concurred, and Beauregard made the appointment on January 28, 1865.[2] Exactly a month later, Bedford Forrest was promoted to lieutenant general.

Forrest was also on Sherman's mind. On January 21, he wrote to Thomas, "I suppose Forrest is again scattered to get horses and men, and to divert attention. I would like to have Forrest hunted down and killed, but doubt if we can do that yet."

By this time, Lieutenant Colonel Jesse Forrest had recovered from the wound he had suffered at Athens and returned to duty. Bedford quickly moved to restore law and order in much of the department and made Jesse his point man in the effort. Bedford ordered that soldiers caught committing crimes against the general public were to be punished "even to extermination." He reminded his men that "kindness to bad men is cruelty to the good." Outlaws were caught and hanged; hundreds of deserters were returned to their units, but Forrest's men could not be everywhere at once, and the plague of lawlessness continued to rage, especially in isolated, rural areas.

Forrest knew the end of the war was near. "[I]t will only be a question of time as to when General Lee's lines at Petersburg will be broken, for Grant is wearing him out with unlimited resources of men and money..." Although he realized there was little hope, Forrest acted as if there were hope in abundance. He gave most of his men a twenty-day furlough, instructing them to return home and rest and get new clothes and replacement mounts. They were promised another twenty-day furlough within the next twelve months if they returned with a well-armed and mounted recruit. This order was issued on January 1. The men left immediately, some of them riding all night through a terrible snowstorm, so they could spend a little more time at home. Sul Ross's men remained on duty because they were from Texas and thus could not return home. At the end of twenty days, most of Forrest's men returned to their units. In some regiments, all of them did.

Forrest did what he could to rationalize his forces. He ordered that no one leave camp, to minimize desertion. Old men and boys were conscripted or allowed to enlist. But it was not enough.

In 1861, excluding slaves, the North had a white population advantage of almost 4 to 1 over the South. In addition, it had sufficient money to hire tens of thousands of foreign mercenaries, including 200,000 from Germany, 150,000 from Ireland and 60,000 from Great Britain and Canada. African-Americans provided 190,000 more, including 70,000 free blacks from the North and 120,000 mostly former slaves from the South. By early 1865, it was able to bring the full weight of its numerical, monetary and industrial

Major General James H. Wilson (1837–1925), the Union commander who finally defeated Nathan Bedford Forrest. After Selma, his troops seized Columbus, Georgia, and Andersonville, and captured Jefferson Davis.

superiority to bear. Forrest did what he could to rationalize his forces. He ordered that no one leave camp, to minimize desertion. He reassigned all white teamsters to combat units and replaced them with black Confederates. The South had lost the initiative on all fronts. Not even Nathan Bedford Forrest could assume the offensive. Instead, he had to consider how to face threats from multiple directions, including Memphis, Vicksburg, Baton Rouge, and northern Alabama as well as from General E. R. S. Canby's army west of Mobile. In all, he had seven-five thousand Yankees with which to contend. He and Taylor were certain that the main blow would come from Wilson in north Alabama, but they had no way of knowing if there would be more than one offensive or from where. Forrest therefore, kept his command somewhat scattered, with plans to concentrate against General Wilson when he attacked.

While Forrest waited, James H. Wilson assembled the largest and best equipped cavalry corps to ever appear on the North American continent. He had ruthlessly confiscated all of the horses and mules he could get his hands on in Tennessee and Kentucky. Even the governor of Tennessee and vice president-elect of the United States, Andrew Johnson, lost his carriage horses to Wilson. By February, sixteen thousand of Wilson's twenty-seven thousand men were mounted with more horses arriving every day. He organized them into five divisions. Even more impressively, thirteen thousand of them were armed with Spencer Repeating carbines, which used metallic cartridges—instead of paper ones—and were (and remain) considered the best individual combat weapon of the war. To meet the Federal onslaught, Forrest had less than ten thousand men in his entire department. And his was the last organized body of Confederate troops in the region. General Hood resigned on January 13 and, the following month, the Army of Tennessee (now under Joseph E. Johnston's command) was sent to North Carolina to protect Lee's rear against General Sherman.[3]

Camp life is monotonous and boring. In order to conserve his resources as he waited for the action, Forrest placed a ban on horseracing and prohibited the recreational discharge of firearms, leading to even more boredom. One day, several of the bored troopers marked off a course—right in front of the general's headquarters—and raced horses in defiance of the order. Forrest and his staff came out to watch, and the corps commander cheered and even placed bets. After the last race, the men raised three cheers for General Forrest. As they turned to ride off, however, the guards arrested them. Those involved in the racing spent the rest of the day carrying heavy fence posts as punishment, Lieutenant Willie Forrest among them. He recalled how sore his shoulders were afterward, but at least he and his comrades weren't bored.

In February 1865, Forrest held seven thousand Federals prisoner in the interior of Mississippi. On February 17, General Thomas sent his provost marshal, Colonel John G. Parkhurst, under a flag of truce to discuss a possible prisoner exchange, or at least shipping shoes, uniforms and blankets to them with Forrest. Thomas also sent Captain Lewis M.

Hosea with him. A recent West Point graduate, Hosea was ordered to "keep his eyes open" and gain whatever military intelligence he could about the Rebels, the state of the surrounding countryside, and especially the current mindset of General Forrest.

Parkhurst, Hosea, and a guard of twenty men left Eastport, Mississippi on February 21 and were well below Corinth before they ran into their first Rebel outpost. They were taken to Rienzi, where Forrest met them, accompanied by Charles Anderson (now a major) and Judge Robert L. Caruthers, the governor-elect of Tennessee, whose authority was limited to wherever there were Confederate Tennessee soldiers. The meeting began at 9 p.m. on February 23. Forrest made a point to dress well (he probably wore the uniform sent to him by General Washburn) because he did not want the Yankees to know how destitute the Confederate Army really was. The conversations continued until 4 a.m. Hosea later wrote home about Forrest:

> I was at the time…struck by what then seemed the 'aristocratic mien' of General Forrest…The general effect is suggestive of notables of the Revolutionary times…and to our unaccustomed eyes the rich gray uniform with its embroidered collar…added much to the effect produced.
>
> I could not but observe the quickness of apprehension and decision displayed by Forrest in seizing the entire thought intended to be conveyed…To think quickly and concretely, and to decide likewise, seemed to be his mental habit. There was about his talk and manner a certain soldierly simplicity and engaging frankness and I was frequently lost in real admiration.
>
> His habitual expression seemed rather subdued and thoughtful, but when his face lighted up with a smile, which ripples all over his features, the effect is really charming…His language indicates a very limited education, but his impressive manner conceals many otherwise notable defects…He invariably omits the final 'g' in the termination 'ing,' and many words

The University of Alabama, 1859. The Rotunda and every building in this photograph was burned by Wilson's raiders on April 4, 1865.

are inexcusably mispronounced, and he always uses the past participle in the place of past tense in such words as 'see' (as 'I seen' instead of 'I saw') etc...In a very short time, however, these pass unnoticed. He speaks of his success with a soldierly vanity, and expresses the kindliest feelings toward prisoners and wounded.

When the Yankees mentioned that Wilson was a West Point graduate, Forrest replied that he knew nothing of West Point tactics; everything he knew came from active campaigning. Forrest did note, however, "I always make it a rule to get there first with the most men." Later, imaginative authors changed this statement to "Git thar furstest with the mostest men." He also expressed his opinion that revolvers were much superior to sabers, and that he said would count it a favor if Thomas and the Union commanders would hang every guerrilla they got their hands on.

Forrest and his Northern guests eventually reached an agreement vis-à-vis the prisoner exchange. As part of the deal, the Yankees ran food relief trains to the citizens of Corinth and surrounding area, which had been so devastated by the war. Forrest gave his word that none of it would be taken for military use.

Rain delayed the exchange. March 1865 was one of the wettest months on record, and the rain washed out the railroad in several places.

That month, too, Wilson began his long-anticipated offensive in northern Alabama. There was little doubt that one of its objectives would be Selma, Alabama. It possessed large iron-working plants (by Confederate standards), arsenals, metal working shops, and even a small navy yard. Except for Richmond and the Shreveport, Louisiana-Marshall, Texas area, it was the most significant industrial site still in Rebel hands. It was connected by rail to the iron and coal region around Elyton (now Birmingham), and it had rail and river links to Meridian, Montgomery, Mobile, and the eastern Confederacy.

Wilson crossed the swollen Tennessee River on March 18 with four divisions—twenty-two thousand men,[4] along with three batteries of horse artillery, 250 wagons and a pontoon bridge train. He marched eighty miles through the moun-

Nathan Bedford Forrest near the end of the war.

tainous part of northern Alabama in four days, began to cross the Black Warrior River near Jasper on March 22, and reached Elyton by March 30. Meanwhile, he sent a brigade under John T. Croxton to burn the state university at Tuscaloosa.

Forrest had already moved Chalmers and two of his three brigades east to defend Selma. On March 26, he ordered Jackson to Tuscaloosa, eighty miles north of Selma, where he would be in position to attack Wilson's flank and rear. Unfortunately, Wilson's scouts intercepted a dispatch to Jackson. Wilson thus learned Forrest's plans and knew that, if he moved quickly, he would be able to burn the pontoon bridge over the Watauga, isolating Jackson on the wrong side of the river and forcing him to look for another way to join Forrest. If he moved quickly enough, he would perhaps prevent Forrest from concentrating against him. Wilson did move quickly. Less than three thousand of Forrest's cavalrymen were up when the main blow fell.

On the morning of March 31, Wilson captured Montevallo and destroyed four iron furnaces, a rolling mill and five coal mines. Then, at

1 p.m., Wilson attacked the Rebel forces south of the town. The defenders consisted of Roddey's small brigade, Crossland's very small Kentucky
brigade, and a handful of militia units under Brigadier General Dan
Adams. Thus began a running battle that would last forty-eight hours,
almost without pause, and end fifty miles south of where it began.

Vastly outnumbered, Forrest fought as fiercely as possible, in the
apparent hope that ferocity itself could somehow substitute for a lack of
men. He engaged the Yankees at Ebenezer Church north of Plantersville
with his Escort and very little else—less than one hundred men. Four
companies of the Seventeenth Indiana Mounted Infantry attacked him,
and the combat was soon swords against revolvers. In the melee, Forrest,
who was riding the magnificent King Philip, made an appealing target.
After he shot one Yankee dead, five more attacked him. The general
fought with his revolver until he was forced to use it to parry a saber
blow, which severed the hammer of his revolver. A Rebel private shot
and killed this man before he could strike at Forrest again. Forrest turned
to flee, but found Yankees to the front and on each side of him—and a
two-horse wagon blocking the road. Without missing a beat, however,
King Philip jumped the wagon, clearing it by several feet. Everyone who
saw the leap was astonished.

Now, only Captain James D. Taylor of the Seventeenth Indiana faced
Forrest. He slashed the general's right arm; the left-handed Forrest ran
him clean through. "If that boy had known enough to give me the point
of his saber, instead of the edge, I should not have been here to tell you
about it," Forrest told General Wilson later.

The next clash occurred at Bogler's Creek near Plantersville and
around the town itself, where Forrest and two thousand men fought nine
thousand extremely well-armed Union soldiers. The vaulted Wizard of
the Saddle was finally defeated in the field. Some of his men were cut off
and had to break out to the west. They escaped but had, in effect, been
pushed off the battlefield. Forrest fell back into Plantersville, where he
and Dan Adams went directly into the telegraph office and wired General
Taylor, "The Yankees are coming!" They had just finished when the
Northerners poured into the town. Adams escaped, but Forrest was

jumped by a "big Dutchman." He kept cutting the general with a sword which, fortunately, was not sharp "... but it made me mighty mad." Forrest pistol got caught and he could not draw it until he had been struck several times. When he finally did get it out, he dropped his reins, grabbed the man by the hair, and fired two rounds into him.

Red Jackson, meanwhile, was looking for another way to cross the river. Just then, Brigadier General Croxton's U.S. brigade crossed the road to Selma. It passed right through Jackson's division, between the rear of his cavalry and the front of his artillery and wagon train. Croxton turned north, followed by Jackson, who was off on the military equivalent of a wild goose chase. On March 31, Jackson was only fourteen miles further from Selma than Wilson. On April 1, Jackson was fifty-three miles from the town, and Wilson was only nineteen miles away. Jackson's bad move also allowed another Union detachment from McCook's division to capture and burn the Cahawba River Bridge, over which Forrest and his Escort had already crossed. It was now impossible for Jackson to join Forrest via the Montevallo-Selma Road, as planned.

General Taylor was in Selma on April 2. About 10 a.m., he recalled, "Forrest fought as if the world depended on his arm. He appeared, horse and rider covered with blood, and announced the enemy was at his heels, and that I must move at once to escape capture. I felt anxious for him, but he said he was unhurt and would cut his way through, as most of his men had done."

At Forrest's insistence, General Taylor boarded his train at 2 p.m. and headed back for Meridian. It was good that Forrest was so insistent as Taylor's train was immediately pursued by the Yankees and he escaped by an eyelash.

Wilson now bore down on Selma with 13,500 men. Forrest had only 3,000 men to defend three and one half miles of earthworks—1,600 of them were untested Alabama militia. He posted Roddey on the right, Armstrong's brigade on the left and the militia in the middle. The militia did not want to fight. Forrest gave them two choices: they would occupy the center or he would toss them into the river. At 4 p.m., when the Yankees attacked, however, they collapsed immediately. At the cost of

359 men, Wilson crushed the hopelessly outnumbered defenders and took almost two thousand prisoners. Again, Forrest had to cut his way out. He and the Escort held open the escape route (the Montgomery Road (over the Alabama River) for the rest of the cavalry. Near Burnsville, Forrest killed another Union soldier, his thirtieth and final kill of the war.

As night fell, Forrest was searching for a bivouac site for the remnants of his command when he heard women screaming. Most of the Escort rushed to a nearby house and found eight Union soldiers ripping the clothes off three women they intended to rape. The Federals cried for mercy, but no quarter was given and all eight were shot down immediately. Some historians consider this an atrocity. I disagree. Shooting would-be rapists is the best thing to do with them.

That same night, Lieutenant George Cowan learned from a captured Yankee that a detachment of the Fourth U.S. Cavalry was camped nearby. Soldiers from this regular unit had murdered the popular Captain Sam Freeman two years earlier, and Forrest's men had neither forgotten nor forgiven the crime. After persuading Forrest to remain behind, Cowan attacked. Amazingly, the Yankees did not post guards. Forrest's men fell on them with, as General Thomas described it, "the ferocity of a wild Indian," killing thirty men and taking five prisoners.

Later that night, Forrest and the Escort escaped down the Burnsville Road and travelled across country to Plantersville, where they captured a Union hospital. Forrest paroled the nurses and lightly wounded and did not bother the doctors and the more seriously wounded.

Wilson, in the meantime, requested a truce and a meeting with Forrest. The Rebel general, Wilson recalled, was depressed and had his arm in a sling. "Well, General," Forrest said when he met the young officer, "you have beaten me badly, and for the first time, I am compelled to make such an acknowledgement."

"Our victory was not without cost," Wilson graciously replied. "You put up a stout fight, but we were too many and too fast."

Wilson asked Forrest to surrender. He refused, but the meeting nevertheless became very cordial. "We were treating each other like old acquaintances, if not old friends," Wilson recalled. They even dined together.

The next day, Forrest moved west to Marion, where he found "several" of his brigades and his artillery on April 4. Wilson headed for Montgomery, which he reached on April 12, and then to Georgia. Forrest moved on to Gainesville, where his command enjoyed several days of rest.

The war was winding down. Richmond had fallen the same day Selma did. A week later, Robert E. Lee surrendered at Appomattox. Jefferson Davis fled south, hoping to join up with Forrest and to form a new army under him and Kirby Smith in the Trans-Mississippi. Wilson's men would later capture him.

Perhaps realizing that there was a chance that he might fall in what apparently were the last days of the war, Forrest wrote a reflective letter to his son Willie. In it, he attributed his survival in battle due to the prayers of his wife and mother, and he called upon his son to shun his father's "wicked and sinful ways." He wrote:

> If I have been wicked and sinful myself, I would rejoice in my heart to see you leading the Christian life which has adorned your mother... What I desire most of you my son is never to gamble or swear... As I grow older I see the folly of these two vices, and beg that you will never engage in them... Be honest, be truthful, in all your dealings with the world. Be cautious in the selection of your friends. Shun the society of the low and vulgar. Strive to elevate your character and to take a high and honorable position in society... Keep this letter prominently before you... should we meet no more on earth.[5]

On April 29, Dick Taylor boarded a railroad handcar at Meridian, and two of his soldiers "pumped" him to a farm twelve miles north of Mobile, where he met General Canby. A Union band struck up "Hail Columbia," but a considerate Canby ordered the tune changed to "Dixie." Not to be outdone, Taylor requested that they return to the original tune.

The two generals agreed on surrender terms based on the agreement reached between Sherman and Johnston in their first meeting in North Carolina. Taylor sent Forrest word that hostilities had ceased. According to the agreement, if the U.S. government did not accept the terms of the accord, fighting could resume upon forty-eight hours' notice.

The U. S. government did indeed renounce the Sherman-Johnston agreement. Taylor and Canby met again at Citronelle, forty miles north of Mobile, on May 4, and reached new terms, which Taylor praised for their "liberality and fairness." On May 6, he signed the dispatch, ordering Forrest to surrender. But no one was sure he would. Sherman, for example, wrote to Grant, "…we will have to deal with numberless bands of desperadoes, headed by such men as Mosby, Forrest, Red Jackson, and others, who know not and care not for danger and its consequences." To his wife, Sherman wrote, "There is great danger of the Confederate armies breaking up into guerrillas, and that is what I most fear. Such men as Wade Hampton, Forrest, Wirt Adams, etc., never will work and nothing is left for them but death or highway robbery. They will not work and their negroes are all gone, plantations destroyed, etc."

General Sherman never did get Nathan Bedford Forrest quite right.

After Lee and Joe Johnston surrendered, Forrest went for rides on two successive nights, considering his options. He took Major Charles Anderson with him as a sounding board. Many of the men were war-weary, while others wanted to fight on. Going to Mexico was an option. The life of a guerrilla sounded romantic to the young, but Forrest knew it was miserable existence. When they came to a fork in the road, Anderson asked which way. "Either. If one road led to hell and the other to Mexico, I would be indifferent as to which to take."

Anderson pled for surrender. He pointed out that the general had a duty to the young men and should lead them in the direction of peace. After listening, Forrest said, "That settles it." He turned his horse toward his base.

Back in camp, he was met by Mississippi Governor Charles Clark and former Tennessee Governor Isham Harris, who called upon him to fight on. "You men can do as you damn well please," Forrest responded. "I'm a-goin' home. Any man who is in favor of a further prosecution of this war is a fit subject for a lunatic asylum and should be sent there immediately."

Ever the realist, Nathan Bedford Forrest knew it was time to quit. The Federals made no effort to humiliate the capitulating Rebels. No Federal officer even entered Forrest's camp, and his men were given the same terms as Lee and Johnston. Forrest's battle flag, made from the bridal dress of a lady from Aberdeen, Mississippi, was cut into small bits, which were given to the soldiers.

On May 9, Forrest issued a farewell address to his troops.

Reason dictates and humanity demands that no more blood be shed...It is your duty and mine to lay down our arms— submit to the powers that be and aid in restoring peace and establishing law and order throughout the land...Civil War, such as you have passed through, naturally engenders feelings of animosity, hatred, and revenge. It is our duty to divest ourselves of such feelings; and as far as it is in our power to do so, to cultivate friendly feelings toward those with whom we have so long contended and heretofore so widely, but honestly differed. Neighborhood feuds, personal animosities, and private differences should be blotted out; and when you return home, a manly straightforward course of conduct will secure the respect even of your enemies. Whatever your responsibility may be to government, to society, or to individuals meet them like men...I have never, on the field of battle, sent you where I was unwilling to go myself; nor would I now advise you to a course of action which I felt myself unwilling to pursue. You have been good soldiers; you can be good citizens. Obey the laws, preserve your honor, the government to which you have surrendered can afford to be, and will be magnanimous.

Thus, one of the most brilliant soldiers America has ever known put his sword back in its scabbard.

# CHAPTER 20

# AFTER THE WAR

*Blindly accepting historical "truths" without vigorous
challenge is a perilous path to understanding real history.*
　　　　　　　　　　　　　　　　　—Stephen Hood

After he disbanded his command, Forrest took the train back
to Memphis. Immediately after the war, railroad executives
let the paroled ex-soldiers and refugees ride home for free, so
practically every inch of the passenger cars were full. Suddenly there was
a violent lunge. The train had run off the tracks. Fortunately, it was not
going fast. The habit of command was now deeply ingrained in Forrest
and he immediately began issuing orders. He told everyone to exit the
cars and organized work gangs to lift it back onto the rails. The first
attempt failed; then someone told the general that there were still men
in the cars.

Forrest immediately lost his temper. He yelled into the car, "If you
damned rascals don't get out here and help get this car on the track, I
will throw every one of you through the windows!" Then he entered the
car to carry out his threat. The men immediately scrambled out, and,
soon, the train was back on the tracks

"I went into the army worth a million and a half dollars," Forrest recalled. "I came out of the war pretty well wrecked, completely used up, shot all to pieces, crippled, a beggar." He told a reporter what he wanted to do. "Where I live, there are plenty of fish, and I'm going to take a tent along, and I don't want to see anyone for twelve months." This was wishful thinking on the general's part, and he knew it. In late May 1865, Forrest left Grenada, Mississippi, with twenty of his former slaves and headed for Sunflower Landing, the site of Green Grove, his three-thousand-acre plantation, where he and Mary began rebuilding their lives and shattered fortunes.

As soon as the war was over, he put in his first crop of corn, which yielded well. Meanwhile, Mary raised chickens and planted a garden. In September, Forrest reopened his sawmill in Coahoma County, Mississippi. Not only did this provide money for him, but also supplied jobs for people who needed them. He also rented much of his plantation land to veterans, both Northern and Southern.

Forrest's war horse, King Philip, came home with the general after the war and Forrest ordered that no saddle ever touch his back again. Like his owner, he never really lost his martial ardor. In August 1866, a troop of Yankee cavalry passed by General Forrest's plantation. They had been out on an unrelated errand and rode a little out of their way to see the home of the fearsome Rebel general. They intended no harm and were more tourists than anything else. Unfortunately, King Philip was grazing in the front yard, eating the tender young grass, and he did not know that the war was over. He did what he always did when he saw blue coats: he attacked them. The startled Yankees tried to keep out of his way, but he stood up on his hind legs, snorting and trying to kick them. The Northerners prepared to defend themselves. One Yankee was severely kicked and threatened to kill the horse. Seeing this, Jerry, Bedford's servant, rushed out with a pitchfork to defend King Philip, belligerently yelling at the Yankees to leave General Forrest's horse alone.

Bedford rode up at that moment and helped to restore peace. When the horse was calmed down and safely in the stable, the Union captain joked with Forrest. "General," he said, "now I know how to account for your successes. Your Negroes fight for you and so do your horses."[1]

The retired war horse was occasionally forced to endure the indignity of being a carriage horse. One day, while the family was visiting in Memphis, Mary and some of her friends decided to go shopping. They were having a happy day until King Philip looked up and saw a platoon of Memphis Police recruits forming up on the sidewalk. They were not Yankees but their uniforms were blue and that was enough for him. His ears went back, his tail went up, he snorted with hate and down the sidewalk he went, at full speed, ignoring the screaming women in the carriage. Shoppers dropped their packages and gentlemen jerked their ladies out of the path of the charging war horse, who had blood in his eyes. The recruits heard the commotion and, seeing the rampaging and rapidly advancing steed, they broke formation and fled down alleys, ducked into doorways and took cover behind water troughs, in order to escape. In the end, King Philip stood proudly on the spot previously occupied by the "enemy," all alone except for the hysterical ladies, who were still screaming. King Philip definitely knew how to break up an enemy formation—or ruin a shopping trip. This noble beast died of colic in 1867 or early 1868 and was buried on Forrest's Mississippi plantation.

In time, seven former Union officers rented land from him. Having ex-Federal officers as friends and business partners helped him attract free blacks to work his farm and gained him credibility in the eyes of the federal government. One of these officers was Major B. E. Diffenbocher of Missouri, General Hatch's former quartermaster. Hatch was understandably not well disposed toward the man who had thrashed him several times, but after he actually got to meet Forrest, he was won over. He noted that Forrest accepted the result of the war and was honestly doing his part to bind the nation's wounds. Soon he was one of Forrest's business partners.

Forrest made a friend of former U.S. Major General Frank Blair.[2] When the two met in Memphis, Blair found him to be nothing like what he expected. Blair wrote to his brother, Montgomery Blair (Lincoln's postmaster general), "I have conceived a very great personal attachment for Forrest...His noble bearing since the war and accepting without complaint the results and using his powerful influence to make others accept in the same spirit, has inspired me with the respect and admiration I have not felt for any other man." Later, he endorsed Forrest's application for a pardon.

Not every Northerner was as magnanimous as Blair and Hatch. Many were calling for the execution of Confederate leaders, and Forrest of Fort Pillow was near the top of their lists of those to be hanged. Strangely enough, the arrest of a Confederate admiral played a role in the resurrection of the charges.

Raphael Semmes had commanded the raider *Alabama*, which destroyed sixty-five Union merchant ships and sank a warship before it was finally sunk off the French coast in June 1864. Semmes made his way back to Richmond via Cuba and Texas, was named commander of the Naval Brigade, and became an admiral and brigadier general simultaneously. He surrendered with Johnston's army at Durham Station, North Carolina.

After the war, Northern insurance and shipping interests wanted Semmes hanged for piracy, and federal authorities arrested him for treason in December 1865. This action raised hackles not only in the South, but in the North as well. The Northern newspapers (led by the *New York Tribune*) and a large part of the general public did not think Semmes deserved execution. They correctly pointed out that the only Yankees Semmes ever killed were aboard Union warships which he engaged in fair combat. He always made sure that the sailors from the unarmed merchant ships he captured were safety aboard the *Alabama* before he sank their ships. As prisoners, they were well treated and released in accordance with the naval law of the day. Why, the editorials asked, was Semmes jailed while Forrest—responsible for the massacre at Fort Pillow—remained free?

Friends of General Forrest fearing that he might be arrested, tried, and executed, raised a significant amount of money in his behalf and sent him a letter of credit with the intention that he use it to go to Europe and stay there until the trouble had passed. Forrest sent back the letter and informed his benefactors, "This is my country. I am hard at work upon my plantation, and carefully observing the obligations of my parole. If the Federal government does not regard it, they'll be sorry."

In the meantime, Colonel Sam Tate and other acquaintances of Andrew Johnson approached the president on the sly and asked him what the government planned to do about Forrest. Lincoln's successor assured them that Forrest would not be arrested or harassed. Bedford, meanwhile, told the Federal officials in Memphis that he intended to share whatever fate awaited his people.

Fortunately for him, Semmes was as good a sea lawyer as he was a sea raider. He argued that he had been legally paroled in April 1865, as an admiral *and* a general. He thereafter could not be tried unless the United States itself violated the terms of his parole. The Federal government could find no way around his defense and released Semmes in April 1866.[3]

Meanwhile, Forrest rented land on his plantation to former Union officers, who had an open invitation to visit his home on Sundays, and they frequently did so. He also employed and rented land to two hundred black farmers, and he began to turn it into profit. Members of U.S. General Oliver O. Howard's Freedman's Bureau inspected Forrest's plantation, and General Howard himself concluded that the ex-Rebel general was "disposed to do everything that is fair and right for the Negroes" and was doing all he could to help his black renters and employees, and that all were treated fairly and justly. The U.S. Army, however, thought he was giving "injurious indulgences" to his black employees. (He was an overly generous man.) They ordered him to stop being so or there would be severe repercussions. Forrest ignored them. But trouble soon raised its ugly head.

Thomas Edwards was a black tenant on Forrest's plantation and, according to black and white witnesses alike, he was insolent and hot-tempered. The trouble began when Edwards confronted Forrest's foreman, Major Diffenbocher, over a pay dispute. During the argument, the major confronted Edwards about his habitual wife-beating, pointing out cruelty toward women was against Forrest's rules of conduct. Edwards heatedly refused to change his behavior. "I will beat my wife whenever I please," Edwards proclaimed. "I do not care a G****mn for General Forrest or any other G****mn man. If General Forrest or any other man attempts to interfere with me, I will cut his guts out."

Tensions exploded on March 31, 1866. Some stagnant pools of water had accumulated near the workers cabins and, because he feared cholera, Forrest wanted them drained. After he explained to the African-Americans the dangers to the health of their families posed by the rancid water, they quickly grabbed their shovels and hoes and began to dig drainage ditches. Edwards walked by at that moment and refused to join in the work, screaming at Forrest said he was going to his cabin to eat his dinner; furthermore, if it was not ready, his wife would pay for it. Soon the air was pierced by the familiar sound of a woman's screaming and the cracking of Edwards's whip upon her back.

True to his nature, Forrest reacted immediately, entering the cabin and ordering Edwards to stop abusing his wife. Edwards responded that he would beat her any time he pleased and cursed Forrest. Forrest responded that Edwards did not cease beating his wife, he would deal with him physically. When Edwards resumed his beating, Forrest picked up a broom handle and popped him on the head. Edwards then drew a knife and slashed at Forrest, cutting his hand. Forrest knocked Edwards to the floor and, as the wife beater rooted about for his weapon, Forrest picked up an axe. When Edwards charged again, Forrest hit him in the head with the axe, killing him instantly.

Self-defense? Murder? Forrest was content to let the courts decide. He sent for the sheriff, whose deputy arrived several hours later.

Of the two hundred freedmen working on the plantation, most were content with Forrest as an employer. After the Edwards incident, Forrest offered to release all of them from their contracts. Only eighteen accepted the offer. There was, however, a disgruntled group of workers who looked upon Edwards as their leader. Several of them gathered around Forrest's house that night, lit bonfires, and demanded Forrest come out. He did— armed with a pair of pistols. He told them that the law would settle the matter, but he would shoot anyone who threatened him. He then went back inside. No one pressed the issue. About midnight, Deputy Wirt Shaw arrived. He knocked cautiously on the door and identified himself. Forrest promptly let him in. The two men decided that it would be best to wait until morning to go into town, which they did without incident.

They went to Sunflower Landing and boarded a steamboat to take Forrest to the magistrate. On board the boat was a large contingent of Northern soldiers. With his easy manner, he was soon laughing and socializing with his former enemies. When they learned that Forrest was under arrest, they offered to free him and toss the deputy into the Mississippi River. But Forrest insisted on handling the matter legally. He was booked and released on $10,000 bail, pending trial.

Forrest was tried in October 1866. The judge was black, and the jury was racially mixed. Mrs. Edwards defended her husband, which sadly is fairly common among abused wives, swearing that Edwards had never beaten her. However, all the other witnesses, black and white—including Captain N. D. Collins of the local Freedman's Bureau, who thought Forrest far too lenient and benevolent toward his black tenants—supported Forrest's version of events. Several blacks testified that Edwards was indeed a wife beater. The jury acquitted Forrest on October 11.

Meanwhile, Forrest's financial problems had begun to dog Forrest. The combination of legal fees, low market prices, poor crop production and abundant generosity left him deeply in debt. He filed for bankruptcy in Memphis on February 5, 1868, and gave up all of his property to his creditors.

In 1865, gangs of "carpetbaggers" (Northerners who had come south to enrich themselves as the South's expense) and "scalawags" (Southern collaborators), freed slaves, and desperate veterans roamed the countryside, extorting, pillaging, robbing, and raping and murdering. They burned hundreds of homes and plundered farms. People abandoned farms out of fear, and others were afraid to go out at night. In some places, women were not safe on the public sidewalks in broad daylight. On a business trip to Chicot County, Arkansas, Forrest witnessed a gang of "bloodthirsty and riotous blacks" force whites out of their homes at gunpoint, rob them, and then burn their houses. Many of the officers who governed the five military districts into which the South had been divided after the war—and in which the Army governed—were unsympathetic, believing that the Southerners were getting what they deserved for being rebels. General Forrest later recalled that he received as many as fifty letters a day from his old soldiers in which they complained that their friends and relatives were being murdered, wives and daughters were being insulted, and criminals were roaming the countryside at night, burning gins, mills and occasionally dwellings.

In this lawless situation, it is hardly surprising that former Rebels began to take matters into their own hands, setting up a Nineteenth-Century version of neighborhood watch patrols. They operated at night, protecting their friends and families against the marauders.

This atmosphere of violence and lawlessness also bred the Ku Klux Klan. The group began innocently enough with six former Confederate cavalrymen who liked to play poker and consume drink together. The still shambolic Southern economy meant that many men were unemployed or underemployed, and time hung heavily on their hands. John Calhoun Lester, a former captain in the Third Tennessee Infantry, turned to his friends and said, "Boys, let's start something to break this monotony. Let's start a club of some kind."[4] They did. Some people later erroneously stated that Nathan Bedford Forrest was the founder of the Ku Klux Klan. In fact, the Klan was formed by Major James R. Crowe,[5] Captains Lester and John B. Kennedy,[6] Lieutenant Calvin Jones, and Privates Richard Reed (also a lawyer) and Frank O. McCord, the editor of the Pulaski *Citizen* in the law offices of Judge Thomas Jones on Christmas Eve, 1865, in Pulaski, Tennessee.[7] "Ku Klux" was a corruption of the Greek word "kuklos," meaning circle. "Klan" was added as an alliteration—put another way, because it sounded good. Initially, it was a social club, formed for the amusement of its small membership. Soon, however, it grew into a protective organization. At first, membership was limited to former Confederate soldiers who had surrendered at the end of the war or were Union prisoners at the time. As the organization grew, however, it attracted some very unsavory characters.

By 1866, the purposes of the KKK had expanded to include protecting Southerners from carpetbaggers, scalawags, and criminals. Many of the citizen patrols that had already been organized merged with the KKK, which grew like wildfire. The Klan, however, had no real central leadership and lacked form and organization. Before long, some of its members began their own criminal careers under the auspices of the Klan. This upset those who thought that Tennessee and the rest of the South needed a paramilitary organization to protect their families and their homes from lawlessness. One Klan meeting was attended by sixteen former Confederate generals.[8]

The KKK was a secret organization, so the full set of records that historians love never existed. We do know, however, that it was soon headed by George Washington Gordon, a former Confederate brigadier general who commanded an infantry regiment or brigade in all of the major battles on the Western Front until Franklin, where he was wounded and captured.[9] He reportedly is the man who told Forrest about the Klan.

Initially, when the war ended, Washington had no formal set of policies guiding reconstruction and initially simply left it up to the Army to deal with the conquered South. In March 1867, however, Congress

William G. "Parson" Brownlow (1805–1877), the Scalawag governor of Tennessee. Although he was a former Methodist preacher and slave owner, he advocated the extermination of former Confederates and their families. Naturally, he and Bedford Forrest hated each other.

began passing a series of Reconstruction Acts, some of the provision of which were harsh. Tensions in Tennessee were further heightened after William G. "Parson" Brownlow became governor. A former Methodist minister, newspaper editor and slave owner who declared that slavery was "ordained by God," he nevertheless remained fiercely pro-Union. In 1861, his anti-secessionist rhetoric led to his arrest. He petitioned Confederate Secretary of War Judah P. Benjamin for his release, promising to leave the South if it were granted. Benjamin set him free. Brownlow then toured the North, where he made a name for himself by his stridently anti-Southern speeches. He returned to Union-occupied East Tennessee in 1863 and was elected governor in 1865. Former Confederates were not allowed to vote in this election—nor were free blacks for that matter. Free blacks were allowed to vote in 1867, however, and their votes helped give Brownlow a second term. He ruled almost as a dictator, established martial law in the state, and spoke openly of seizing the land of Confederate veterans and giving it to Unionists and freedmen.

More ominously, Brownlow spoke of exterminating former Confederates. In one postwar speech, he declared,

> I am one of those who believe that the war ended too soon. We have whipped the Rebels, but not enough. The loyal masses constitute an overwhelming majority of the people in this country, and they intend to march again on the South, and intended the second war shall be no child's play. The second army of invasion will, as they ought to do, make the

entire South as God formed the earth, without form or void. They will not, and ought not to, leave one Rebel fence rail, outhouse, one dwelling, in the [eleven] seceded states. As for the Rebel population, *let them be exterminated.* When the second war is wound up, which should be done swift destruction, let the land be surveyed and sold out to pay expenses.

It was not the only speech he gave along these lines.

Meanwhile, former Confederate generals John B. Gordon and John C. Brown had assumed positions of leadership of the Klan. A prominent Tennessee leader was Captain John Morton, Forrest's former chief of artillery. Forrest approached him and asked permission to join, and his former captain swore his general in to the organization.

Organizations often change over time. The Democratic Party of 1860, for example, was the party of slavery. After the war, it was the party of white supremacy. In the 1920s, it was heavily influenced by the Ku Klux Klan. In 1960, it was the party of segregation. This is no longer true. Similarly, the Ku Klux Klan of 1866 was not the same as the Klan of 2015. Although the original KKK reflected the racial attitudes of its time, it was not formed to campaign against blacks. Its original mission statement, for example, claimed it was "an instrument of Chivalry, Humanity, Mercy and patriotism" which saw as one of its primary goal to "relieve and assist the injured, oppressed, suffering, and unfortunate, especially widows and orphans of Confederate soldiers; and to support the United States Constitution and Constitutional Law."

A delegation of former Confederate officers, headed by Major General John B. Gordon of Georgia, traveled to Lexington, Virginia, where Robert E. Lee was serving as president of Washington College. They asked General Lee to assume command of the KKK. Lee refused because of his poor health. Then someone suggested Forrest. This sounded like a great idea to General Lee, who sent Forrest a message, urging him to accept leadership. A secret meeting was held in the Maxwell House hotel in Nashville in the spring of 1866.[10] It is fairly certain that Forrest was elected leader and the first Grand Wizard of the KKK at this meeting.[11]

The title apparently was a tribute to his wartime nickname, "the Wizard of the Saddle."

Under his leadership, the Klan transformed from a protective association into a political and paramilitary group—and occasionally a vigilante organization (vigilantism was a tradition on the frontier, where Forrest grew up). Clearly from the beginning, Forrest intended for the Klan to be a military force that would fight if Brownlow tried to use the state militia and the U.S. Army to put his plans for extermination into action.

The notion that the carpetbaggers and radical Republicans would deliberately start a second Civil War sounds far-fetched today; to the people of the South in the late 1860s, it seemed a very real and very frightening possibility. It did because Brownlow was not alone in advocating retribution. Thaddeus Stevens, the Speaker of the U.S. House of Representatives, said, "The South's land must be seized and divided and conveyed to loyal men, black or white." Former Union general Benjamin F. "Spoons" Butler[12] called for a second war "and woe to him who oppose us!" Governor Richard Yates of Illinois also advocated a second war "to finish the good work." Carpetbagger Governor Andrew J. Hamilton of Texas and Senator Jim Lane of Kansas, among others, openly declared that they wanted another war.

Forrest took their words seriously. He had to. In a speech in Brownsville, Tennessee, he said that he believed Governor Brownlow was seeking to pass laws that lumped all former Confederates together and make it legal for anybody to shoot them on sight. If these laws were passed, Forrest declared, there would be another war, although he himself did not want it. He ended the speech by declaring that "If they bring this war upon us, there is one thing I will tell you—that I shall not shoot any Negroes so long as I can see a white Radical to shoot, for it is the Radicals who will be to blame for bringing on this war."

In September 1866, Brownlow's legislature passed the first Anti-Ku Klux Klan Law, which mandated a $500 fine and a minimum of five years imprisonment for anyone found to be a member of the organization. Another law gave the governor the power to call out the state militia to enforce this law. Forrest, of course, refused to back down. "Brownlow says he will bring his militia down here and get us," Forrest told his men. "I say, let him fetch them, and you boys will be ready to receive them." He also said that he would look upon an activation of the militia as a declaration of war and, in that event, he could raise forty thousand Klansmen in Tennessee and 550,000 throughout the South in five days. He also declared the Klan a "protective political military organization."

Brownlow and his cronies, however, were not willing to risk their own lives in a battle with a reconstituted Forrest's cavalry, and a civil war was averted, although both sides maintained a threatening posture.

In another speech, Forrest said, "I loved the old government in 1861. I love the old Constitution yet. I think it the best government in the world if administered as it was before the war. I do not hate it. I am opposing now only the radical revolutionists who are trying to destroy it. I believe that party to be composed as I know it is in Tennessee of the worst men on God's green earth—men who would not hesitate at any crime and who have only one object in view and that is to enrich themselves."

In the election of 1868, Forrest was chosen as a delegate to the Democratic National Convention in New York City. On the trip north, a mob assembled at one of the railroad stations along the route. Its leader declared that he was going to thrash "that butcher Forrest." Seeing trouble, the conductor (a former Union soldier) asked Brigadier General Basil Duke, a delegate from Kentucky and former second-in-command of Morgan's raiders, to ask Forrest to keep his seat during the stop. Forrest calmly agreed, stating that these were not the first people to threaten his life, and he saw nothing to get excited about. When the ringleader barged onto the train, however, Forrest rose to the threat.

"I never in my life witnessed such an instantaneous and marvelous transformation in any one's appearance," General Duke wrote later. "Erect and dilated, his face the color of heated bronze, and his eyes flaming, blazing. He strode rapidly down the aisle toward the approaching champion, his gait and manner evincing perfect, invincible determination."

"Where is that butcher, Forrest?" the man yelled.

Suddenly the general was upon him. "I'm Forrest!" he roared. "What do you want?"

The combination of Forrest's transformation, sudden appearance, physical stature, and obvious willingness to fight, completely unnerved the man, who immediately ran away. Forrest chased him and yelled for him to come back. The man kept running, losing his hat in the process. At that point, Forrest stopped and laughed. The mob also laughed, somewhat nervously.

This was Forrest's first visit to New York, and he and his son, Willie, who accompanied him, were apparently unaware that the newspapers had announced the general was in town. As they were out exploring the city, a crowd formed around them. Forrest didn't think anything of it until he heard someone say, "That's him! That's the Rebel, General Forrest!" Bedford and Willie tried to walk away, but the crowd, which had grown to the hundreds, blocked their path. Tired of being surrounded by so many curious people, in his famous battlefield voice, Forrest yelled, "Get out of my way, G*****n you!" Such was the power of Forrest's voice and presence that the crowd instantly dispersed. It did so quickly in fact that some of those in the rear were knocked down by those in the front as they tried to get away.

Bedford played little public role in the convention and made no speeches. Behind the scenes, he supported his fellow Tennessean, Andrew Johnson. When his state's delegation realized that the president could not win, it switched its support to New York Governor Horatio Seymour, who won the nomination on the Twenty-Third ballot, but was defeated by Ulysses S. Grant in the general election. Forrest's friend, Frank Blair, was the unsuccessful vice presidential nominee. Possibly as a reward for his support, before he left office, Johnson granted Forrest a full pardon on July 17, 1868.

The next morning, an angry woman, knocked on the door of his hotel room before Forrest had gotten his boots on. She was described as "a typical New England old maid," tall and thin, with a Bible in one hand and an umbrella in the other. Bursting past William, she charged up to the general. "Are you the Rebel General Forrest? And if so, why did you murder those wonderful colored folks at Fort Pillow? Tell me, sir! I want no evasive answer!"

"Yes, madam. I killed the men and women for my soldiers' dinner and ate the babies myself for breakfast. Best meal I ever had." The woman ran screaming from the room.

Meanwhile, in order to advance his presidential ambitions, Judson Kilpatrick, who had commanded Sherman's cavalry during the March to the Sea, launched a number of particularly hateful attacks at Forrest. Among the many atrocities he accused Forrest of committing, accused Forrest of nailing blacks to fences and burning them to death. Forrest ignored the first attacks but, after a while, he finally had enough. He sent an open letter to the newspapers, denouncing General Kilpatrick "as a blackguard, a liar, a scoundrel and a poltroon." He noted that Kilpatrick was portraying himself as a hero to the Northern people. If he was so courageous, Forrest said, let him prove it. He challenged him to a duel on horseback with sabers. Kilpatrick declined on the thin excuse that Forrest wasn't a gentleman. His apparent timidity—if not outright cowardice—in the face of Forrest's challenge appears to have fatally damaged his political career.[13]

On February 25, 1869, Brownlow's second term as governor ended, and he became a United States Senator.[14] His successor, DeWitt Senter, sought to work with the Democrats and was conciliatory to men like Forrest.[15] After he announced his intention to restore the voting rights of former Confederates and to disband Brownlow's State Guard, Forrest essentially ordered the Klan to disband, issuing General Order Number One, which read:

> Whereas, the Order of the KKK is in some localities being perverted from its original honorable and patriotic purposes; And whereas, such a perversion of the Order is in some instances defeating the very objectives of its origin, and is

becoming injurious instead of subservient to the public peace
and public safety for which it was intended, and in some cases
is being used to achieve personal benefit and private purposes,
and to satiate private revenge by means of its masked features.
It is therefore ordered and decreed, that the masks and cos-
tumes of this order be entirely abolished and destroyed. And
every Grand Cyclops shall assemble the men of his Den and
require them to destroy in his presence every article of his
mask and costume and at the same time shall destroy his own.
And every man who shall refuse to do so shall be deemed an
enemy of this Order, and shall be treated accordingly. And
every man who shall hereafter be seen in mask or costume,
shall not be known or recognized as a member of this order;
but shall be deemed an enemy of the same.

It is presumed that this decree was authored by Forrest himself.
He was always a man who supported law and order. "There was no
further need for it" he commented later, "…the country was safe."
As the order indicates, he also wanted to ensure that no one committed crimes under the ostensibly honorable cover of the Klan. Yet,
despite ordering its disbandment and decrying its baser elements,
Forrest was never able to disassociate himself entirely from the Ku
Klux Klan—and more important from the second manifestation of
the Klan.

Certain branches of the KKK lived on under such names as the
Constitutional Union Guards, the Pale Faces, the White Brotherhood,
the White League and the Knights of the White Camelia. A few KKK
dens lingered on until 1877, but the original Ku Klux Klan effectively
ceased to exist and faded into history. One of its founders, Captain
John Calhoun Lester, put it very well when he wrote, "There never
was, before or since, a period of our history when such an order could
have lived. May there never be again!"

In 1915, D. B. Griffith produced and directed the infamous film,
"Birth of a Nation" (originally titled, "The Clansman"). Its contents

were so incendiary that it led to several race riots, propelled the NAACP into national prominence—and led to the birth of the second Ku Klux Klan, which was (and is) largely a terrorist organization. Had it not pirated the name of the original KKK, we might look upon the original Ku Klux Klan completely differently than we do today. But it did. To associate Nathan Bedford Forrest's name with the deprivations of the Klan of the Twentieth and Twenty-First centuries is wrong, but many people do so, even though it was created almost four decades after his death, and he clearly had nothing to do with it.

In 1871, Forrest was forced to testify before Congress about the Ku Klux Klan. Apparently, he felt no obligation to share what he knew with the government, which he believed was stirring up trouble in the South. He repeatedly claimed he did not remember events or things, and would only divulge the names of people who were already dead. He later confessed that he "lied like a gentleman." To his credit, however, his political and racial views continued to evolve.

In August 1873, two white men attended a barbecue hosted by freedmen in Trenton, Tennessee. After they ate, they refused to pay. This led to a race riot, after which sixteen blacks were arrested. Shortly thereafter, a lynch mob of approximately seventy-five whites broke into the jail and hanged the sixteen African-Americans. At a public meeting in Memphis, Forrest lambasted the crime, describing the criminals as "marauders who disgrace their race by this cowardly murder of Negroes." He volunteered to round up these murderers personally if the state gave him the authority to do so. Former Confederate General John C. Brown, who was governor at the time, actually thought about it, but decided against it.

The fact is that, although he reflected the racial views of his upbringing and his times, Nathan Bedford Forrest never hated black people. He made substantial contributions to a black Baptist church on Beale Street in Memphis. As early as 1867, his railroad employed four hundred blacks, mostly as laborers, but some as foremen, conductors, and even architects and engineers. By 1875, Forrest was publicly declaring that blacks should be free to enter any profession they chose without restriction. In the mid-1870s, he even remarked that African-Americans should have the unrestricted right to vote.[16]

After the war, Forrest never regained the prosperity he had enjoyed in the antebellum years. In 1866, he and C. C. McCreanor contracted to complete the Memphis & Little Rock Railroad from Madison (on the St. Francis River) to DeValls' Bluff on the White River. It had to traverse the difficult Crowley Ridge and L'Anguille River bottoms, but they were successful and the first train ran in 1868. Along the route, he built a town, which was incorporated as Forrest City, Arkansas, in 1870. It now is the county seat of St. Francis County with a population of fifteen thousand. The railroad was not particularly profitable, however.

In 1867, Forrest became president of the Planters Life Insurance Company after his plantation failed and his sawmill was taken over by creditors. Despite his vigorous work, the company went bankrupt in 1868. He also set up a road paving firm called Forrest, Montgomery & Company. It won a road paving contract from the city of Memphis, to be financed by bond sales. A third of the project was completed when Memphis—still economically crippled by the war—could no longer meet its obligations. Forrest and his partners had no choice but to withdraw from the project.

After his bankruptcy in 1868, Forrest purchased an interest in the Cahaba, Marion & Memphis Railroad, which soon became the Selma, Marion & Memphis Railroad. Forrest became president of the firm, named former Colonel Edmund W. Rucker its superintendent, and immersed himself in the activities of the railroad for the next five years.

Forrest envisioned that the proposed railroad would extend 280 miles, running from Memphis to the iron and coal producing areas in central and northern Alabama. Forrest needed $25,000 per mile to build the line, but only managed to raise $16,000 per mile by 1872. He nevertheless began laying track, counting on the revenue generated by the railroad to make up the difference. By 1873, some of the track had been laid in Alabama and the rail bed had been graded and ties laid from Memphis to Holly Springs, Mississippi.

Things finally were looking up for Forrest. He gave generously to disabled Confederate veterans, the widows and orphans of his former soldiers, and former Rebels who were down on their luck. He even donated $5,000 in railroad stock (more than $70,000 in today's debased currency) to the founding of Vanderbilt University. Then everything fell apart. A yellow fever epidemic swept the nation in 1872 and 1873, and the Panic of 1873 threw the country into a financial depression.[17] Forrest's railroad collapsed financially and he resigned as president in 1874.

On September 10, 1870, Forrest, while traveling on the riverboat *Shenandoah Herald*, encountered his old nemesis, William Tecumseh Sherman, who was now general-in-chief of the United States Army. They greeted each other as old acquaintances, if not quite friends, and enjoyed a private conversation. Most of the exchange between them remained private, but Sherman was overheard telling Forrest that, before and during the Atlanta campaign of 1864, he not only filled Sherman's every waking moment, but occupied his dreams as well. Forrest replied that, if Richmond had given him the permission he asked for, he would have turned Sherman's nightmares into reality.

After the S M & M Railroad fell into receivership, Forrest was looking for employment. At that same time, it appeared that the United States was about to go to war with Spain over Cuba. Forrest wrote to Sherman and offered his services. Sherman wrote a glowing letter of recommendation for Forrest to the War Department and informed President Grant that, if war came, he wanted Forrest to command the American cavalry. He told Grant that if Forrest caused them half as much trouble as he had caused us, he would be a tremendous asset for the U. S. Army. He wrote Forrest a warm letter in response and told him that he would be honored to serve side-by-side with him.

Fortunately or unfortunately, the crisis was averted. War with Spain did not come for twenty-five years. Forrest, meanwhile, took his remaining money and leased a double log cabin on President's Island, south of

Memphis, which is the longest island in the Mississippi River. It was twelve miles long and thirty-two thousand acres in area in 1874. He leased out about 117 convicts from Shelby County to work his plantation, which was 1,300 acres in size. He organized the convicts with military efficiency, cleared eight hundred acres and planted corn, cotton, potatoes, and millet. He and Mary cultivated their vegetable garden.

Forrest had now come full circle. He was again living in a log cabin—and he didn't even own this one. Whereas he seemed to have the Midas touch before the war, now everything Forrest tried seemed to fail. He was poor—not unlike his entire region. In 1860, six of the nation's eleven richest states in terms of per capita income were Southern. Not one has made the top ten since the end of the war, although Texas—God bless it—may soon do so.

Some people will not look up to God until they hit rock bottom. During the war, when pressed by Christian friends about his lack of a genuine relationship with Christ, Forrest would respond that he did not have time for it, but perhaps he would consider it after the war. In November 1875, Nathan Bedford Forrest ran into an old friend, Lieutenant Colonel Raleigh R. White, the former commander of the Fourteenth Tennessee Cavalry and briefly a brigade commander. He was only twenty-five years old when the war ended.[18] "So what have you been up to these days?" Forrest asked. White responded that his life had dramatically changed. Although not a Christian during war, he was now a Baptist minister, "preaching the gospel of the Son of God." Forrest commented that he was considering becoming a Christian himself and that they should talk about it some time. White's response was, why not right now? The two stepped into the lobby of a nearby bank and discussed salvation for more than an hour, and prayed on their knees. Afterward, much to Mary's delight, Bedford decided to be baptized. Mary Forrest was a member of the First Cumberland Presbyterian Church (also known as the Court Avenue Cumberland Presbyterian Church) in Memphis. And it was there about a week later, on the evening of Sunday, November 14, Reverend George Tucker Stainback baptized Nathan Bedford Forrest.[19]

Later that year, Forrest was invited to attend the meeting of the Independent Order of Pole-Bearers Association, an early civil rights organization made up of black people in the Memphis area, including several of Forrest's former soldiers. Now greatly aged and growing feeble, he rose slowly and was presented with a bouquet of flowers by young black lady named Lou Lewis. He said,

Bedford Forrest late in life.

> Ladies and gentlemen I accept the flowers as a memento of reconciliation between the white and colored races of the Southern states. I accept it more particularly as it comes from a lady, for if there is anyone on God's earth that loves ladies I believe it is myself. [Laughter]
>
> I came here with jeers of some white people, who think that I am doing wrong. I believe I can exert some influence, and did much to assist people in strengthening fraternal relations, and shall do all in my power to elevate every man and to depress none. I want to elevate you to take positions in law offices, in stores, on farm, and wherever you are capable of doing. I have not said anything about politics today. I don't propose to say anything about politics. You have a right to elect whom you please; but vote for the man you think best...Do as you consider right and honest in electing men for office.
>
> I do not come here to make you a long speech, although invited to do so by you. I am not much of a speaker, and my business prevented me from preparing myself. I came to meet you as friends, and welcome you to the white people. I want you to come nearer to us. When I can serve you I will do so.

We have but one flag, one country; let us stand together. We
may differ in color, but not in sentiment.

Many things have been said about me which are wrong,
and which white and black persons here, who stood by me
through the war, can contradict. Go to work, be industrious,
live honestly and act truly, and when you are oppressed, I'll
come to your relief. I thank you, ladies and gentlemen, for this
opportunity you have afforded me to be with you, and to
assure you that I am with you in heart and in hand.

Amid thunderous applause, the former slave trader and Grand Wizard of the Ku Klux Klan performed an unprecedented act—he bent down
and kissed Miss Lewis on the cheek. This was an unheard of gesture of
respect for a white man to pay to a black woman in that day and time.
Nathan Bedford Forrest had indeed come a long way. He even led a
ceremony at Elmwood Cemetery in Memphis, to decorate the graves of
Union soldiers buried there.

Sadly, Forrest's attempts to bring about racial harmony met with
staunch opposition from many quarters. The Cavalry Survivors Association—the first post-war Confederate fraternal organization—unanimously voted to condemn his Pole-Bearers speech, and several newspapers
added their condemnations. The *Macon Weekly Telegraph* denounced
it as a "disgusting exhibition." The *Charlotte Observer* said that "We
have infinitely more respect for [General James] Longstreet, who frater-
nizes with negro men on public occasions, with the pay for the treason
to his race in his pockets, than with Forrest and Pillow, who equalize
with the negro women, with only 'futures' in payment."[20] Exactly what
he meant by "futures," the North Carolina editorialist did not say.

As mentioned previously in this book, Forrest enjoyed gambling, and
he was good at it. Once, after the war, when the family was down to its
last $10, Forrest left home with plans to gamble his way out of a par-
ticular debt he could not pay. He succeeded.

On another occasion, Forrest had co-signed a note for a friend for
$2,500. The friend defaulted, the note came due, and Forrest could not

cover it. He decided to win the money at a poker table. As he left, Mary tried to dissuade him. She told him that while he was gone she would be on her knees with her Bible in her hand, praying for him to renounce gambling. Forrest said that he would stop as soon as he won the required amount. That evening, as soon as he won what he needed, he picked up his money to leave the table. The other gamblers tried to talk him into staying. Forrest refused. "My wife is sitting at home with the Bible on her knee. I told her I would quit as soon as I had enough money to pay my debt of honor. I am never going to gamble again." He never did.

Meanwhile, in 1872, Forrest became a grandfather when Nathan Bedford Forrest II, was born in Oxford, Mississippi. He would pass away in Memphis in 1931. William had graduated from Ole Miss after the war and married Jane Taylor Cook (1847-1882) in 1868. The couple has two more children and lived nearby.[21] Willie was a railroad executive until his death on February 7, 1908. He suffered a fatal stroke while watching a play about the Ku Klux Klan. He was stricken just as the actor playing his father entered the stage.

The war and the hard times afterward had taken their toll on Forrest. He was not yet forty-four years old when the war ended but physically he was much older than that. "His iron constitution was simply too depleted to work at the level he was accustomed to," Kastler wrote later, "but his determination and work ethic prevented him from slowing down. Eventually something would have to give, and it would be Forrest's body." By 1875, he was suffering from diabetes, "inflammation of the stomach" and diarrhea.

His failing health caused Forrest to frequently "take the waters" at Hurricane Springs, near Tullahoma, Tennessee. While he was there in 1876, Charles Anderson visited him. "There was a mildness in his matter, a softness of expression, and a gentleness in his words that appeared to me strange and unnatural. At first I thought his bad health but that brought about the change, but then I remembered that when sick or wounded he was the most restless and impatient man I ever saw. Soon I told him that there was something about him I couldn't understand, that he didn't appear to me to be the same man I used to know so well. He

Captain Willie Forrest

was silent for a moment, and then seem to divine my trouble, and, halting suddenly, he took hold all volatile of my coat and turned me squarely in front of him, raising his right hand with that long index finger…extended, he said, 'Major, I'm not the man you were with so long and knew so well. I hope I am a better man. I've joined the church and I'm trying to live a Christian life…Mary has prayed for me night and day for many years, and I feel now that through her prayers my life has been spared, and to them I am indebted for passing safely through so many dangers.'" This was their final meeting.[22]

Joseph Wheeler also visited him in his last years and noticed a change in Forrest's demeanor. "Every line parsing just about harshness had disappeared, and he seemed to possess in those last days the gentleness of expression, the voice and manner of a woman."

In 1877, Forrest was losing weight rapidly, despite the fact that he was always hungry and ate constantly (those who suffer from certain forms of diabetes exhibit these symptoms.) Forrest knew he was dying. In April of that year, he went to Hot Springs, Arkansas, again to "take the waters," but it did little good. When he returned to Memphis, he dropped all the lawsuits he had filed against his former railroad. His attorney, John T. Morgan, a former wartime comrade, tried to talk him out of it.[23] "I am broken in health and in spirit, and have not long to live," Forrest said. "My life is a battle from the start. It was a fight to achieve a livelihood for those dependent upon me in my younger days, and independence for myself when I grew up to manhood, as well as in the terrible turmoil of the Civil War. I have seen too much of violence, I want to close my days at peace with all the world, as I'm now at peace with my Maker." He further told that he intended to live a peaceful and a better life for the remainder of his days. Although assured by his distinguished attorney that the suits were favorable to his interests, he persisted in their abandonment, saying that he would not leave his only son a heritage of contention.

Bedford's home on President's Island burned down in 1877 and Forrest spent his final days in the Memphis home of his brother Jesse at 399 Union Street, which was closer to medical care. He now barely weighed one hundred pounds and could not walk without help. He also suffered from chronic diarrhea (possibly dysentery), high blood pressure, and malarial fever.

By now he could no longer work or take part in social or civic affairs, but he worked up enough strength to make one last public appearance on September 21, 1877, when he addressed a reunion of the Seventh Tennessee Cavalry, which he had joined as a private sixteen years before. In his final days, he was visited by Jefferson Davis, who also was living in Memphis. Davis's last call occurred the day before Bedford died.

Just before the end, Colonel Meriwether took his young son, Lee, to visit the man who had once threatened his life. "As we walked away from that house," young Meriwether recalled, "my father's eyes dimmed with tears as he said to me, 'Lee, the man you saw dying will never die. He will live in the memory of men who love patriotism, and who admire genius and daring.'"

On October 29, 1877, just before 7 p.m., Forrest's last earthly thoughts turned to the one person who had loved and supported him through it all. "Call my wife," he said to Colonel Meriwether, and closed his eyes, never to open them again. He died peacefully at 7:15 p.m.

Forrest's funeral was held on Halloween Day, and was attended by twenty thousand people. At his request, he was buried in his Confederate uniform and his processional extended for three miles. At least three thousand of the mourners were black, and some place their number at more than six thousand. He was taken to Elmwood Cemetery in a hearse

Mary Forrest, 1873, holding her grandchild, Nathan Bedford Forrest II. After Willie's first wife died young, she helped him raise his three children. She was a devoted wife, mother, surrogate mother, and a thoroughly wonderful Christian lady. Photo from Find-a-Grave, posted by Dwayne Sessom, 6/1/2015.

drawn by four black horses, with Jefferson Davis and Governor James D. Porter riding in a carriage behind it.

During their ride, Porter said to Davis, "History has accorded General Forrest the first place as a cavalry leader in the War Between the States, and has named him as one of the half-dozen great soldiers of the country."

"I agree with you," the former president replied. "The trouble was that the generals commanding in the Southwest never appreciated Forrest until it was too late. Their judgment was that he was a bold and enterprising partisan raider and rider. I was misled by them, and I never knew how to measure him until I read his reports on his campaign across the Tennessee River in 1864. This induced a study of his earlier reports, and after that I was prepared to adopt what you are pleased to name as the judgment of history."

"I cannot comprehend such lack of appreciation after he fought the battle at Brice's Cross Roads in June of 1864," the governor responded. "That battle was not a cavalry raid, nor an accident. It was the conception of a man endowed with a genius for war."[24]

"That campaign was not understood in Richmond," Davis sadly recalled. "The impression made upon those in authority was that Forrest had made another successful raid, but I saw it all after it was too late."

The veterans of the Escort Company led the funeral procession, with former Lieutenant George L. Cowan at their head. Fire station and church bells tolled, and the local artillery fired ceremonial salutes. The guns were commanded by Major J. C. Thrall, who had once directed the Arkansas Rats of Mouton's battalion. The pall bearers were members of Forrest's staff and President Davis. Rev. George Stainback, the pastor of Cumberland Presbyterian, delivered the eulogy. "Lieutenant General Nathan Bedford Forrest, though dead, yet speaketh," Stainback declared. "His acts have photographed themselves upon the hearts of thousands, and will speak there forever." Southern newspapers mourned his passing, while some Northern newspapers declared good riddance.

Mary Forrest ascended to heaven on January 22, 1893, at age sixty-seven, and was buried next to her husband. She and Bedford were reinterred on Nathan Bedford Forrest Park in Memphis, in the medical district, on November 11, 1904. A beautiful statue of Forrest astride his horse Roderick overlooked their graves, until it was removed by the ignorant and uneducated, and the corrupt Memphis political thugs and grave desecrators who pander to them. It was made in Paris and took three years to complete. The inscription reads:

> Those huff beats die not on fame's crimson sod
> but will live through her song and her story.
> He fought like a titan and struck like a God,
> and his dust is our ashes of glory.

There is a great deal of truth in this. He indeed fell upon his adversaries like a thunderbolt from a clear blue sky. In some indefinable way, his subordinate commanders became "little Forrests" and the common soldier, serving under Forrest, often fought like a hero. Uncommon bravery and ferocity became routine, and his veterans never ceased to praise him for making them more than they were. As one of his men said later, a man serving under Forrest during the last year and a half of the war was no ordinary man. Years after his death, one of his old soldiers recalled, "He rode into my heart…and he rides there still."

# NOTES

## CHAPTER 1: FRONTIERSMAN TO MILLIONAIRE

1. The height of the average man in 1860 was 5' 7".
2. They were: Mary (born 1828), John Nathan (1829), William Hezekiah (called Bill) and Mildred (1831), Aaron H. and Jesse Anderson (1833), Isaac (1835) and Jesse Edward (1838).
3. Miriam even cooked Sunday meals on Saturday, to keep the Sabbath holy. The Old Testament in particular discouraged work on the Sabbath.
4. Jack Hurst, *Nathan Bedford Forrest: A Biography* (New York: Random House, Inc., 1994).
5. Luxton (c. 1798-June 5, 1863) died in Memphis and is buried in the Forrest family plot in Elmwood Cemetery, but has no grave marker.
6. In the 1850s, Hernando, Mississippi, was about twenty-two miles from Memphis.
7. A marriage proposal this early in a relationship would be considered highly unusual in today's society, but this was not the case on the

319

Nineteenth Century American frontier, where things happened quickly and events like this occurred much more frequently.

8.    Phrenology is a pseudoscience based on the theory that a person's psychological and intellectual aptitudes, abilities and tendencies can be determined by measuring certain parts of his or her skull. It is not taken seriously by most scientists today.

9.    Forrest also owned a second home in Memphis which employed seven slaves, mostly female.

## CHAPTER 2: FIRST BLOOD

1.    The company was soon sent to Fort Wright, sixty-five miles north of Memphis, to undergo training.

2.    This figure does not include the Confederate forces in Missouri and Arkansas, which were also under Johnston's command.

3.    Adam R. Johnson later became a brigadier general and Martin (who was only twenty-one years old in 1861) became a colonel.

4.    Mollie Morehead married in 1866 and died in childbirth four years later. The United Daughters of the Confederacy named a chapter after her.

5.    Forrest's scouts had estimated the Union strength at five hundred. They were pretty close to the mark. About four hundred Federals were engaged. They were commanded by eighteen-year-old Major Eli H. Murray (1843-1896), who was later territorial governor of Utah (1880-86). Forrest probably had 250 men when the battle ended.

6.    Charles Clark (1811-77) was a wealthy plantation owner. He was later seriously wounded at Shiloh and Baton Rouge, and was promoted to major general of Mississippi State troops in 1863. He was the last Confederate governor of Mississippi (1864-65) (see Chapter XIX).

## CHAPTER 3: I'LL BE DAMNED IF I'LL SURRENDER

1.    The Cumberland joins the Ohio below Paducah; the Tennessee empties into it at the town.

2.    Fort Henry was one of the worst cited positions in American military history. Half of it was flooded on February 6. Had Grant

waited two days, however, he could not have captured it, because the entire fort was under water on February 8.

3. Robert M. "Bob" Martin (1840-1901) became a colonel (at age twenty-three) and commanded the Tenth Kentucky Cavalry Regiment in Morgan's cavalry. When the rest of the command was captured in the Ohio raid, Martin broke out with four hundred men and escaped via West Virginia and east Tennessee. He directed partisan operations in Kentucky until he was severely wounded in 1864. After he recovered, he was sent to Canada, where he directed Confederate clandestine operations and was involved in a plot to burn New York City. After the war, he made and lost several fortunes and spent thirteen years as a warehouse inspector in Brooklyn.

4. Of the 14,805 Confederates in the fort, 327 were killed and 1,127 were wounded and evacuated before the fort fell. Three hundred fifty wounded were captured. The Federals lost about five hundred killed and 2,100 wounded of the twenty-seven thousand engaged.

5. President Davis relieved Floyd of his command on March 11, 1862. He was never reemployed.

## CHAPTER 4: SHILOH

1. A bullet passed through Johnston's leg but, thinking it was just a flesh wound, the general ignored it. It had, in fact, nicked his popliteal artery. By the time he realized the wound was serious, it was too late to save him, and he bled to death. Ironically, earlier in the battle, he had dispatched his personal physician to attend some wounded Yankees, so he had no trained medical help when he needed it. Jefferson Davis, a close personal friend, later stated that Johnston's death was "the turning point of our fate." They were cadets together at West Point and later fought together at Buena Vista.

2. Albert Sidney Johnston is buried in the Texas State Cemetery in Austin, Texas, just down Republic Hill from Stephen F. Austin. His casket is covered by a polished marble sarcophagus, which is one of the most beautiful I have ever seen.

3.      John Cabell Breckinridge (1821-1875) was a Kentucky politician
        and former vice president of the United States (1857-1861). Initially
        he was pro-Union, but after he visited wounded Kentucky
        Confederate soldiers who had been captured at Bull Run, President
        Lincoln ordered his arrest, despite the fact he was a sitting United
        States Senator. Tipped off by friends, Breckinridge promptly fled
        behind Southern lines, where he was greeted as a hero and was
        commissioned brigadier general. He later became the last
        Confederate secretary of war (1865).

## CHAPTER 5: THE MURFREESBORO RAID

1.      Halleck reduced Grant to second-in-command. The future president
        was very upset by the demotion.
2.      From his old regiment, Forrest was allowed to retain his staff and
        twenty scouts under the command of his brother, Captain William
        (Bill) Forrest.
3.      Oaklands was built in 1831 by Colonel Harden Murfree, after
        whom the town was named. It is still extant.
4.      William Richardson (1839-1914) of Huntsville survived the war and
        became a state judge and U.S. Congressman (1900-1914). He had
        gone from jail to Congress. Today, this usually works the other way
        around.
5.      Forrest's staff held a brief birthday party for him at Oaklands that
        evening before heading for McMinnville.
6.      In those days, Mississippi, Tennessee, Alabama, and parts of
        Louisiana and Florida were considered "the south-west."
7.      His grandson, Colonel Andrew Jackson III (1834-1906), was
        commander of the First Tennessee Heavy Artillery Regiment at
        Vicksburg. He is now buried as the Hermitage.
8.      Bull Nelson was severely wounded in this battle but escaped. He
        was murdered by Brigadier General Jefferson C. Davis in a
        Louisville hotel the following month. Nelson had earlier relieved
        Davis of command for dereliction of duty. Prior to the war, Nelson
        had been a naval officer for twenty-one years.
9.      The typical Confederate regiment had ten companies.

10. Breckinridge's infantry was commanded by Roger W. Hanson (born 1827), who had worked so well with Forrest at Fort Donelson. He was captured when the fort fell and later exchanged. Promoted to brigadier general on December 13, he was mortally wounded at Stone River on January 2, 1863, and died two days later.

11. John died in 1867 and is buried in Elmwood Cemetery, Memphis. He had served with the famous Mississippi Rifles in Mexico.

12. Despite being sixty-two years old, the elder Rambaut joined the Confederate Army as a captain of artillery.

13. Rambaut returned to Memphis at the end of the war. He founded a stockyard and fertilizer company and was involved in several other businesses. He was also president of the Memphis School Board. A father of six, he died in 1896.

14. Mrs. Helm was the former Emilie Todd, half-sister to Mary Todd Lincoln. Abraham Lincoln was very fond of her husband, Ben Helm, to whom he offered the job of paymaster of the Union Army in 1861. Helm, however, formed the First Kentucky Cavalry for the Confederacy. Later a brigadier general, he was killed at Chickamauga. Lincoln said that the day he learned of Helm's death was his worst day of the war.

15. Severson retired in 1864 and was replaced by Warren, who had previously worked for General Polk.

16. After the war, Morton studied medicine and was valedictorian when he graduated from the University of Tennessee. He later engaged in journalism and farming, and was assistant secretary of agriculture for Tennessee (1882-86) and Tennessee secretary of state (1901-09). He lived in a mansion just south of Nashville, which had been slightly damaged by shrapnel during the war. Morton saw the scars on his house every time he left or returned home. The shells that caused the damage had been fired from his own guns in 1864. Morton died at his daughter's home in Memphis (where he spent his twilight years) in 1914 and is buried in Mount Olivet Cemetery, Nashville.

17. Confederates usually elected their company and regimental officers and commanders.

18.    After the war, Boone was sheriff of Lincoln County and warden of
       the State Prison in Nashville. A temperance man, he died in
       Booneville in 1898.

## CHAPTER 6: THE WEST TENNESSEE RAID

1.    Another of his spies was Ohio-born Virginia "Ginny" Moon (b.
      1844), who smuggled medical supplies to Forrest's cavalry until
      1863, when she was captured. She was saved because of the
      intercession of her sister's boyfriend, U.S. General Ambrose
      Burnside. She spent the rest of the war in Ohio. Ginny had sixteen
      different fiancées during her spy career, mostly Union officers. Post-
      bellum, she was a famous Memphis philanthropist who was noted
      for her work in combating Yellow Fever epidemics. She even
      appeared in a couple of Hollywood movies before her death in
      1925. She is buried in Elmwood Cemetery, not far from the Forrest
      family plot.
2.    Ingersoll later became the attorney general of Illinois. Despite his
      controversial views, many considered him the greatest public
      speaker of his day. People paid $1 to hear him speak, a huge sum at
      that time.
3.    This included Biffle's Ninth Tennessee Cavalry, Cox's battalion and
      Freeman's battery.
4.    Davies (1809-1899) was a New Yorker and a West Point classmate
      of Robert E. Lee. Davies, however, left the army in 1841 and did not
      rejoin it until 1861.
5.    Thomas Alonzo Napier was born in 1837 and was a company
      commander in the Forty-Ninth Tennessee Infantry Regiment in late
      1861. Captured at Fort Donelson, he escaped while being
      transported to Johnson's Island. He then raised five companies of
      guerrilla cavalry behind Union lines. He was a small man noted for
      his abundant energy.

## CHAPTER 7: FAILURE AT FORT DONELSON

1.    Abner C. Harding (1807-1874) was born in Connecticut and moved
      to Illinois, where he practiced law. A member of the Illinois
      legislature (1848-1850), he was involved in the railroad business for

twelve years. He became colonel of the Eighty-Third Illinois
Infantry Regiment and was simultaneously named commander of
Fort Donelson in 1862.

2.    Harding was promoted to brigadier general for bravery after his
defense of Fort Donelson. He later commanded the post of
Murfreesboro. He was a member of the U. S. House of
Representatives from 1865 to 1869, where his main activity was to
promote railroads in Illinois.

## CHAPTER 8: THOMPSON'S STATION AND BRENTWOOD

1.    Van Dorn had five brigades under Brigadier Generals Forrest, William
T. Martin, and George B. Cosby, and Colonels (later Brigadier
Generals) Frank C. Armstrong and John W. Whitfield—a total of
6,500 men. Armstrong and Winfield's brigades came under a division
commanded by Brigadier General William H. "Red" Jackson.

2.    For 152 years, historians (who were misled by Dr. Peters and his family)
believed Van Dorn was murdered for having an adulterous affair with
Peters' wife. This was not the cause. Had Peters shot everyone who
fooled around with Mrs. Peters' and her 15-year-old daughter, whom
he impregnated. The baby was Van Dorn's fourth illegitimate child. All
of this and more is revealed in Bridget Smith's book, *Where Elephants
Fought* (Mechanicsburg, Pennsylvania: 2015).

## CHAPTER 9: THE PURSUIT OF THE JACKASS BRIGADE

1.    Streight's command consisted of his own Fifty-First Indiana
Infantry, Colonel Gilbert Hathaway's Seventy-Third Indiana
Infantry, Colonel Otis Lawson's Third Ohio Infantry, Lieutenant
Colonel Andrew Rodgers's Eighty-First Illinois Infantry and two
companies of Alabama (Union) cavalry. In all, he had about three
thousand men.

2.    Roddey's birth date and year are unknown, but it was around the
time his father was killed in an altercation in Moulton, Alabama, in
1824. Like Forrest, he had little formal education. He was a county
sheriff (1846-1852) and a steamboat owner before the war. He
burned his steamboat to keep it out of Yankee hands, raised a
company of Confederate cavalry and fought at Shiloh. He recruited

the excellent Fourth Alabama Cavalry Regiment later that year. Roddey was named commander of the District of Northern Alabama in December. He and Forrest liked each other and worked well together.

3.  Starnes was sick and McLemore was acting commander of the Fourth Tennessee.

4.  A vidette is a mounted sentry, posted in advance of outposts.

5.  Mr. Samson had died in 1859. His only son, Rufus, was a soldier in the Nineteenth Alabama Infantry Regiment.

6.  Emma Samson was born on August 16, 1847. She married Private Christopher B. Johnson of the Tenth Alabama Infantry Regiment in 1864. They moved to Callaway (now Little Mound), Texas in 1876. They had seven children. Mr. Johnson died in 1887 and Emma passed away on August 9, 1900. She is buried in the Little Mound Cemetery in back of the Baptist Church.

7.  Captain J. Harvey Mathes wrote that Forrest said "Enough to blow you to pieces in thirty minutes."

8.  Streight (1828-1892) was sent to Libby Prison in Richmond but, along with 107 others, escaped ten months later. A somewhat corpulent man, he got stuck in the tunnel and had to be pulled back. He took off his coat, vest and shirt and tried again, this time successfully. He made his way back to Union lines, where he was given command of an infantry brigade and a brevet promotion to brigadier general. Later he was a successful furniture manufacturer and business owner in Indianapolis, an Indiana state senator and unsuccessful candidate for governor. His wife, a nurse, was also captured at Lawrence's Plantation but was immediately released.

9.  As late as May 27, Lincoln telegraphed Rosecrans and wanted to know "Where is Forrest's headquarters?" Rosecran didn't have a clue.

10. Morton and Gould had both been captured at Fort Donelson and had been prison mates. They had been schoolmates before that. Morton thought Gould was a man of "rare courage and efficiency."

# CHAPTER 10: RIVER OF DEATH

1.  Most volunteers were members of the Fourth Alabama Cavalry, which had served under Forrest and had considerable respect for him.

2.  The government would not purchase the excellent rifles for the brigade, so Wilder asked the men if they would purchase them for themselves. They unanimously agreed to do so. Wilder then took out a personal loan for the rifles at $35 a rifle and issued them to his men. He was planning to take the money out of their pay, but an embarrassed Lincoln administration repaid the loan before the colonel could do this. The average white Union private was paid $13 per month. African-American privates were paid three dollars less. Despite his accomplishments, Colonel Wilder (1830-1871) was never promoted to brigadier general, although he was given a brevet to that rank. He resigned from the army in October 1864 due to dysentery. He moved to Tennessee after the war and became a very successful businessman. He was born in New York but moved to Indiana before the war.

3.  On the other hand, the reader might argue that, had he been facing Lee and/or Jackson, Rosecrans would not have made such careless dispositions. There you have me. You are probably right.

4.  W. H. T. Walker graduated from West Point in 1837 and had a distinguished career in the regular army. He was killed in action near Atlanta on July 22, 1864.

5.  Berry was assigned to the staff but was not with Forrest for long. The following month he was shot through the left lung and was left to the clemency of the enemy. They sent him to a prison in southern Ohio, but he escaped by jumping off a moving train. He reached Kentucky, raised a company of sixty-four men (twenty-three of them escaped prisoners) and went into the guerrilla warfare business.

6.  Longstreet's third division, commanded by Major General George Pickett, was in North Carolina at the time. In any case, it had been severely depleted at Gettysburg.

7.  William McLemore (1830-1908), the goat of the Battle of Parker's Crossroads, had since redeemed himself and had been promoted to colonel. He would be a brigade commander at the end of the war. A

lawyer from Franklin, Tennessee, he became a judge after the surrender.

8.    Hindman (1828-1868) was a former congressman from Arkansas and a good divisional commander. He criticized Bragg, however, so he had to go. He was later restored to command by Joseph E. Johnston. Hindman was critically wounded in the Atlanta campaign and unable to perform field duty thereafter. After the war, he was murdered by Carpetbagger agents. He formerly commanded the Trans-Mississippi Department (1862-63).

## CHAPTER 11: FORREST CREATES AN ARMY: THE SECOND WEST TENNESSEE RAID

1.    McDonald's battalion was the former Third Tennessee Cavalry Regiment—Forrest's original command. It was now commanded by Captain (soon to be Major) P. T. Allin. Lieutenant Colonel Charles McDonald was killed on October 7, 1863, during Wheeler's disastrous raid into western Tennessee.

2.    This rumor turned out to be untrue. Jeffrey had been wounded and captured. He was exchanged fairly quickly and resumed command of his regiment, which joined Forrest's corps in early 1864.

3.    They were not officially designated as such until February 1864. The Twentieth Tennessee was also known as the Fifteenth Tennessee Cavalry Regiment.

4.    The commander of the Nineteenth Tennessee Cavalry, Wisdom (1836-1905) was five foot tall and weighed 250 pounds. Born in McNary County, he practiced law in Prudy and moved to Indian Territory (now Oklahoma) after the war. He was a member of the Mississippi State Senate in the early 1870s.

## CHAPTER 12: OKOLONA

1.    Smith made enormous contributions to the field of scientific engineering, especially to the underpinnings of skyscrapers and bridges. He built the world's first all steel bridge across the Missouri and played a role in the construction of every skyscraper built in Chicago prior to 1910.

2.	Waring (1833-1898) joined the Union Army at age twenty-eight, as a major in the Thirty-Ninth New York Volunteer Infantry. Transferred to the cavalry in August 1861, he became colonel of the Fourth Missouri (Union) Cavalry. Young described him as "gallant, good-natured and a fierce fighter," and praised "his courage of the very highest order." In civilian life, he became one of the greatest sanitary engineers in U.S. history. He was street commissioner of New York City in 1898, when he went to Cuba near the end of the Spanish-American War. Here he died of yellow fever.

3.	The Twelfth Kentucky was part of McCulloch's brigade.

4.	Tyler had two companies—a total of 150 men.

5.	Jeffrey Forrest was born in Tippah County, Mississippi on June 10, 1838. He was a slave trader in Vicksburg prior to the war. He enlisted with Bedford but became a second lieutenant in June 1861 and a captain after Fort Donelson. Promoted to major in late 1862 and colonel in 1863, he was wounded and captured at Bear's Creek, Alabama on October 26, 1863. He was subsequently paroled and exchanged. He married Sallie Dyche of Aberdeen, Mississippi, during the war.

6.	Initially buried in Aberdeen, Jeffrey was reinterned in Elmwood Cemetery in Memphis in 1868. Another of Bedford's brothers, Lieutenant Colonel Aaron H. Forrest, the commander of the Sixth Battalion, Mississippi State Troops, would die of pneumonia at Dresden, Tennessee, on or about April 25, 1864.

# CHAPTER 13: THE THIRD WEST TENNESSEE RAID

1.	The brigade consisted of the Third, Seventh and Eighth Kentucky Cavalry Regiments.

2.	After several years in the U.S. Congress, James R. Chalmers died in 1898. He was buried in Elmwood Cemetery in Memphis, not far from the first grave of Nathan Bedford Forrest.

3.	Hurst was already rich. He was a major slaveholder and he and his brothers owned a sixty square mile (38,400 acre!) plantation extending to the Tennessee River. Locally it was called "the Hurst nation." But Colonel Hurst still misused his position to expand his wealth.

4. Colonel Wisdom commanded the Nineteenth Tennessee Cavalry.
5. Hawkins (1818-1880) was eventually exchanged. He was commanding cavalry in Kentucky at the end of the war. A native of Columbia, Tennessee, he later served as Congress (1865-71) as a Republican.
6. A Mexican War veteran, he had been critically wounded at Shiloh.
7. Crossland (1827-1881) was a pre-war farmer, lawyer, legislator and sheriff. Called "as plain as the proverbial 'old shoe' and an accomplished gentleman," he "had the unfortunate habit to stop the flight of a bullet in almost every conflict in which he was engaged." He became a judge and a congressman after the war.
8. Mason Brayman (1813-1895) was later territorial governor of Idaho (1876-80).

## CHAPTER 14: FORT PILLOW

1. Travelling via the Mississippi River, Fort Pillow was eighty miles from Memphis. Since 1864, the river has moved about two miles to the west.
2. Two ten-pounder rifled Parrotts, two twelve-pounder howitzers and two six-pounders.
3. Bradford's father was an anti-Jackson political ally of Davy Crockett and once ran unsuccessfully for Congress against James K. Polk.
4. Black troops were granted no such luxury. They were forced to sleep in tents. Discrimination was widespread in the Union Army and was the rule, rather than the exception.
5. Shaw had been one of Bradford's prisoners but had recently escaped.
6. He was called Black Bob because of the color of his hair and to distinguish him from his cousin, "Red Bob," who also rode with Forrest.
7. The *New Era* had six twenty-four-pounders.
8. Unfortunately, Clark did not say if he heard Forrest give this order, or if he heard it from a third party who attributed it to Forrest, in which case it must be regarded as hearsay.
9. Washburn was the youngest of three distinguished brothers. Israel Washburn was the wartime governor of Maine, and Elihu, a congressman from Illinois, was the chairman of the Military Affairs

Committee and an early patron of Ulysses S. Grant. Cadwallader himself served three terms as a congressman from Wisconsin. (At one time, all three brothers served in Congress together.) Cadwallader resigned to join the army. Later he was governor of Wisconsin and founder of General Mills.

## CHAPTER 15: "THE MOST PERFECT BATTLE": BRICE'S CROSS ROADS

1.  Lee replaced General Polk on May 9. Bishop Polk commanded a corps under Joseph E. Johnston until June 14, 1864, when he was killed in action.
2.  Henry (1804-1880) and Davis attended law school together. Fort Henry, Tennessee, was named in his honor.
3.  Sherman estimated that it would take 160 railroad cars of supplies per day to supply his armies. On the other hand, Sherman calculated, if each of his wagons carried two tons of supplies twenty miles a day, he would need to assemble 36,800 wagons, complete with six mule teams and teamsters, to supply his Atlanta offensive—which was clearly impossible.
4.  Sturgis's primary objective was to kill Forrest. His secondary objective was to destroy—or at least neutralize—Forrest's Cavalry Corps. His first geographical objective was to cut the Mobile & Ohio Railroad and then capture Tupelo. He also wanted to destroy as much of the Southern infrastructure as possible.
5.  Davis was a prominent local attorney. Colonel McMillen headquartered in his house.
6.  Chalmers's Mississippi Battalion (aka the Eighteenth Mississippi Cavalry Battalion) was commanded by Lieutenant Colonel Alexander H. Chalmers (1829-1872), the brother of General James Chalmers. It was later upgraded to the Eighteenth Mississippi Cavalry Regiment. Like the general, Alexander Chalmers was a very good officer.
7.  Bell reduced the odds somewhat by designating every eighth man a horse-holder. Normally it was one out of every four.
8.  During the Civil War, African-Americans were called "colored" and their units were officially designated USCT (United States Colored

Troops). Former slaves who were not in the army were called "contrabands" by the Yankees.

9.  Captain Morton also reported that eight hundred of the 1,300 black troops escaped.

10. The Sixteenth Tennessee was commanded by Colonel Andrew Wilson. Jesse Forrest was its lieutenant colonel.

11. Sturgis remained unemployed for the rest of the war. After the war, he reverted to his regular army rank of lieutenant colonel. Most of his post-war service was in the west, including a tour of duty as commander of the U.S. Seventh Cavalry. He was succeeded in this post by his lieutenant colonel, George Armstrong Custer. He retired from the army for age in 1886 and died in St. Paul, Minnesota, in 1889. He is buried in Arlington National Cemetery.

12. According to Forrest's report. There are 120 graves in the Confederate Cemetery at Brice's Cross Roads. Some of these no doubt died after the battle. In those days before antibiotics, even minor wounds sometimes became infected and resulted in death.

# CHAPTER 16: "THERE WILL NEVER BE PEACE": TUPELO AND THE MEMPHIS RAID

1.  A game similar to horseshoes except they tossed a circular iron ring or a rope.

2.  Because of feints from Union forces at Vicksburg and Baton Rouge, Lee was not yet up from central and southern Mississippi, but Smith was certain that he would join Forrest—as indeed he did.

3.  Colonel Falkner (1825-1889) was the great-grandfather of novelist William Faulkner, who won the Pulitzer Prize twice. He fought in the Mexican War, was a militia general, was wounded at the First Manassas, and commanded the Seventh Mississippi Cavalry (aka First Mississippi Partisan Rangers). The regiment was disbanded in 1863 because of its poor combat record and Falkner was left unemployed. After the war, he was a lawyer, railroad builder and state legislator. He was killed by a former business partner.

4.  Donelson was the son of Brigadier General Daniel S. Donelson, C.S.A., who died of camp fever in 1863.

5.  Maury was born in Fredericksburg, Virginia in 1822 and graduated from West Point in 1846. He fought in Mexico and remained in the army until 1861. He served as Van Dorn's chief of staff and was promoted to brigadier general after distinguishing himself at Pea Ridge. He fought at Iuka and Corinth and, after briefly serving in Vicksburg and in East Tennessee, he was transferred to Mobile, where he remained for the rest of the war. He was promoted to major general on November 4, 1862. Later he founded the Southern Historical Society and was U.S. minister to Columbia. He died in 1900.

6.  Buckland (1812-1892) was an Ohio lawyer and former commander of the Seventy-Second Ohio Volunteer Infantry Regiment. He helped save Sherman's corps at Shiloh, which led to his promotion to brigadier general. He fought well in the Vicksburg campaign and was named district commander of Memphis in January 1864. A Republican, he served two terms in Congress after the war (1865-1869), and was later director of the Union Pacific Railroad. Rutherford B. Hayes was his law partner.

## CHAPTER 17: RIDING AGAINST SHERMAN

1.  Lyon was promoted to brigadier general on June 14, 1864.

2.  Bell would be promoted to brigadier general on February 28, 1865.

3.  Neely (1816-1894) and Green (1829-1906) were cashiered on October 4, 1864. Neely returned to Bolivar County, Tennessee, where he was a physician and became sheriff after the war. Green returned to farming in Tennessee and later became a newspaper editor. Stewart was apparently not cashiered but was unemployed for the rest of the war. Duckworth (1834-1915) was a postwar Methodist preacher and physician in Brownsville, Tennessee.

4.  McDonald's battalion was redesigned Twenty-Sixth Tennessee Cavalry Battalion shortly thereafter. Kelley (1833-1909), who was known as "Forrest's fighting preacher," was minister at a variety of churches after the war. He also served as trustee of Vanderbilt University.

5.  Roddey's reinforcements were led by Colonel William L. Johnson, a top-notch commander who had impressed Forrest at Brice's Cross

Roads. A pre-war steamboat owner, Johnson (1827-1891) previously commanded the Fourth Alabama Cavalry. Two of his brothers were killed during the war and one died in Union prison camp. Like Forrest, Johnson was a fierce warrior and once killed a Union colonel in a saber fight. After he downed him, he tried to save the colonel's life by dressing his wound, but was unsuccessful. Forrest was so impressed with his courage that he presented him with a beautiful black charger. Johnson accepted the gift, but preferred to use his old warhorse in combat.

6.   Most of the 125 white POWs were members of the Third Tennessee (Union) Cavalry Regiment.

7.   Andrew McGregor was born on August 13, 1832 and commanded Company G, Fourth Tennessee Cavalry. He died on September 23, 1910, and is buried in Lebanon, Tennessee.

8.   Named for the Union governor of Tennessee and current Republican vice presidential nominee, Andrew Johnson.

9.   The Tennessee River is nine hundred miles long and is the fifth largest river in the United States.

10.  Forrest thought very highly of General Lyon.

11.  Hinson's 1,200 acre plantation, Bubbling Springs, lay on the edge of Fort Donelson.

12.  Rucker's brigade and Lieutenant H. H. Briggs's battery.

## CHAPTER 18: THE NASHVILLE CAMPAIGN

1.   Red Jackson (1935-1903) graduated from West Point in 1856. He commanded the Seventh Tennessee Cavalry in Van Dorn's Holly Springs raid and was promoted to brigadier general at the end of 1862. Post-war he became famous as a thoroughbred horse breeder.

2.   Edwin S. Walton graduated from college in 1855. As a lieutenant, he was severely wounded at Vicksburg in 1863. He was a successful planter near Sardis, Mississippi, after the war and was still alive in 1887.

3.   Palmer was a resident of Murfreesboro and had served as mayor from 1855 to 1859. Before the war, Sears was a professor of mathematics at the University of Louisiana (now Tulane).

4. Bate (1826-1905), who had little education, started out as a clerk on a steamboat. He was later governor of Tennessee (1883-87) and U.S. senator (1887-1905).
5. No relation to Captain Morton.
6. Colonel Barteau had been severely wounded earlier in the day when a Yankee bullet broke his leg. He was out of action for the rest of the war. Later a Memphis lawyer, he died in 1900 and is buried in Elmwood Cemetery.
7. Alley would later marry and father nine children. He died in 1912.
8. Rucker (1835-1924) became one of the South's most successful industrialists. He was also a railroad owner and bank president. Fort Rucker, Alabama, the home of U.S. Army's helicopter school, was named in his honor.
9. Edward C. Walthall (1831-1898) was born in Virginia but grew up in Holly Springs, Mississippi, which was his home the rest of his life. He commanded the Twenty-Ninth Mississippi Infantry at Corinth and in the Perryville campaign, and was promoted to brigadier general in late 1862. He fought at Chickamauga and Chattanooga, and distinguished himself as Confederate commander in the "Battle Above the Clouds" (which it was not). Wounded here, he returned to duty and commanded his brigade and later a division in the battles around Atlanta. He had two horses shot out from under him at Franklin. He was a United States senator from 1885 until his death. Walthall rose from lieutenant to major general in three years.
10. Buford did not recover until March 1865. His division was temporarily merged with Chalmers's. He was reorganizing his command when the South surrendered. He returned to his beautiful farm in Kentucky and resumed breeding and raising thoroughbred horses. In the 1870s, he suffered a series of financial and personal tragedies, including the loss of his farm and the deaths of his wife and only son. Depression set in and he committed suicide on June 9, 1884.
11. Frank C. Armstrong (1835-1909) was the son of an army officer and was born at Choctaw Agency, Indian Territory. Educated at Holy Cross Academy in Massachusetts, he was commissioned directly into the army in 1854. He fought on the Northern side at

the First Manassas but joined the C.S. Army in August 1861. He
fought at Pea Ridge before becoming colonel of the Third Louisiana
Infantry. Later he transferred to the cavalry and served under
Stephen Lee, Wheeler, Sterling Price and Forrest. He was promoted
to brigadier general on January 20, 1863. Armstrong worked for the
Bureau of Indian Affairs after the war.
12. Dr. and Mrs. Peters were currently separated—at least
    geographically. They reconciled after the war.

## CHAPTER 19: THE LAST BATTLE

1. Beauregard was commander of the Department of the West, which
   included Hood's army and Taylor's Department of Mississippi,
   Alabama and East Louisiana, as well as the Mobile garrison. His
   was a vague and nebulous assignment, however, because he did not
   actually command forces and had little real power.
2. His official title was commander of the Cavalry Department of
   Mississippi, Alabama and East Louisiana. West Tennessee was
   added to this title—apparently by Forrest himself.
3. Hood was succeeded by Richard Taylor, who was acting
   commander from January 13 to February 22, 1865, when he was
   succeeded by Johnston.
4. Wilson's divisions were commanded by Brigadier Generals Edward
   Hatch, Eli Long, Edward M. McCook and Emory Upton. His fifth
   division, commanded by Joseph F. Knipe, had been transferred to
   Canby's command, which was driving on Mobile.
5. William Forrest was promoted to captain just before the end of the
   war.

## CHAPTER 20: AFTER THE WAR

1. Jerry was in charge of the forty-three slaves (later free men) who
   went to war with General Forrest. He was called "G'ineral" by the
   other blacks.
2. Francis P. Blair, Jr. (1821-1875) was engaged in a cotton venture in
   Mississippi which was ultimately unsuccessful. He had commanded
   the XV and XVII Corps in the March to the Sea. He later served as
   U.S. Senator from Missouri (1871-73).

3.  Admiral Semmes (1809-1877) became an Alabama judge and practiced law in Mobile after the war. After all of his adventures, he died from eating a bad oyster.

4.  Lester (1840-1903), a life-long bachelor, was a lawyer with a distinguished combat record. He later served in the Tennessee legislature.

5.  Crowe (1838-1911) served with the Fourth Alabama Infantry and the Thirty-Fifth Tennessee Infantry. He fought in several battles, was wounded three times, and commanded a battalion of sharpshooters. It was he who originated the term "Ku Klux Klan."

6.  Kennedy (1841-1913) was also a veteran of the Third Tennessee Infantry and was a *bona fide* war hero. He was severely wounded three times and was captured and escaped. After the war he spent twenty-two years as the clerk of a circuit court.

7.  Calvin Jones, who was also a lawyer, was Judge Jones's son. The judge was not present. Calvin had been adjutant of the Thirty-Second Tennessee Infantry Regiment during the war.

8.  Some of the more prominent Klansmen included Brigadier Generals John C. Brown of Pulaski (later the governor of Tennessee); A. H. Colquitt, George T. Anderson, and A. R. Lawton. Former Lieutenant General William J. Hardee of Alabama was a member. Former Brigadier General Albert Pike was reportedly the Klan's chief judicial officer, but this information was taken from a source that is not particularly reliable.

9.  George W. Gordon (1836-1911) was a surveyor before the war. Elected to Congress in 1906, he was the last Confederate general to sit in that body. He died in office and is buried in Elmwood Cemetery, Memphis.

10. The Maxwell House burned down in 1961.

11. There is no documentation for this, but old Klansmen tell us it was so.

12. Butler (1818-93) was called "Spoons" because, as military dictator of New Orleans, he changed residences frequently. When Butler left and the owners of a particular mansion were allowed to return home, much was missing. The silverware was always gone. A poor

general, U.S. Grant fired him in January 1865. By then, Butler was a rich man.

13. Kilpatrick (b. 1836) ran for Congress and lost. He changed his political affiliation twice but was unable to gain any credibility. He finally managed to secure an ambassadorship to Chile, where he feuded with General Hurlbut, the ambassador to Peru. He died in Chile in 1881.

14. Brownlow went on to serve as a U.S. Senator (1869-1875).

15. DeWitt C. Senter (1830-1898) was a lawyer and popular Methodist preacher. He was a member of the Tennessee Senate (1851-52) and U. S. House of Representatives (1855-61). He strongly opposed secession and advocated the establishment of a separate East Tennessee state within the Union. He was arrested by Confederate authorities and imprisoned for several months. He was elected to the Tennessee state senate in January 1865, became its president, and succeeded Brownlow. He was reelected in 1869, but was forced to retire from politics in 1871.

16. As far as I have been able to determine, the only other former Confederate general to ever take this position was P. G. T. Beauregard.

17. The Yellow Fever Epidemic lasted until 1879. Among its victims were General John Bell Hood, his wife, and one of their ten children.

18. White (1840-1911) was born in Independence, Missouri, and joined the Confederate Army in 1861, against his father's objections. After distinguishing himself in the war he became a medical doctor but, largely because of the influence of his devout wife, he was ordained in 1873. He later moved to Texas, where he was especially active in ministering to African-Americans. He is buried in Temple.

19. Dr. G. T. Stainback, D.D., (1829-1902) had been an assistant professor of Latin and Greek at Ole Miss, where he had taken his doctorate in 1855. He had been a preacher in Columbus, Mississippi, for years, and was a chaplain in the Confederate Army before coming to Cumberland. Forrest respected him. Like Mary, he had been working to converse Bedford to Christianity, and he studied Bible with Forrest after his conversion. Stainback later

returned Columbus, where he died and is buried. The father of seven, he was a Grand Master of the Grand Lodge of Grand Masons in Mississippi.

20. James Longstreet (1821-1904) was a scalawag after the war and the only senior Confederate Army general to join the Republican Party. Named adjutant general of Louisiana in 1872, he faced the anti-Reconstruction White League in the Battle of Liberty Place in New Orleans in 1874, directing city policemen and African-American militia. Despite the fact that he had artillery and Gatling guns, Longstreet was quickly defeated and taken prisoner. He was spared only because of his previous Rebel service. He left Louisiana shortly thereafter and settled in Gainesville, Georgia, where he was a postmaster and farmer. Later he was U.S. ambassador to the Ottoman Empire.

21. After Jane's death, Willie married Hallie Fairies (1869-1912).

22. After the war, Charles Anderson returned to work for the Nashville & Chattanooga Railroad. He left it in 1879, when he began to have serious health problems. He then managed his farm until his death in 1908. He had been born in Kentucky in 1825.

23. John Tyler Morgan (1824-1907) was a brigadier general and served on the Eastern and Western Fronts. He was a leader in the white supremacy movement and was U.S. senator from Alabama from 1877 until his death. His was buried in Selma.

24. James David Porter (1828-1912) was born in Paris, Tennessee. He served as General Pillow's adjutant in 1861 and was later Cheatham's chief of staff. He became a judge after the war before being elected governor twice (1874 and 1876), during which he established the South's first medical school for blacks. Later he was U.S. assistant secretary of state and ambassador to Chile.

# BIBLIOGRAPHY

Allardice, Bruce S. *Confederate Colonels*. Columbia: University of Missouri Press, 2008.

Ashdown, Paul, and Edward Caudill. *The Myth of Nathan Bedford Forrest*. Lanham, Maryland: Rowman & Littlefield, 2006.

Barrow, Charles K., J. H. Segars and R. B. Rosenburg. *Black Confederates*. Gretna, Louisiana: Pelican Publishing Co., 2001.

Bearss, Edwin C. *Forrest at Brice's Crossroads and in North Mississippi in 1864*. Dayton, Ohio: Morningside Bookshop, 2001.

Beck, Brandon H. *The Battle of Okolona*. Charleston, S.C.: The History Press, 2009.

Bedwell, Randall, ed. *May I Quote You, General Forrest?* Nashville, Tennessee: Cumberland House, 1997.

Berry, Thomas F. *Four Years with Morgan and Forrest*. Oklahoma City: The Harlow-Ratliff Co., 1914.

Bradley, Michael R. *Forrest's Fighting Preacher: David Campbell Kelley of Tennessee*. Charleston, S.C.: The History Press, 2011.

Bradley, Michael R. *Nathan Bedford Forrest's Escort and Staff.* Gretna, Louisiana: Pelican Publishing Co., 2009.

Bradley, Michael R. *They Rode With Forrest.* Gretna, Louisiana: Pelican Publishing Co., 2012.

Bradshaw, Wayne. *The Civil War Diary of William R. Dyer: A Member of Forrest's Escort.* BookSurge Publishing, 2009.

Brady, Cyrus T. *Three Daughters of the Confederacy.* New York: G. W. Dillingham, 1905.

Brooksher, William R. and David K. Snyder. *Glory at a Gallop: Tales of the Confederate Cavalry.* Gretna, Louisiana: Pelican Publishing Co., 2002.

Brown, Andrew. "The First Mississippi Partisan Rangers, C.S.A." *Civil War History.* Vol. 1, No. IV (December 1955): pp. 371–400.

Browning, Robert M., Jr. *Forrest: The Confederacy's Relentless Warrior.* Dulles, Virginia: Brassey's, Inc. 2004.

Bryan, Charles E., Jr. "I Mean to Have Them All": Forrest's Murfreesboro Raid. Civil War Times Illustrated. Vol. 12 (January 1974): pp. 27–34.

Cadwallader, Sylvanus. *Three Years With Grant.* New York: Knopf, 1955.

Castel, Albert. The Fort Pillow Massacre: A Fresh Examination of the Evidence." *Civil War History.* Vol. IV, No. 1 (March 1958): pp. 37–50.

Chalmers, James R. "Forrest and His Campaigns." *Southern Historical Society Papers,* Vol. VII (October 1879): pp. 451–86.

Cimprich, John. *Fort Pillow, a Civil War Massacre and Public Memory.* Baton Rouge: L.S.U. Press, 2005.

Cisco, Walter Brian. *War Crimes Against Southern Civilians.* Gretna, Louisiana: Pelican Publishing Co., 2007.

"Concerning the Nathan Bedford Forrest Legend." *Tennessee Folklore Society Bulletin,* September 1938.

Confederate Veteran. Various numbers and volumes.

Cooling, Benjamin F. "The Attack on Dover, Tennessee." *Civil War Times Illustrated.* Vol. 2 (August 1963): pp. 11–13.

Cottrell, Steve. *Civil War in Tennessee*. Gretna, LA: Peilican Publishing Co., 2001.

Cozzens, Peter. *This Terrible Sound: The Battle of Chickamuga*. Chicago: University of Illinois Press, 1992.

Crocker, H. W., III. *The Politically Incorrect Guide to the Civil War*. Washington, D.C.: Regnery, 2008.

Cunningham, O. Edward. *Shiloh and the Western Campaign of 1862*. Gary D. Joiner and Timonty B. Smith, ed.s. New York: Savas Beatie, 2007.

Currotto, William F. *Wizard of the Saddle: Nathan Bedford Forrest*. N.p.: Patchwork Books, 1996.

Daniel, Larry J. *Shiloh: The Battle That Changed the Civil War*. New York: Simon and Schuster, 1997.

Davis, Orlando and Rev. Samuel Agnew. "The Civilian Side" in Robert Selph Henry, ed. *As They Saw Forrest: Some Recollections and Comments of Contemporaries*. Jackson, Tennessee: McCowat-Mercer Press, 1956: pp. 245–50.

Davis, William C. *Look Away: A History of the Confederate States of America*. 2002. New York: Free Press, 2003.

Davison, Eddy W., and Daniel Foxx. *Nathan Bedford Forrest: In Search of the Emigma*. Gretna, LA: Pelican Publishing Co., 2007.

Dawson, Sarah Morgan. *A Confederate Girl's Diary*. London: William Heinemann, 1913.

Dinkins, James. "An August Sunday Morning in Memphis" in Robert Selph Henry, ed. *As They Saw Forrest: Some Recollections and Comments of Contemporaries*. Jackson, Tennessee: McCowat-Mercer Press, 1956: pp. 251–68.

Dinkins, James. *Personal Recollections and Experiences in the Confederate Army, 1861 to 1865*. Cincinnati: The Robert Clark Co., 1897.

Duke, Basil W. *Reminiscences of General Basil W. Duke, C.S.A.* New York: Doubleday, Page and Co., 1911.

Dyer, John P. *"Fighting Joe" Wheeler*. Baton Rouge: L.S.U. Press, 1941.

Eckenrode, Hamilton J. *Life of Nathan Bedford Forrest*. Richmond, Virginia: B. F. Johnson Publishing Co., 1918

Edmonds, George. *Facts and Falsehoods Concerning the War in the South, 1861–1865.* Memphis: A. R. Taylor and Co., 1904.

Eicher, David J. *The Longest Night: A Military History of the Civil War.* New York: Simon and Schuster, 2002.

Evans, Clement. *Confederate Military History.* Atlanta: Confederate Publishing Company, 1899. 12 volumes.

Fisher, John E. *They Rode With Forrest and Wheeler: A Chronicle of Five Tennessee Brothers.* Jefferson, N.C.: McFarland & Company, Inc., 1995.

Foote, Shelby. *The Civil War, A Narrative: Fort Sumter to Perryville.* New York: Random House, 1958.

Foote, Shelby. *The Civil War, A Narrative: Fredericksburg to Meridian.* New York: Random House, 1963.

Foote, Shelby. *The Civil War, A Narrative: Red River to Appomattox.* New York: Random House, 1974.

Freeman, Douglas S., ed. Lee's Dispatches. New York: G. P. Putnam's Sons, 1935.

Gauss, John. *Black Flag! Black Flag! The Battle of Fort Pillow.* Lanham, Maryland: University Press of America. 2003.

Gentry, Claude. *General Nathan Bedford Forrest: The Boy and the Man.* Macon, Georgia: Magnolia, 1972.

Gott, Kendall D. *Where the South Lost the War: An Analysis of the Fort Henry-Fort Donelson Campaign, February 1862.* Mechanicsburg, PA: Stackpole Books, 2003.

Grant, Ulysses S. *Personal Memoirs of U. S. Grant.* New York: Charles L. Webster & Co., 1892.

Groom, Winston. *Shiloh, 1862.* Washington, D.C.: National Geographic, 2012.

Hafendorfer, Kenneth A. *Nathan Bedford Forrest: The Distant Storm— The Murfreesboro Raid of July 13, 1862.* Louisville, Kentucky: K H Press, 1997.

Hancock, Richard R. *Hancock's Diary, or a History of the Second Tennessee Cavalry, C.S.A.* Nashville: Brandon Printing Co., 1887.

Henry, Robert Selph, ed. *As They Saw Forrest: Some Recollections and Comments of Contemporaries*. Jackson, Tennessee: McCowat-Mercer Press, 1956.

Henry, Robert Selph. *"First with the Most" Forrest*. Indianapolis: Bobbs-Merrill Co., 1944.

Heritage Not Hate Productions. "A Tribute to Our Black Confederate Heroes." Utube. Accessed 2015.

Horn, Stanley F. *Invisible Empire: The Story of the Ku Klux Klan, 1866–1871*. Boston: Houghton Mifflin Co., 1939.

Hubbard, John Milton. "Notes" in Robert Selph Henry, ed. *As They Saw Forrest: Some Recollections and Comments of Contemporaries*. Jackson, Tennessee: McCowat-Mercer Press, 1956: pp. 137–223.

Hubbard, John Milton. *Notes of a Private*. St. Louis, Missouri: Nixon Jones, 1911.

Hughes, Nathaniel C., Jr., Connie Walton Moretti and James M. Browne. *Brigadier General Tyree H. Bell, C.S.A.: Forrest's Fighting Lieutenant*. Knoxville: University of Tennessee Press, 2004.

Hughes, Nathaniel C., Jr. *Liddell's Record*. Dayton, Ohio: Morningside House, Inc., 1985. Reprint ed., Baton Rouge: L.S.U. Press, 1997.

Hurst, Jack. *Men of Fire: Grant, Forrest and the Campaign That Decided the Civil War*. New York: Basic Books, 2008.

Johnson, Adam R. *The Partisan Rangers in the Confederate States Army*. Louisville, Kentucky: George G. Fetter, 1904.

Johnson, Robert U., ed. *Battles and Leaders of the Civil War*. New York: The Century Co., 1884–1886. 4 volumes.

Johnston, Joseph E. *Narrative of Military Operations Directed During the Late War Between the States*. New York: D. Appleton and Company, 1874.

Jordan, Thomas, and J. P. Pryor. *The Campaigns of General Nathan Bedford Forrest and Forrest's Cavalry*. 1868. Reprint ed., New York: Di Capo Press, 1996.

Kennedy, James Ronald and Walter Donald Kennedy. *The South Was Right*. Gretna, Louisiana: Pelican Publishing Co., 1994. 2nd edition.

Ladnier, Gene. *General Nathan Bedford Forrest on Fame's Eternal Battlefield*. Charleston, S.C.: BookSurge, 2001.

Langsdon, Phillip. *Tennessee: A Political History*. Franklin, Tennessee: Hillsboro Press, 2000.

Lash, Jeffery N. *A Politician Turned General: The Civil War Career of Stephen Augustus Hurlbut*. Kent, Ohio: Kent State University, 2003.

Lester, John C., and Daniel L. Wilson. *Ku Klux Klan: Its Origins, Growth and Disbandment*. New York: Neale Publishing, 1905.

Lindsley, John Berrien. *The Military Annals of Tennessee.: Confederate*. Nashville: J. M. Lindsley & Co, 1886.

Logsdon, David R., ed. *Eyewitnesses at the Battle of Franklin*. 1988. Nashville, Tennessee: Kettle Mills Press, 2000.

Longacre, Edward G. *A Soldier to the Last: Major General Joseph Wheeler in Blue and Gray*. Sterling, VA: Potomac Books, Inc., 2007.

Losson, Christopher. *Tennessee's Forgotten Warrior: Frank Cheatham and His Confederate Division*. Knoxville, Tennessee: University of Tennessee Press, 1989.

Lytle, Andrew Nelson. *Bedford Forrest and His Critter Company*. 1951. Reprint ed., Nashville, Tennessee: J. S. Sanders and Company, 2002.

Maness, Lonnie E. *An Untutored Genius: The Military Career of General Nathan Bedford Forrest*. Oxford, Mississippi: Guild Bindary Press, 1990.

Mathes, J. Harvey. *General Forrest*. New York: D. Appleton and Co., 1902.

Maury, Dabney H. *Recollections of a Virginian in the Mexican, Indian, and Civil Wars*. New York: Charles Scribner's Sons, 1892.

McDonough, James L. *Nashville: The Western Confederacy's Final Gamble*. Knoxville: University of Tennessee Press, 2004.

McDonough, James L. *Shiloh—In Hell Before Night*. Knoxville, Tennessee: University of Tennessee Press, 1977.

McDonough, James L., and Thomas L. Connelly. *Five Tragic Hours: The Battle of Franklin*. 1983. Knoxville, Tennessee: University of Tennessee Press, 2001.

McKenney, Tom C. *Jack Hinson's One-Man War: A Civil War Sniper.* Gretna, LA: Pelican Press, 2009.

McMurry, Richard M. *John Bell Hood and the War for Southern Independence.* Lincoln, Nebraska: University of Nebraska Press, 1992.

McPherson, James. *Battle Cry of Freedom: The Civil War Era.* Oxford: Oxford University Press, 1988.

McWhitney, Grady, and Judith Lee Hallock. *Braxton Bragg and the Confederate Defeat.* Tuscaloosa, Alabama: University of Alabama Press, 1991. 2 volumes.

Morton, John W. *The Artillery of Nathan Bedford Forrest's Cavalry.* Nashville, Tennessee: Publishing House of the M. F. Church, South, Smith and Lamar, agents, 1909.

Porter, James D. *The Military History of Tennessee, War of 1861–65.* Nashville: 1899. Republished as Volume VIII in Clement Evans's *Confederate Military History.*

Rambaut, Gilbert V. "Forrest at Shiloh" in Robert Selph Henry, ed. *As They Saw Forrest: Some Recollections and Comments of Contemporaries.* Jackson, Tennessee: McCowat-Mercer Press, 1956: pp. 54–65.

Robuck, J. E. *My Own Personal Experiences and Observations as a Soldier in the Confederate Army During the Civil War, 1861–1865.* N.p.: Leslie Print and Publishing Co., 1911.

Rollins, Richard, ed. *Black Southerners in Gray: Essays on Afro-Americans in Confederate Armies.* Redondo Beach, CA: Rank and File Publishing, 1994.

Seabrook, Lochlainn. *A Rebel Born: A Defense of Nathan Bedford Forrest.* Franklin, Tennessee: Sea Raven Press, 2012.

Seabrook, Lochlainn. *Nathan Bedford Forrest: Southern Hero, American Patriot.* Franklin, Tennessee: Sea Raven Press, 2007.

Segars, J. H., and Charles Kelly Barrow. *Black Southerners in Confederate Armies: A Collection of Historical Accounts.* 2001. Gretna, Louisiana: Pelican Publishing Co., 2007.

Sherman, William T. *Memoirs of W. T. Sherman.* New York: Charles Scribner's Sons. 1894.

Smith, Bridget. *Where Elephants Fought*. Mechanicsburg, PA: 2015.

Smith, Jeffrey K. *The Wizard of the Saddle: Nathan Bedford Forrest*. North Charleston, South Carolina: CreateSpace Independent Publishing Platform, 2015.

Southern Historical Society Papers. Volumes 1–42 (1876–1916).

Speer, William S. *Sketches of Prominent Tennesseans*. Nashville, Tennessee: Genealogical Publishing Co., 1888.

Starnes, James W. *Forrest's Forgetton Horse Brigadier*. Westminister, Maryland: Heritage Books, 1995. [H. Gerald Starnes]

Sworp, Wiley. *The Confederacy's Last Hurrah: Spring Hill, Franklin and Nashville*. New York: Harper Collins, 1992.

Thomas, Emory. *The Confederate Nation, 1861–1865*. New York: 1974.

*Union Army, The*. Volume VIII. *Biographical*. Madison, Wisconsin: Federal Publishing Co., 1908.

United States Congress. Joint Select Committee on the Conduct of the War. *Fort Pillow Massacre, April 21, 1864*. Washington, D.C.: 1864.

United States Government. List of Staff Officers of the Confederate States Army. Washington, D.C.: United States Government Printing Office, 1891.

Walsh, George. *"Those Damn Horse Soldiers": True Tales of the Civil War Cavalry*. New York: Forge, 2006.

Ward, Andrew. *River Run Red: The Fort Pillow Massacre in the American Civil War*. New York: Viking Press, 2005.

Waring, George E., Jr. *Whip and Spur*. New York: Doubleday and McClure, 1897.

Warner, Ezra J. *Generals in Blue: Lives of the Union Commanders*. Baton Rouge: L.S.U. Press, 1964.

Warner, Ezra J. *Generals in Gray: Lives of the Confederate Commanders*. Baton Rouge: L.S.U. Press, 1959.

Weaver, Rev. John. "General Nathan Bedford Forrest." Internet lecture accessed 2013.

Willett, Robert L. *The Lightning Mule Brigade*. Carmel, Indiana: Guild Press, 1999.

Willis, Brian Steel. *A Battle from the Start: The Life of Nathan Bedford Forrest*. New York: Harper Collins, 1992.

Willis, Brian Steel. *The Confederacy's Greatest Cavalryman: Nathan Bedford Forrest*. Lawrence, Kansas: University of Kansas Press, 1998.

Wilson, Florence. "Forrest, the Matchless Rider." Nashville Banner, July 7, 1935.

Witherspoon, William. *Reminiscences of a Scout, Spy and Soldier of Forrest's Cavalry*. Jackson, Tennessee: McCowat-Mercer Printing Co., 1910.

Witherspoon, William. "Reminiscences of '61 and '65" in Robert Selph Henry, ed. *As They Saw Forrest: Some Recollections and Comments of Contemporaries*. Jackson, Tennessee: McCowat-Mercer Press, 1956: pp. 68–100.

Witherspoon, William. "7th Tennessee C.S.A. vs. 7th Tennessee U.S.A." in Robert Selph Henry, ed. *As They Saw Forrest: Some Recollections and Comments of Contemporaries*. Jackson, Tennessee: McCowat-Mercer Press, 1956: pp. 101–111.

Witherspoon, William. "Tishomingo Creek" in Robert Selph Henry, ed. *As They Saw Forrest: Some Recollections and Comments of Contemporaries*. Jackson, Tennessee: McCowat-Mercer Press, 1956: pp. 112–136.

Witherspoon, William. *Tishomingo Creek or Bryce's Cross Roads*. Jackson, Tennessee: Privately published by the author, 1906.

Wolseley, Field Marshal Viscount. "On Forrest" in Robert Selph Henry, ed. *As They Saw Forrest: Some Recollections and Comments of Contemporaries*. Jackson, Tennessee: McCowat-Mercer Press, 1956: pp. 17–53.

Woodward, Steven. *Jefferson Davis and his Generals: The Failure of the Confederate Command in the West*. Lawrence, Kansas: 1990.

Wright, John D. *The Language of the Civil War*. Westport, CT: Oryx, 2001.

Young, Bennett H. *Confederate Wizards of the Saddle*. Boston: Chapple Publishing Co., 1914.

Young, J. P. *The Seventh Tennessee Cavalry (Confederate)*. Nashville: Publishing House of the M. E. Church, South, 1890.


## INTERNET SOURCES:

Davis, Susan L. *Authentic History of the Ku Klux Klan, 1869–1877*. New York: 1924. Digitized by Internet Archive, 2012. Accessed, 2015.

Lester, John C., Rev. D. L. Wilson and Walter L. Fleming. *The Ku Klux Klan: Its Origin, Growth and Disbandment*. Originally published in 1905. Digitized by the Gutenberg EBook Project, 2010. Accessed, 2015.

http://explorekyhistory.ky.gov. "Battle of Sacremento."

http://fortbentonblogshot.com/2012/08/in-shadow-of-colonel-nathan-bedford_26.html.

http://old.nationalreview.com/hanson/hanson040502.asp.

http://scvcamp741.tripol.com/causes/causes2.htm.

https://www.youtube/watch?v=FZyVVm316cU, accessed 2014.

www.findagrave.com

www.kentuckytourism.com/ …battle-of-sacremento.

www.southernheritage411.com/be.php/nw=037.

# ABOUT THE AUTHOR

**D**r. Samuel W. Mitcham, Jr. attended Northeast Louisiana University, North Carolina State, and the University of Tennessee, where he received his doctorate. A former army helicopter pilot and company commander, he is a graduate of the U.S. Army's Command and General Staff College. An internationally recognized authority on military history, he was a visiting professor at West Point and has guest lectured at the Air War College, the General Staff College of the Marine Corps, and several other institutions. He was a professor at Henderson State University, Georgia Southern University and the University of Louisiana at Monroe, and has written more than 30 books of military history. His works have been translated into German, Japanese, Russian, Hungarian, Bulgarian, Spanish, Polish, and Chinese. Several have been main or alternate selections of the Military Book Club and the British Military Book Club. His recent Civil War book, *Richard Taylor and the Red River Campaign*, was selected by three book clubs. Dr. Mitcham has appeared on the History Channel and on CBS, and is a holder of the Jefferson Davis Gold Medal for Excellence in the Writing and Research of Southern History.

# INDEX

## A

Able, John, 17
Adams, Dan, 284, 288
*Alabama*, 294
Anderson, Charles W., 68–70, 81,
    83, 91–92, 99–100, 128, 133,
    167–68, 180, 182, 184–85, 230,
    245, 251, 281, 288, 313
Anderson, James Patton, 14
*Anna*, 252
Armstrong, Frank C., 98, 100–2,
    114, 118–19, 128, 131, 140,
    273, 285

## B

Bacon, Albert G., 30

Banks, Nathaniel P., 149
Barteau, Clark R., 155–56, 180,
    184–85, 203, 205–6, 208, 220,
    248, 256
Bate, William B., 266
Battle of Chickamauga, 72
Battle of Murfreesboro, 72, 89
Battle of Princeton, 68
Battle of Shiloh, 51, 134, 176
Baxter, Max, 86–87
Beauregard, P. G. T., 2, 22, 48–49,
    53–54, 60, 175, 257, 277–78
Beck, Miriam, 5
Bell, Tyree, 139, 145, 204, 212,
    235
Benjamin, Judah P., 300
Berry, Thomas F., 129

Biffle, Jacob, 78, 80, 107, 110, 117

Blair, Frank, 294, 304

Blanton, J. C., 30

Boone, Nathan, 72, 143, 246

Booth, Lionel, 177–79, 181, 184–85, 191

Bradford, Theodore F., 178, 179, 181–85, 188

Bradford, William F., 177

Bragg, Braxton, 22, 60, 62–66, 71, 75–76, 82, 89–90, 92, 95, 103–4, 106, 118–19, 121–28, 130–35, 137–38, 140, 169, 193, 196–98, 237

Brannan, John M., 128

Brayman, Mason, 171

Breckinridge, John C., 49–50, 66

Brent, George William, 133

Brewer, Theodore F., 174

Brice, William, 201

Brice's Cross Roads, 73, 194, 200–3, 206, 210–13, 218, 316

Brown, John C., 264, 301, 307

Brown, Joseph E., 114, 197

Browne, Thomas, 121

Brownlow, William G., 300, 302–3, 305

Bruyere, Jean de la, 1

B-17 bombers, 1

Buckland, Ralph P., 167–69, 225, 228

Buckner, Simon B., 35, 38–42, 71, 126

Buford, Abraham, 164–65, 167, 170–71, 174–75, 196, 205–6,

219–21, 235, 239, 247, 250–52, 255, 259, 263, 265–67, 269, 272

"Bull Pups," 205–6, 267

Burnside, Ambrose, 75, 126

Butler, Benjamin F., 302

**C**

Cadwallader, Sylvanus, 2, 192, 194

Calhoun, John C., 221, 298, 306

Campbell, Wallace, 241

Canby, Edward R. S., 176, 197, 279, 287–88

Carlyle, Thomas, ix

*Carondelet*, 37, 67

Caruthers, Robert L., 281

Catton, Bruce, 2

Cavalry Survivors Association, 312

Chalmers, Alec, 227–28

Chalmers, Alexander H., 227

Chalmers, James R., 48, 164, 166

*Charlotte Observer*, 312

Cheatham, Benjamin F., 48, 81, 129, 133, 264, 274–75

Cimprich, John, 188

Civil War, ix–x, 2, 4–5, 9, 31, 49, 60, 63, 85, 90, 127, 165, 177, 194–95, 228, 243, 250–51, 264, 289, 302, 314

Clark, Achilles V., 185

Clark, Charles, 28, 288

Cleburne, Pat, 133, 175, 165

Coburn, John, 97–98

Collins, N. D., 297

Colt Repeating Rifles, 149

Confederates, 3, 37–38, 47, 49, 59, 73, 90, 92, 98–99, 106, 108,

127, 130, 152, 168, 170, 179, 182, 184, 190, 208, 218, 220, 223, 250, 252, 259–60, 267, 279, 300, 302, 305

Cooch, Daniel W., 190

Cook, Jane Taylor, 313

Cooper, Samuel, 124, 165–66, 278

Cowan, James B., 70, 79, 127, 134–35, 158–59

Cowan, Samuel, 12–13, 79

Cox, N. N., 86

Crews, James M., 171

Crittenden, John J., 23

Crittenden, Thomas L., 125–27, 131

Crittenden, Thomas T., 55, 57

Crossland, Edward, 170, 220, 284

Crowe, James R., 299

Croxton, John T., 246, 260, 283, 285

Curtis, Samuel, 82

**D**

Dashiell, George, 70

Davies, Thomas A., 82, 84

Davis, A. N., 30

Davis, Jefferson, x, 2, 39, 47, 54, 118, 124–25, 130, 133–34, 137–39, 165–66, 191, 193, 197–98, 201, 223, 236–37, 279, 287, 315–17

Dawson, William A., 253

D Company, 177

Dibrell, George G., 66, 78, 80, 85, 106–7, 128, 131

Diffenbocher, B. E., 293, 296

Dinkins, James, 32, 146, 183, 226–27, 229, 272

Distinguished Flying Cross, 1

Dobbs, William, 169

Dodge, Grenville M., 83–84, 104–7, 109

Donaldson, Samuel, 70

Don Carlos, 44–45, 48–49, 54, 60, 62–65, 70, 75, 123

Dorn, Earl Van, 82, 95, 97–101, 103, 107, 118, 275

Douglas, Edwin, xi, 86–87

Duckworth, William L., 169–70, 188, 235–36

Duffield, William, 55–56, 58–59

Duke, Basil, 126, 303

Dunham, Cyrus L., 84–86

Dyson, James, 11

**E**

Eighteenth Mississippi Cavalry Regiment, 220

Eighth Tennessee Cavalry Regiment, 69, 106

Eleventh Tennessee, 106

*Elfin*, 254

Elliott, Jonas, 241

Elliott, Washington L., 247

Escort Company, 65, 72–73, 77, 85–86, 98, 124, 138, 153–54, 158, 167, 208, 231, 316

**F**

Falkner, William, 153, 175, 220

Fifteenth Tennessee, 253

Fifth Mississippi Cavalry, 187

Fifty-Fourth Virginia Infantry, 267

First Georgia, 72

First Kentucky Cavalry, 54

First Missouri Light Artillery, 178

First Tennessee, 100

Floyd, John B., 35–36, 38–43

Foote, Andrew H., 35–36, 40

Foote, Shelby, 2

Forrest, Bill, 69, 107–8, 226–27, 229

Forrest, Jesse, 226, 228, 241, 278

Forrest, Jonathan, 10

Forrest, Miriam, 7

Forrest, Nathan Bedford, vii, ix–xi, 1–25, 27–33, 35–45, 47–51, 53–73, 75–93, 95, 97–103, 105–19, 121–35, 137–47, 149–61, 163–74, 177, 179–83, 185–99, 201–33, 235–57, 259–60, 262–89, 291–317

Forrest, Nathan Bedford, II, 313, 316

Forrest, William, 6, 24

"Forrest's Cavalry Corps," 23

"Forrest's Old Regiment," 24

"Forrest's Tennessee Cavalry Battalion," 23

Fort Donelson, 33, 35–36, 39–43, 45, 62, 68–69, 71, 89–91, 93, 95

Fort Heiman, 250–52

Fort Pillow Massacre, 181, 187, 189

Forty-Third Illinois Volunteer Infantry Regiment, 80

Fourteenth Tennessee Cavalry, 241, 310

Fourteenth Tennessee Infantry, 251

Fourth Alabama, 80, 85, 138

IV Corps, 128, 260

Fourth Mississippi Cavalry, 100

Fourth Regulars, 156

Fourth Tennessee Cavalry, 132

Fourth U.S. Cavalry, 286

Fourth U.S. Regulars, 102

Fowler, Orson, G., 18–19

Freedman's Bureau, 295, 297

Freeman, Samuel, xi, 68, 71, 78, 80, 85, 97, 101–2, 286

Fuller, John W., 84–85

## G

Gallaway, Matthew C., 70

Garfield, James A., 103, 105

Gaus, Jacob, 158, 183, 207, 227, 267

Gholson, Samuel J., 151, 160, 198

Goodman, Walter A., 181, 270

Gordon, George Washington, 299

Gordon, John B., 301

Gould, Andrew, 118–19

Gracey, Frank M., 253–54

Granger, Gordon, 98–100, 103, 121–22, 131, 246

Grant, Ulysses S., 2, 33, 35–43, 45, 47–49, 51, 53, 75–76, 78–79, 82, 84, 86–87, 118, 125, 140, 151, 161, 191, 198, 230, 246, 251, 256, 259, 263, 268, 278, 288, 304, 309

Green, John U., 235

Grierson, Benjamin, 143, 150, 152, 155–56, 159–60, 171–72, 191, 195–96, 199, 202–5, 218, 221, 231–32, 277
Griffith, D. B., 306

## H

Halleck, Henry, 45, 53–54, 62, 82, 197, 268
Hamilton, Andrew J., 302
Hamner, James H., 29
Hancock, R. R., 152, 156, 275–76
Hanson, Roger, 38
Hardee, William J., 48–49, 133, 197
Harding, Abner C., 91–92
Harris, George W. D., 168–69, 174
Harris, Isham, 22, 61, 288
Harrison, Isham, 220
Hatch, Edward, 232, 260, 268, 271, 293–94
Hathaway, Gilbert, 114
Hawkins, Isaac A., 169–70
Helm, Benjamin Hardin, 69
Henderson, Thomas, 69, 169, 249
Henry, Gustavus Adolphus, 197
Hicks, Stephen G., 170, 175
Hill, A. P., 194
Hill, Charles S., 70
Hill, D. H., 130–31, 133
Hindman, Thomas C., 133
Hinson, John W., 250–51, 254
"Homegrown Yankees," 78
Hood, John Bell, 22, 130, 150, 223, 237–39, 244, 257, 260, 262, 264–66, 268–77, 280

Hood, Stephen, 291
Hooker, Joseph, 257
Hosea, Lewis M., 281
Howard, Oliver O., 295
Howe, J. H., 213
Hubbard, John Milton, 16, 141, 201, 225
Huggins, Jacob, 128
Hurlbut, Samuel, 82, 139–41, 151, 172, 175–78, 190–91, 225–27, 231
Hurst, Fielding, 167–69, 171, 173
Hurst, Jack, 186
Hurst, Melocky, 167

## I

Independent Provisional Brigade, 104–5
Ingersoll, Robert, 78–79

## J

Jackson, Andrew, 62,
Jackson, Stonewall, 126, 194, 211–12, 236–37
Jackson, William Red, 98, 118, 259, 263, 265–67, 269, 272–73, 283, 285, 288
Johnson, Adam R., 25
Johnson, Andrew, 22, 69, 280, 295, 304
Johnson, Bushrod R., 35–36
Johnson, Ludwell, 125
Johnson, William L., 202

Johnston, Albert Sidney, 22, 24, 31, 33, 35, 43–45, 47–49, 69, 99,

Johnston, Joseph E., 2, 95, 118, 138–40, 191, 196–97, 212–13, 223, 280, 288–89, 294

Jones, Calvin, 299

Joy, Charles G., 216

*J. W. Cheeseman*, 252

# K

Kelley, David C., 24, 27, 29, 31, 36, 41, 48, 50–51, 221, 236, 239, 241–42, 252, 262, 265, 276

Kennedy, John B., 184, 299

Kentucky Brigade, 192, 203, 220, 235, 284

*Key West*, 254

Kilpatrick, Judson, 305

Ku Klux Klan, 298–99, 301–2, 306–7, 312–13

# L

Landis, A. L., 271–72

Lane, Jim, 302

Lanning, George H., 178

Larkin, James, 90

Lathrop, William, 242

Lawler, Michael K., 84

Laws, John, 5–6

Leaming, Mack J., 180

Lee, Robert E., x–xi, 2, 64, 66, 75, 99, 104, 125–26, 130, 139, 150, 165, 191, 198, 219, 221, 259,

262, 269, 278, 280, 287–89, 301

Lee, Stephen D., 138, 140, 146, 153, 171, 192–93, 196–97, 199, 202, 216, 218–21, 223, 262, 269, 275

Lester, Henry C., 55, 59

Lester, John Calhoun, 298–99, 306

Liddell, John, 63

Lightning Brigade, 127

Lilly, John C., 42, 51

Lincoln, Abraham, 2, 20–21, 39, 65, 69, 72–73, 87, 90, 99, 103, 171, 175–76, 190, 192, 198, 205, 216, 222, 294–95

Little, Montgomery, 72, 85, 98

Logan, John A., 268

Long, J. B., 158

Longstreet, James, 130–31, 133, 312

Loring, W. W., 213

Lowe, William W., 84

Luxton, James Horatio, 9

Lyon, Hiram, 203, 205, 207

Lyon, Hylan B., 235, 250, 254

Lytle, Andrew Nelson, 55

# M

*Macon Weekly Telegraph*, 312

Mainfort, Robert C., Jr., 188

Mann, John G., 70

Marshall, James, 185

Martin, Robert M., 28, 38, 132

Mathes, James Harvey, 42, 68

Matlock, William, 10–11

Maury, Dabney H., 219, 223, 236, 250

*Mazeppe*, 251

McClellan, George B., 194, 263

McClernand, John A., 37–38

McCook, Alexander McDowell, 70, 125, 131, 285

McCord, Frank O., 299

McCreanor, C. C., 308

McCree, James, 172

McCulloch, Black Bob, 145, 153–54, 157–58, 160, 179–80, 183, 188, 220, 222, 235–36, 239

McDonald, Charles, 124

McGregor, Andrew, 244–45

McLaws, Lafayette, 130, 132

McLemore, William S., 84, 107, 132

McMillen, William L., 195, 199, 202, 206, 208, 218

McPherson, James B., 213

Minnis, J. B., 242

Mitcham, Grover, ix–x

Montgomery, Mary Ann, 11–12

Montgomery, Richard, 12

Montgomery, William H., 12

Morgan, James D., 246

Morgan, John Hunt, 63, 126, 238

Morgan, John T., 314

Morse, James K., 11

Morton, G. H., 267

Morton, John W., 61, 78

Mower, Joseph A., 213, 215

Murfreesboro, 43, 53–57, 60, 62–64, 66, 72, 89, 97, 121, 260, 266, 268

**N**

Napier, Theodore A., 81, 85

Napoleon, x, 5, 19, 45, 103, 137, 273

"Navy Sixes," 150

Neely, James J., 171–72, 220, 224, 226, 228, 235

Nelson, William, 62–64

*New Era*, 185

Nineteenth Alabama Infantry, 90

Nineteenth Michigan, 99

Ninety-Third Indiana Infantry Regiment, 195

Ninth Michigan Infantry Regiment, 55

Ninth Mississippi Infantry Regiment, 165

Ninth Tennessee, 109

**O**

Odom, H. C., 231

Okolona, 139, 149, 151–52, 155–57, 160–61, 163, 166, 199, 202, 218, 222

110th USCT Regiment, 241

Owens, William, 55–56

**P**

Palmer, Joseph B., 266

Parker, William J., 277

Parkhurst, John G., 56, 59, 72, 280–81

Patton, George S., Jr., 32, 89, 155

Pegram, John, 128, 131

Pemberton, John C., 75, 79, 82, 95
Peters, Jessie, 275
Pickett, George, 39, 194
Pillow, Gideon, 22, 35–42, 118, 140, 175, 312
Pillow, Granville, 109
*Pittsburg*, 37
Pointer, Henry, 115–16
Polk, Leonidas, 22, 24, 64, 122, 128, 131–33, 141, 145–46, 153, 160, 163–66, 197
Porter, David, 78
Prentiss, Benjamin H., 48

### R

Rambaut, Gilbert, 68, 122, 220
Reed, Richard, 299
Reed, Wiley, 187
Richardson, Robert V., 139
Richardson, William, 56
Rieckhoff, Herbert, 33
Roddey, Philip D., 105–9, 114, 219–20, 239–40, 242, 248, 277, 284–85
Rommel, Erwin, x, 2, 61, 89, 155, 213
Roosevelt, Theodore, 72
Rosecrans, William S., 65, 75–76, 89, 101, 103–4, 121–28, 130–32, 266–67
Ross, Sul, 273, 278
Rounds, Oliver Cromwell, 55, 57
Rousseau, Lovell H., 244, 246, 266–67

Rucker, Edmund W., 201–7, 219–20, 235–36, 238–39, 241, 252, 256, 262, 268–69, 308
Ruegen Island, 1
Russell, Milton, 85, 113–16, 156–57, 220

### S

Samson, Emma, 111–13
Saunders, James C., 53, 57
Schofield, John M., 150, 246, 260, 262–65
Sears, Claudius W., 266
Seay, George E., 220
Second Colored Light Artillery, 184
Second Kentucky, 124
Second Kentucky Infantry Regiment, 38
Second Manassas, 64, 194
Second Tennessee Cavalry Regiment, 180
Second U.S. Colored Troops Light Artillery Battalion, 177
Seddon, James, 118, 197–98
Semmes, Raphael, 294–95
Senter, DeWitt, 305
Seventh Indiana Cavalry, 156
Seventh Tennessee Cavalry Regiment, 16, 21, 73, 167
Seventy-Third Indiana Infantry, 114
Severson, C. S., 70
Seymour, Horatio, 304
Shafter, William R., 98

Shaw, A. J., 180, 297
Shaw, Wirt, 297
Sheets, James W., 108, 203, 244
*Shenandoah Herald*, 309
Sheridan, Philip H., 97–98, 130, 150, 232, 263
Sherill, L. J., 220
Sherman, William T., 2–4, 45, 49–51, 75, 138, 149–53, 160, 171, 175–76, 190–91, 193–98, 212–13, 215, 222–23, 232–33, 235, 237–40, 243–44, 246–47, 249, 256, 259–60, 263, 278, 280, 288, 305, 309
Sixteenth Army Corps, 144
XVI Corps, 82, 139, 141, 144, 176, 260
Sixth Illinois Cavalry, 230
Sixth Mississippi, 220
Sixth Tennessee Cavalry, 167, 169
Sixth U.S. Colored Troops Heavy Artillery Battalion, 177
Smith, A. J., 140, 190, 215, 223, 226, 231, 235, 246, 260
Smith, Edmund Kirby, 53
Smith, Green Clay, 100
Smith, John E., 213
Smith, Kirby, 53–54, 60, 64, 287
Smith, William Sooy, 149, 160
Spencer Repeating Rifles, 123, 127
Stainback, George, 310, 317
Stanley, David S., 101–2, 125, 260, 263
Starnes, James W., 29, 78, 80, 83, 85, 98, 100–2

Starr, Matthew, 230
Steedman, James B., 246–48
Stevens, Thaddeus, 302
Stevenson, Carter L., 269
Stevenson, John D., 140
Stewart, Francis M., 235
*St. Louis*, 36–37, 82, 257
Stoneman, George, 194
Strange, John P., 68, 80, 86, 157–58, 220, 230, 242
Streight, Abel D., 103–11, 113–17, 210, 271
Sturgis, Samuel, 191–92, 194–95, 199, 201–2, 204–5, 207, 210–13, 217
Sullivan, Jeremiah C., 76–81, 84, 86
Syrus, Publilius, 1, 75, 149, 277

**T**

Tate, Sam, 295
Tate, Thomas, 154, 159
*Tawah*, 254
Taylor, A. K., 19
Taylor, James D., 284
Taylor, Richard, 191, 236–37
Taylor, Zachary, 236–37
Tenth Tennessee, 98
Third Arkansas Cavalry, 97
Third Illinois Cavalry, 228
Third Kentucky, 253
Third Minnesota, 55, 58
Third Tennessee Cavalry Regiment, 24, 45, 48, 167
Third Tennessee Infantry, 298

Third West Tennessee Raid, 167, 173

Thirteenth Tennessee Cavalry, 167, 177, 179

Thirty-Ninth Iowa Infantry, 85

Thirty-Third Indiana Infantry, 97

Thomas, DeWitt, 195

Thomas, George H., 63, 246, 260

Thompson, Alice, 97

Thompson, Sam, 170

Thrall, J. C., 255–56, 316

Thucydides, 21

Trezevant, Edward B., 98

Turner, Robert, 113

Twelfth Kentucky Cavalry, 175

Twelfth Missouri Cavalry, 226

Twentieth Tennessee Cavalry Regiment, 140

Twenty-Second Wisconsin Infantry Regiment, 99

XXIII Corps, 257, 260

Tyler, H. A., 154, 202, 205, 207, 275

# U

*Undine*, 252–53

Unionist, 24, 78, 90, 108, 156, 171, 173, 179, 242, 300

USS *Conestoga*, 27

USS *Louisville*, 37

# V

Veatch, James C., 191

*Venus*, 252–53

# W

Wade, Benjamin F., 190

Walker, W. H. T., 129

Walthall, Edward C., 270, 273–74, 276

Walton, Edwin S., 262

Waring, George E., 151–52, 154–57, 160, 196–97, 204, 206, 211, 213

Warren, Alexander, 70

Washburn, C. C., 191–92, 194, 196–97, 209, 212, 222, 225–28, 230–31, 246, 250, 281

Watkins, Sam, 265

Watson, Mack, 211–12

Webster, Joseph D., 246

Wharton, John, 56, 69, 72, 89–92

Wheeler, Joseph, 65, 71, 89–93, 95, 103, 122–24, 131, 133, 238–40, 243, 249, 314

White, Josiah S., 21

White, Raleigh R., 241, 310

Whitney, Eli, 6

Wick, S. M. Van, 25

Wilder, John T., 123, 127

Williams, Minnick, 100, 228

Wilson, Andrew N., 156

Wilson, James H., 260, 263, 279–80

Winbush, Louis Napoleon, 73

Winslow, Edward, 196

Wisdom, Drew W., 141, 168, 205

Wisdom, John H., 113

"Wizard of the Saddle, the," 4, 62, 82, 107, 146, 166, 194, 216, 219, 233, 246, 249, 284, 302

Wolseley, Viscount, 2, 31
Wood, Thomas J., 130
Woodward, Thomas G., 124
Wright, Eric, 72

**Y**

Yates, Richard, 302